T0295534

Leading Reliable Healthcare

Leading Reliable Healthcare

Edited by
Bandar Abdulmohsen Al Knawy

CRC Press
Taylor & Francis Group
Boca Raton London New York

CRC Press is an imprint of the
Taylor & Francis Group, an **informa** business
A PRODUCTIVITY PRESS BOOK

CRC Press
Taylor & Francis Group
6000 Broken Sound Parkway NW, Suite 300
Boca Raton, FL 33487-2742

© 2018 by Taylor & Francis Group, LLC
CRC Press is an imprint of Taylor & Francis Group, an Informa business

No claim to original U.S. Government works

Printed on acid-free paper

International Standard Book Number-13: 978-1-138-19751-0 (Hardback)
International Standard Book Number-13: 978-1-3152-7758-5 (eBook)

This book contains information obtained from authentic and highly regarded sources. Reasonable efforts have been made to publish reliable data and information, but the author and publisher cannot assume responsibility for the validity of all materials or the consequences of their use. The authors and publishers have attempted to trace the copyright holders of all material reproduced in this publication and apologize to copyright holders if permission to publish in this form has not been obtained. If any copyright material has not been acknowledged please write and let us know so we may rectify in any future reprint.

Except as permitted under U.S. Copyright Law, no part of this book may be reprinted, reproduced, transmitted, or utilized in any form by any electronic, mechanical, or other means, now known or hereafter invented, including photocopying, microfilming, and recording, or in any information storage or retrieval system, without written permission from the publishers.

For permission to photocopy or use material electronically from this work, please access www.copyright.com (http://www.copyright.com/) or contact the Copyright Clearance Center, Inc. (CCC), 222 Rosewood Drive, Danvers, MA 01923, 978-750-8400. CCC is a not-for-profit organization that provides licenses and registration for a variety of users. For organizations that have been granted a photocopy license by the CCC, a separate system of payment has been arranged.

Trademark Notice: Product or corporate names may be trademarks or registered trademarks, and are used only for identification and explanation without intent to infringe.

Library of Congress Cataloging-in-Publication Data

Names: Al Knawy, Bandar Abdulmoshen, author.
Title: Leading reliable healthcare / Bandar Abdulmoshen Al Knawy.
Description: Boca Raton ; London : Taylor & Francis, 2018. | "A CRC title, part of the Taylor & Francis imprint, a member of the Taylor & Francis Group, the academic division of T&F Informa plc." | Includes index.
Identifiers: LCCN 2017022041| ISBN 9781138197510 (hardback : alk. paper) | ISBN 9781315277585 (ebook)
Subjects: LCSH: Medical errors--Prevention. | Medical care--Quality control. | Health facilities--Safety measures.
Classification: LCC R729.8 .A44 2018 | DDC 610.28/9--dc23
LC record available at https://lccn.loc.gov/2017022041

Visit the Taylor & Francis Web site at
http://www.taylorandfrancis.com

and the CRC Press Web site at
http://www.crcpress.com

Contents

Foreword ... vii
Preface ... ix
Acknowledgments ... xi
About the Contributors ... xiii

1 Organizational Safety Culture ... 1
SALLIE J. WEAVER AND HANAN H. EDREES

2 Operational Excellence ... 25
SUSAN MASCITELLI, STEPHEN S. MILLS, MICHAEL BIERL, AND RYAN LE

3 Efficient Clinical Practice ... 45
SANDRA L. FENWICK, KATHY J. JENKINS, JOHN G. MEARA, CHRIS NEWELL, ANNE STACK, SARA TOOMEY, AND CYNTHIA HAINES

4 Successful Patient Outcomes ... 71
CALEB FAN, SAMI EL-BOGHDADLY, AND MARTIN A. MAKARY

5 High Reliability Organizations ... 83
FRANK FEDERICO, AMELIA BROOKS, AND HANAN H. EDREES

6 Information Technology: A Neural Network for Reliable Healthcare ... 111
HEE HWANG

7 Healthcare Education and Training to Support a Responsive Healthcare System: Canadian Perspectives ... 123
STEVE SLADE, TANYA HORSLEY, AND ANDREW PADMOS

8 Integration of Primary Healthcare and Hospitals ... 135
F.D. RICHARD HOBBS AND CLARE J. TAYLOR

9 Performance Parameters ... 155
JULES MARTIN, ALISON ALSBURY, AND WILL REYNOLDS

10 Quality and Cost in Healthcare: Improving Performance ... 189
BRUNO HOLTHOF

11 Leadership through Crisis ... 205
BANDAR AL KNAWY

12 Health System Innovation and Reform 217
TARA DONNELLY

13 The Financial Aspects of Leading a Reliable Healthcare System 231
CHRIS HURST

Index 241

Foreword

Plenty of books debut each year, promising to be the definitive guide to change management in healthcare. In fact, the shelves in my office at Johns Hopkins Medicine are crammed full of such texts. Yet few of these volumes pull off what Dr. Bandar Al Knawy has managed with this edition—namely, compiling insightful, practical perspectives from experts around the globe who have pioneered innovations in medical practice and clinical operations in the name of providing consistently excellent care.

Medical professionals can glean a number of lessons from the examples gathered herein, whether it be a snapshot of how the National Health Service in England has managed to maximize primary care networks or a glimpse into how one Saudi Arabian hospital responded to a MERS outbreak in the emergency department. These are concise takes on critical issues, grounded in real-world examples and up-to-date theory. The result is not merely an enlightening read but a patently useful one, as the book prompts readers to examine our own practices and consider how we might apply the principles of high reliability in our own health systems.

What strikes me in reading this refreshingly global volume is the universality of many of the issues confronting leaders in healthcare. Apollo 9 astronaut Russell Schweikart once said that when you look down on earth from space, what strikes you is that it is all one system, with no actual borders or boundaries. No matter where we live or practice medicine, the experience of providing—and receiving—healthcare has far more commonalities than differences. While there certainly are variations across cultures, many of us are encountering comparable challenges today as we attempt to curb the cost of care while at the same time working to keep growing numbers of patients well.

We are all on this path together, and it is critical that we get it right. We owe it to our patients and our fellow taxpayers (in the United States, healthcare expenditures have come to consume nearly 18% of our gross domestic product without a proportionate boost in outcomes), not to mention the next generation of medical professionals who will inherit the systems we are reshaping today.

So what, exactly, is our commitment to them? Above all, this book contends, we need to engineer systems that reliably deliver safe, high-quality care by monitoring our performance, providing transparent feedback, and continually improving.

Al Knawy et al. define high-reliability organizations as those that achieve outstanding levels of safety and performance despite operating in high-risk environments. Medicine is advancing at a more rapid pace than ever in human history, and as medicine becomes more complex more quickly, opportunities for error abound. My Johns Hopkins colleague Dr. Marty Makary, one of this book's contributors, set off alarm bells in the field in 2016 with his finding that medical error is *the third-leading* cause of death in the United States. Moreover, preventable errors cost the

United States tens of billions of dollars each year, costs for which insurance companies and other payers are increasingly reluctant to reimburse care providers.

Now more than ever, we have to bear down on the science of healthcare delivery. For many years, patient-safety research was seen as the less-glamorous cousin to other types of scientific inquiry, but that is beginning to change. For their part, Dr. Makary and his co-authors here make a compelling case: "In a given year, more lives may be saved through the use of a procedure checklist than the number of lives saved by the newest chemotherapy." Incremental improvements in care delivery may not garner as much hype as a sexy new pill or the discovery of a genetic marker of disease, but they can save many lives nonetheless.

Advances in safety science are not the only thing we have going for us as we work to ensure high reliability. We also have powerful 21st-century tools at our disposal, with the electronic health record, mobile health apps, and other technologies. As Hee Hwang points out in Chapter 6, "Advances in IT have provided new opportunities to pursue the triple aims of improving the patient care experience, improving the health of the population, and reducing per capita healthcare costs." With petabytes of data capacity and muscular analytics, we are uniquely empowered to monitor our quality and efficiency and pinpoint areas for improvement. This book sheds light on how to target those efforts to maximize reliability.

Despite our best efforts, we never will eliminate errors altogether. As William Osler famously said, "The practice of medicine is an art, not a trade." Along with the humanism that makes medicine so powerful—the physician's intuition, the doctor–patient touch—comes the potential for human error. That is why our organizations must "aim to be harm-free rather than error-free," an important distinction laid out by Frank Federico and Hanan Edrees in Chapter 5. In other words, we absolutely must take steps to minimize errors, but we also need to foster a culture where it is commonplace to discuss errors openly, not just in the name of accountability but in the interest of addressing issues early and learning from our mistakes.

While this book charts some promising routes on the path to high reliability in healthcare, most of us still have a considerable distance to travel as we implement change initiatives. It is up to all of us to apply these ideas at home—and to share, far and wide, the lessons learned along the way—to arrive at a place where excellence is assured for each and every patient.

Paul B. Rothman, MD
Dean/CEO, Johns Hopkins Medicine

Preface

It seems that whatever the country, its politics, and its preferred healthcare system, leaders of the modern world face similar challenges to ensure never less than reliable standards of care for patients, their families, and their carers. As a leader of one of the largest and most complex healthcare organizations in the Middle East, I recognize the need to equip managers, current and future, with the practical knowledge to build and sustain a reliable healthcare system.

While there are many publications concerning the theory behind the "high reliability organization," few concentrate on real practical examples, their application, and their potential learnings. This book aims to strike a balance between theory and practice, being descriptive, informative, and detailed, while encouraging and prompting the reader to explore his or her own thinking and practice.

Contributors have been carefully selected to represent various international healthcare systems with unique and pioneering characteristics. All contributors understand the global and diverse nature of healthcare and are all frontline leaders of repute.

The concept of reliability has been used to describe a system with nearly harm-free care and one that delivers the same outcomes every single time, regardless of complexity or of the behavior of those who deliver and receive it. This book looks to develop this definition, as it aims to provide healthcare leaders with the "know-how" to build a reliable healthcare system covering key areas of quality and safe patient care. The leaders of highly reliable healthcare systems must be able to design a structure to deliver consistently on all aspects of quality healthcare, whether it is timeliness, efficiency, safety, or culture.

Authoring, coordinating, and editing this book has been a journey that has lasted for almost one year. It was one that filled me with excitement, learning, and hard work. I would like to convey my thanks to all the contributors for their efforts. It is my hope that *Leading Reliable Healthcare* will add value and inspire healthcare managers and clinical leaders, responsible for shaping and delivering health systems, to improve the standard and quality of patient care across the world.

Acknowledgments

I would like to express my heartfelt gratitude to those who inspired me the most in seeing this book to fruition:

My parents; my wife, Haya; my children, Abdulmohsen, Mona, Mohammad, Musaad, and Najla; and all employees of the Health Affairs, Ministry of National Guard, for their commitment to serve our patients.

This book is for you.

About the Contributors

Bandar Al Knawy is the Chief Executive Officer of Health Affairs, Ministry of National Guard, a premier healthcare organisation with five tertiary medical facilities and 40 primary healthcare clinics composed of around 25,000 employees across the Kingdom of Saudi Arabia. In addition, the President of King Saud bin Abdulaziz University for Health Sciences, with 11 dedicated health science colleges distributed in three different campuses with a total of 10,000 students. He is also the General Supervisor for the National Dialysis Charity Project and a member of the National Health Services Council. From 2009 until January 2015, he served as the General Supervisor for the Royal Clinics of the late King Abdullah Bin Abdulaziz Al Saud, Custodian of the Two Holy Mosques.

Dr. Al Knawy is a strong advocate of patient safety and quality of care and oversaw the launch of multiple high-impact initiatives such as the Annual National Patient Safety Forum and the Saudi Medication Safety Program, among others. Under the management and direction of Dr. Al Knawy, the health sciences university and King Abdullah International Medical Research Centre commissioned their state-of-the-art facilities. He recently led a system-wide implementation of the Electronic Health Record project to cover all medical services.

Dr. Al Knawy has published scientific articles and was the guest editor for the *Clinics in Liver Disease—Healthcare Associated Transmission of Hepatitis B & C Viruses*, February 2010. He has also edited two books, *Hepatology: A Practical Approach,* (Elsevier 2005), and *Hepatocellular Carcinoma: A Practical Approach* (CRC 2009).

Alison Alsbury has, for the past two years, been leading workforce and resource modeling nationally, as workforce modeling lead for the new care models team. She has always worked freelance, and her varied career has focused on the management of substantial change in highly complex stakeholder environments. Alison's economic and language abilities took her first into high-level European strategic and policy consulting, then into aiding utilities to deal with the complex regulatory frameworks required by privatisation. Her first public sector experience came from three roles in regeneration, leading high-profile public–private sector partnerships.

For the past 12 years, her roles have all been focused around transformation in health, social care, and the voluntary sector, using her system economic skills. She has worked in every possible health sphere: senior assignments at NHS England, the Department of Health, and with several Royal Colleges.

Michael Bierl is Director of Strategic Alliances & Global Services for NewYork-Presbyterian Hospital. In this capacity he directs domestic and global growth initiatives for the hospital through its regional hospital network, partnerships with employers, international alliances, and digital health. Michael previously worked for The Boston Consulting Group advising international healthcare corporations on strategic and operational matters. He also worked on a joint venture with Johns Hopkins Medicine to develop digital diabetes interventions. Michael holds an MS in Health Economics from the London School of Economics and Political Science, UK, and a BS in Healthcare Management from the University of Bayreuth, Germany.

Amelia Brooks is the director of Patient Safety–Europe at the Institute for Healthcare Improvement (IHI). She has expertise in quality improvement, patient safety, human factors, analytics for improvement, and safety culture. Amelia joined the IHI in January 2016 as a director in the patient safety team, where her role includes teaching, diagnostics, and on-site coaching for organizations. She is also now IHI's regional director for the Europe region and lives in the United Kingdom. Amelia leads a number of the IHI's European programs and oversees all regional activity. Prior to joining the IHI, Amelia worked in strategic and operational roles in the patient safety and improvement fields, including frontline roles as a quality improvement specialist. Prior to joining the IHI, she led the design, development, and implementation of a regional patient safety collaborative in England.

Tara Donnelly is chief executive of the Health Innovation Network, which speeds up the best in health and care across South London. The Health Innovation Network is one of 15 Academic Health Science Networks (AHSNs) established in the United Kingdom in 2013. AHSNs exist to spread innovation at pace and scale across the healthcare system. Tara is an improvement enthusiast with an extensive background in leadership roles within the NHS and third sector. She has spent the past 18 years at board level, including at University College London Hospitals NHS Foundation Trust; as a nonexecutive director at Macmillan Cancer Support, the leading UK charity for people living with cancer; as chief executive at the West Middlesex University Hospital; and as deputy chief executive and director of operations at the Whittington Hospital. Her first role in the NHS was as a ward housekeeper when she was 18, prior to studying at King's College London.

Hanan H. Edrees is a quality and patient safety manager at the King Abdullah Specialist Children's Hospital in the Ministry of National Guard–Health Affairs, Kingdom of Saudi Arabia. She is an associate faculty member at the Johns Hopkins University–Bloomberg School of Public Health. Dr. Edrees holds a doctorate in healthcare management and leadership from Johns Hopkins University, a master's degree from Georgetown University, and an undergraduate degree from George Mason University. Dr. Edrees has led several patient safety initiatives—nationally and internationally. She has also consulted for the World Health Organization and the Abu Dhabi Health Services Company (SEHA), and was a project manager at the Johns Hopkins Armstrong Institute for Patient Safety and Quality.

Sami El-Boghdadly has been working at King Abdulaziz Medical City as director of OR and day care services and a consultant in general and laparoscopic surgery for the past 11 years. He graduated with an MBChB from Alexandria University in 1974; LRCP, MRCS (London, England) in 1997; FRCS (London) in 1979; and received FACS from the United States in 1989 and Diploma in Medical Education, Dundee, United Kingdom, in 1995. Throughout his career as director of OR and day care, he has done well in introducing state-of-the-art technologies. Other than that, he is also an assistant professor of surgery at King Saud bin Abdulaziz University for Health Sciences. He is an active member of the Advanced Trauma Life Support (ATLS) program, conducting courses in and outside the Kingdom. In addition, participation in the National Surgical and Quality Improvement Program (NSQIP) by the American College of Surgeons is his brainchild.

Caleb Fan is a native of Gaithersburg, Maryland, and is currently a fourth-year medical student at the Johns Hopkins University School of Medicine. He recently matched into otolaryngology head and neck surgery at the Icahn School of Medicine at Mount Sinai, where he will continue his training. Caleb, along with his colleagues, was the first to demonstrate an association between safety culture and surgical outcomes. He is passionate about quality and safety in medicine and is eager to advance the field within the realm of otolaryngology.

Frank Federico is vice president and senior safety expert at the Institute for Healthcare Improvement in Cambridge, Massachusetts. His primary areas of focus include patient safety and the application of reliability principles in healthcare. He is also faculty for the Patient Safety Executive Development Program. He is chair of the National Coordinating Council for Medication Error Reporting and Prevention (NNC MERP), and vice-chair of the Joint Commission Patient Safety Advisory Group. Mr. Federico is an executive producer of *First, Do No Harm*, part 2: "Taking the Lead." He served as director of pharmacy at Children's Hospital, Boston. He is coauthor of the IHI white paper *Respectful and Effective Crisis Management*, and contributing author to *Achieving Safe and Reliable Healthcare, Strategies and Solutions*. He has authored a number of articles focusing on patient safety. Frank Federico coaches teams and lectures extensively, nationally and internationally.

Sandra L. Fenwick leads the nation's foremost independent pediatric hospital and the world's leading center of pediatric medical and health research. Ms. Fenwick has been a driving force in improving the effectiveness and efficacy of the care provided at Boston Children's while at the same time reducing the costs of care. Through a combination of hospital affiliations, outpatient specialty care centers, community health centers and regional partnerships, she has helped create a children's health network providing high-quality pediatric care in local settings. She has also expanded its commitment to and investment in both basic, translational, and clinical research and care innovation as well as prevention efforts focused on asthma, obesity, mental health, and violence.

Cynthia Haines, MBA, is senior vice president, international services at Boston Children's Hospital (BCH) and is responsible for the leadership of BCH's international programs and initiatives including international patient services, medical education, collaborations, and global health. Cynthia previously held progressive leadership positions at the Children's Hospital of Philadelphia and at Stanford Children's Health. Earlier in her career, Cynthia worked in healthcare management consulting and investment banking. Cynthia holds an MBA from the University of Chicago Booth School of Business.

F.D. Richard Hobbs. As well as being professor and head of the Nuffield Department of Primary Care Health Sciences, Professor Richard Hobbs is also the national director of the NIHR School for Primary Care Research (2009–) and was codirector of the quality and outcomes (QOF) review panel from 2005–2009. He sits on many national and international scientific and research funding boards, including the council of the British Heart Foundation (until 2012), the board of the British Primary Care Cardiovascular Society, and is president of the European Primary Care Cardiovascular Society (EPCCS).

His research interests focus on cardiovascular epidemiology and clinical trials, especially relating to vascular and stroke risk, and heart failure. Overall, Professor Hobbs' publications include 28 book chapters, 13 edited books, and over 350 original papers in peer-reviewed journals such as

The Lancet, *Annals of Internal Medicine*, *BMJ*, *Atherosclerosis*, *EHJ*, and *Stroke*. His research has impacted on international health policies and clinical guidelines. Within the NHS, he has consulted on national service frameworks for CHD, atrial fibrillation, and heart failure and several National Institute of Clinical Excellence (NICE) reviews. He has provided clinical care in inner-city general practice for over 30 years.

Bruno Holthof is the Chief Executive Officer of Oxford University Hospitals Foundation Trust (OUHFT). OUHFT employs 12,000 staff across four hospital sites and 44 other locations. Before OUHFT, he was CEO of the Antwerp Hospital Network from January 2004 until September 2015. During this period, he transformed ZNA into the most profitable hospital group in Belgium. Before becoming a CEO, he was a partner at McKinsey and Company. During this period, he served a wide range of healthcare clients in Europe and the United States and gained significant expertise in the areas of strategy, organization, and operations. Bruno Holthof is a member of the board of Barco, a public listed company providing visualization solutions for professional markets and a member of the board of Armonea, a European private care home provider. He holds an MBA from Harvard Business School and an MD/PhD from the University of Leuven.

Tanya Horsley is the associate director of the research unit at the Royal College where she leads efforts to professionalize research and scholarship activities and programs corporately. Dr. Horsley completed her PhD in health and rehabilitation sciences at the University of Western Ontario, followed by a postdoctoral fellowship at the Centers for Disease Control. Dr. Horsley's research explores the formalization of integrated knowledge translation for the cocreation, use, and influence of research and complex systems of care with a particular focus on multi-stakeholder engagement and organizational contexts. She is faculty at the University of Ottawa, School of Epidemiology, Public Health and Preventive Medicine, proudly serves on several national and international committees and contributes as an associate editor to the *Journal of Continuing Education in the Health Professions* and the *Canadian Medical Education Journal*.

Chris Hurst is a chartered accountant with 25 years' board experience, gained in both executive and non-executive roles. He has worked in and with healthcare organizations for over 20 years and previously worked in the banking and IT sectors and in local and central government. In 2012, he resigned from his role as Finance Director for Health & Social Care Services in Wales to set up Dorian3d Ltd.—a business specializing in providing strategic and financial consultancy, and executive coaching and mentoring services, to both public and private sector clients. Prior to working in Wales, Chris was the deputy chief executive and finance director at the Oxford Radcliffe Hospitals NHS Trust for nine years. He is currently a non-executive trustee of the UK Healthcare Financial Management Association (HFMA), a non-executive director of Oxford Health NHS Foundation Trust and sits on a private sector technology board. Chris is a past member of the Secretary of State's Advisory Committee for (NHS) Resource Allocation in England and has been an independent expert advisor to a number of healthcare businesses, including Philips' new healthcare technologies division. He has traveled to the United States, South Africa, Australia, and Sweden to study healthcare systems.

Hee Hwang is chief information officer and associate professor of pediatric neurology at Seoul National University Bundang Hospital (SNUBH), Korea. He graduated from Seoul National University College of Medicine in 1996 and was a visiting scholar at the MEG center and epilepsy surgery program of Cincinnati Children's Hospital, Ohio, United States. He has been in charge of the development and management of electronic health record (EHR) systems at SNUBH since 2004. His major interests are the usability of EHR systems, health information exchange, and clinical intelligence.

Kathy J. Jenkins is professor of pediatrics at Harvard Medical School. Dr. Jenkins is executive director of the Center for Applied Pediatric Quality Analytics at Boston Children's Hospital, where she is also a senior faculty member in the Department of Cardiology. She is the immediate past chair of the Congenital Heart Public Health Consortium, a former chair of the Adult Congenital and Pediatric Cardiology Council, and a current member of the Women in Cardiology Leadership Council. She has led several national quality projects, including the NCDR Impact Registry, the National Pediatric Cardiology Quality Improvement Collaborative, and the ACPC QNet project. Dr. Jenkins is project director for the International Quality Improvement Collaborative for Congenital Heart Surgery in Developing World Countries. She has an extensive background in measurement and risk adjustment for pediatric health outcomes.

Ryan Le is an analyst in the Strategic Alliances & Global Services Department at NewYork-Presbyterian Hospital. His work is primarily centered on advancing international patient care for the hospital while continuing to improve organizational effectiveness domestically. He is particularly interested in the implications of technology across the industry and helps support digital health initiatives within NYP. Ryan holds a master of health administration from the Johns Hopkins Bloomberg School of Public Health and a BS in biology from The College of New Jersey.

Martin A. Makary is the creator of "The Surgery Checklist," publishing its first description and subsequently serving on the WHO Safe Surgery Saves Lives committee and leading the WHO workgroup in creating global measures of surgical quality. Dr. Makary has published over 200 scientific articles, including the first description of "frailty" as a medical condition influencing patient outcomes, and the original studies on safety culture measurement in healthcare. He is a leading voice for physicians, writing in *The Wall Street Journal*, *Newsweek*, and *TIME* magazine. Dr. Makary is *The New York Times*-bestselling author of *Unaccountable*, a book about quality and price transparency in healthcare. Dr. Makary is a surgical oncologist specializing in minimally invasive pancreatic surgery. At Johns Hopkins, he has served as the endowed chair of gastrointestinal surgery, the director of surgical quality and safety, and founding director of the Johns Hopkins Center for Surgical Outcomes Research and Clinical Trials. He currently serves as the chief of the Johns Hopkins Center for Islet Transplantation and executive director of *Improving Wisely*, a Robert Wood Johnson Foundation project to lower healthcare costs in the United States by creating measures of appropriateness in healthcare.

Jules Martin is a clinician with extensive experience as a board director serving on the boards of CCG's and major providers as a chief operating officer and chief executive. Her varied career has focused on service and system improvement, having worked in a number of acute NHS hospitals including district, teaching, integrated providers, and foundation trusts. In Jules' early career, she worked clinically within the NHS. During her tenure, Jules has transformed organizations that have been struggling with complex agendas in difficult health sectors to achieve system-wide change. Her portfolio within the acute hospital settings has included organizational turnaround and financial recovery. She joined the Central London Clinical Commissioning Group (CCG) as the managing director. The CCG is part of the largest commissioning collaboration in London known as North West London.

Susan Mascitelli, RN, is senior vice president, patient services, and liaison to the board of trustees for NewYork-Presbyterian. She is responsible for NewYork-Presbyterian's patient experience and patient-centered care infrastructure, oversees the Department of Patient Services, and is the executive sponsor for Integrative Health and Wellbeing. Ms. Mascitelli also acts on behalf of the president and Chief Executive Officer as official liaison to NewYork-Presbyterian's board of trustees. In addition, she has administrative responsibility for NewYork-Presbyterian's volunteer, chaplaincy, pastoral care, ethics, and administrator-on-call functions. Over the past 30 years, Ms. Mascitelli held leadership roles in many of NewYork-Presbyterian's quality, patient safety, and regulatory initiatives and has served NewYork-Presbyterian in progressive levels of patient care and management, beginning as a general staff nurse in the CCU, then senior staff nurse, patient representative, assistant director, director, and vice president of patient services. Ms. Mascitelli obtained her undergraduate degree in nursing from Columbia School of Nursing and a certificate in executive leadership from Harvard Business School.

John G. Meara. As plastic surgeon-in-chief at Boston Children's Hospital, Dr. Meara provides family-centered care for patients with a wide variety of complex congenital anomalies. Dr. Meara dedicates the majority of his time to direct patient care, and about one-third of this schedule to research and innovation. Dr. Meara is a prominent researcher in cleft lip and palate and craniofacial anomalies, a leader in developing global health and public policy initiatives, and an advocate for continuous improvement in department administration and hospital leadership.

Stephen S. Mills is a seasoned healthcare professional with over 40 years of experience providing expert solutions to boards of trustees and senior-level executives. Mr. Mills served as the president and chief executive officer of NewYork-Presbyterian Hospital Queens for 21 years. During his tenure, he was responsible for directing the vison strategic plan and financial and program operations for the 535 bed facility with an operating budget of $650 million and 3,700 employees. From 1994–2016, he also served as the President and Chief Executive Officer for the Silvercrest Center for Nursing and Rehabilitation, a 320-bed skilled nursing facility with a $50 million budget. Under the management and direction of Mr. Mills, both NewYork-Presbyterian Hospital Queens and the Silvercrest Center experienced substantial financial viability, major facility expansions and significant network growth. Mr. Mills began his career at The New York Hospital (before acquisition by NewYork-Presbyterian Hospital), taking on progressive positions until he was appointed senior vice president of network affairs. He also served as the executive vice president and director of the New York Hospital Care Network. Mr. Mills received a bachelor of arts degree from Columbia University and a master of healthcare administration from Tulane University.

Chris Newell is the senior director of learning and development at Boston Children's Hospital. He is also a senior research fellow at Boston University School of Management and a founder of the Institute for Global Work. Prior to his role at Boston Children's, he was the chief collaboration officer at Keane Inc., founder of the Lotus Institute, and cofounder of the IBM Institute for Knowledge Management. Chris has a doctorate in psychology from William James University.

Andrew Padmos served as senior mentor, thought leader, and coauthor of Chapter 7. Educated in political sciences and economics at the University of Toronto and in medicine at McMaster University, Dr. Andrew Padmos completed specialty training in internal medicine and hematology in 1976. A hematologist by profession, Dr. Padmos practiced in Riyadh, Saudi Arabia from 1978–1993, where he developed a bone marrow transplant program while managing a large clinical program in hematology and oncology. He has served as CEO of the Royal College of Physicians and Surgeons of Canada since September 2006. As CEO of the Royal College, Dr. Padmos has led an ambitious agenda of change, development, and expansion to enhance post-graduate medical education and training, membership engagement and recognition, volunteer programs, health policy, external relations, and international outreach.

Will Reynolds is an award-winning senior health and social care manager. A specialist in demand management who enjoys tackling complex problems and developing creative solutions, Will was part of two separate teams that won back-to-back Management Consultancy Association Awards (winning the MCA Award for 'Change Management in the Public Sector' in 2012 and then the 'Customer Engagement' award in 2013). With over a decade of experience working directly for the public sector and as a senior management consultant, Will joined NHS Central London CCG as Head of Planned Care.

Steve Slade was primary author, researcher, and content planner for Chapter 7. As director of health systems and policy at the Royal College of Physicians and Surgeons of Canada, Mr. Slade leads the organization's effort to serve as a trusted source of data and evidence about the specialty medical workforce. While serving as a senior executive at the Association of Faculties of Medicine of Canada, he cochaired Canada's multi-stakeholder Physician Resource Planning Task Force Technical Steering Committee. In the roles of senior consultant and project manager, Mr. Slade led trailblazing physician workforce research at the Canadian Institute for Health Information and College of Family Physicians of Canada. Mr. Slade was a student of computer science and biostatistics at the University of Toronto and completed his undergraduate degree in psychology at York University.

Anne Stack is the clinical chief, Division of Emergency Medicine at Boston Children's Hospital. Dr. Stack's research interests include the evaluation of resource utilization and standardization of care in the emergency department. Her recent work has focused on the development and implementation of evidence-based guidelines for care in the pediatric emergency department. She is an expert in quality improvement. Dr. Stack received her MD from Harvard Medical School. She completed a residency in pediatrics and a fellowship in pediatric emergency medicine at Boston Children's Hospital. Dr. Stack has recently served as cochair of the PEM Special Interest Group of the Academic Pediatric Association. She is currently cochair of the Evidence-Based Guideline Committee of the Committee on Quality Transformation of the Section of PEM of the American Academy of Pediatrics. Dr. Stack joined the faculty of the Division of Emergency Medicine at Children's Hospital in 1993.

Clare J. Taylor is a part-time academic GP and NIHR Academic Clinical Lecturer. She is an active member of Council at the Royal College of General Practitioners (RCGP). She was Chair of their Associates in Training Committee and went on to establish and lead the RCGP First 5 initiative, which supports new GPs through the formative years of independent practice.

Sara Toomey is an assistant professor at Harvard Medical School and at the Division of General Pediatrics at Boston Children's Hospital. She is a general pediatrician and health services researcher. Dr. Toomey's research focuses on studying the factors that affect the quality of pediatric care. She has studied how receiving care in a patient-centered medical home (PCMH) relates to healthcare quality for children with chronic conditions. She is the managing director of the AHRQ/CMS-funded Center of Excellence for Pediatric Quality Measurement at Boston Children's Hospital. As part of the center's work, she is also a member of the core team tasked with developing a measure of pediatric inpatient experience of care, the Pediatric Consumer Assessment of Healthcare Providers and Systems (Pediatric HCAHPS) Survey. She is also the principal investigator on a career development award project, "Racial/Ethnic Differences in Parent Perspectives of Pediatric Inpatient Care," that extends the Pediatric HCAHPS project to examine racial/ethnic disparities in parent experience of pediatric inpatient care.

Sallie J. Weaver is an industrial-organizational psychologist and program director in the Healthcare Delivery Research Program (HDRP) at the U.S. National Institutes of Health National Cancer Institute (NCI). She is working with the NCI Healthcare Teams Initiative that aims to improve the outcomes and experiences of people facing cancer through research examining teaming in cancer care and translation of evidence-based team performance interventions into practice. Dr. Weaver's interests and research focus on organizational factors that influence team performance, and interventions designed to optimize patient safety, care quality, and coordination both within and across health system boundaries. Before joining NCI in October 2016, Dr. Weaver was an associate professor at the Johns Hopkins University School of Medicine and core faculty at the Armstrong Institute for Patient Safety and Quality. She also retained joint appointments at the Johns Hopkins Bloomberg School of Public Health's Department of Health Policy and Management, Carey School of Business, and School of Nursing. She earned her MS and PhD in psychology from the University of Central Florida and her postdoctoral master of health science in epidemiology from the Johns Hopkins Bloomberg School of Public Health.

Chapter 1

Organizational Safety Culture

Sallie J. Weaver and Hanan H. Edrees

Contents

1.1 Introduction: Organizational Culture and High Reliability ... 2
1.2 What Is Organizational Culture? ... 3
1.2.1 Definitions of Safety Culture ... 3
1.2.2 Models Examining the Inputs, Emergence, and Outcomes of Safety Culture and Climate ... 5
1.2.2.1 Reiman's Layers of Culture Model ... 5
1.2.2.2 Zohar's (2003) Multilevel Model of Safety Climate ... 6
1.2.2.3 High Reliability Organizing and Safety Culture: The 3 Es Model ... 8
1.2.3 Patient Safety Culture and Outcomes ... 10
1.3 Leadership and Organizational Culture ... 10
1.4 Tools for Measuring Patient Safety Culture ... 11
1.4.1 Patient Safety Culture and Climate Assessment Tools in Healthcare ... 11
1.5 Interventions and Strategies for Building Cultures of Patient Safety ... 14
1.6 Barriers to Developing and Sustaining Safety Cultures ... 16
1.7 Application: A Case Study of Transformation and Building a Culture of Resilience After the MERS–CoV Outbreak at the Ministry of National Guard Health Affairs (NGHA), Kingdom of Saudi Arabia ... 16
1.7.1 Background ... 16
1.7.2 The MERS–CoV Outbreak ... 17
1.7.3 Transformation and Building a Culture of Resilience ... 17
1.8 Conclusions and Lessons Learned ... 17
References ... 20

The only thing of real importance that leaders do is create and manage culture.

Edgar Schein
Professor Emeritus, MIT Sloan School of Management

1.1 Introduction: Organizational Culture and High Reliability

Healthcare leaders have a lot to learn from organizations that achieve outstanding levels of safety and performance despite operating in high-risk environments. Such organizations include oil and gas production, nuclear power, aviation, and military operations. Originally defined by organizational scholars Karlene Roberts, Todd LaPorte, and Gene Rochlin as "high reliability organisations" (HROs; see Chapter 5), these organizations have mastered the ability to anticipate the unexpected, adapt, and produce reliably safe, high-quality outcomes despite the significant complexity and inherent risk in their work (Rochlin et al. 1987). HROs offer a benchmark for healthcare leaders and care delivery systems. While healthcare shares levels of complexity and risk with these industries, patients continue to experience preventable harm and patients and their loved ones still report uncoordinated, suboptimal care (Aranaz-Andrés et al. 2011; Bouafia et al. 2013; The Joint Commission 2015; Wilson et al. 2012; Jha et al. 2010).

Thanks to theoretical and empirical work by Kathleen Sutcliffe, Karl Weick, Tim Vogus, and others, we now have an enriched understanding of how HROs function, learn, and adapt, and more nuanced insights into the underlying assumptions and values that shape how their leaders and frontline team members approach their work (Weick and Sutcliffe 2007; Weick and Sutcliffe 2015). These theories emphasize that the pathway to reliably safe outcomes involves: (1) practicing a series of cognitive and behavioral habits that can be identified as mindful organizing; (2) reliability-enhancing work practices; and (3) actions that enable, enact, and elaborate a culture of safety and a climate of trust and respect (Sutcliffe et al. 2016). While contextual factors at multiple levels interact to influence care processes and outcomes (see Figure 1.1), research has shown that organizational

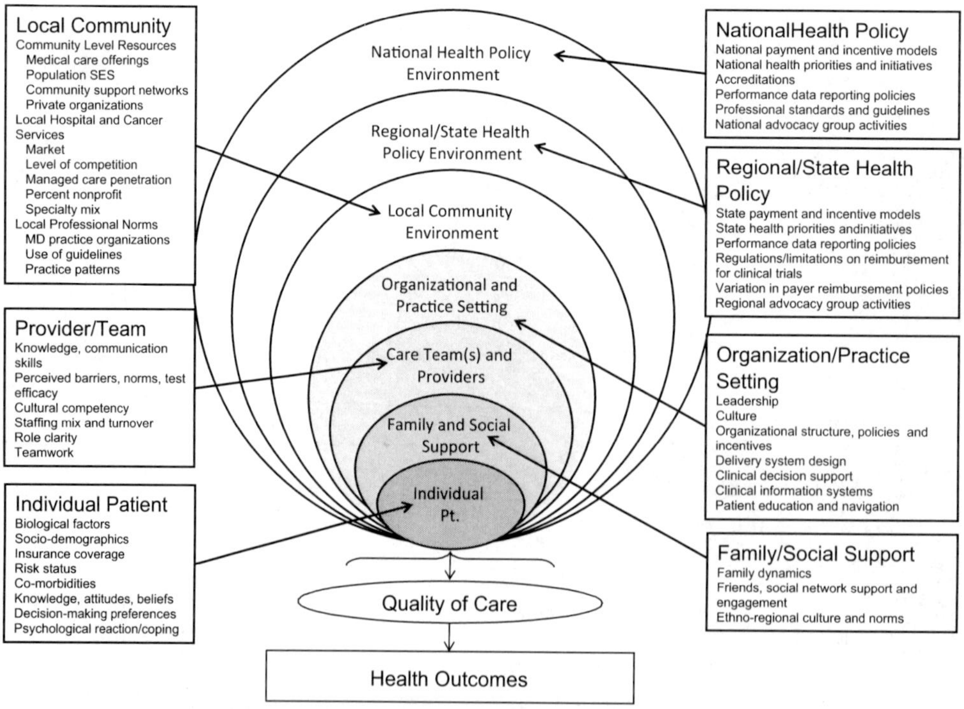

Figure 1.1 Multilevel model of contextual factors influencing care delivery. (Adapted from Taplin, S. H., et al., *JNCI Monographs*, 2012, 2, 2012.)

culture influences a broad range of issues including (1) the situations and cues that clinicians, staff, and administrators perceive or interpret as indicators of potential harm; (2) a willingness to speak up with concerns, questions, and ideas about opportunities for improvement (also known as a sense of psychological safety [Nembhard and Edmondson 2006]); and (3) motivation to participate in improvement work. Given the foundational role culture plays in developing the habits and practices of mindful organizing and reliably safe outcomes, it is fitting to begin this text for healthcare leaders with a chapter dedicated to organizational culture. Chapter 5 provides an in-depth discussion of other aspects of HROs and related principles.

We provide an overview of the state of the science and practice related to patient safety culture and leadership strategies for strengthening culture and addressing challenges associated with punitive cultures. We also discuss practical issues related to assessing patient safety culture in practice. First, we describe the fundamental definitions and models of organizational culture and related concepts of patient safety culture and climate in the healthcare context. We discuss the antecedents and factors that influence how cultures emerge, develop, and change over time, as well as the outcomes linked to culture in the healthcare context. Third, we relate these overarching concepts to the notion of mindful organizing and draw insights and guiding principles from research on high reliability organizing. Finally, we summarize the existing evidence on the leadership strategies and interventions thought to influence organizational culture.

1.2 What Is Organizational Culture?

Culture can be defined as the set of shared beliefs, assumptions, values, norms, and artefacts shared among members of a given group such as an organization, profession, department, unit, or team (Ouchie and Wilkins 1985; Pettigrew 1979; Schein 2010; Schneider et al. 2013; Guldenmund 2000). Organizational culture reflects the learned tacit set of assumptions and related behavioral norms that members of a given organization would describe as "how we do things here," "why we do these things in this way here," and "what we expect around here" (Schein 2010; Weick and Sutcliffe 2007). Organizational culture colors the lens through which members formulate their mental model of "the right thing to do" in a given situation and their perceptions of which types of decisions or actions may be praised and which may be frowned upon. It is the compass that clinicians, staff, and administrators use to guide their behaviors, attitudes, and perceptions on the job (Zohar and Luria 2005; Schein 2010). This is why culture is a critical aspect of developing and sustaining reliably safe care and why it is important for healthcare leaders to mindfully manage the culture in their organization, department, unit, or team as part of their work.

1.2.1 Definitions of Safety Culture

HROs develop strong safety cultures (Bierly 1995; Weick and Sutcliffe 2015) and emphasize collective accountability for identifying and addressing system issues that contribute to undesirable outcomes (Weaver et al. 2014). Safety culture refers to one facet of a larger, overarching organizational culture. While multiple definitions exist, safety culture can be defined as "those aspects of organisational culture which impact attitudes and behaviours related to increasing or decreasing risk" to organizational members and to the individuals and communities served by the organization (Guldenmund 2000, p. 250). An organization's overarching culture tends to encompass aspects such as how internally versus externally focused an organization tends to be and the degree to which flexibility and discretion are valued relative to factors such as stability and control (Cameron and Quinn 2011). Within that larger culture, the concept of *safety culture* focuses specifically on the way that risk, safety, and occupational health are approached and valued within a given organization or group (Guldenmund 2014; Guldenmund 2000). The related construct of *patient safety culture* further sharpens this focus and refers to the values, beliefs, assumptions, behavioral norms, symbols, rites, and rituals specifically related to patient safety (Waterson 2014; Guldenmund 2014). Patient safety culture is a multidimensional concept that generally manifests in (1) communication patterns and language related to patient safety; (2) feedback, reward, and corrective action practices related to patient safety; (3) formal and informal leader actions and expectations related to patient safety; (4) teamwork processes and collaboration norms; (5) resource allocation practices; and (6) error detection, correction, and learning systems (Schein 2010). Finally, the related but distinct concept of *patient safety climate* refers specifically to clinician and staff perceptions of the more observable aspects of patient safety culture including policies and procedures and the degree to which leaders and colleagues prioritize patient safety in their daily work (Zohar 2010; Zohar et al. 2007; Waterson 2014). For parsimony, we will use the term *patient safety culture* for the remainder of this chapter, bearing in mind the nuanced differences between these concepts despite the fact that they are often used interchangeably in practice.

It is important to emphasize that patient safety culture is only one aspect of an organization's overarching culture and that organizational attitudes and norms related to patient safety are shaped, at least in part, by this overarching organizational culture. One of the most widely cited frameworks used to conceptualize and measure general organizational culture is the Competing Values Framework (CVF) (Cameron and Quinn 2011). The CVF describes four dimensions or "types" of general organizational culture: (1) group cultures (those that emphasize and value teamwork, inclusion, participation, and share rewards); (2) entrepreneurial (cultures that value innovation, are tolerant of risk-taking in the name of innovation, and reward individual achievement or initiative); (3) hierarchical (those that value and emphasize order and predictability, reward rule-following, and use primarily rank-based rewards); and (4) rational or production-oriented cultures (those that value fair exchange and reward in return for accomplishing goals). General organizational culture measures based on the CVF are empirically associated with the patient safety climate in the acute care context. For example, a study of 30 Veteran's Administration hospitals in the United States found that those hospitals with more group-oriented cultures (e.g., those in which collegiality, shared decision-making, and participation by all were valued) and entrepreneurial cultures (e.g., those in which innovation, learning, and adaptability were valued) also had more desirable patient safety climates (Hartmann et al. 2009; Singer et al. 2009). The same study found that hospitals with more hierarchical cultures had lower, less desirable patient safety climates. This was some of the earliest work to provide empirical evidence for the recommendation that leaders work to promote group- or team-oriented cultures and to change attitudes and norms that feed hierarchical cultures.

Later work adapted the CVF framework to also include quality-oriented, patient-centered, and physician-centered cultural dimensions (Nembhard et al. 2012). Applying this extended framework to a sample of eight multispecialty medical groups, cultural variation was visible both within and between the groups. Specifically, qualitative analyses demonstrated the presence of subcultures and potentially conflicting cultural orientations; for example, strong patient-centered and physician-centered orientations existed simultaneously within the same group. These findings underscore the complexity of organizational culture and highlight that multiple subcultures often coexist within the same organization. It also highlights that some aspects of organizational culture might interact or conflict with other aspects. This suggests that healthcare leaders must also pay attention to potential alignments and misalignments between the various dimensions of their overarching organizational culture.

1.2.2 Models Examining the Inputs, Emergence, and Outcomes of Safety Culture and Climate

Numerous theoretical and conceptual models have been developed to attempt to describe safety culture, how it emerges, and the factors that influence its emergence and fluctuations over time. While a comprehensive review of these models is beyond the scope of this chapter, we describe three of these models to provide an overview of (1) the layers that make up safety culture, (2) the inputs or factors that influence culture, (3) the processes through which culture emerges and changes, and (4) associated outcomes. We encourage interested readers to see Guldenmund (2014) for an in-depth review and history of organizational culture models.

1.2.2.1 Reiman's Layers of Culture Model

Most theoretical models of patient safety culture build on models of general organizational culture to characterize culture as a dynamic state rather than an end point or outcome, a critical point for healthcare leaders to consider (Reiman et al. 2010; Guldenmund 2014; Schein 2010). These conceptual models emphasize that a culture of safety is not a final destination but a continuous journey that emerges and continually develops through interactions between different factors at multiple levels of a given organization. For example, Teemu Reiman and colleagues (2010) synthesized cultural models in the organizational and safety sciences to create a multilevel framework, and in doing so identified three layers of factors that together enable a culture of safety to emerge between members of a given organization, unit, or team: (1) organizational dimensions, (2) social processes, and (3) psychological dimensions. Organizational dimensions included factors such as actions of organizational leadership and immediate supervisors related to safety, collaboration, and information flow between units and professional groups; cooperation practices; resource management; management of change; and organizational learning practices. Social processes included those processes that affect how information and practices observed by frontline providers are interpreted, the social factors that shape daily practices, and how meaning is created. For example, collective sensemaking, normalization, processes related to creating and maintaining social identities, and adaptation of procedures or norms to fit a unit or department's local context all play a role in shaping what members of a given organization or group view as potential patient safety risks. Third, psychological dimensions refer to individual-level factors that create the foundation for an individual's motivation and propensity to pay attention to or prioritize safety-oriented behaviors during their daily work. Examples include a sense of control over and perceived meaningfulness of one's work, and a knowledge of hazards or risks and the means to achieve safe outcomes. A knowledge of shared goals and requirements helps to create a mind-set and attitude alert to the possibility of potential hazards and mindfulness of patient safety as a shared goal. As depicted in Figure 1.2, this model emphasizes that these three dimensions interact, with the organizational dimensions creating the preconditions for the psychological dimensions and providing cues or triggers for the social processes. The social processes play a key role in helping frontline care providers to interpret and attribute meaning to the organizational dimensions, and the psychological dimensions direct and steer the organizational dimensions. This model is valuable in highlighting the complex range of factors and processes that interact to create organizational culture and draw

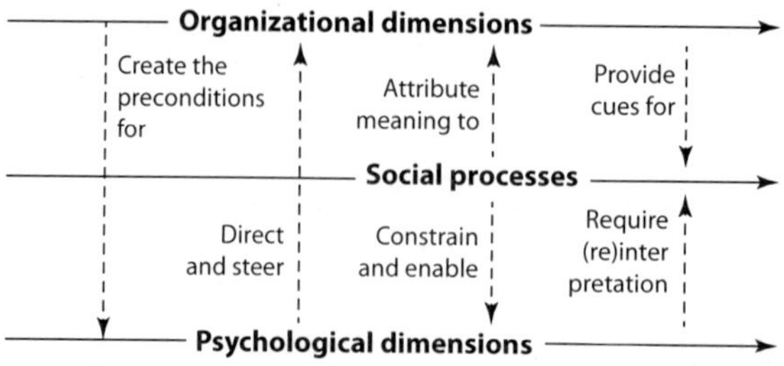

Organizational dimensions:
Organizational management system
Actions of the management to promote safety
Actions of the immediate supervisor
Practices of cooperation
Communication and information flow
Practices of organizational learning
Management of competencies and training
Management of resources
Management of change
Management to third parties/subcontractors
Collaboration and information flow between units
Collaboration and information flow between professional groups

Social processes:
Collective sensemaking
Social identity maintenance
Optimizing and local adaptation
Normalization of cues
Embedding of conceptions

Psychological dimensions:
Perceived meaningfulness of one's work
Sense of control over one's own work and results
Knowledge of organizational and group expectations concerning one's work
Sence of personal responsibility over one's own work and its results
Knowledge of the hazards and hazard mechanisms that can turn potential hazards into actual harm
Knowledge of safety and means to achieve it
Knowledge of the organizational core task, its constraints, and requirements

Figure 1.2 Multilayered model of safety culture. (Reprinted with permission from Reiman, T., et al., *Quality and Safety in Healthcare*, 19, 1, 2010.)

attention to the role organizational leaders play in demonstrating patient safety as a goal that is prioritized, valued, and resourced.

1.2.2.2 Zohar's (2003) Multilevel Model of Safety Climate

Dov Zohar, a leading organizational safety scientist, developed a multilevel model of safety climate (see Figure 1.3) that offers four important insights (Zohar 2003; Zohar 2010; Zohar et al. 2007). First, this model builds on published theories and studies examining climate strength to emphasize that a safety climate is born out of frontline perceptions of the degree to which espoused values (i.e., what leaders and colleagues say is important) align with enacted values (i.e., what leaders, colleagues, and influential others actually do in their day-to-day work). The model suggests, for example, that frontline clinician perceptions of the degree to which their organization prioritizes patient safety is based on the degree to which the statements made by organizational and departmental leaders about patient safety actually align with the behaviors and decisions these leaders make in practice. This model is helpful for understanding that safety culture or climate is stronger when espoused and enacted values are aligned and weaker when they are not. For example, the model suggests that the organizational safety climate is stronger when leaders say that patient safety is their number one priority (an espoused value) and then also choose to allocate protected time or resources that enable frontline clinicians and staff to lead patient safety initiatives (an enacted value). Empirical evidence demonstrates that stronger safety climates are better predictors of patient safety practices related to medication administration and emergency resuscitation (Zohar et al. 2007). In practice, such evidence informed recommendations to examine both the level (e.g., the mean or percentage of positive response among members of given unit, department, or organization) and strength (e.g., the standard deviation of scores among members of a given group or more advanced metrics of within-group agreement like the Rwg(i) statistic [James et al. 1993; LeBreton and Senter 2007]) of patient safety climate survey results (Ginsburg and Oore 2016; Vogus 2016).

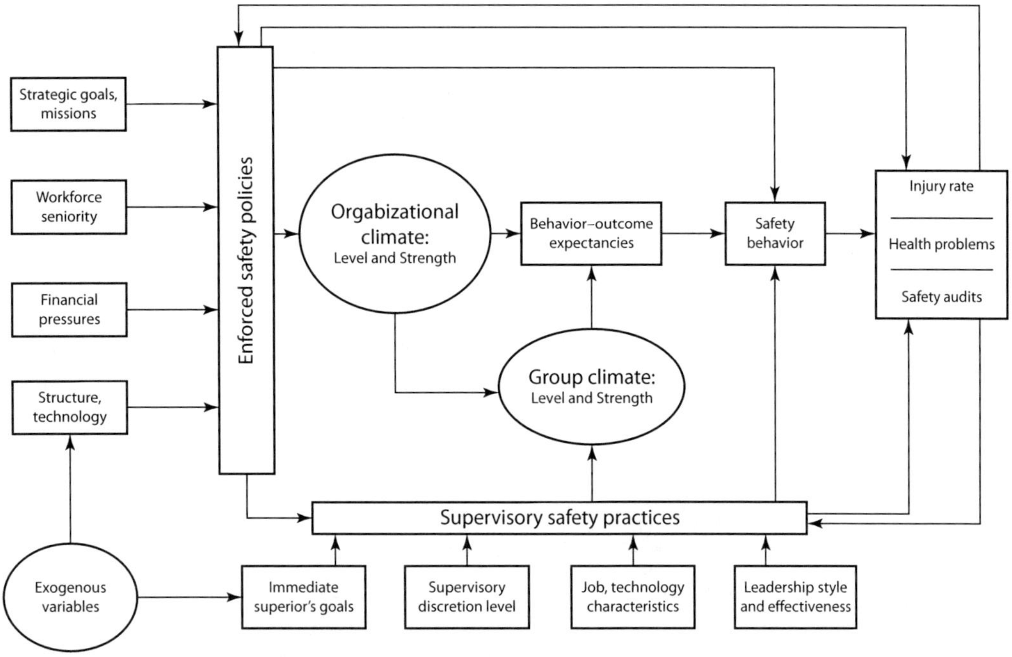

Figure 1.3 Zohar's multilevel model of safety climate. (Reprinted with permission from Zohar, D., *Handbook of Organizational Health Psychology*, American Psychological Association, Washington, DC, 2003.)

Second, this model incorporates theory and evidence demonstrating that safety culture is a multilevel phenomenon, meaning that (1) units, departments, and other groups develop their own safety-oriented subcultures; and (2) frontline clinicians and staff can differentiate the degree to which safety is prioritized at the organizational level from the degree to which it is prioritized at their local unit, department, or team level. For example, implementation of organizational-level safety policies and procedures requires substantial interpretation by local unit and departmental leaders as well as by frontline staff. Differences in how organizational policies are interpreted as well as differences in local unit or department history, variation in disciplines that work together in a given unit or department, and numerous other factors contribute to significant differences in safety-related norms across work areas that make up a single organization (Zohar 2010). For example, studies of acute care facilities in the United States suggest that scores on survey-based measures of patient safety culture can differ between units in the same hospital by 20% or more (Huang et al. 2010; Huang et al. 2007; Sorra and Dyer 2010; Hartmann et al. 2009). Similar variation has also been documented between different disciplines or professional groups working in the same unit or department. These variations have important implications for the evaluation of safety culture in practice and leadership strategies for strengthening a safety culture. These are discussed in more detail below.

Zohar's model also outlines factors that influence frontline team member perceptions of safety culture at both the organizational and local unit, department, or team level. For example, organizational-level goals, strategy, structure, technology, workforce factors, and the decisions and behaviors of senior or executive leaders critically influence the enforcement of organizational safety policies. These factors, as well as when, how, and for whom organization-level safety policies are perceived as being enforced, can influence team member perceptions of their organization's orientation toward patient safety. Comparatively, the goals of local supervisors or mid-level leaders, their leadership style and effectiveness, and the characteristics of the local unit or department (e.g., level of acuity, structure, degree of multidisciplinary collaboration, etc.) have a more direct influence on team member perceptions of the local safety culture in their specific unit, department, or team. The model suggests that organizational safety culture and local unit or department-level safety culture interact to shape frontline clinician and staff expectations about the degree to which their behaviors affect or influence safety outcomes. This in turn influences the probability that they will prioritize safety over other competing goals (e.g., efficiency and throughput) in their daily work.

While this model was originally developed to focus on occupational health outcomes and the physical safety of organizational employees, it certainly has implications for leaders aiming to understand and build a strong culture of patient safety. Overall, this model highlights the importance of aligning espoused values with decisions and behaviors practiced daily by leaders. Additionally, it reminds leaders to pay attention to overarching organizational culture as well as local unit, department, or team culture. Different factors influence culture at these levels, and the model emphasizes the need to activate both senior organizational leaders and mid-level leaders in efforts to build strong safety cultures.

1.2.2.3 High Reliability Organizing and Safety Culture: The 3 Es Model

The concept of high reliability organizing originated in research examining organizations operating in high-risk environments that were successful in maintaining low rates of error and stakeholder harm despite operating under extreme conditions. Described by Karlene Roberts, Todd LaPorte, and Gene Rochlin as "high reliability organisations or HROs," organizations including military naval ships; nuclear power, oil, and gas operations; and airlines were found to master the capacity to remain sensitive to and successfully adapt to the unexpected in ways that allowed them to maintain reliably safe outcomes with relatively low rates of catastrophe (Rochlin et al. 1987). Later work by Kathleen Sutcliffe, Karl Weick, and others revealed that such organizations achieve these reliably safe outcomes by developing and practicing "mindful organizing," or a shared orientation toward collective mindfulness in their daily work that includes paying attention to weak signals that may suggest the potential for unintended consequences and processes that facilitate adaptation, resilience, and teamwork (Sutcliffe 2011; Weick et al. 1990; Weick and Sutcliffe 2015). This work underscored that high reliability was not necessarily the product of rigid, detailed standardized protocols and enforced compliance. Instead, *reliably safe outcomes* were the product of relatively flexible procedures enacted successfully thanks to a shared underlying mind-set that emphasized sensitivity to weak signals, deference to experience, and novel insights rather than rote deference to formal hierarchy, a learning orientation, an appreciation for systems, and an understanding of interdependencies, and a commitment to adaptation and resilience (Weick and Sutcliffe 2007; Sutcliffe et al. 2016).

However, while healthcare organizations have aimed to reduce the occurrence of errors within their systems, patients continue to be harmed. While some organizations succeed in various process improvement projects, many healthcare provider organizations continue to be challenged by lapses into "mindless" organizing and struggle to maintain high levels of safety, quality, and clinical excellence. For example, many process improvement projects include a specific timeline with a start and end date, while organizing for high reliability is an iterative and continuous process. A detailed discussion of the science of HROs and related practices appears in Chapter 5 by

Federico, Brooks, and Edrees and highlights the importance of creating a strong safety culture as a foundational element of HROs. In the current chapter, we draw attention to a conceptual model developed by Tim Vogus and Kathleen Sutcliffe and rooted in research examining HROs and theories of mindful organizing that describe the pathways through which a culture of patient safety and mindful organizing can emerge or change over time (Vogus et al. 2010). This model is critical in reinforcing the notion that mindful organizing "must be treated as a culture, as well as a set of principles that guide practice" (Weick and Sutcliffe 2015, p. 137).

The "3 Es" model outlines how organizational members contribute to developing and sustaining a culture of safety and mindful organizing through practices that can be organized into three categories: (1) enabling, (2) enacting, and (3) elaborating practices (Vogus et al. 2010). As shown in Table 1.1, this model suggests that formal and informal leaders can help to enable a safety culture by drawing attention to patient safety as an organizational and personal priority as well as working to support frontline team members in identifying safety issues that have affected patient care or may pose risks.

In doing so, leaders enable clinicians to prioritize specific safety issues and empower them to speak up when there is potential patient harm. Once these safety issues have been identified, staff will be able to translate them into meaningful improvements. As a result, they become part of a practice in which staff actively make changes to improve patient care. Thus, it is the commitment and—more importantly—the action of leaders that enable a culture of safety.

While enabling a culture of safety might seem promising on its own, it is not sufficient. The 3 Es model emphasizes that organizations must enact a safety culture by creating an environment in which staff can openly communicate and report errors to leadership. If staff are able to highlight patient safety issues, they can then tackle them by utilizing problem-solving resources in their local work areas. Moreover, organizational members that enact a safety culture adopt the mind-set and practices of mindful organizing. These concepts are explained in more detail in Chapter 5. Finally, elaborating

Table 1.1 Components of the 3 Es Model of Enabling, Enacting, and Elaborating a Culture of Patient Safety

Component	Description
Enabling	Leaders enable safer practices through • Directing attention to patient and staff safety • Creating psychologically safe contexts where staff feel safe to speak up and act in ways to improve patient safety
Enacting	Frontline staff enact a safety culture through • Speaking up respectfully and accurately representing emerging concerns and possible threats to patient safety • Mobilizing resources or taking actions to resolve potential threats to safety
Elaborating	Leaders and staff implement practices that • Rigorously reflect on and learn from safety outcomes, including near misses. This also includes critically analyzing and learning from critical incidents that occur in other units or departments and other, external, healthcare organizations. • Use feedback to modify enabling practices and enacting processes.

Source: Adapted from Vogus, T.J., et al. *Academy of Management Perspectives*, 24, 60, 2010.

practices focus on learning and the use of this learning to inform future practices. Elaborating practices include those that engage leaders, clinicians, and staff in reflecting on safety outcomes and using the feedback to change and modify the practices that enable and enact a safety culture.

A culture of safety that adequately adopts the principles of high reliability organizing is a culture built on trust, a learning orientation, humility, and continuous process improvement. Trust can be strengthened when organizational leaders and team members eliminate blame for system failures, encourage staff to report, react in a timely fashion to address system defects, and communicate these improvements. The interplay between the three components of trust, learning-oriented reporting, and support for improvement work can strengthen a culture of patient safety and facilitate reliably safe outcomes (Chassin and Loeb 2013; Sutcliffe et al. 2016).

1.2.3 Patient Safety Culture and Outcomes

Studies using surveys to measure clinician and staff perceptions of patient safety culture demonstrate small to medium associations between perceptions of culture and a variety of care processes, patient outcomes, and clinician outcomes including (1) voluntary incident reporting by clinicians and staff (Itoh et al. 2014; El-Jardali et al. 2014; Martinez et al. 2015; Sorra and Dyer 2010); (2) adherence to standard infection precaution guidelines (Hessels and Larson 2016); (3) adverse events (e.g., medication errors, care-related urinary tract infection rates [Hofmann and Mark 2006; Mardon et al. 2010; Singer et al. 2009]); (4) hospital readmission rates (Hansen et al. 2011); (5) patient satisfaction and perceptions of their care experience (Sorra et al. 2014; Hofmann and Mark 2006); (6) employee engagement (Daugherty et al. 2016); and (7) clinician job-related injury (e.g., back injuries [Gimeno et al. 2005; Cook et al. 2016; Hofmann and Mark 2006]). Such findings align with the conceptual models discussed above that emphasize culture and climate as relatively distal contextual influences that likely interact with other contextual and individual-level factors to shape safety-oriented behaviors and outcomes in practice.

From a practice perspective, it is important to consider two additional issues. First, the level or unit of analysis often varies between studies. For example, several studies examine associations between hospital-level safety culture survey scores and hospital-level outcomes (e.g., Mardon et al. 2010; Sorra et al. 2014; Wagner et al. 2013), while other studies examine the association between unit- or department-level measures of safety culture and outcomes (e.g., Huang et al. 2010; Sexton et al. 2006; Daugherty et al. 2016; Sexton et al. 2011). Leaders and health services researchers should be mindful of the ecological fallacy, that is, mistakenly inferring that the associations observed in organizational or hospital-level analyses play out in exactly the same way or with the same degree of association at unit or departmental level (or vice versa). Second, these studies and practitioner-oriented models of organizational change (such as John Kotter's eight-step model of leading change) eloquently underscore that culture change comes last (Kotter and Heskett 1992; Kotter 2012). That is to say, the concept of "culture change" really means developing specific leadership and organizational practices that model, reinforce, and reward a mindful, team-oriented, safety-focused approach first, and that as these become instantiated as new habits, attitudes, and norms, these culture changes will solidify.

1.3 Leadership and Organizational Culture

The models described in Section 1.2 demonstrate a broad range of factors that influence how cultures emerge, develop, and change over time. However, the conceptual and empirical evidence clearly points to the role that formal and informal leaders play in developing and sustaining a culture of patient safety. Formal leaders are individuals with a formal leadership title (e.g., manager, supervisor, director, and executive), while informal leaders include individuals that may lead without a formal title thanks to their expertise, tenure, social ties, or other mechanisms. Both empirical and qualitative evidence demonstrate that the attitudes and actions of both formal and informal leaders can influence several key constructs underlying reliably safe outcomes including (1) psychological safety, or the degree to which team members feel it is safe to speak up with concerns, novel information, or novel ideas (Nembhard and Edmondson 2006); (2) organizational learning (Edmondson 2004; Tucker et al. 2007); (3) clear, shared goals and accountabilities related to patient safety and care quality (Keroack et al. 2007; Wachter and Pronovost 2009); (4) the perceived priority of safety and quality relative to other goals (Keroack et al. 2007); (5) a climate of trust and mutual respect (Sutcliffe et al. 2016); and (6) heedful interrelating, a shared mind-set that values understanding the upstream and downstream implications of one's own daily work (Sutcliffe 2011; Weick and Sutcliffe 2015).

From a practical perspective, the next logical question is: how do leaders influence these things? Edgar Schein (2010) articulated two primary mechanisms by which leaders shape culture, summarized in Table 1.2. Primary mechanisms generally refer to the behavioral tools most available to leaders and under their immediate, personal control. Schein argues that these are the tools that are most visible and salient to others. Secondary mechanisms refer to visible yet potentially less immediately malleable mechanisms.

1.4 Tools for Measuring Patient Safety Culture

A positive safety culture is one in which transparency, learning from system defects, and continuous process improvement become an integral part of daily practice. Arguably, one part of mindfully managing culture involves assessing it in some way and using the insight gained to identify how best to strengthen areas of weakness and to leverage areas of strength. Surveys designed to capture clinical and nonclinical staff perceptions about patient safety and practice norms are one commonly adopted strategy for evaluating organizational patient safety culture in healthcare. A detailed overview of the multitude of metrics available is outside the scope of this chapter. However, we provide a brief summary of several metrics commonly used in practice but also point readers to more in-depth reviews that provide detailed discussions of the psychometric properties of the tools and other expert panel findings (Flin et al. 2006; Flin 2007; Jackson et al. 2010; Parker et al. 2015).

1.4.1 Patient Safety Culture and Climate Assessment Tools in Healthcare

As discussed above, safety climate is defined as the surface layers or visible factors that manifest in practice thanks to the underlying patient safety culture. Patient safety climate surveys capture staff perceptions and beliefs about patient safety as an organizational and local unit or work area priority (Waterson 2014). In line with theoretical models defining climate as a group-level construct, survey responses are collected at an individual level and aggregated to create unit-level, departmental-level, and organizational-level scores (Sorra and Dyer 2010). These results can be used to analyze trends over time, examine variation, and benchmark against other similar care-delivery organizations.

Examples of the numerous surveys and assessment tools used to assess patient safety climate and related concepts include

- Patient Safety Cultures in Healthcare Organizations (PSCHO; Singer et al. 2007)
- Multiple versions of the Survey on Patient Safety Culture (SOPS; Nieva and Sorra 2003):

Table 1.2 Mechanisms for Developing and Embedding a Culture of Safety

Mechanisms	Examples
Primary Mechanisms	
What leaders pay attention to, measure, and direct attention toward on a regular basis	• Leaders pay attention to, comment on, and ask questions about patient safety and quality-improvement efforts • Clear, just accountability systems exist for patient safety • Organizational goals and improvement priorities are centrally established in partnership with clinical leadership; decisions regarding tactics to improve are decentralized and clinician-driven • Executive, department, and unit leadership accept responsibility for quality and safety within their areas of oversight • Leaders link patient safety, care quality, and service excellence together and emphasize them as integral to competitive advantage and superior care
How leaders react to near misses, critical incidents, events, and crises	• Leaders exhibit and encourage a learning orientation that aims to understand what happen, why, and what can be learned
How leaders allocate resources and time	• Protected, paid time for leading or participating in the development, design, implementation, and/or evaluation of quality and safety improvement efforts is prioritized
Deliberate role modeling, teaching, coaching	• Leaders are passionate about patient safety, quality, and service excellence
How leaders allocate rewards and status	• Leaders frequently recognize clinician and nonclinician contributions to safety at every level
How leaders recruit, select, promote, and sanction	• Leaders select and promote people with skills in quality and safety improvement • Expectations regarding professional behavior and participation in improvement activities are salient and clearly articulated to clinical and nonclinical team members • Leaders swiftly deal with unprofessional behavior and behaviors that undermine a culture of safety in a just manner, based on predefined expectations and accountability structures
Secondary Mechanisms	
Organizational design and structure (e.g., organizational chart, reporting and approval structures)	• Leaders design governance structures and practices that minimize conflict between organizational missions (e.g., in an academic medical center), service lines, and functional areas

(*Continued*)

Table 1.2 (Continued) Mechanisms for Developing and Embedding a Culture of Safety

Mechanisms	Examples
Organizational policies, systems, and procedures	• Organizational policies and procedures outline clear roles and responsibilities for all organizational team members related to patient safety and quality • Policies and procedures are developed with a systems view of errors in mind, providing provisions for adaptation and revision
Organizational rites and rituals	• Leaders facilitate organizational rituals that reinforce the espoused priority of patient safety and quality improvement and actively participate in these activities
Stories about important people or events	• Leaders share local stories that reinforce the value of continuous improvement and the role team members at all levels of the organization play in patient safety, care quality, and service excellence
Physical layout and space	• Leaders ensure that there is space for patient safety and quality improvement work to occur • Building layout and structural issues that contribute to patient safety concerns are prioritized
Formal statements about organizational mission, vision, values	• Patient safety and care quality, as well as a commitment to continuous improvement, are emphasized in organizational-, department-, and unit-level statements of mission and values

Source: Pronovost, P. J., et al. *The New England Journal of Medicine*, 355, 2725, 2010; Schein, E. H., *Organizational Culture and Leadership*, Jossey-Bass, Hoboken (NJ), 2010; Vogus, T. J., et al., *Academy of Management Perspectives*, 24, 60, 2010; and Keroack, M. A., et al., *Academic Medicine*, 82, 1178, 2007.

  - Hospital Survey on Patient Safety Culture
  - Medical Office Survey on Patient Safety Culture
  - Nursing Home Survey on Patient Safety Culture
  - Community Pharmacy Survey on Patient Safety Culture
  - Ambulatory Surgery Centre Survey on Patient Safety Culture
- Safety Attitudes Questionnaire (SAQ; Sexton et al. 2006)
- Veteran's Administration Patient Safety Culture Questionnaire (VHA PSCQ; Burr et al. 2002)
- Culture of Safety Survey (CSS; Weingart et al. 2004)
- Medication Safety Self-Assessment (MSSA; Smetzer et al. 2003),
- Safety Organizing Scale (SOS; Vogus and Sutcliffe 2007)
- Manchester Patient Safety Framework (MaPSaF; National Health Service [United Kingdom] 2006)
- Strategies for Leadership: An Organizational Approach to Patient Safety (SLOAPS; VHA Inc. 2000)

The majority are surveys that use multiple questions to elicit respondent perceptions about several dimensions (or aspects) of patient safety culture including leadership, policies, staffing, teamwork, communication, organizational learning, safety, and reporting adverse events. Operationally, the SAQ and the collection of SOPS surveys are two of the most commonly used surveys in healthcare (Profit et al. 2016). Both surveys have been translated and adapted for use internationally. The MaPSaF and SLOAPS tools provide a different approach for evaluating culture. These tools are not surveys, but instead use culture maturation frameworks that define specific types or degrees of cultural maturation and ask respondents to evaluate the level of maturity their own organizational culture or climate aligns best with. These tools are designed to facilitate open discussion and group self-assessment using a discussion to consensus model, rather than asking individual respondents to complete a survey. The MaPSaF is widely utilized in the National Health Service (NHS) in the United Kingdom to support organizational leaders and clinicians in prioritizing their efforts to create a mature, open, and fair patient safety culture (Carthey 2014). When deciding which approach or tool to utilize, operational patient safety leaders and organizational survey administrators should understand that each tool has inherent strengths and weaknesses.

In addition to these tools, which have demonstrated reasonable, evidence-based psychometric properties, some healthcare organizations choose to develop hybrid surveys in which they adapt, modify, or create their own survey tools in an effort to elicit perceptions of local priority areas or adapt existing surveys for specific populations. However, organizations should be careful when choosing this route or when making modifications to existing tools as this can significantly impact the validity and reliability of the data collected using such hybrid or in-house assessment tools. For example, rather than selecting individual items or questions from existing measures, expert guidance suggests selecting and including all of the items that make up a particular dimension of interest. Ideally, pilot testing and examining the psychometric properties of the hybrid survey to ensure reliability and validity should follow any adaptations or the creation of a hybrid survey. Several recommendations and guidelines for adapting such assessment tools have been published by the Agency for Healthcare Research and Quality (AHRQ) (Sorra et al. 2016) and The Leapfrog Group (The Leapfrog Group 2016b).

Accreditation agencies, including the Joint Commission and Joint Commission International (The Joint Commission 2016) and others, have strongly recommended that organizations regularly measure workforce perceptions of patient safety culture. Regular assessment can facilitate staff awareness regarding organizational interest in sustaining a positive and strong culture of patient safety. Regular assessment also can provide administrative and clinical leadership with insight into patterns of safety within and across units or work areas, informing resource allocation and strategic planning. While a detailed discussion is outside the scope of this chapter, practical guides for conducting survey-based organizational assessments are available (e.g., AHRQ SOPS survey user guides: https://www.ahrq.gov/professionals/quality-patient-safety/patientsafetyculture/index.html).

1.5 Interventions and Strategies for Building Cultures of Patient Safety

Existing evidence points to several strategies for establishing a positive, patient safety-focused culture, most of which focus on leadership, teamwork, and behavioral change rather than technologies. For example, leadership or executive rounding, structured educational programs, team-based strategies, multifaceted unit-based programs, and multicomponent organizational interventions have been examined as strategies designed to elaborate a culture of safety in healthcare organizations (Morello et al. 2012; Weaver et al. 2013). Examples of these strategies are summarized in Table 1.3. Additional strategies include carefully considering patient safety culture survey results and other organizational data prior to introducing new initiatives or interventions. Given that

Table 1.3 Strategies and Interventions for Developing and Sustaining a Culture of Patient Safety

Strategy	Description	Examples and related citations
Leadership/executive rounding	Leadership or executive rounds allow senior leadership to visit patient care areas and engage with frontline healthcare providers in an effort to address safety concerns and opportunities for improvement. Demonstrates senior leadership commitment to safety, increases visibility, and can help resource-improvement initiatives	Patient safety rounding by senior leaders that engages senior leaders in communication with frontline healthcare providers (Thomas et al. 2005; Tucker and Singer 2014)
Structured educational programs and norm-facilitating tools	The purpose of structured educational programs is to change teamwork practices to improve patient outcomes. Norm-facilitating tools focus on building empowerment, commitment, and collaboration among team members	Pre-briefs and checklists (e.g., Allard et al. 2011; Treadwell et al. 2014); clinical leadership educational program (Ginsburg et al. 2005)
Team-training strategies	These strategies aim to (1) Assess the underlying factors that affect teamwork, such as knowledge, skills, and attitudes (2) Develop structured methods to strengthen teamwork, communication, collaboration, and leadership among teams	TeamSTEPPS™ (Team Strategies and Tools to Enhance Performance and Patient Safety) (King et al. 2008)
Multifaceted unit-based programs	These types of programs include several interventions that promote patient safety culture	The Comprehensive Unit-Based Safety Program (CUSP) (Pronovost et al. 2006; Berenholtz et al. 2014)
Multicomponent organizational interventions	These types of interventions often employ changes implemented at multiple system levels	These may include changes in governance or reporting structure, interdisciplinary daily rounding, leadership/executive walk arounds, etc.

patient safety culture is a multidimensional concept, the evidence suggests that multicomponent interventions designed to include several strategies under one organizational initiative (such as focusing on the goal of improving communication while implementing teamwork tools or training and interdisciplinary rounds as well as executive/leadership rounds) tend to demonstrate more robust effects (Sacks et al. 2015; Weaver et al. 2013).

1.6 Barriers to Developing and Sustaining Safety Cultures

While numerous efforts have focused on establishing positive patient safety cultures, there continue to be barriers and challenges to developing these cultures. Some barriers include:

- Poor implementation of organizational strategies or initiatives that aim to improve patient safety culture (Morello 2013). This will ultimately lead to staff disengagement in future organizational efforts and will create distrust within the organization.
- Limited evidence on the effectiveness of patient safety culture interventions and their impact on organizational cost (Weaver et al. 2013). Further research is needed to evaluate and quantify the cost-effectiveness of specific interventions used to improve patient safety culture such as the adoption of teamwork and communication tools as well as the implementation of organizational initiatives and their impact on patient outcomes and experiences.
- Challenges in engaging frontline healthcare providers when a top-down management approach to safety is being used (Waterson 2014).
- Mandatory requirements from regulators and/or accrediting bodies that determine organizational performance based on the quantity of patient safety and quality improvement projects and initiatives. This will result in pressurizing staff to create projects that are not sustainable rather than focusing on improving patient safety (Waterson 2014).
- Lack of multidisciplinary teamwork among clinicians. Healthcare providers continue to work in silos because of the way in which the traditional educational system has failed to support multidisciplinary training.
- Perceptions of an organizational culture of blame in which there continues to be a stigma attached to reporting and addressing errors (Edrees 2017).
- Lack of established error-reporting systems, lack of clarity on what or how to report, and lack of timely feedback create distrust within the organization (Edrees 2017).
- Lack of leadership support in developing patient safety unit-based projects and organizational initiatives.

1.7 Application: A Case Study of Transformation and Building a Culture of Resilience After the MERS–CoV Outbreak at the Ministry of National Guard Health Affairs (NGHA), Kingdom of Saudi Arabia

1.7.1 Background

The Ministry of National Guard Health Affairs is a large, tertiary academic medical center located in the Kingdom of Saudi Arabia. It has five main campuses across the country with the largest based in Riyadh, which includes a 1,000 plus bed hospital, research center, and health sciences university. NGHA has provided healthcare services to the Saudi Arabian National Guard personnel and their dependents for many years.

1.7.2 The MERS–CoV Outbreak

In July 2015, NGHA–Riyadh experienced one of the largest Middle East Respiratory Syndrome coronavirus (MERS–CoV) outbreaks, which led to the closure of the hospital in August 2015. The outbreak revealed several system issues that had been building for some time: overcrowding and boarding in the emergency department, poor infection control practices, mismanagement of healthcare services, and delays in the identification and handling of suspected cases. As a result, the organization responded to this emergency by establishing a command and control center and emergency plan to oversee and address these challenges in a timely fashion (see also Chapter 11). Fortunately, the organization was declared free of MERS–CoV in October 2015.

1.7.3 Transformation and Building a Culture of Resilience

Many lives were lost during the outbreak. Several healthcare providers were infected and harmed. The community lost trust in the organization's ability to provide optimal care. In an effort to redefine care delivery, rebuild trust, and strengthen the organizational culture after the outbreak, the Chief Executive Officer, His Excellency Dr. Bandar Al Knawy, introduced and led the NGHA Transformation Program with a vision that focused on changing the culture to prioritize patient care and providing the "Right Care, Right Now." The Transformation Program provided a shared purpose for staff to engage in improving patient care at NGHA. The organization collectively agreed on zero tolerance of patient harm. Moreover, the leadership aimed to achieve excellence by partnering with frontline staff and administrators to identify system challenges and mitigate patient harm.

The Transformation Program included and was succeeded by several transformation efforts including and not limited to the Patient Outcomes Workshop, TeamSTEPPS training, and the "Perfect Week" initiative. These initiatives provided staff with an opportunity to transparently address factors affecting organizational culture such as organizational policies, communication, teamwork, event reporting, the decisions of senior executives, and others. Table 1.4 details several strategies that were implemented in an effort to develop a strong culture of safety at NGHA.

As mentioned above, formal and informal leaders play a significant role in creating a strong culture of patient safety and sustaining highly reliable care. Given the MERS–CoV outbreak, there was a need for the NGHA leadership to effectively manage organizational culture by introducing the aforementioned initiatives. As a result, staff were engaged and empowered, clinicians were able to identify system defects and mitigate patient harm, leaders and department heads were able to handle patient flow through streamlined admissions and discharge processes, and all staff were reeducated on the importance of infection control guidelines and practices.

1.8 Conclusions and Lessons Learned

A culture of safety is a relatively dynamic state that continuously emerges and evolves through the decisions and actions used by organizational leaders and frontline staff to enact their values and beliefs about the priority of patient safety relative to sometimes competing goals. Overarching organizational culture and more localized departmental, unit, professional, and team cultures

Table 1.4 Case Study: Strategies for Developing and Sustaining a Strong Safety Culture at NGHA

Strategy	Examples and description
Structured educational program	Patient outcomes workshop: This two-day workshop was led by international experts to provide clinical decision-makers and improvement leaders with an understanding of the fundamentals of outcomes-based healthcare
Team-based strategies	TeamSTEPPS training: The purpose of this workshop was to educate clinical leads and decision-makers on an evidence-based set of communication and teamwork tools used to improve patient outcomes
Multicomponent organizational interventions	1. NGHA Transformation Program: The purpose of this organization-wide program was to lead organizational change and build resilience within the system. The areas of focus included transforming emergency care, nursing, bed management, obstetric care, infection control, patient outcomes, and patient experience 2. Perfect Week: The purpose of this one-week initiative was to improve health services, streamline patient flow, and provide timely and effective care. Some of the existing challenges identified in the system included • Delays in consultations • High bed-occupancy levels • Long length of stay • Boarding in the emergency department • Delays in obtaining and communicating critical lab results, and others Several interventions to address these challenges were documented and implemented in the Health Affairs Rules of Excellence in Clinical Care (HARECC), to include • Leadership/executive rounding • Multidisciplinary ward rounds/patient rounds to be concluded by noon • Specified start time for operating room procedures/surgeries • Morning leadership huddles • Clear discharge planning • Escalation procedures in the event of delays in care

color the context in which care is delivered, influencing clinician behaviors, attitudes, and cognitions on the job. Healthcare organizations that thoughtfully develop and maintain strong cultures of safety and mindfully organize and prioritize mutual respect learn faster and achieve more reliably safe outcomes for their patients. Over 50 years of research examining culture in the organizational and safety sciences emphasizes that leaders—both those with a formal leadership title and informal leaders that may lead without a formal title thanks to their expertise, tenure, social ties, or other mechanisms—play critical roles in developing and sustaining a commitment to and culture of patient safety. Additionally, there is evidence to support the efficacy of several interventions as methods to improve frontline clinician and staff perceptions of the culture of safety in their work area and institution (Sacks et al. 2015; Weaver et al. 2013).

So what does the evidence suggest that health system leaders do to facilitate a strong culture of safety in their daily leadership practices? First and foremost, the evidence emphasizes that leaders must strive to align their stated goals of delivering safe, high-quality care with their decisions and actions. Strong cultures of safety can emerge when business decisions align with stated safety and quality goals, while weak cultures persist when leaders state such goals but appear to prioritize patient throughput and financial performance over these goals in organizational business decisions. For example, providing paid, protected time for clinicians to lead or participate in quality improvement work sends clear, salient signals that leaders are actively prioritizing improvement goals. Additionally, leaders can ensure that promotional and privileging criteria, selection criteria, and organizational policies include clear expectations about participation in quality and safety initiatives and that clinical staff have opportunities to develop competencies in quality improvement and change management. Second, leaders should strive to facilitate a learning orientation toward near misses and the weak signals that indicate potential system vulnerabilities. For example, when undesired outcomes happen, it is important for leaders to deliberately role model asking questions about what happened rather than about who is at fault, and coaching others to do the same (see also Chapter 11; Weick and Sutcliffe 2015; Sutcliffe et al. 2016). This includes building event-reporting systems that facilitate continuous learning and that can be easily used to identify or priorities improvement efforts. Leaders must also speak transparently and openly about safety and quality concerns, improvement strategies, and efforts to improve that have succeeded, as well as those that may not have gone as planned.

Existing evidence also highlights that leaders should employ a variety of strategies to remain connected to the work of frontline clinicians. This includes regularly evaluating clinician and staff perceptions of the culture in their work area and in the broader organization. It also includes spending time with frontline clinicians and patients to learn about their concerns and experiences firsthand through executive rounding or other shadowing methods. To be successful, however, the findings from these assessments must lead to active problem solving and demonstrable action by leadership to address the issues identified (Tucker and Singer 2014). Finally, leaders should aim to create and reinforce a culture in which their authority or the authority of others is not a barrier to speaking up or acting in the name of safety. This includes clearly defining expected behavior and standards of professional conduct as well as committing to upholding them personally. It also means holding others accountable when these standards are violated. Studies of behaviors that undermine a culture of safety, including intimidating or disruptive behaviors, show that such behaviors are often present in healthcare professionals in positions of power. Leaders must clearly identify types of disruptive behavior that are not acceptable, clearly define the escalating repercussions for engaging in unacceptable behaviors, and be willing to hold others accountable, especially their peers and fellow leaders. Doing so in a just and fair way requires humble, courageous leadership as well as tact and skills in assertive yet nonaggressive communication methods.

These recommendations are likely to be neither surprising nor groundbreaking, but they require sustained attention, mindful practice, and investment. Many are codified in the accreditation and leadership standards of The Joint Commission (2016) and Joint Commission International (2014), as well as in the rating systems used by The Leapfrog Group (2016a) and other healthcare delivery stakeholders. Enacting the practices or mind-sets described in this chapter simply to comply with these standards, however, undermines the very concept of organizational culture. Culture is about the values and assumptions that implicitly guide daily clinical and leadership practice. The models and evidence summarized in this chapter demonstrate that leadership alone does not create or sustain a culture or climate of patient safety but that the actions, decisions, and attitudes of formal and informal leaders play an important role in shaping organizational culture.

References

Allard, J., A. Bleakley, A. Hobbs, and L. Coombes. 2011. Pre-surgery briefings and safety climate in the operating theatre. *BMJ Quality & Safety* 20 (8): 711–17.

Aranaz-Andrés, J. M., C. Aibar-Remón, R. Limón-Ramírez, A. Amarilla, F. R. Restrepo, O. Urroz, O. Sarabia, et al. 2011. Prevalence of adverse events in the hospitals of five Latin American countries: Results of the 'Iberoamerican Study of Adverse Events' (IBEAS). *BMJ Quality & Safety* 20 (12): 1043–51, BMJ Publishing Group Ltd.

Berenholtz, S. M., L. H. Lubomski, K. Weeks, C. A. Goeschel, J. A. Marsteller, J. C. Pham, M. D. Sawyer, et al. 2014. Eliminating central line-associated bloodstream infections: A national patient safety imperative. *Infection Control and Hospital Epidemiology* 35 (1): 56–62.

Bierly, P. E. 1995. Culture and high reliability organizations: The case of the nuclear submarine. *Journal of Management* 21 (4): 639–56.

Bouafia, N., I. Bougmiza, F. Bahri, M. Letaief, P. Astagneau, and M. Njah. 2013. Ampleur et Impact Des Évènements Indésirables Graves Liés Aux Soins: Étude D'incidence Dans Un Hôpital Du Centre-Est Tunisien. *Pan African Medical Journal* 16: 68.

Burr, M., J. S. Sorra, V. F. Nieva, and T. Famolaro. 2002. *Analysis of the Veteran's Administration (VA) National Center for Patient Safety (NCPS) FY 2000 Patient Safety Questionnaire*. Rockville (MD).

Cameron, K. S., and R. E. Quinn. 2011. *Diagnosing and Changing Organizational Culture Based on the Competing Values Framework*. 3rd ed. San Francisco: Jossey-Bass.

Carthey, J. 2014. Improving safety culture in healthcare organizations. In *Patient Safety Culture: Theory, Methods, and Application*, edited by Patrick Waterson, 139–158. Burlington, VT: Ashgate.

Chassin, M. R., and J. M. Loeb. 2013. High-reliability health care: Getting there from here. *Milbank Quarterly* 91 (3): 459–90.

Cook, J. M., M. D. Slade, L. F. Cantley, and C. J. Sakr. 2016. Evaluation of safety climate and employee injury rates in healthcare. *Occupational and Environmental Medicine* 73 (9): 595–99.

Daugherty B., E. Lee, L. I. Paine, P. Murakami, C. Herzke, and S. J. Weaver. 2016. Associations between safety culture and employee engagement over time: A retrospective analysis. *BMJ Quality & Safety* 25 (1): 31–7.

Edmondson, A. C. 2004. Learning from failure in health care: Frequent opportunities, pervasive barriers. *Quality & Safety in Health Care* 13 (Suppl 2) (December): ii3–9.

Edrees, H., M. N. Mohd Ismail, B. Kelly, C. A. Goeschel, S. M. Berenholtz, P. J. Pronovost, A. A. Alobaidli, and S. J. Weaver. 2017. Examining influences on speaking up among critical care healthcare providers in the United Arab Emirates. BMJ Quality Conference Proceedings: Patient Safety Forum. March. Ministry of National Guard Health Affairs.

El-Jardali, F., F. Sheikh, N. A. Garcia, D. J., and A. Abdo. 2014. Patient safety culture in a large teaching hospital in Riyadh: Baseline assessment, comparative analysis and opportunities for improvement. *BMC Health Services Research* 14 (January): 122.

Flin, R. 2007. Measuring culture in healthcare: A case for accurate diagnosis. *Safety Science* 45: 653–67.

Flin, R., C. Burns, K. Mearns, S. Yule, and E. M. Robertson. 2006. Measuring safety climate in health care. *Quality & Safety in Health Care* 15 (2): 109–15.

Gimeno, D., S. Felknor, K. D. Burau, and G. L. Delclos. 2005. Organizational and occupational risk factors associated with work related injuries among public hospital employees in Costa Rica. *Occupational and Environmental Medicine* 62 (5): 337–43.

Ginsburg, L., and D. G. Oore. 2016. Patient safety climate strength: A concept that requires more attention. *BMJ Quality & Safety* 25 (9): 680–87.

Ginsburg, L., P. G. Norton, A. Casebeer, and S. Lewis. 2005. An educational intervention to enhance nurse leaders' perceptions of patient safety culture. *Health Services Research* 40 (4): 997–1020.

Guldenmund, F. W. 2000. The nature of safety culture: A review of theory and research. *Safety Science* 34 (1): 215–57.

Guldenmund, F. W. 2014. Organizational safety culture principles. In *Patient Safety Culture: Theory, Methods, and Application*, edited by Patrick Waterson, 15–42. Surrey, UK: Ashgate.

Hansen, L. O., M. V. Williams, and S. J. Singer. 2011. Perceptions of hospital safety climate and incidence of readmission. *Health Services Research* 46 (2): 596–616.

Hartmann, C. W., M. Meterko, A. K. Rosen, S. Zhao, P. Shokeen, S. J. Singer, and D. M. Gaba. 2009. Relationship of hospital organizational culture to patient safety climate in the Veterans Health Administration. *Medical Care Research and Review* 66 (3): 320–38.

Hessels, A. J., and E. L. Larson. 2016. Relationship between patient safety climate and standard precaution adherence: A systematic review of the literature. *Journal of Hospital Infection* 92 (4): 349–62.

Hofmann, D. A., and B. Mark. 2006. An investigation of the relationship between safety climate and medication errors as well as other nurse and patient outcomes. *Personnel Psychology* 59: 847–69.

Huang, D. T., G. Clermont, J. B. Sexton, C. A. Karlo, R. G. Miller, L. A. Weissfeld, K. M. Rowan, and D. C. Angus. 2007. Perceptions of safety culture vary across the intensive care units of a single institution. *Critical Care Medicine* 35 (1): 165–76.

Huang, D. T., G. Clermont, L. A. N. Kong, L. A. Weissfeld, J. B. Sexton, K. M. Rowan, and D. C. Angus. 2010. Intensive care unit safety culture and outcomes: A US multicenter study. *International Journal for Quality in Health Care* 22 (3): 151–61.

Itoh, K., H. B. Anderson, and K. L. Mikkelsen. 2014. Safety culture dimensions, patient safety outcomes, and their correlations. In *Patient Safety Culture: Theory, Methods, and Application*, edited by Patrick Waterson, 67–98. Burlington, VT: Ashgate.

Jackson, J., C. Sarac, and R. Flin. 2010. Hospital safety climate surveys: Measurement issues. *Current Opinion in Critical Care* 16 (6): 632–38.

James, L. R., R. G. Demaree, and G. W. Schmidt. 1993. R Wg : An assessment of within-group interrater agreement. *Journal of Applied Psychology* 78 (2): 306–09.

Jha, A. K., N. Prasopa-Plaizier, I. Larizgoitia, and D. W. Bates. 2010. Patient safety research: An overview of the global evidence. *Quality and Safety in Health Care* 19 (1): 42–47.

Joint Commission International. 2014. *Joint Commission International Accreditation Standards For Hospitals.* OakBrook, Joint Commission Resources.

Keroack, M. A., B. J. Youngberg, J. L. Cerese, C. Krsek, L. W. Prellwitz, and E. W. Trevelyan. 2007. Organizational factors associated with high performance in quality and safety in academic medical centers. *Academic Medicine* 82 (12): 1178–186.

King, H. B., J. Battles, D. P. Baker, A. Alonso, E. Salas, J. Webster, L. Toomey, and M. Salisbury. 2008. TeamSTEPPS(TM): Team strategies and tools to enhance performance and patient safety. In *Advances in Patient Safety: New Directions and Alternative Approaches (Vol. 3: Performance and Tools)*, edited by K. Henriksen, J. B. Battles, M. A. Keyes, and M. L. Grady. Rockville, MD: Agency for Healthcare Research and Quality.

Kotter, J. P. 2012. *Leading Change*. 2nd ed. Boston: Harvard Business School Press.

Kotter, J. P, and J. L. Heskett. 1992. *Corporate Culture and Performance*. New York: Simon and Schuster.

LeBreton, J. M., and J. L. Senter. 2007. Answers to 20 questions about interrater reliability and interrater agreement. *Organizational Research Methods* 11 (4): 815–852.

Mardon, R. E., K. Khanna, J. Sorra, N. Dyer, and T. Famolaro. 2010. Exploring relationships between hospital patient safety culture and adverse events. *Journal of Patient Safety* 6 (4): 226–32.

Martinez, W., J. M. Etchegaray, J. Thomas, G. B. Hickson, L. S. Lehmann, A. M. Schleyer, J. A. Best, J. T. Shelburne, N. B. May, and S. K. Bell. 2015. 'Speaking up' about patient safety concerns and unprofessional behaviour among residents: Validation of two scales. *BMJ Quality & Safety* 24 (11): 671–80.

Morello, R. T., J. A. Lowthian, A. L. Barker, McGinnes, D. Dunt, and C. Brand. 2013. Strategies for improving patient safety culture in hospitals: A systematic review. *BMJ Quality & Safety*, 22(1):11–18.

National Health Service UK. 2006. Manchester patient safety framework. *Guidance Report # 0199.*

Nembhard, I. M., and A. C. Edmondson. 2006. Making it safe: The effects of leader inclusiveness and professional status on psychological safety and improvement efforts in health care teams. *Journal of Organizational Behavior* 27 (7): 941–966

Nembhard, I. M., S. J. Singer, S. M. Shortell, D. Rittenhouse, and L. P. Casalino. 2012. The cultural complexity of medical groups. *Health Care Management Review* 37 (3): 200–213.

Nieva, V. F., and J. Sorra. 2003. Safety culture assessment: A tool for improving patient safety in healthcare organizations. *Quality & Safety in Health Care* 12 Suppl 2 (December): ii17–23.

Ouchie, W. G., and A. L. Wilkins. 1985. Organizational culture. *Annual Review of Sociology* 11: 457–83.

Parker, D., M. Wensing, A. Esmail, and J. M. Valderas. 2015. Measurement tools and process indicators of patient safety culture in primary care. A mixed methods study by the LINNEAUS collaboration on patient safety in primary care. *The European Journal of General Practice* 21 Suppl (sup1). Taylor & Francis: 26–30.

Pettigrew, A. M. 1979. On studying organizational cultures. *Administrative Science Quarterly* 24 (4): 570–581.

Profit, J., H. C. Lee, P. J. Sharek, P. Kan, C. C. Nisbet, E. J. Thomas, J. M. Etchegaray, and B. Sexton. 2016. Comparing NICU teamwork and safety climate across two commonly used survey instruments. *BMJ Quality & Safety* 25 (12): 954–61.

Pronovost, P. J., R. Demski, T. Callender, L. Winner, M. R. Miller, J. M. Austin, S. M. Berenholtz, and National Leadership Core Measures Work Group. 2013. Demonstrating high reliability on accountability measures at The Johns Hopkins Hospital. *The Joint Commission Journal on Quality Improvement* 39 (12): 532–44.

Pronovost, P. J., D. Needham, S. Berenholtz, D. Sinopoli, H. Chu, S. Cosgrove, B. Sexton, et al. 2006. An intervention to decrease Catheter-Related Bloodstream Infections in the ICU. *The New England Journal of Medicine* 355 (26): 2725–32.

Reiman, T., E. Pietikainen, P. Oedewald, and E. Pietikäinen. 2010. Multilayer approach to patient safety culture. *Quality and Safety in Healthcare* 19 (5): 1–5.

Rochlin, G. I., T. R. LaPorte, and K. H. Roberts. 1987. The self-designing high-reliabilty organization: Aircraft carrier flight operations at sea. *Naval War College Review* (Autum): 76–90.

Sacks, G. D., E. M. Shannon, A. J. Dawes, J. C. Rollo, D. K. Nguyen, M. M. Russell, C. Y. Ko, and M. A. Maggard-Gibbons. 2015. Teamwork, communication and safety climate: A systematic review of interventions to improve surgical culture. *BMJ Quality & Safety* 24 (7): 458–67.

Schein, E. H. 2010. *Organizational Culture and Leadership*. 4th ed. Hoboken, NJ: Jossey-Bass.

Schneider, B., M. G. Ehrhart, and W. H. Macey. 2013. Organizational climate and culture factors. *Annual Review of Psychology* 64 (1): 362–88.

Sexton, J. B., S. M. Berenholtz, C. A. Goeschel, S. R. Watson, C. G. Holzmueller, D. A. Thompson, R. C. Hyzy, J. A. Marsteller, K. Schumacher, and P. J. Pronovost. 2011. Assessing and improving safety climate in a large cohort of intensive care units. *Critical Care Medicine* 39 (5): 934–39. doi:10.1097/CCM.0b013e318206d26c.

Sexton, J. B., R. L. Helmreich, T. B. Neilands, K. Rowan, K. Vella, J. Boyden, P. R. Roberts, and E. J. Thomas. 2006. The safety attitudes questionnaire: Psychometric properties, benchmarking data, and emerging research. *BMC Health Services Research* 6: 44.

Singer, S. J., A. Falwell, D. M. Gaba, M. Meterko, A. Rosen, C. W. Hartmann, and L. Baker. 2009. Identifying organizational cultures that promote patient safety. *Health Care Management Review* 34 (4): 300–311.

Singer, S. J., S. Lin, A. Falwell, D. Gaba, and L. Baker. 2009. Relationship of safety climate and safety performance in hospitals. *Health Services Research* 44 (2 Pt 1): 399–421.

Singer, S. J., M. Meterko, L. Baker, D. Gaba, A. Falwell, and A. Rosen. 2007. Workforce perceptions of hospital safety culture: Development and validation of the patient safety climate in healthcare organizations survey. *Health Services Research* 42 (5): 1999–2021.

Smetzer, J. L., A. J. Vaida, M. R. Cohen, D. Tranum, M. A. Pittman, and C. W. Armstrong. 2003. Findings from the ISMP medication safety self-assessment for hospitals. *Joint Commission Journal on Quality and Safety* 29 (11): 586–97.

Sorra, J., and N. Dyer. 2010. Multilevel psychometric properties of the AHRQ hospital survey on patient safety culture. *BMC Health Services Research* 10: 199.

Sorra, J., L. Gray, S. Steagle, T. Famolaro, N. Yount, and J. Behm. 2016. *AHRQ Hospital Survey on Patient Safety Culture: User's Guide*. Rockville, MD: Agency for Healthcare Research & Quality.

Sorra, J., K. Khanna, N. Dyer, R. Mardon, and T. A. Famolaro. 2014. Exploring relationships between patient safety culture and patients' assessments of hospital care. *The Journal of Nursing Administration* 44 (3): S45–53. doi:10.1097/NNA.0000000000000118.

Sutcliffe, K. M. 2011. High reliability organizations (HROs). *Best Practice & Research. Clinical Anaesthesiology* 25 (2): 133–44.

Sutcliffe, K. M., L. Paine, and P. J. Pronovost. 2017. Re-examining high reliability: Actively organizing for safety. *BMJ Quality & Safety* 26 (3): 248–251.

Taplin, S. H., R. Anhang Price, H. M. Edwards, M. K. Foster, E. S. Breslau, V. Chollette, I. Prabhu Das, S. B. Clauser, M. L. Fennell, and J. Zapka. 2012. Introduction: Understanding and influencing multilevel factors across the cancer care continuum. *JNCI Monographs* 2012 (44): 2–10.

The Joint Commission. 2015. Sentinel Event Data: Root Causes by Event Type. Oakbrook Terrace, IL: Joint Commission Resources.

The Joint Commission. 2016. Patient Safety. In *Comprehensive Accreditation Manual for Hospitals*, PS1–PS54. Oakbrook Terrace, IL: Joint Commission Resources.

The Leapfrog Group. 2016a. 2016 Leapfrog hospital survey. http://www.leapfroggroup.org/survey-materials (accessed October 1, 2016).

The Leapfrog Group. 2016b. The Leapfrog Group hospital survey: Guidelines for a culture of safety survey that demonstrates validity, consistency, and reliability. http://www.leapfroggroup.org/sites/default/files/Files/Guidelines_CultureSurvey_20170401_0_0.pdf (accessed April 1, 2017).

Thomas, E. J., J. B. Sexton, T. B. Neilands, A. Frankel, and R. L. Helmreich. 2005. The effect of executive walk rounds on nurse safety climate attitudes: A randomized trial of clinical units. *BMC Health Services Research* 5 (1): 28.

Treadwell, J. R., S. Lucas, and A. Y. Tsou. 2014. Surgical checklists: A systematic review of impacts and implementation. *BMJ Quality & Safety* 23 (4): 299–318.

Tucker, A. L., I. M. Nembhard, and A. C. Edmondson. 2007. Implementing new practices: An empirical study of organizational learning in hospital intensive care units. *Management Science* 53 (6): 894–907.

Tucker, A. L., and S. J. Singer. 2014. The effectiveness of management-by-walking-around: A randomized field study. *Production and Operations Management* 24 (2): 253–271. doi:10.1111/poms.12226.

VHA Inc. 2000. Strategies for leadership: An organizational approach to patient safety. http://www.aha.org/content/00-10/VHAtool.pdf (accessed April 1, 2017).

Vogus, T. J. 2016. Safety climate strength: A promising construct for safety research and practice. *BMJ Quality & Safety* 25: 649–52.

Vogus, T. J., and K. M. Sutcliffe. 2007. The safety organizing scale: Development and validation of a behavioral measure of safety culture in hospital nursing units. *Medical Care* 45 (1): 46–54. doi:10.1097/01.mlr.0000244635.61178.7a.

Vogus, T. J., K. M. Sutcliffe, and K. E. Weick. 2010. Doing no harm: Enabling, enacting, and elaborating a culture of safety in health care. *Academy of Management Perspectives* 24: 60–77.

Wachter, R. M., and P. J. Pronovost. 2009. Balancing 'no Blame' with accountability in patient safety. *New England Journal of Medicine* 361 (14): 1401–6.

Wagner, C., M. Smits, J. Sorra, and C. C. Huang. 2013. Assessing patient safety culture in hospitals across countries. *International Journal for Quality in Health Care* 25 (3): 213–21.

Waterson, P. 2014. Patient safety culture: Setting the scene. In *Patient Safety Culture: Theory, Methods, and Application*, edited by Patrick Waterson, 1–14. Burlington, VT: Ashgate.

Weaver, S. J., X. X., Che, P. J., Pronovost, C. A., Goeschel, K. C., Kosel, and M. A. Rosen, 2014. Improving patient safety and care quality: A multiteam system perspective. In *Pushing the Boundaries: Multiteam Systems in Research and Practice*, 35–60. Emerald Group.

Weaver, S. J., L. H. Lubomksi, R. F. Wilson, E. R. Pfoh, K. A. Martinez, S. M. Dy, and L. H. Lubomski. 2013. Promoting a culture of safety as a patient safety strategy: A systematic review. *Annals of Internal Medicine* 158 (5 Pt 2): 369–74.

Weick, K. E., and K. M. Sutcliffe. 2007. *Managing the Unexpected*. 2nd ed. San Francisco: Jossey-Bass.

Weick, K. E., and K. M. Sutcliffe. 2015. *Managing the Unexpected*. 3rd ed. Hoboken, NJ: Wiley & Sons.

Weick, K. E., K. M. Sutcliffe, and D. Obstfeld. 1990. Organizing for high reliability: Processes of collective mindfulness. In *Research in Organizational Behavior*, edited by R. S. Sutton and B. M. Staw, Volume 1, 81–123. Greenwich, CT: JAI Press.

Weingart, S. N.,. Farbstein, R. B. Davis, and R. S. Phillips. 2004. Using a multihospital survey to examine the safety culture. *Joint Commission Journal on Quality and Safety* 30 (3): 125–32.

Wilson, R. M., P. Michel, S. Olsen, R. W. Gibberd, C. Vincent, R. El-Assady, O. Rasslan, et al. 2012. Patient safety in developing countries: Retrospective estimation of scale and nature of harm to patients in hospital. *BMJ* 344: e832.

Zohar, D. 2003. Safety climate: Conceptual and measurement issues. In *Handbook of Organizational Health Psychology*, edited by James C. Quick and Lois E. Tetrick, 123–42. Washington, DC: American Psychological Association.

Zohar, D. 2010. Thirty years of safety climate research: Reflections and future directions. *Accident; Analysis and Prevention* 42 (5): 1517–22.

Zohar, D., Y. Livne, O. Tenne-Gazit, H. Admi, and Y. Donchin. 2007. Healthcare climate: A framework for measuring and improving patient safety. *Critical Care Medicine* 35 (5): 1312–17.

Zohar, D., and G. Luria. 2005. A multilevel model of safety climate: Cross-level relationships between organization and group-level climates. *The Journal of Applied Psychology* 90 (4): 616–28. doi:10.1037/0021-9010.90.4.616.

Chapter 2

Operational Excellence

Susan Mascitelli, Stephen S. Mills, Michael Bierl, and Ryan Le

Contents

2.1 Introduction 25
2.2 Implementation of Policies and Procedures 26
2.3 Supply Chain Management 28
2.4 Establishing a Departmental Performance Management Program 31
2.5 Automation of Improvement 34
2.6 Exceed Expectations of Patient Satisfaction 36
2.7 Lean Management/Six Sigma (Measures of Productivity) 39
2.8 Staff Recruitment/Retention and Staff Engagement/Empowerment 40
References 44

2.1 Introduction

Over the past few decades, healthcare systems across the globe have experienced rapid and transformational changes. The advent of the information age has enabled major advances in care delivery, leading to improved patient outcomes and significantly reduced recovery times. Procedures once requiring major resources and extended hospital stays can now be completed in a matter of hours within an outpatient setting. From an industry perspective, the shift away from fee-for-service toward pay-for-performance has placed increasing pressure on providers to offer the highest quality of care. Recent legislation has further expanded the scope of this responsibility to ensure greater accessibility of care at an affordable price.

Despite this fluctuating landscape, however, the principle that healthcare organizations are accountable for the services they provide has not wavered. To ensure success, standardized systems have been put in place for organizations to monitor, measure, and improve performance over time. These processes are directly related to their ultimate pursuit of operational excellence. From facilities management to physician recruitment, this concept plays a vital role in every aspect of the industry. Because of its widespread impact, operational excellence can often appear very broad and almost intangible when viewed at a systematic level. For example, how can a healthcare system consisting of two major flagship hospitals, 10 different locations, and thousands of employees hope to achieve optimal efficiency? Additionally, where does one begin when attempting to address this issue?

This example refers to the size and scope of the NewYork–Presbyterian healthcare system. For 16 years, NewYork–Presbyterian has maintained the title of the number one healthcare provider in New York City and currently stands as the number six hospital in the United States, according to the 2016–2017 U.S. News and World Report (2016). Serving more than two million patients each year, it follows that the health system utilizes proven methods to ensure quality, accessibility, and affordability. Over the years, these measures have constantly changed and improved to best fit the needs of the population served by the hospital.

In this chapter, we outline major concepts and ideas that must be considered when seeking to improve operational excellence and illustrate them with case examples of some of the challenges faced within the NewYork–Presbyterian system. By sharing best practice with the international healthcare community, we hope to foster clear and honest communication centered on strategies that are truly able to improve the care delivered to patients. As a general note, all changes made to an organization should always take into account specific goals, target populations, and the external environment.

2.2 Implementation of Policies and Procedures

The implementation of policies and procedures refers to the creation of guidelines to direct company activities. They ensure that appropriate actions are being taken to carry out the organization's mission. These defined rules ultimately dictate the appropriate code of conduct for employees and yield the greatest value when properly followed. In a healthcare setting, policies are divided into clinical and nonclinical categories. Despite clear differences between the two, they each follow similar frameworks for determining a particular problem and following the necessary steps to address the issue.

The application of new clinical guidelines is particularly challenging because of the complexity of many medical conditions and the variety of treatment options available. Factoring in the difficulty in obtaining a consensus among medical providers, standardizing a single course of action is often very demanding. Medicine is a dynamic field that focuses on unique patient factors and inherently favors varying opinions. Clinical protocol development should, therefore, offer sufficient structure to act as a framework but also leave room for physician discretion. According to a manual developed by the American Academy of Otolaryngology for the translation of evidence-based practices into clinical standards, several major stages are required for successful implementation:

1. Definition of scope
2. Involvement of major stakeholders
3. Gathering evidence-based practices
4. Implementation of new guidelines
5. Ongoing evaluation
6. Continuous process improvement

Facilitating active conversation between executives and physicians while completing these steps allows the most effective and practical guidelines to be developed (Rosenfeld et al. 2013).

When starting any major project, a proper definition of scope is required in order to determine a functional workflow. This begins with a candid discussion regarding a particular area of concern such as why hospital-acquired infections (HAIs) are rising or what the current standards are for maintaining sterile environments. These types of questions form the basis of how major stakeholders will be chosen. Guidelines are only as effective as the number of people that follow them. Naturally, receiving input and feedback is essential to ensuring overall compliance. Clinical protocols require careful physician oversight and the proper collection of evidence-based practices before moving forward. Once implemented, however, the final two steps of the process require revision and alterations in practice over time. Given the speed with which new findings and techniques are discovered, ongoing evaluations help to translate industry best practices into better medical care.

A brief example illustrating the importance of these processes examines the effect of clinical pathways on the management and treatment of inpatient asthma. To better standardize care across a large academic medical center, a general consensus from providers was developed in accordance with national standards. The key features within this pathway for asthma treatment of the hospital's pediatric population were:

- A nurse-driven protocol for weaning bronchodilators
- Peak flow measurements (for children over five) every four hours, before and after nebulization
- Asthma teaching essentials, including spacer and peak flow meter training, beginning on the day of admission
- Prescriptions for home therapies given to families before discharge
- Early contact between the attending physician and private medical doctor to establish a plan for asthma management and to improve coordination of care

Following implementation and improvement over time, these new protocols resulted in a 13-hour reduction in the average length of hospital stay (Johnson et al. 2000). This example highlights how the implementation of clinical best practices creates an opportunity to drastically improve patient outcomes.

From a nonclinical perspective, policies and procedures also have a significant impact on the operational efficiency of an organization. Health systems typically consist of large institutions employing thousands of individuals. As a result, rigorous protocols must be established. The process by which these rules are created shares many similarities with the steps needed to develop clinical guidelines; they both rely on the identification of a particular issue, involvement of senior leadership, and frequent updates. The primary difference, however, lies in the direct link of these policies to an organization's overall mission. Nonclinical policies govern the relationships between all members of the hospital regardless of position or rank and ultimately influence the working environment. This impact on culture makes proper planning and execution a major key to success.

Many healthcare organizations today have policies deeply rooted in the foundation of the system as a whole. To maintain specific standards, it is the responsibility of senior leadership to frequently revisit these rules and revise them to better fit industry changes. As part of a recent system-wide initiative to improve clinical quality across NewYork–Presbyterian, procedures related to the maintenance of a sterile environment were closely examined. To determine the best course of action, specific project groups consisting of physicians, nurses, and administrators were formed. These teams focused on the use of hospital data to develop solutions necessary for the reduction of HAIs. Process improvement workshops and workflow analyses found that the risk of contamination within operating rooms (ORs) could be a major patient safety concern.

To proactively address the HAI issue, a new initiative was developed to standardize the color of scrubs within restricted areas enterprise-wide. These restricted zones cover all ORs, central sterile processing departments, women's units, and preoperative rooms. All staff members entering these areas are required to change into sterile burgundy scrubs that cannot be worn into or out of any building. Providers not wearing burgundy scrubs within the designated areas can as a result be immediately identified as a potential risk to patients undergoing surgery. To ensure proper sanitation guidelines, the scrubs are also specifically laundered by the hospital. Elimination of the green or blue scrubs typically found within ORs in favor of a more distinctive color empowers all members of the workforce to take part in hospital quality control. These clear visual cues allow staff to stay alert and manage threats to patient safety as they happen.

As with any major policy update at the systematic level, a structured rollout plan is necessary for proper implementation. The new scrub initiative would be enforced across the main campuses of the NewYork–Presbyterian network. Such large-scale changes require buy-in from senior leadership and an understanding of the process from middle management. To best engage all those affected by the decision, informative presentations were first made to physicians and staff to facilitate local discussion. OR committees, perioperative steering committees, and town halls were all established to better understand the logistics associated with this transition. E-mail communications with talking points were also distributed to managers so that frequent progress updates could be relayed to frontline staff before any changes occurred. These new regulations were enforced through collaboration with hospital security. From a logistical perspective, the procurement office at the hospital was also engaged to ensure proper distribution and selection of the new scrubs. All of these actions were carried out prior to any changes so that all stakeholders could be involved.

The burgundy scrub initiative at NewYork–Presbyterian serves as an exemplar of how proper execution of the steps required to deliver organizational change can ensure the smooth rollout of a new procedure. Any policy, whether large or small, should take those affected and any potential impact on the ability to carry out specific responsibilities into account. A clear understanding of the workforce allows a culture to develop that is dedicated to providing the best care to all patients.

2.3 Supply Chain Management

Supply chain management refers to the process by which goods and services are delivered to a consumer. This includes the negotiation of contracts for all component products and services utilized to create the final goods and services consumed. Within healthcare, the most common use of the term centers on the movement of goods throughout a hospital, how they are utilized along the way, and how the contracts for those goods and services are negotiated. Because of the volumes in which these items are used, costs typically consume a large proportion of total expenses. As such, standardization and waste reduction across the supply chain in a particular system provide a significant opportunity to improve an organization's bottom line. Historically, hospital supply chains focused on direct relationships with a number of different producers. In the 1980s, hospitals—borrowing practices from independent farmers and retail chains—began to use group purchasing organizations (GPOs). GPOs exploit the buying power of multiple individual businesses by combining them into one larger buying group, through which major discounts can be negotiated on behalf of the smaller organizations that are unable to do so independently (McKone-Sweet et al. 2005).

Leveraging buying power through GPOs has eliminated the need for small individual hospitals to form relationships with multiple producers. Streamlining supply acquisition through one primary source not only enhances efficiency but drives the greatest value. This shift in the power balance toward the purchaser has also been furthered by recent technological advances. Through investment in information technology (IT) systems, many organizations no longer need to rely on suppliers to understand their purchasing patterns and utilization rates (Cohn and Hough 2008; see also Chapter 10). Establishing hospital-wide sourcing departments enables direct accessibility to data and helps inform decision-making through a standardized process. Centralizing procurement efforts is effective in both maintaining the strength of the GPO and ensuring that all suppliers are held accountable to a consistent level of quality.

In many cases, the size of an organization often dictates the necessity to use a GPO. Large, stand-alone enterprises may have the volume to negotiate discounts without the need for systems. However, independent of how purchasers approach a certain producer, effective contract negotiation remains a priority in preliminary discussions to achieve the most competitive prices. The initial structuring of a contract requires a fundamental understanding of both supply utilization within an organization and the market trends for the product. This assumes that before arriving at the negotiating table, hospitals have gathered sufficient data on usage to properly inform any major decisions. Most negotiation models within the United States require commitments from healthcare systems to purchase a given volume or share of a product for specific discounts to be given in return. For brands essential to operation and that require standardization across the business, this is often the best strategy to maintain efficiency. When purchasing products that are easily interchangeable between suppliers and that do not require certain specifications, other models may be better. Independent of the type of agreement reached, it is always the responsibility of the purchasing organization to perform due diligence and anticipate any potential consequences of a long-term contract.

As intuitive as many of these ideas may seem, implementation of these concepts within healthcare has historically lagged behind other industries. The complexity of care delivery in hospitals has created a number of barriers to the development of a supply chain management strategy. There is little in terms of accepted best practice or literature tailored specifically to healthcare systems. Operationally, several barriers have prevented wide acceptance of supply chain concepts. Across many organizations, a failure of full buy-in from leadership has hindered their ability to find executive champions for the concept. As a result, many supply chain management initiatives do not have a clear vision and experience difficulties when choosing the most appropriate performance metrics (McKone-Sweet et al. 2005). Even when the most appropriate indicators are chosen, data use is still limited because of the rate of incorporation of new technologies into healthcare organizations.

Another major challenge in the application of supply chain concepts is poor physician engagement, which often results in a culture of mistrust. Across any hospital, clinical supplies typically make up the largest proportion of the expense base (Schneller and Smeltzer 2006). Therefore, target goals for cost management programs focus on how providers are using supplies to deliver quality care. Across the healthcare industry as a whole, this is not a particularly new issue. Administrators attempting to reduce costs have long been skeptical of clinician preferences for supplies. In a similar manner, providers have viewed administrators as solely focused on improving the bottom line. Addressing these generalizations requires a shift in attitude combined with consistent communication. From the perspective of hospital supply chain professionals, preconceived notions regarding physician choices of supplies typically arise from suppliers using clinicians for marketing or research activities. Emphasis on this within the hospital management literature has given rise to the idea that the interests of the physician are better aligned with suppliers than with the hospital.

Complicating the issue further are the difficulties associated with evaluating and comparing different medical devices. Since they are trained to operate clinical equipment, clinicians will usually have the best understanding of which brands provide the greatest benefit to patients.

Therefore, clear dialogue between procurement professionals and providers must use evidence-based approaches to effectively identify options that best suit the hospital's needs (Schneller and Smeltzer 2006). In addition, there are many cases in which physician preference represents the only factor distinguishing one product over another. A healthy relationship can allow suppliers to be selected that take the concerns of both administrator and clinician into account.

Those employing best practices across the industry have established organization-wide sourcing departments to serve as a point of contact for relationships both within and outside the enterprise. Many institutions use value analysis teams for clinical supply purchasing. To determine the most appropriate course of action, these groups consider the potential impact of a particular product on clinical metrics such as length of stay or infection rate. At NewYork–Presbyterian, these value analysis teams have been replaced by a physician executive (MD/MBA qualified) that manages sourcing specialists responsible for cost reduction in specific areas (Cohn and Fellows 2011). The appointment of an individual that understands the dynamics associated with both parties provides a clear and simple solution. Under the direction of this procurement and sourcing expert, all products across the hospital are sorted into clinical and nonclinical categories, each of which headed by a director responsible for maintaining a specific expense base through the management of category contracts, supplier relationships, and technology integration.

In terms of structure, the strategic sourcing department within the NewYork–Presbyterian system also differs from those found in other large academic medical centers in its scope of responsibilities. As a whole, the department has a greater degree of involvement in other areas of the business compared with similar organizations. For example, NewYork–Presbyterian has a clinical technology projects group within its strategic sourcing department tasked with equipment planning for major building projects. While many organizations relegate this function to other departments, placing it within strategic sourcing helps reinforce the idea of waste elimination as an enterprise priority. By remaining innovative in its approach, NewYork–Presbyterian has the ability to deliver better results in the long term.

With over $500 million spent each year on clinical supplies, this area has been the primary focus of major cost reduction efforts. The success of the strategic sourcing department and its ability to generate major savings can be attributed to the degree of physician involvement. To bridge the administrator-clinician gap, sourcing specialists communicate directly and daily with the end users of the projects they are working on. Active engagement in the form of e-mail, face-to-face meetings, and teleconferences allows for informed and streamlined decision-making. Over the years, the breadth of service lines interacting with the sourcing team has grown tremendously. Equal importance has been given to all clinical categories regardless of their contribution to the spending base (Cohn and Fellows 2011). This commitment to relationship building has enabled full buy-in of the stakeholders needed to execute organizational efficiency.

Extensive investment in the resources and time required to fully involve operational leaders in sourcing department activities has not only improved the corporate culture but also resulted in major financial benefits. To best quantify results over time, the success of cost reduction projects has been measured by the amount of money saved from operational budgets following completion. Since 2004, this calculation has resulted in annual savings of $10 million–13 million. As a portion of net patient revenue, strategic sourcing initiatives have decreased overall hospital expenditure on supply costs by 4.5% from 2004 to 2009 (Cohn and Fellows 2011).

With mounting pressure from recent legislative changes to reduce overall healthcare costs, supply chain management concepts are playing an increasingly important role in healthcare systems across the country. For long-term sustainability, approaches to cost reduction must utilize effective strategies to engage staff enterprise-wide. From contract negotiation to ongoing process improvement, a culture focused on generating value and eliminating waste is essential to financial success.

2.4 Establishing a Departmental Performance Management Program

Hospital performance management uses quantitative data and accurate reporting methods to best achieve a desired result or outcome. It enables both frontline staff and senior leadership to identify key areas for improvement and the creation of tangible goals. When implemented correctly, performance management tools provide the most accurate snapshot of the quality of care delivered by an organization. There has also been a steadily increasing need for such programs due to policy changes in the United States. Additional financial incentives have been awarded to hospitals that show consistent improvement, and many accreditation standards are based on specific measures. More than ever, public reporting of quality measures has motivated the use of performance management techniques. Patients can now self-educate through the information available on the Internet and can take healthcare into their own hands. Websites such as "Hospital Compare" (Centers for Medicare and Medicaid Services) require hospitals accepting money from public programs to make certain standards freely available. This enables transparency between medical institutions and individuals seeking care.

Developing a departmental performance management program begins with an evaluation of an organization's priorities. Specific target areas need to be established. A comprehensive and continuous understanding of the strengths and weaknesses within a particular department is essential to maintaining long-term success. Once department leadership agrees on these goals, appropriate metrics aligned to these targets must be chosen. Key performance indicators (KPIs) should be based on a variety of existing measures from nationally recognized programs such as the National Quality Forum (NQF) and the Healthcare Effectiveness Data and Information Set (HEDIS). According to the Health Resources and Services Administration (HRSA 2012), four different types of performance measures can and should be selected: (1) a quantitative measure defining a specific system and its effectiveness on the care of service given to a patient; (2) *outcome*, a direct measure of a patient's health status resulting from care at the particular organization; (3) *balancing*, which measures changes to one area of a system to ensure that another area is not being negatively affected; and (4) *structure of care*, which quantifies an aspect of the organization based on its ability to provide care.

The most efficient performance measurement systems can take each of these measures into account to provide a suitable balance. Following this process, a proper benchmarking method must also be established. The best way to accurately quantify improvements over time is to first generate a set of baseline standards. Measures for comparison typically utilize national averages and regional standards to quantify success, for example, Medicare costs or New York State Institutional Cost Reports. Once established, concrete goals with certain targets can be reached. When setting these base values, it is important to recognize that effective decision-making can only occur if data are visualized in an actionable manner. Errors in the translation of raw data to a presentable format can misinform. Frequent reviews and quality checks are the best way to ensure that the most truthful picture of a specific department is being presented.

With ever-increasing advances, IT has become integral to both streamlining and maintaining all the aspects of a departmental performance management program. The use of institution-wide scorecards enables proper performance management and takes the future vision of a particular healthcare organization into account. Scorecards examine different parts of the hospital and develop specific actionable targets. The complexity of these systems prevents only a single perspective from being examined as a means of overall improvement. Poor performance measures are not directly tied to one root cause but are usually the result of multiple issues. A balanced scorecard accounts for this by addressing multiple factors that can affect organizational health. These may include topics such as revenue cycle, strategic operations, or clinical quality. Once chosen, a deeper examination of specific measures in each category allows for the creation of a department-specific dashboard.

Dashboards differ from balanced scorecards because they focus on departmental monitoring rather than management. Therefore, they do not necessarily provide a clear picture of the final goal related to organizational objectives. What they do offer, however, is a direct connection to data sources and real-time progress tracking. Dashboards relay information in a graphical format and allow for accurate results (Hansel and Seaman 2012). They are often presented in a variety of different ways based on specific metrics to better identify problem areas. These measures can provide insights into department processes that can guide decision-making.

In 2010, the passing of the Patient Protection and Affordable Care Act forced healthcare organizations to reexamine the quality and affordability of the care being delivered. With the drastic expansion of federal programs to help cover the 32 million uninsured Americans, operational efficiency became a major subject of interest. The ability to effectively manage performance targets and reduce costs was essential to maintaining a healthy bottom line in the midst of significant reimbursement reductions. In recognition of these changes and their potential financial impact, NewYork–Presbyterian launched an initiative in 2011 to curb spending system-wide and grow profitability despite major health reforms. Termed HERCULES (Hospital, Efficiency, Revenue Cycle, Clinical Utilization, Length of Stay, Enhanced Sourcing), this project focused on establishing accountability standards within various service lines to deliver a cost reduction of $150 million in three years.

Initial analyses showed that the hospital had the means to reduce the cost of care through a more efficient system. Seizing this opportunity to reduce cost structure while simultaneously improving quality and patient experience, senior leadership organized the HERCULES project into six core teams, each focused on goals specifically tailored to a certain department: Length of Stay, Operational Excellence, System and Access, Clinical Resource Optimization, Supply Utilization, and Revenue Cycle. Implementation of evidence-based best practices from both previous experiences and industry experts enabled the identification of numerous projects within each category.

Following the development of these changes, a structure was put into place to operationalize each improvement. Executive sponsors were chosen to help guide implementation and establish ownership, clear communication, and direction from whomever was essential to engage staff, leadership, and doctors. In any major enterprise-wide project, progress is the result of small improvements multiplied across many departments. Individual actions repeated on a wider scale slowly become part of the larger culture. The importance of proper performance management using the appropriate techniques and metrics mentioned above cannot be overstated. A deeper dive into one of the many projects associated with a specific core HERCULES team area illustrates these processes in practice.

Within HERCULES, the role of the Operational Excellence team was to facilitate workflow improvement and create new processes to improve care delivery. Taking this into consideration, one of the key questions addressed was labor efficiency. In order to determine optimal utilization of the current workforce, a thorough knowledge of what drives departmental activities and costs was first required. An understanding of demand patterns enables comparison with existing staffing plans and helps determine excess capacity. In this particular project, baseline measurements of potential volume were first calculated using procedure numbers from machine utilization (CT, x-ray, MRI, etc.) from the previous year. By contrasting this with maximum procedure capacity, a utilization percentage for each machine was generated. Using data from this exercise combined with the average number of procedures performed on an hourly basis, the most optimal staffing model was developed. When viewed graphically against current staffing, the areas for potential cost savings become apparent. Shown in Figure 2.1 is an example of such a comparison of these practices using mock data.

From 7 a.m. to 2 p.m., current staffing levels are approximately two times the volume of procedures actually performed. Reducing the number of workers during this period or repurposing staff to other departments allows the greatest financial gain.

Following the collection of these results, HERCULES staff members and senior leadership developed solutions at both hospital-wide and departmental levels. On a broad scale, prioritization of these programs depended on the relationship between potential financial benefit and implementation complexity. Significant dollar targets focused resources on quick wins to better align current expenditure with industry-wide benchmarks. Cost reduction efforts to improve labor efficiency began with decreasing overtime hours, which was identified as the greatest opportunity for success given its low implementation difficulty. Strategies to achieve this goal included increasing the number of positions to provide support, utilizing float pool workers as a substitute for staff off sick or on leave, and changing shift hours to incorporate more evening employees.

Despite its enterprise-wide scope, the HERCULES project represents an excellent example of how results can be achieved through a structured performance management program with accountability. After meeting the original goal of $150 million in three years, the initiative has continued to grow and develop. Long-term sustainability of HERCULES through carefully selected

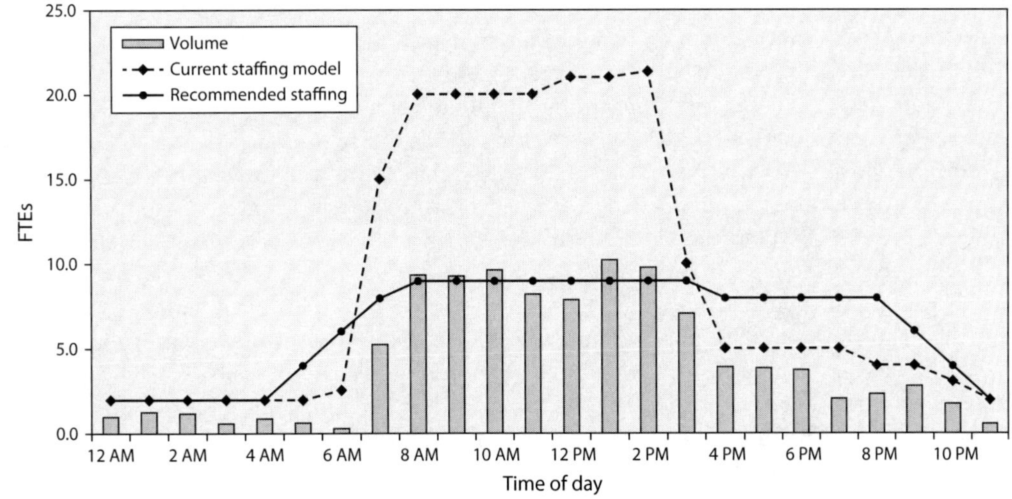

Figure 2.1 An example of the HERCULES process using mock data. The average number of procedures in progress is overlaid with current staffing and a model of recommended staffing.

metrics and process improvements has enabled the entire NewYork–Presbyterian system to better invest in providing quality care to its patients. The importance of establishing the proper buy-in from all stakeholders from the top downward cannot be overstated. Ultimately, change can only be delivered by those working on the frontline, and involving these people who are assessed in the performance measurement process is the best way to ensure accurate results and to boost morale.

2.5 Automation of Improvement

Technology has had an impact on virtually every industry. Drastic improvements in technology have enabled both physicians and administrators to effectively monitor the status of their organization or department while improving the quality of services delivered. From a patient's perspective, breakthroughs in IT have improved access to providers while reducing time spent waiting for care. Today, operational excellence is enmeshed with the ability to successfully implement and utilize the latest technologies.

However, one of the greatest challenges associated with these advances is employee pushback. This reluctance to accept new ideas has created a large barrier to their adoption. Historically, healthcare has been an industry that is slow to change. Given the nature of medicine, it follows that best practices are only accepted when there is almost full certainty that no negative consequences will occur. This stability has allowed clinical care to be standardized across the country but poses a major threat to innovation with IT. Factoring in the difficulty in obtaining physician champions, it follows that the rate of technology implementation within healthcare is slower than that observed in other industries.

Government efforts to stimulate the adoption of new technology have included financial incentives to organizations demonstrating meaningful use of technologies such as electronic health records (EHRs, see Chapter 6). In 2009, the Health Information Technology for Economic and Clinical Health (HITECH) Act was passed, expanding on the goal of President Bush's American Recovery and Reinvestment Act (ARRA) to install EHRs nationwide. At the time of the ARRA, only about 20%–21% of physicians had adopted basic EHR technology (Hoggle et al. 2010), but the HITECH Act increased this significantly to about 50% (Hsiao and Hing 2012). Within large academic medical centers, adoption is significantly higher, a testament to the resources typically dedicated to improving technological innovation within these organizations.

As more data begin to surface regarding the ability of automation to improve quality and reduce costs, a large market has developed within the healthcare innovation space. Of particular relevance to operational excellence is the increased use of mobile health (mHealth) technologies by physicians to deliver better outcomes. While devices used to track daily exercise goals such as the FitBit are extremely widespread, applications and programs specifically targeted for clinical use have yet to see the same popularity. That said, the use of telehealth for electronic consultations is quickly gaining traction across large academic medical centers in the United States. Patients now have the opportunity to have a consultation with a nationally ranked physician in the comfort of their home using mobile devices, web cameras, and so on. For those unable to easily return to the hospital or travel long distances, this alternative allows for unparalleled accessibility to high-quality care. With the ability to remotely manage and follow up more cases, telehealth practices can drive patient volume while still meeting clinical quality targets.

Recognizing the impact of technology on both patient satisfaction and care delivery, NewYork–Presbyterian launched a comprehensive suite of digital solutions called NYP OnDemand with its medical school partners ColumbiaDoctors and Weil Cornell Medicine. Using a mobile phone, tablet, or computer, patients across the world now have access to the premier services offered by the hospital in four different ways: a remote second opinion platform, digital follow-up appointments, virtual urgent care and emergency room visits, and inter-hospital consultations. Each of these programs uses the latest technological advances to fundamentally change how people receive their care. From a quality perspective, NYP OnDemand's accessibility allows physicians to see patients in minutes. In cases such as stroke, where the window of time before irreversible brain damage is short, these types of services are essential for full recovery. Future improvements to NYP OnDemand are crucial to expanding both access and quality.

For many healthcare organizations, automation of improvement does not simply mean the utilization of the latest technologies but also revisiting past processes to determine where new innovations may fit in. In 2013, NewYork–Presbyterian Queens, a 535-bed acute care community teaching institution, needed to expand its pharmacy department to better serve the rising volume of patients within its diverse community. Combined with new regulations on intravenous compounding, an entirely new workroom was required. Additionally, the new pharmacy would allow the implementation of barcode medication administration by nursing staff to reduce medication administration errors (see also Chapter 6).

Initial concepts around the design of the new pharmacy focused all workflows around the future acquisition of three robotic dispensing systems. To determine the most appropriate system, six institutions across the New York City metropolitan area were examined. Factors that were considered in the selection of the dispensing robot included

- Reduction in dispensing errors
- Efficiency
- Consistency
- Staff redirection/workflow changes
- Inventory management
- Around-the-clock availability
- Barcoding capabilities
- Recycling returned doses

During hospital visits, it quickly became apparent that only two primary systems met industry best practices. In the end, the SwissLog PillPick/BoxPicker system was the best fit for the anticipated workflow of the new pharmacy.

The SwissLog package comprises several separate machines, each with designated tasks. The PillPick 1 and 2 robots distribute oral solids and other small-volume parenteral vials. PillPick 1 serves as the primary dispensing robot and divides the medication orders into specific types. These doses are sequentially dispensed onto a PickRing (double check this with authors) in the order that they will be administered throughout the day. Each PickRing consists of two unique bar codes to identify both the patient and the drug, thereby ensuring that nurses cannot substitute the same medications for different patients. The PillPick 2 primarily functions as a packaging robot for the large volume of medications purchased by the hospital in mass quantities to optimize savings. Individual lots of these bulk drugs are packaged into canisters that can only be accessed by the PillPick system or administrator once sealed. Each robot is routinely stocked with a seven-day supply of medication.

Excluding the time spent vetting and selecting different systems, implementing the SwissLog robots into the new NewYork–Presbyterian Queens pharmacy took about three months. Since then, significant results have been observed in both waste reduction and duplicate elimination.

The ability to recycle medications that are returned after patient discharge has also enabled 15% of all dispensed doses to be recovered. With robotic assistance, returned medications can be sorted appropriately and stored efficiently. This process alone has resulted in estimated annual savings of $180,000. Additionally, the new inventory space provided by the robots has enabled the use of bulk medication containers and an annual saving of $156,000 compared with the previous individual unit packaging. To date, the new pharmacy system has dispensed five million doses without error.

Overall, the adoption of robotic technology in the pharmacy has been extremely beneficial in terms of both cost and waste reduction. The ultimate success of the project can in no small way be attributed to acceptance by pharmacy employees of an entirely different workflow. From beginning to end, major restructuring of existing processes was necessary to ensure optimization of the new system. This willingness to adopt new and better practices and provide feedback on the design of the improved pharmacy ensured that major bottlenecks and inefficiencies were quickly addressed. Transparency between leadership and employees facilitated an honest conversation focused on the best interests of all involved. As a whole, the introduction of the SwissLog system eliminated a number of tedious tasks for pharmacists and technicians, enabling full use of their skills and training. Utilizing employees to their full potential not only improves efficiency but also creates a positive atmosphere for growth.

2.6 Exceed Expectations of Patient Satisfaction

The U.S. healthcare system increasingly links reimbursement to patient satisfaction. Successful hospitals must not only offer a high standard of clinical care but also an excellent experience. This typically extends far beyond the patient, from assisting the family in their understanding of particular diagnoses to working with insurance companies to ensure proper billing. Patient satisfaction plays a pivotal role in a healthcare organization's overall strategy. How the general public views a certain system directly affects its decisions to receive treatment from it. Both clinicians and administrators are responsible for creating an environment that promotes excellent communication between the care team and patients while promoting better clinical outcomes. In an industry primarily built through word of mouth, poor patient experiences can reduce volumes and have significant financial impacts.

In order to measure and quantify patient perspectives, the Centers for Medicare and Medicaid Services (CMS) developed the Hospital Consumer Assessment of Healthcare Providers and Systems (HCAHPS) survey. The primary objective of HCAHPS was to empower the general public as a healthcare consumer. Widespread reporting of these results not only enables patients to select the best institutions but also makes the healthcare provider accountable by establishing a standardized comparison method. Combined with the increasing financial incentives for organizations with higher ratings and better outcomes, HCAHPS serves as an effective tool for motivating positive change.

The survey randomly samples all patients discharged within the past year. CMS regulations require at least 300 patients per 12-month reporting period. The 27 questions featured in the assessment take the following indicators: (i) composite measures (communication with nurses, communication with doctors, responsiveness of hospital staff, pain management, communication about medicines, discharge information, care transition); (ii) individual items (cleanliness of hospital environment, quietness of hospital environment); and (iii) global items (hospital rating, hospital recommendation).

These 11 categories represent core measurements within the HCAHPS Summary Star Rating system, a methodology developed by CMS to aggregate multiple items into a single averaged score out of five stars (Centers for Medicare 2015). The HCAHPS rating is then publicly displayed on Hospital Compare, a CMS-funded website that reports on government-collected healthcare data and allows consumers to directly compare providers participating in the program.

The expanding role of patient satisfaction within healthcare has also led to the creation of new administrative structures to assure good performance. In many hospitals across the country, designated chief experience officers are responsible for the development and implementation of an overall service strategy. This requires thorough knowledge of government regulations on reimbursement and the ability to view healthcare delivery through the lens of an average patient. Traditionally, quality and patient safety have dictated the comprehensiveness of healthcare delivery. Inseparable from these two measures, however, is the concept of service; the perception of one's quality of care is built upon a balance of service, safety, and quality. A provider closely following evidence-based clinical guidelines in a manner that reduces the most risk can still negatively impact hospital performance if he or she cannot communicate effectively with a patient. As a rule of thumb, improvement in the patient experience and satisfaction overall should focus on the development of an overall strategy rather than focusing on individual tactics.

One of the greatest challenges with patient satisfaction is that it measures interactions that often occur when no one is looking. Without proper buy-in from providers, it is very easy to simply ignore hospital-set recommendations on improving the patient experience. Developing the proper service infrastructure must become a priority before any major changes can occur. The foundation of any service strategy is contingent upon senior management endorsement, identification of KPIs, accountability, and the use of evidence-based best practices. Essential to all of these elements, however, is the understanding and standardization of interactions with patients and their impact on perception. An effective chief experience officer is able to tailor a service strategy for a healthcare organization based on its environment, patient population, and size.

Strategy development first begins with gathering data from patient experience surveys and establishing improvement priorities and targets. Once targets are established, best practices can be selected from the published literature to implement to achieve targets. Consulting previous hospital patient satisfaction data enables senior leadership to identify problem areas when determining improvement targets. Comparing scores with benchmarks from similar competitors across the country serves as a baseline standard from which targets can be set. Leveraging HCAHPS star rankings and different assessment tools can also provide an accurate indication of current organization performance. As the industry begins to place stricter regulations on patient quality, additional CAHPS tools for different healthcare settings are likely to become mandatory.

The underlying goal of a strategy in any context, regardless of industry, is to integrate certain behaviors into organizational culture. Launching new plans for service improvement should, therefore, focus on long-term sustainability and tracking success over time. Changing behavior requires constant reinforcement and communication. The general trend in yearly performance, assuming proper implementation, can be seen in Figure 2.2.

As one might expect, the first year following a strategy go-live is met with instability and large fluctuations in staff performance. The length of time over which this occurs is highly dependent on the ability of employees to adapt to new changes. Initial resources required for

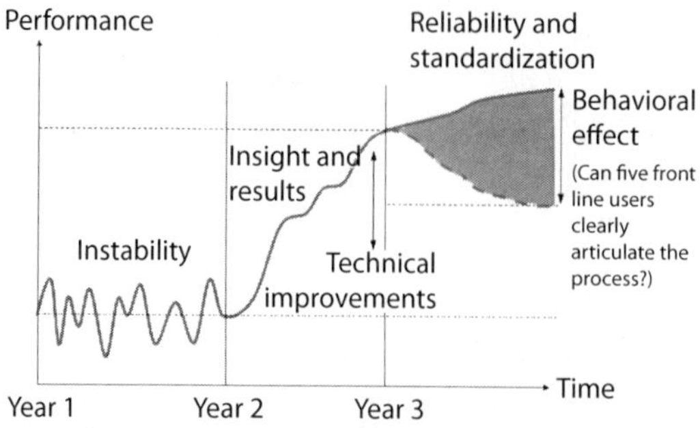

Figure 2.2 General trend in yearly performance assuming proper implementation of patient satisfaction improvements. (Source: Studer Group. 2012. Evidence-based leadership digging deeper. Presentation.)

education and training inevitably cause inefficiencies. Over time, however, performance begins to stabilize as policies once considered new become second nature and part of the workflow. The beginning of the third year requires improvements by senior leadership as front-end users recognize and report ways to streamline the process. Optimal performance occurs when the strategy becomes natural behavior. A rule of thumb for tracking optimal progress is the number of individuals that can clearly explain new policies and the reasons why they are more efficient.

With respect to its size and scope, the NewYork–Presbyterian system faces a large number of challenges that significantly affect both the scalability and effectiveness of major patient satisfaction initiatives. Its status as an academic medical center serving a large and diverse urban patient population has required a targeted approach to changing how care is delivered. Following the development of an overall strategy, the service team must help develop specific annual target metrics for each service line to meet. This involves a transparent conversation with both administrators and providers at the departmental level. To best facilitate improvement, departmental performance is benchmarked with historical data from previous years. Once the appropriate data are collected and analyzed, correlation analysis enables the most important priorities to be identified. It is the responsibility of the service team to determine the most effective evidence-based best practices specific to each functional unit. Collaboration across an entire department enables an overall strategy to be cascaded down to individuals. Establishing accountability for patient satisfaction measures through the use of a designated liaison also facilitates a transfer of ownership from the service team member to the department itself. Monthly meetings and formal partnerships between service team members and clinical area liaisons enable consistency to be promoted throughout the organization.

There is little doubt that influencing behavior requires major resource investments and thorough management of people, processes, and projects. Changing established work habits always carries anxiety and stress. Proper staff engagement and support from both leaders and their employees throughout transition periods, however, can result in major successes.

The healthcare industry is fundamentally built on the relationship established between provider and patient. It is the mission and obligation of hospitals to help promote an environment conducive to effective care. Above all, patients must feel safe and confident within the hospital setting. Cultivating the patient experience is not simply stating the things a patient wants to hear, but rather a means of ensuring that patients trust the treatment they are about to receive. The effort required to sustain this over time is a small price to pay for the reward of improving a patient's stay.

2.7 Lean Management/Six Sigma (Measures of Productivity)

Healthcare organizations are facing extreme pressure to provide the best care possible using available resources. The need for innovative delivery systems has forced many leaders to look outside the industry for new ideas. With origins in the Toyota production system, the concept of Lean management offers an approach to optimizing existing processes through waste reduction. Six Sigma, on the other hand, focuses on product quality by eliminating variation in the manufacturing process. Taken together, "Lean Six Sigma" concepts have the ability to significantly enhance performance.

The idea of Lean production was first conceived as a production philosophy intended to create the best method for delivering the same high-quality product time and time again (Joosten et al. 2009). To do this, individual elements contributing to the overall process were examined to determine value. For Toyota, this meant the application of shop floor tools to authorize movement along the assembly and serve as quality measure checkpoints. This enabled managers to identify major problem areas. Any actions or elements along the workflow that did not improve existing processes were immediately eliminated in the hope of achieving the optimal goal of perfect value with zero waste (Rooney and Rooney 2005).

Applying this method to healthcare is often difficult because of the complexity of the products and services delivered by hospitals and clinics. Lean management in this context takes an expanded definition beyond simple operations. The success of a healthcare organization in Lean implementation requires a culture that emphasizes efficiency as one of its primary goals. To facilitate this, transparency must be established between senior leadership and staff to enable meaningful conversations about increasing value. At the same time, there must be a fundamental understanding of one's role in the improvement of care delivery. Those directly involved with patients on the frontline are the only ones that can truly improve the quality of the services delivered. It is their responsibility to ensure that they are following best practices and protocols to provide the best possible experience. The role of managers fundamentally differs because those in leadership positions are not able to directly reduce waste or drive value. Instead, these individuals are responsible for creating an environment that promotes their workforce to adopt particular ways of thinking (Berwick 2003). The true challenge in the development of a Lean organization is establishing the culture necessary for long-term success.

Because of the difficulty and resources required to fully implement Lean principles, many organizations have begun to take a different approach to quality improvement by using Six Sigma. While this method still takes the value added to a particular workflow into account, Six Sigma focuses on the number of defects per million opportunities. Using statistical analysis, the optimal level of performance is given as 3.4 defects per million opportunities or six standard deviations below the mean (Bandyopadhyay and Coppens 2005). Unlike Lean management, Six Sigma specifically uses a data-driven approach to promote meaningful change. Major decisions are only made after past statistics and trends have been consulted.

Given Six Sigma's emphasis on concrete evidence in the form of numbers, quantifying the human aspect of healthcare can present a major challenge. To help solve this issue, four primary indicators have been used to determine a healthcare organization's performance: service level, service cost, customer satisfaction, and clinical excellence according to the Six Sigma DMAIC Quality Improvement Model (Lazarus and Neely 2003). Originally developed by Robert Galvin, former CEO of Motorola Inc., the DMAIC model sets specific action items based on the following definitions (Bandyopadhyay and Coppens 2005):

- *Define*: select target consumer, identify key problem areas, and provide objectives necessary for success
- *Measure*: collect the data and quality characteristics needed to determine baseline metrics for improvement
- *Analyze:* utilize analytical tools to transform the gathered data into actionable items
- *Improve*: allocate the resources needed to effectively carry out the action items previously determined through analysis
- *Control*: continuously monitor processes over time to ensure improvements are maintained

The use of Six Sigma as a means to improve business operations has translated into financial gain for some of the largest corporations across the world. From General Electric to Citibank, the basic principles of the concept can be tailored to almost any type of business. When applied to healthcare, however, the adoption of Six Sigma has been fairly slow compared with other industries because it relies on human factors as measurements of outcome. These factors constantly change because they relate to individual diagnosis and treatment plans. From a patient satisfaction perspective, process standardization poses a major challenge because of the unpredictability of human behavior. For measurement and data-driven processes such as Six Sigma, attempting to quantify such results requires creativity and innovation.

Across the NewYork–Presbyterian health system, Lean management and Six Sigma principles are utilized at both the hospital and departmental level to help reach target metrics. Clinical systems engineers are process and systems redesign experts that serve in advisory roles for these projects and help guide any potential projects. These individuals are typically Six Sigma-certified Black and Green belts that help engage frontline staff by identifying gaps in current processes, designing the ideal state, and teaching methodologies. For any potential improvement event across the hospital requiring the engagement of a clinical systems engineer, the typical timeline is as shown in Figure 2.3.

Using the same structured and proven process for each new project, both frontline staff and the clinical systems engineer can easily identify key problem areas. It is important to recognize that in any organization, quality and safety experts cannot carry out the solutions that they help to develop; only staff members with specific responsibilities influence real change. Long-term success after the support of a process improvement expert can only be maintained with a clear understanding by departmental leaders and their staff. Since the introduction of these principles, many successes have been observed across the hospital. A future goal includes integrating these concepts within the entire healthcare system.

2.8 Staff Recruitment/Retention and Staff Engagement/Empowerment

No organization can function correctly without dedicated staff. Employees form the cornerstone of an organization and act as the drivers for achieving company goals. It is, therefore, the responsibility of senior leadership to develop a healthy work environment that keeps staff engaged in their work and allows them to be recognized for their efforts. Successful organizations consistently accomplish this

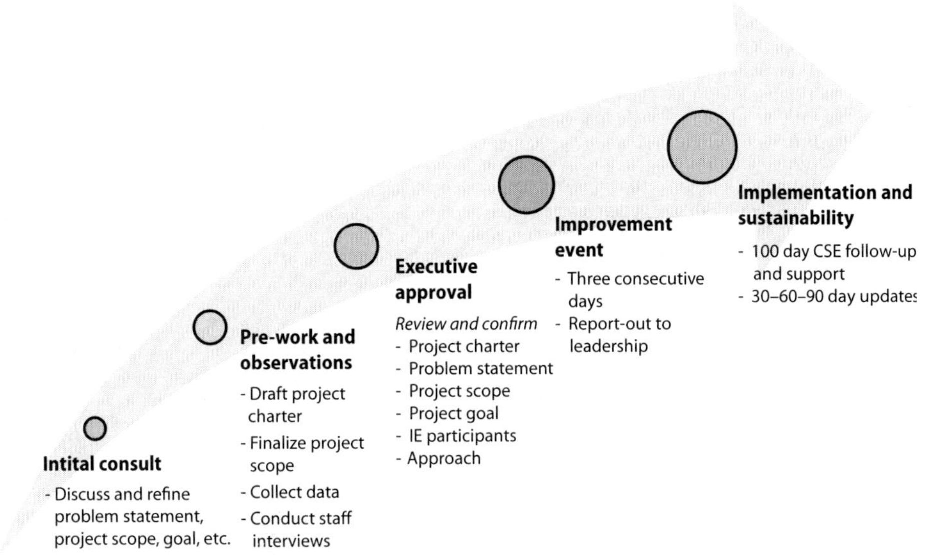

Figure 2.3 Timeline of an improvement event involving a clinical systems engineer. (Source: NYP Quality and Safety).

through employee feedback and engagement. At the end of the day, happy employees not only strive to do more outside of their job descriptions, but also foster a positive and encouraging atmosphere.

The healthcare industry's recent legislative policies have placed an emphasis on tying pay-for-performance measures to financial reimbursement. As these changes slowly take shape, hospitals are quickly realizing the impact of poor job satisfaction on their bottom line. Successful healthcare systems must place equal importance on being both an employer and provider of care. To date, U.S. Health and Human Services has estimated that the Affordable Care Act has reduced the number of uninsured individuals by 20 million. Coupled with the declining numbers of new healthcare providers over the past few years, workforce efficiency is vital for delivering the same quality of care.

Inspiring employees to do their best work begins at the very core of the business itself. Senior leadership must develop a vision for their business that incorporates the values and beliefs of all stakeholders. Maintaining intrinsic motivation over time requires establishing a company purpose that extends far beyond profit. Within healthcare, providers are often subject to long hours, difficult patients, and low levels of appreciation. This declining level of job satisfaction is cited as the primary reason for high turnover rates, especially within nursing (Laschinger 2012). A single unified mission spanning an entire organization promotes a sense of community among employees. Each individual is responsible for contributing a small part to the larger goal of providing the best clinical care for each patient. Commitment to a collective objective places company goals above one's own personal interests. Over time, repeated actions emphasizing these values become ingrained into organizational standards.

Once a hospital's mission is determined and its core principles are prioritized, effective talent recruitment is needed to ensure success. This process begins with the identification of what is most important to prospective employees. Leveraging an organization's strengths enables differentiation from competitors and a better reputation within the job market. Employees are attracted to companies that provide significant roles, adequate work-life balance, and opportunities for professional growth (Macken and Hyrkas 2014). It is a common misconception that remuneration is one of the most important motivators for performance and retention. While a competitive salary or extensive benefits package certainly influences retention, people are ultimately driven by meaning in their careers (Pfeffer 1998). The right combination of these elements provides the greatest incentive for new employees to join the organization.

After potential new members of the workforce have submitted their applications, the hospital must fully understand the skill set needed to thrive within the vacant position. Careful screening of candidates requires a thorough understanding of an individual's experiences and ability to integrate into the existing culture. A structured interview process that seeks to identify competencies is the best way to ensure future success. Directly related to the importance of culture is the concept of motivational fit. Targeted questions dividing this fit into categories such as job, organization, and location enable hiring managers to better understand the factors that best contribute to a candidate's personal satisfaction. In terms of practical skill sets, applicants must also be able to provide substantive examples of selected traits such as time management, leadership, and adaptability.

Despite the difficulties that may arise in recruiting talent, however, one of the greatest challenges associated with workforce management is the long-term retention of staff. All organizations, no matter how large, have a commitment to ensuring the happiness of their workers. This applies to both new hires and established professionals alike. In 2013, NewYork–Presbyterian recognized the importance of employee wellness and launched a steering committee responsible for developing a hospital-wide well-being program. From its very inception, NYP Be Healthy has focused on providing the necessary resources for employees to take better control of their health and serves as just one aspect of NewYork–Presbyterian's employee benefits. When combined with additional benefits such as competitive retirement and savings accounts, life and disability insurance coverage, and multiple tax-advantaged spending accounts, hospital employees truly understand the commitment the system has to its workers. A more comprehensive list of this world-class benefits package is shown in Figure 2.4.

A closer of examination of one of these offerings reveals the level of detail given to the full support of staff members and their families. NYP Be Healthy incorporates a number of different programs that target specific areas within employee support. The first is the use of well-being assessments and biometric screenings. Providing these baseline measures of health allows

Core benefits	Employee support and well-being	Retirement and savings
• Medical • Prescription • Dental • Vision	• Education assistance • Annual well-being assessment • On-site well-being coaches • On-site retirement resources • Financial planning	• Cash Balance • Cash Balance+ • Cash Balance+ Excess • 403(b) • 457(b)

Basic insurance coverages	Optional benefits	Tax advantaged spending accounts
• Basic/supplemental life insurance • Spouse life insurance • Child life insurance • Long-term disability	• Voluntary short term disability • Universal life insurance • Critical illness coverage • Pet insurance • Identity theft protection • Auto and home insurance • Legal	• Dependent care • Health care • Adoption assistance • Mass transit • Commuter parking

Figure 2.4 NewYork–Presbyterian's employee benefits structure. (Source: NYP Be Healthy)

employees to set realistic goals. They also promote a sense of a self-awareness that comes with proper education and enable comparison with other corporations across the country. As of 2015, about 2500 employees within the hospital have participated in the well-being assessment program. Future improvements seek to increase this number while expanding the scope of services offered.

Once employees have identified the opportunities for better health, they can sign up for personalized on-site coaches at each of the NewYork–Presbyterian campuses. These specialized sessions utilize data from well-being assessments to focus on individual health factors. The various categories managed include body mass index (BMI), exercise, stress, blood pressure, and tobacco cessation. Proper management across each of the five groups results in significant cost savings. Over a period of just nine months, coaching sessions have yielded annual savings of about $300,000, not including any improvements in emotional health associated with a positive body image. Similar to well-being assessments, increased traction and penetration of on-site coaching is likely to realize even greater benefits long term.

It is important to understand that in order to be truly effective, employee wellness programs must encompass as many aspects of the health continuum as possible. This can range from stress reduction classes to discounted prices for healthier meals in the cafeteria. NYP Be Healthy takes a holistic approach to the well-being of the NewYork–Presbyterian workforce. Physical health plays an important role in overall happiness, but it is not the only factor. Emotional health, work/life balance, and financial health are all currently addressed in additional offerings such as counseling, backup childcare, and student loan repayments. Organization-wide competitions such as the annual Steps Challenge also foster a sense of community and inclusion across the hospital. Taken together, all of these programs enhance staff retention by addressing absenteeism and turnover.

All successful wellness plans require a carefully structured plan driven by evidence-based practices and data. Utilizing the most appropriate metrics enables success to be measured in a concrete way. To launch the new features of NYP Be Healthy in 2016, three basic steps have been outlined with the appropriate performance indicators: awareness, engagement, and integration, as shown in Figure 2.5.

Following the development of a plan, it is also essential that senior leadership buy into the project. Finding the appropriate executive sponsor to champion the proposed ideas is the fastest way to ensuring both timely implementation and lasting impact. Once this individual has been identified, an oversight structure for enacting the various phases should be formed. Gathering a steering committee with those able to influence critical decision-making materializes the project from a proposed idea to

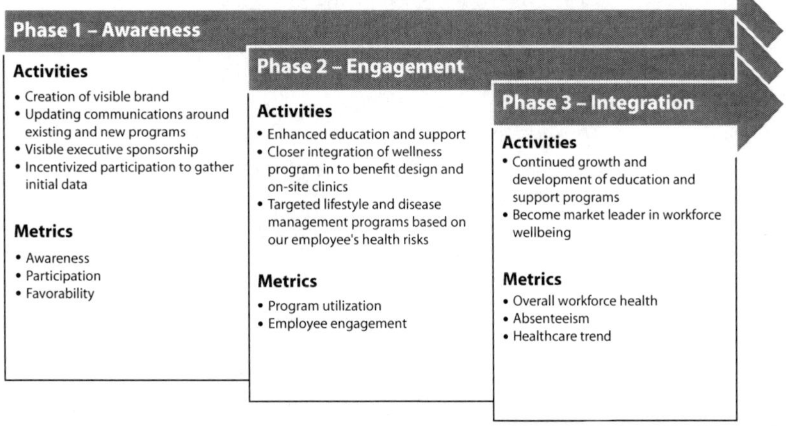

Figure 2.5 Implementation of NewYork–Presbyterian's new Be Healthy features. (Source: NYP Be Healthy).

a real deliverable. Operationally, NYP Be Healthy filtered from top-level management to individual employees through collaboration with department managers spearheading local initiatives. Given the sheer size of the organization, the true success of the project was in the cultural alignment of all those involved and the emphasis on the importance of giving back to employees. For its efforts, New York–Presbyterian Hospital was named one of 2017's top 25 best workplaces in New York by Fortune. Additionally, NYP was also named one of America's Best Employers for 2017 by Forbes.

References

Bandyopadhyay, J. K., and K. Coppens. 2005. The use of six sigma in healthcare. *Intl Journal of Productivity & Performance Management* 5 (1):v1–v12.

Berwick, D. M. 2003. Improvement, trust, and the healthcare workforce. *Quality & Safety in Health Care* 12 (6):448–452.

Cohn, K. H., and S. A. Fellows. 2011. *Getting it Done: Experienced Healthcare Leaders Reveal Field-tested Strategies for Clinical and Financial Success*. Chicago, IL: Health Administration Press.

Cohn, K. H., and D. E. Hough. 2008. *The Business of Healthcare* (Vol. 1). Santa Barbara: Greenwood Publishing Group.

Hansel, J., and N. Seaman. 2012. Building a powerful hospital scorecard by keeping it simple! http://www.hfma.org/brg/pdf/MedeAnalytics_Building%20a%20Hospital%20Scorecard_White%20Paper.pdf.

Health Resources and Services Administration. 2012. Performance management & measurement. http://www.hrsa.gov/quality/toolbox/methodology/performancemanagement/index.html.

Hoggle, L. B., M. M. Yadrick, and E. J. Ayres. 2010. A decade of work coming together: nutrition care, electronic health records, and the HITECH Act. *Journal of the American Dietetic Association* 110 (11):1606–1612. doi:10.1016/j.jada.2010.09.019.

Hsiao, C-J., and E. Hing. 2012. Use and Characteristics of Electronic Health Record Systems Among Office-Based Physician Practices, United States, 2001–2012. *NCHS Data Brief* 111:1–8.

Johnson, K. B., C. J. Blaisdell, A. Walker, and P. Eggleston. 2000. Effectiveness of a clinical pathway for inpatient asthma management. *Pediatrics* 106 (5):1006–1012.

Joosten, T., I. Bongers, and R. Janssen. 2009. Application of lean thinking to health care: issues and observations. *International Journal for Quality in Health Care* 21 (5):341–347. doi:10.1093/intqhc/mzp036.

Laschinger, H.K.S. 2012. Job and career satisfaction and turnover intentions of newly graduated nurses. *Journal of Nursing Management* 20:472–484.

Lazarus, I, and C. Neely. 2003. Six Sigma: Sure to raise the bar A look into methodologies that hold an immediate potential for improving processes in healthcare, because numbers don't lie. *Managed Healthcare Executive* 13 (1):31–33.

Macken, L., and K. Hyrkas. 2014. Work climate, communication and culture – workforce issues and staff retention. *Journal of Nursing Management* 22 (8):951–952. doi:10.1111/jonm.12275.

McKone Sweet, K. E., P. Hamilton, and S. B. Willis. 2005. The ailing healthcare supply chain: a prescription for change. *Journal of Supply Chain Management* 41 (1):4–17.

Medicare, Centers for, and Medicaid Services. 2015. *HCAHPS Star Ratings Technical Notes*. http://www.hcahpsonline.org/Files/HCAHPS_Stars_Tech_Notes_9_17_14.pdf

Pfeffer, J. 1998. Six dangerous myths about pay. *Harvard Business Review* 76:108–120.

Rooney, S. A., and J. J. Rooney. 2005. Lean glossary. *Quality Progress* 38 (6):41–47.

Rosenfeld, R. M., R. N. Shiffman, and P. Robertson. 2013. Clinical practice guideline development manual, a quality-driven approach for translating evidence into action. *Otolaryngology – Head and Neck Surgery* 148:S1–S55.

Schneller, E. S., and L. R. Smeltzer. 2006. *Strategic Management of the Health Care Supply Chain*. Jossey-Bass.

Studer Group. 2012. Evidence-based leadership digging deeper. Presentation.

U.S. News and World Report. 2016. U.S. News & World Report Announces the 2016–17 best hospitals. http://www.usnews.com/info/blogs/press-room/articles/2016-08-02/us-news-announces-the-201617-best-hospitals.

Chapter 3

Efficient Clinical Practice

Sandra L. Fenwick, Kathy J. Jenkins, John G. Meara, Chris Newell, Anne Stack, Sara Toomey, and Cynthia Haines

Contents

3.1 Introduction 46
3.2 Value-Based Healthcare 47
3.2.1 Outcome Measurements 48
3.2.2 Cost 50
3.2.2.1 Time-Driven Activity-Based Costing 51
3.2.3 Evidence-Based Guidelines 55
3.2.3.1 Developing Evidence-Based Guidelines 55
3.2.4 Standardized Clinical Assessment and Management Plans (SCAMPs) to Produce Value 58
3.2.4.1 SCAMP Aims 59
3.2.4.2 SCAMP Methodology 59
3.2.4.3 SCAMP Advantages 59
3.2.4.4 Success Story: Pediatric Critical Asthma SCAMP 60
3.2.4.5 Success Story: Distal Radius Fracture SCAMP 61
3.2.4.6 Value Results 62
3.2.4.7 Network Effects 62
3.2.5 Engaging Physicians in Quality Improvement (QI) 63
3.2.6 Employee Engagement 64
3.2.7 Engaging Pediatric Patients and Their Families 66
3.3 Conclusions 68
Acknowledgments 69
References 69

3.1 Introduction

Boston Children's Hospital was founded in 1869 as a 20-bed facility and is now Harvard Medical School's primary pediatric teaching hospital, ranked the number one children's hospital in the United States (2016–2017) by U.S. News and World Report. It is a globally recognized pediatric center of excellence, not least because it is the world's largest pediatric research enterprise and a global leader in translational research. Boston Children's Hospital focuses on extraordinary care for children with complex and rare medical conditions and is committed to highly reliable, compassionate, patient and family-centered care, as summarized in Figure 3.1.

Boston Children's began its transformation toward value-based healthcare (Moriates et al. 2015) many years ago. As a clinical academic institution, this has meant

- Investing in highly skilled teams of experts who are also active in research and clinical/technological innovations
- Encouraging interdisciplinary, team-based healthcare practices
- Providing cost-effective care at the right time and in the right place
- Continuously improving outcomes

Early on, hospital leaders recognized that transformation is a long series of local experiments and that the innovation that drives transformation occurs on the front line of the enterprise, that is, where care is delivered. More recently, as part of the value-based healthcare journey, Boston Children's launched an enterprise-wide initiative to become a "high reliability organization" (HRO; see Chapter 5), that is, to build a culture that places safety above all other competing priorities and with the ultimate goal of having *zero* events of preventable harm to patients, family members, and employees. At Boston Children's Hospital, "high reliability" means getting things right each and every time by (1) preventing failure in processes, policies, technology, and people; and (2) reducing the probability that errors will occur with a focus on attention to detail, clear communication, and questioning attitudes.

As part of this journey, over 15,000 employees and associated personnel have participated in high reliability training. The organization's leadership launched a series of initiatives to support and reinforce cultural change which is fundamental to the journey to high reliability including

Boston Children's Hospital Profile, 2016

- 404 inpatient beds
- 25,000 inpatient admissions per year
- 557,000 outpatient visits per year
- 60,000 emergency department visits per year
- 26,500 surgeries per year
- 2,418 full time MDs and DMDs
- 2,358 Nursing staff
- 1,100 Research Scientists
- 2 Nobel Prize winners
- 10,000+ employees and associated personnel
- Serve patients from >100 countries

Figure 3.1 Boston Children's Hospital profile (2016).

- "Rounding to Influence," an executive leadership practice occurring once per month, where leaders conduct rounds throughout the hospital to discuss high reliability concepts with frontline personnel
- "Daily Operations Briefings," led by the chief operating and nursing officers along with departmental leaders to review all patient safety incidents occurring in the previous 24 hours
- A comprehensive communication strategy across the enterprise to provide frequent updates to all staff and transparent hospital metrics

These practices have cascaded through the enterprise to ensure that high reliability practices are internalized, language is consistent, and local teams can implement practices independently.

This chapter focuses on efficient clinical practice at Boston Children's Hospital framed within the context of the hospital's journey to ward value-based healthcare and high reliability. Value-based medicine is first discussed and then illustrated with successful examples of clinical practices (time-driven activity-based costing, standardized clinical assessment and management plans) developed by local teams that aim to improve outcomes and care within the context of value-based medicine. We also present the hospital's approach to physician and employee engagement and the role that patients and their families play in efficient clinical practice.

3.2 Value-Based Healthcare

Value lies at the center of highly reliable healthcare institutions, but perceptions of value vary between stakeholders because of the competing goals of providers, payers, and patients (Moriates et al. 2015). In healthcare, patients define value, and improvements for patients ultimately benefit other stakeholders and the health system as a whole (Porter 2010). Value can be defined as the quality of care or patient outcomes divided by the cost of care (Porter 2006) and does not depend on a single measure but rather all relevant patient outcomes and costs throughout the care cycle (Porter 2010).

Value measurement requires taking health outcomes into account; considering cost alone is insufficient, as demonstrated by the global life expectancy and health expenditure per capita in each country shown in Figure 3.2 (International Federation of Accountants 2013). For example, the United States spends about 18% of its gross domestic product (Fuchs 2013, Moriates et al. 2015) and more per capita in current U.S. dollars than almost every other country in the world (International Federation of Accountants 2013), but its outcomes are not as good (Woolf and Aron 2013, Moriates et al. 2015). Up to a third of that spending may not help patients, and the Institute of Medicine (2012) has categorized that waste (from greatest to least) as care that is costly without improving outcomes, inefficient, excessively expensive, accompanied by high administrative fees, fraudulent, or the result of a failure to provide preventive care (Moriates et al. 2015).

Health systems can most effectively be improved by measuring outcomes and improving value for patients (Porter 2010). This can be achieved either by improving health outcomes for the same cost or by lowering cost while maintaining health outcomes (Moriates et al. 2015). Outcomes, by definition, relate to conditions and their common comorbidities, making integrated practice units—that is, connected, multidisciplinary teams with strong leadership and organization—ideal for covering the full care cycle (Porter 2010).

In addition to the clear role for clinicians in driving and improving health outcomes, they also have a responsibility to manage costs, as the burden of healthcare costs affects their own patients (Moriates et al. 2015), and, in some cases, prevents patients from seeking, reaching, or receiving care. For this reason, providers have a duty to improve value and to serve as resources for patients

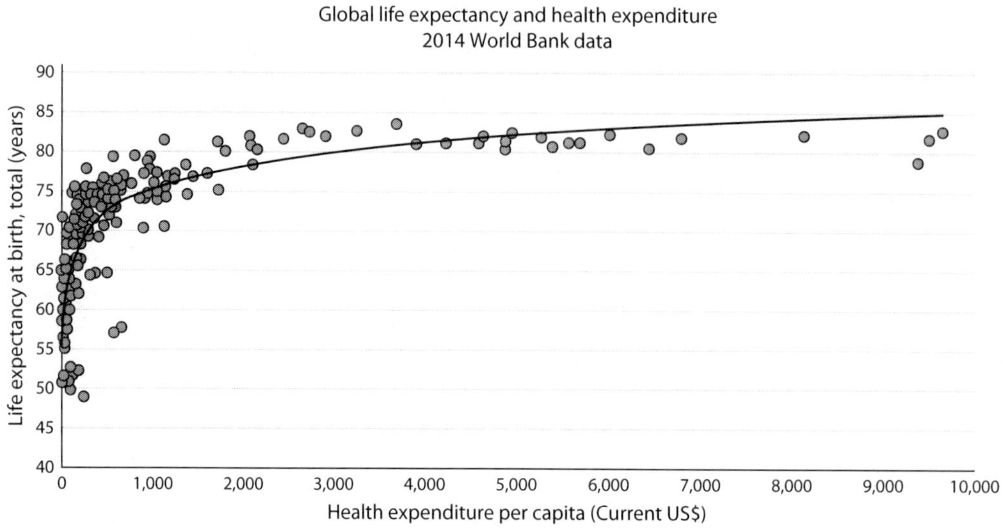

Figure 3.2 Total life expectancy at birth versus health expenditure per capita in current U.S. dollars for each country in the world in 2014, according to indicator data from the World Bank (World Bank 2016).

who are looking for information on healthcare costs (Moriates et al. 2013). The shift in healthcare from volume to value (Porter 2010) may also affect providers financially as some systems move toward a pay-for-performance reimbursement model (Moriates et al. 2015).

3.2.1 Outcome Measurements

Many data collection schemes have been developed around the world to report on health behaviors, outcomes, and access to care. Numerous countries including Brazil, Denmark, and the United States collect data at the national level. While these data may be used for quality improvement (QI) and research, they are not standardized across institutions and thus do not allow for benchmarking. The overarching need to analyze patient outcomes requires comprehensive, international systems that measure what is most relevant to patients including clinical, functional, and patient-reported outcomes over appropriate and relevant time periods. Patient outcomes reflect the patient experience, another important component of value, and help to focus safety and QI efforts.

In order to truly measure quality of care or patient outcomes, healthcare institutions must track their performance using standardized outcome metrics. According to Michael Porter of Harvard Business School, outcome standardization should involve compiling a minimum set of outcomes for a specific medical diagnosis (Porter 2010). Relying on outcomes that reflect specialty services can make it difficult to differentiate the quality of care between providers and to compare patient results among those with and without complex medical conditions (Porter 2010).

Outcome measures that focus on medical specialties and process measures tracking compliance have little to no relevance to patient populations (Porter 2009, Porter and Lee 2013, Porter et al. 2016). Outcomes that matter most to patients are those that track health status, recovery, and sustainability of health throughout the full care cycle (Porter 2009, Porter and Lee 2013, Porter et al. 2016). In this context, the full care cycle refers to the multiple medical specialties involved in the treatment of a specific medical condition (Porter 2009, Porter and Lee 2013, Porter et al. 2016). Measures looking at the full care cycle should not only incorporate clinical outcomes such as postoperative complication rates but also subjective information through patient-reported metrics (Kaplan and Anderson 2003).

Creating a minimum standard outcome set that applies globally to patients with a given medical condition is nontrivial. To create standardized measures that are practical for healthcare institutions worldwide, the Institute for Strategy and Competitiveness at Harvard Business School, the Boston Consulting Group, and the Karolinska Institute founded a nonprofit organization called the International Consortium for Health Outcomes Metrics (ICHOM) (Kaplan and Anderson 2003), which gathers clinical, administrative, and patient representatives to outline the minimum standard set of outcomes that should be collected for a specific medical condition (Kaplan and Anderson 2003).

One example of a core outcome measure set finalized by the ICHOM is the "Cleft Lip and Palate Standard Set" drafted by a working group consisting of several parties including surgeons, parents, and speech therapists, who reached a consensus on the clinical and patient-reported outcomes to be collected for this patient population throughout the entire course of treatment (Kaplan and Anderson 2003). The different outcomes collected during the full cycle of cleft lip and palate care are shown in Figure 3.3. Outcomes that measure the burden of treatment and complications include the number of interventions, complication rates, and the number of hospital readmissions. Outcomes that focus on the degree of health also include patient-reported outcomes and intend to measure

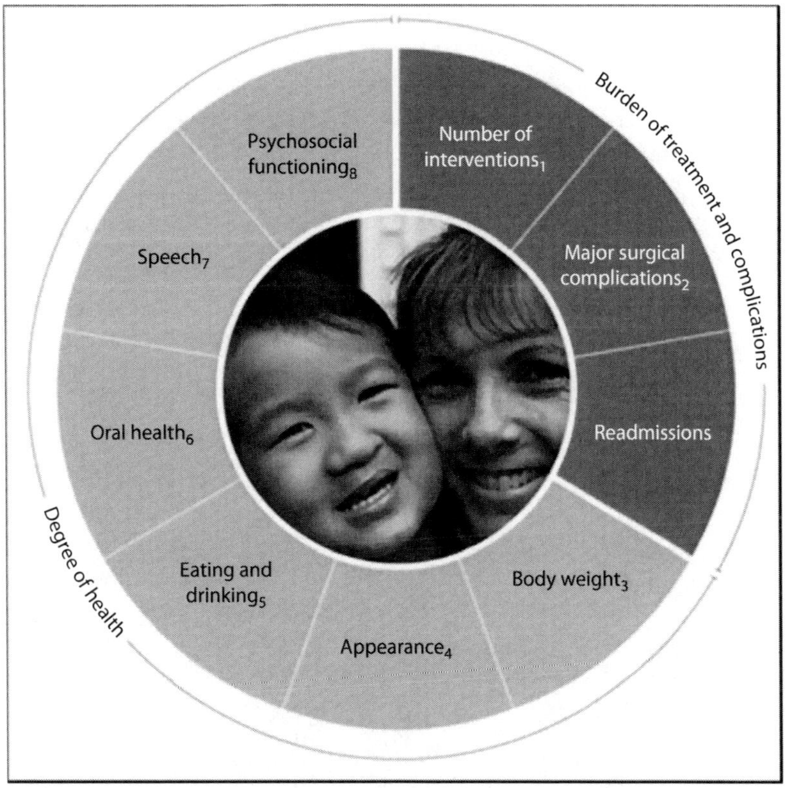

Figure 3.3 Outcomes collected in the ICHOM Cleft Lip and Palate Standard Set, including "Degree of Health" and "Burden of Treatment and Complications" (International Consortium for Health Outcomes Metrics 2012).

physical functionality, psychosocial functionality, and appearance. The time points for collecting each outcome in the care cycle were determined by the working group (Kaplan and Anderson 2003).

The adoption of this and other globally applicable standard sets by more healthcare institutions will allow comparison of performance based on patient outcomes. ICHOM's goal is to produce standard sets that cover over 50% of the global disease burden by 2017 (Kaplan and Anderson 2003).

3.2.2 Cost

In order to create an environment amenable to value-based healthcare, healthcare leaders, and individual providers must improve their understanding of the costs of providing high-quality care. However, it is also important for providers and institutions to understand that this is balanced against the additional resources required to improve the accuracy of costing data, which falls along a continuum as shown in Figure 3.4.

Currently, many managers use off-the-shelf accounting products that are not specifically tailored to the healthcare industry or, in some instances, create internal systems using in-house metrics or calculations to inform the managerial decision-making process. However, an accounting system that is not integrated with the care cycle creates challenges for a management team trying to fulfill a value-based agenda. The ultimate goal is to create a continuous feedback loop between the cost accounting system and clinical operations by connecting granular patient and diagnosis-level data to make real-time changes in care delivery possible.

Two common cost accounting approaches used to create this environment are the "top-down" approach and the "bottom-up" approach. The top-down approach analyses overall organizational operating expenses and attributes these to specific service lines, departments, and even specific occurrences in the organization (Hanover 2014). The bottom-up approach attempts to identify costs beginning at the patient or diagnosis level for a certain type of encounter and has historically been time and cost intensive. More recently, a number of vendors have marketed potential information technology (IT) solutions to help eliminate some of the more detailed costing efforts

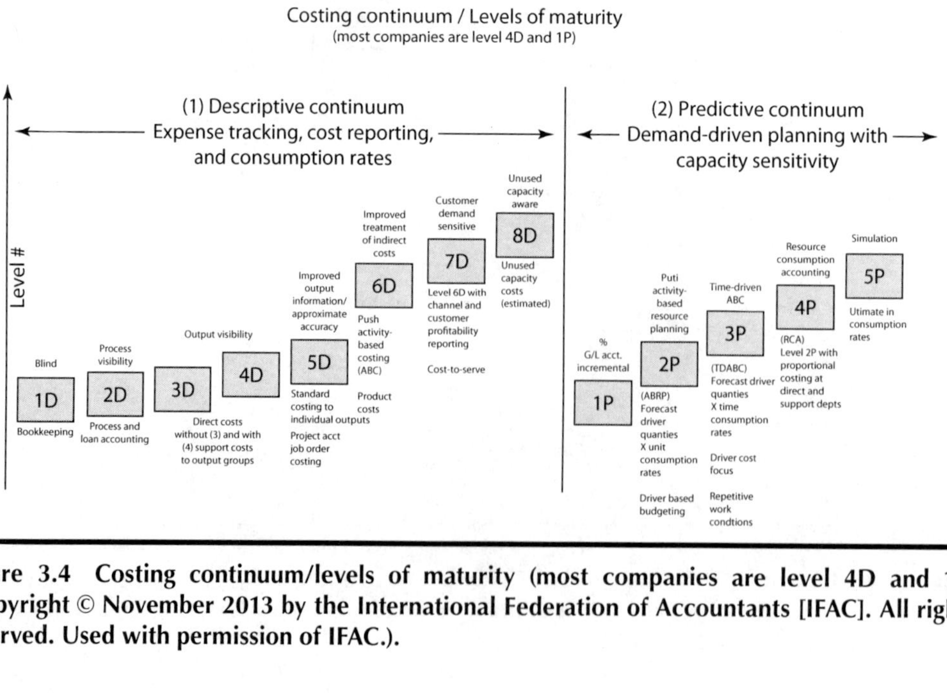

Figure 3.4 Costing continuum/levels of maturity (most companies are level 4D and 1P) (Copyright © November 2013 by the International Federation of Accountants [IFAC]. All rights reserved. Used with permission of IFAC.).

using various methodologies to determine costs including ratio of cost to charge, percentage of total cost, or relative value unit (RVU, a numerical factor assigned to a medical service during coding based on the skill and time required to undertake such a procedure), with varying degrees of success. A hybrid system utilizing allocable direct costs, time-based values, RVU data, and non-charge-related activities provides the most comprehensive, timely, and accurate data (Imus 2014). Boston Children's Hospital has made significant progress in pioneering many of these methodologies, particularly in the area of time-driven activity-based costing (TDABC).

3.2.2.1 Time-Driven Activity-Based Costing

TDABC is a user-friendly version of traditional activity-based costing with the advantages of scalability, accuracy, and decreased data requirements (Kaplan and Witkowski 2014). TDABC requires only two composite data points (Kaplan and Witkowski 2014): (1) the time needed for a particular activity in service delivery, and (2) the unit cost of service provision.

3.2.2.1.1 Process Mapping/Timing

The patient encounter must be mapped to determine the time necessary for healthcare activities. This involves

- Identifying the key steps within a particular activity (which allows for significant flexibility and scalability of this method)
- Distinguishing which personnel are involved in each step
- Determining the time necessary for the different personnel to carry out the steps
- The total time required for the activity

First, a general process map is determined. Then, the time necessary to complete each phase in the process map is estimated or observed and later averaged to determine the expected time required. Process mapping can be developed through direct observation alone or by consensus groups validated by direct observation (Kaplan and Witkowski 2012, Kaplan and Anderson 2007). For example, researchers at Boston Children's Hospital mapped the process of delivery of post-procedural antibiotics (Figure 3.5) (Daniels and Lappi 2016).

The process map of antibiotic delivery was broken into its three component steps. The times for each step were observed nine times, averaged, and summed to yield the mean total time taken to prepare and administer antibiotics for a patient undergoing cleft palate repair (Daniels and Lappi 2016).

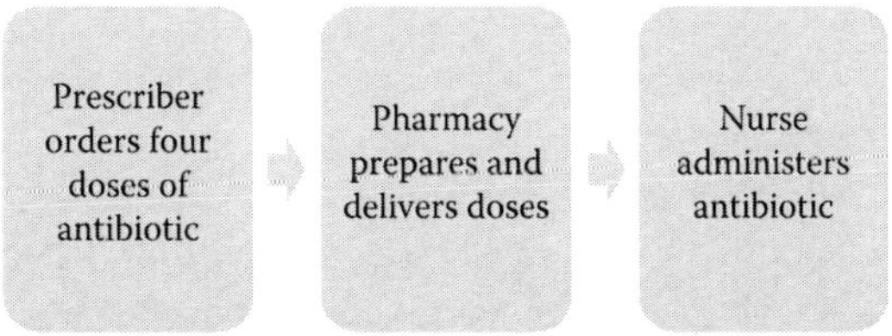

Figure 3.5 Process map for preparing and administering an antibiotic. The process map of antibiotic delivery is broken into its three component steps. The times for each step were observed nine times, averaged, and summed to yield the mean total time to prepare and administer antibiotics for a patient undergoing cleft palate repair (Daniels and Lappi 2016).

3.2.2.1.2 Unit Costs

The unit cost of service provision, also known as the cost of supplying capacity, is unique to each healthcare service entity. In TDABC for healthcare, personnel who perform the activities are assigned costs based upon their salaries, benefits, and associated fixed costs. When totaled, these costs are the numerator of the unit cost of each respective personnel cadre. In cases where there is minimal variability within specific cadres, costs can be averaged for all members. However, in instances where there is significant variability within cadres, it may be necessary to address individual members of the group to distribute costs equitably (Kaplan and Witkowski 2014).

The denominator is the total productive time, which is defined as the nominal time spent at work with vacations, daily breaks, expected sick days, research time, and other factors that reduce actual time spent at work subtracted. These calculations yield the cost of the capacity supplied divided by the practical capacity of the personnel/resources (Kaplan and Witkowski 2014).

3.2.2.1.3 Practical Examples

The Department of Plastic and Oral Surgery (DPOS) at Boston Children's Hospital utilized TDABC to identify the true costs of both providers and patients. The DPOS's first application of TDABC was in primary care, simple surgeries, and complex surgeries. The department mapped every administrative and clinical process required for each patient for three indications (in order of increasing complexity): plagiocephaly, benign neoplasms, and craniosynostosis (cost analysis shown in Figure 3.6; Kaplan and Witkowski 2012). They also calculated the cost of supplying capacity utilizing financial/administrative data (cost worksheet shown in Figure 3.7).

By adopting this approach, the DPOS discovered that the comparatively lower costs of treating plagiocephaly compared with its revenue generation allowed them to provide more complex craniosynostosis care without generating a net loss. Before this discovery using TDABC, the DPOS was considering withdrawing basic plagiocephaly services (Kaplan and Witkowski 2012).

The flexibility and scalability of TDABC allows implementation in lower-income settings and less robust health systems such as those seen in Haiti. At the Hôpital Universitaire de Mirebalais (HUM), Haiti's largest teaching hospital, TDABC was used to determine the actual cost of providing obstetric and cancer care and proved to be more accurate than the standard management accounting system for hospitals (MASH) method of service costing (Kaplan and Mistry 2015). Another example of TDABC's impact was demonstrated at Indus Hospital (IH), Karachi, Pakistan, where free at the point-of-care services have been provided to its population since its foundation in 2007 for over 1,000 patients daily. IH currently functions under a fixed payment model and is using TDABC to discover areas for process improvement and to calculate the actual cost of knee replacements to advocate for their patients and raise funding (Arnquist et al. 2015).

3.2.2.1.4 Future of TDABC

Each efficiency and cost reduction uncovered by TDABC strengthens the argument for its use in value-based healthcare. As highlighted above, the key input for TDABC is the time necessary to perform an activity. In industry, there is increasing use of global positioning systems (GPS) and radio-frequency identification (RFID) to create process maps for production, inventory, and sales (see also Chapter 12) (Kaplan and Witkowski 2012). These practices have made it possible to minimize the expenses associated with TDABC and track costs in real time. As interest in

	Surgeon	Ambulatory service representative (ASR)	Registered nurse (RN)	Clinical assistant (CA)	Total
Compensation: salary, fringes, and bonus	$ 5,500,000	$ 390,000	$ 1,098,500	$ 235,300	$ 7,223,800
Malpractice insurance	220,000	-	-	-	220,000
Billing services	760,000	-	-	-	760,000
Office expenses: rent, utilities, insurance, supplies	400,000	148,200	247,000	123,500	918,700
Total	$ 6,880,000	$ 538,200	$ 1,345,500	$ 358,800	$ 9,122,500
Research and teaching time	25%	-	-	-	0
Clinical time	75%	-	-	-	0
Surgeon clinical expenses	5,160,000	-	-	-	0
Medical supplies	67,200	-	-	-	0
Total clinical costs	**$ 5,227,200**	**$ 538,200**	**$ 1,345,500**	**$ 358,800**	**$ 7,469,700**
Number of employees	10	6	10	5	31.0
Clinical cost per employee	$ 522,720	$ 89,700	$ 134,550	$ 71,760	

Source: Casewriler analysis. All cost numbers in this case have been created artificially by the case writers for illustrative purposes only and not represent actual cost data of the organization.

Figure 3.6 Department of plastic and oral surgery, Boston Children's Hospital: Cost analysis.

Resource	Surgeon	ASR	RN	CA
Weeks per year	52	52	52	52
Less: Vacation and holidays	6	4	4	4
Less: Training and leave	2	2	2	2
Available weeks per year	44	46	46	46
Hours per day	10	8	8	8
Less: Breaks, training, meetings	1.2	1.5	1.5	1.5
Available hours	8.8	6.5	6.5	6.5
Less: Estimate of research and education time (%)	25%	0%	0%	0%
Clinical hours per day	6.6	6.5	6.5	6.5
Clinical minutes available per day	396	390	390	390
Clinical minutes available per year	87120	89700	89700	89700
Annual cost per person	$ 522,720	$ 89,700	$ 134,550	$ 71,760
Capacity cost rate ($ per minute)	$6.00	$1.00	$1.50	$0.80
Personnel process times (minutes)				
Plagiocephaly	18	8	23	5
Neoplasm skin excision	22	55.5	20	5
Craniosynostosis	40	10.5	23	10

Medical diagnosis cost per patient visit	Surgeon	ASR	RN	CA	Total cost	Charge	Average reimbursement	TDABC profit	RCC Cost	RCC Profit
Plagiocephaly	$ 108.00	$ 8.00	$ 34.50	$ 4.00	$ 154.50	$ 350.00	$ 224.00	$ 69.50	$ 210.00	$ 14.00
Neoplasm skin excision	$ 132.00	$ 55.50	$ 30.00	$ 4.00	$ 221.50	$ 350.00	$ 224.00	$ 2.50	$ 210.00	$ 14.00
Craniosynostosis	$ 240.00	$ 10.50	$ 34.50	$ 8.00	$ 293.00	$ 350.00	$ 224.00	$ (69.00)	$ 210.00	$ 14.00

Plastic surgery dept.	
Charges	$ 12,449,500.00
Costs	$ 7,469,700.00
Reimbursement	$ 7,967,680.00
RCC: Ratio of costs-to-charges	$0.60
Average DPOS reimbursement rate	64%

Source: Casewriter analysis. All cost numbers found in this case have been created artificially by the case writers for illustrative purposes only and do not represent the actual cost data of the organization.

Figure 3.7 Department of Plastic and Oral Surgery, Boston Children's Hospital: Cost worksheet.

value-based healthcare and TDABC uptake in health services increases, this type of concurrent costing is likely to become necessary.

Whether low or high resource, highly reliable healthcare institutions rely on high value, which is driven by quality of care per unit cost. There is, therefore, a need to measure standardized outcomes that matter to patients over time periods that matter to patients. Cost of care can be analyzed by TDABC. Health systems can be improved through increased value and, as proposed by the Institute of Healthcare Improvement, this is the "triple aim" of reducing costs while increasing quality and improving the patient experience (Berwick et al. 2008). Some institutions have already experienced progress toward their value-based goals through the creation of a "value management office," which, much like a clinical center of excellence, is driven by a centralized team (Kaplan et al.).

3.2.3 Evidence-Based Guidelines

Evidence-based guidelines (EBGs) are increasingly applied in healthcare to reduce variable delivery of patient care and thereby improve care. Standardization of care processes can improve patient outcomes and reduce unnecessary resource utilization and associated costs. The development of EBGs is the first step in the overall process of improving care. Outcomes must be defined, measured, implemented, and adopted at the local level.

Given the variety of presenting conditions and the need for quick decision-making, emergency departments (EDs) are an excellent setting for EBG implementation. Boston Children's Hospital's ED is a Level I Regional Pediatric Trauma Centre with an annual volume of 60,000 visits.

3.2.3.1 Developing Evidence-Based Guidelines

In this example in Boston Children's Hospital's ED (Akenroye and Stack 2016), ED leadership identified variation in care practices and wide differences in resource utilization for certain conditions. Conditions were prioritized based on the number of patients affected, the potential for high impact (such as a disease with high morbidity and/or mortality rates), the potential for elimination of variation in practice patterns, and the potential for improved efficiency by reducing unnecessary resource utilization. Eleven guidelines were initially identified for development via a process involving ED leadership and EBG physician champions. Guideline scope was established using the PICO framework (patient/problem, intervention, comparison, outcomes), and national guidelines were studied and updated with current evidence and adapted to fit the local context. A team of five physician and nursing colleagues was engaged to provide expert opinion on the scientific validity and usability of each guideline. A structured process was developed for implementation and evaluation of each EBG. In this way, the ED program developed and implemented EBGs that have helped to improve efficiency, reduce resource utilization and costs, and standardize emergency care without jeopardizing patient outcomes.

The success of the ED EBG program was dependent on

- Strong leadership support
- Local presence of guidelines
- Selection of motivated champions
- Development of practical processes for guideline development and implementation
- Peer consensus among a highly academic group
- Rigorous performance monitoring with frequent feedback to stakeholders

Lessons learned included that

- A local EBG program can improve the value of care.
- Developing EBGs is never complete, as evidence continues to emerge and guidelines must be updated.
- Implementation is the most important and challenging phase of an EBG program, and appropriate strategies for the local setting are essential for successful implementation.

The fundamentals of this EBG program can be adapted to other clinical settings. Two case studies are presented below.

3.2.3.1.1 An EBG to Reduce Cranial CTs for Children with Minor Blunt Head Trauma

Cranial computed tomography (CT) is the gold standard for the diagnosis of traumatic brain injury but is reported to be associated with an increased lifetime risk of malignancy. Care for children with minor head injuries was identified as an opportunity to improve care, both to decrease non-value-added resource utilization and to spare children from unnecessary and risky testing. A program was developed to improve clinical care through the translation of published evidence and national guidelines (when available) into local EBGs to improve and standardize practice. The improvement team analyzed key drivers and constructed a multidisciplinary plan to reduce the CT rate by 10% for ED patients with minor blunt head trauma as illustrated in Figure 3.8.

A pediatric emergency physician and nurse developed the initial head trauma guidelines based upon Pediatric Emergency Care Applied Research Network (PECARN) Traumatic Brain Injury (TBI) age-based clinical rules. The guidelines were revised through an iterative process with input from multiple pediatric emergency and neurosurgery attending physicians.

A multidisciplinary team including a physician, a specialized pediatric emergency nurse, a QI expert, and an administrator was assembled to implement the EBG. The key steps of the implementation process were

- Feedback on initial guidelines collected through hour-long multidisciplinary conferences
- Development of a "Head Trauma" electronic order set which included a link to and recommendations from the guidelines

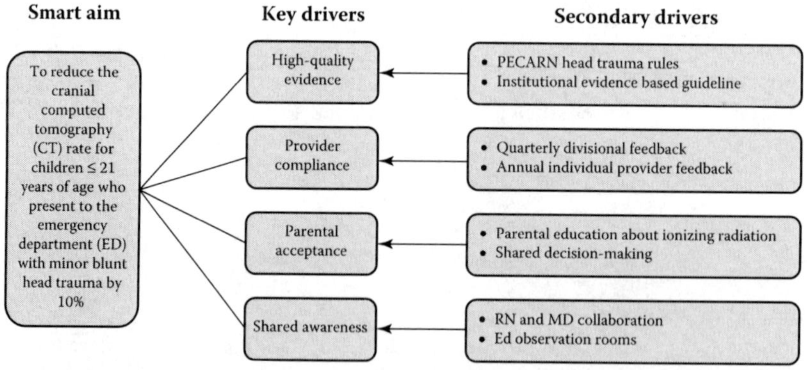

Figure 3.8 Key driver diagram for reduction of cranial CT for minor blunt head trauma. PECARN, Pediatric Emergency Care Applied Research Network (Nigrovic et al. 2015).

- Development of electronic discharge instructions
- Determination and communication of a rollout date
- Individual provider feedback given by EBG champions to improve provider awareness, acceptance, adoption, and adherence

The primary EBG outcome measure was performing a CT during the initial ED visit. The balancing measure was any return to the ED within 72 hours that required hospitalization for management of head injury.

The pre-intervention CT rate was 21%, which dropped to 15% after EBG implementation. After implementation of individual provider feedback on cranial CTs, the rate reduced further to 9%. No ED visits for minor blunt head trauma were identified in the post-intervention period, and the CT scanning rates over the course of implementation are shown in Figure 3.9.

By recognizing the gap that existed between data-driven evidence and change in clinical practice, the implementation strategy was designed to provide clinicians with high-quality decision-making guidelines that integrated into existing workflows. As of 2016, the reduction in head CT rates has continued, highlighting the sustainability of this intervention in the clinical workspace.

3.2.3.1.2 An EBG to Reduce Hospitalizations for Children with Isolated Skull Fractures

Approximately 500,000 children visit U.S. EDs annually for evaluation of head trauma, resulting in nearly 50,000 admissions and $1 billion in healthcare expenditure. Children with isolated skull fractures are at low risk of clinical decompensation. However, and despite this low risk, hospitalization rates for children with isolated skull fractures approach 80% nationally. Hospitalization is associated with increased costs and the potential for medication errors and nosocomial infections, so children should only be hospitalized when clinically necessary. Although some children with isolated skull fractures may require hospital admission for ongoing symptoms or evaluation

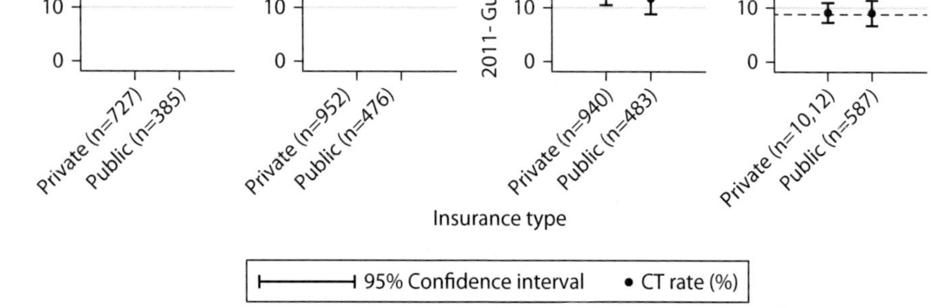

Figure 3.9 Rates of CT scanning for patients with minor head injury by insurance type (Nigrovic et al. 2015).

of non-accidental trauma, outpatient care with close follow-up is a safe option for the majority of children evaluated.

At Boston Children's Hospital, the baseline hospitalization rate for children with isolated skull fractures was similar to the U.S. national average. The ED leadership hypothesized that it could safely reduce hospitalization rates for isolated skull fractures without a significant impact on quality of care, and so established a QI initiative to reduce hospital admissions for isolated skull fractures by at least 20% over a two-year period (Lyons et al. 2016).

An isolated skull fracture was defined as a skull fracture without intracranial injury. The intervention included two steps: (1) the development and implementation of an EBG, and (2) dissemination of a provider survey designed to reinforce guideline awareness and adherence. The primary outcome was hospitalization rate, and the balancing measure was hospital readmission within 72 hours. The PHIS database* was reviewed for trends at other U.S. children's hospitals, which informed the overall intervention goal to reduce hospital admissions by at least 20% from baseline and sustain the reduction.

The EBG was developed through an iterative process with involvement of key stakeholders from multiple disciplines including ED physicians and nurses, neurosurgeons, and social workers. After initial development, education conferences were held for faculty, fellows, and nursing staff to highlight and discuss current evidence and institutional experience. Feedback from these conferences was then used to refine the guideline. At implementation, the guideline was made available in all patient care areas through an accessible online library and nested within the electronic medical record (EMR) "Minor Head Trauma" order set used to order neuroimaging. To reinforce awareness and compliance, multiple education sessions were held, electronic reminders were sent, and departments were provided with biannual updates.

This initiative included a survey to be completed by every ED attending provider caring for a child with an isolated skull fracture. After EBG implementation, attending providers were surveyed at the time of admission on their decision-making for hospitalization. The survey was developed to reinforce EBG awareness, increase adherence, and understand barriers to guideline adherence while identifying focus areas for future QI efforts.

The baseline admission rate was 71%, which decreased to 46% after EBG implementation. No child was readmitted after discharge. Admission rates for children with isolated skull fractures at other similar pediatric institutions over the same time period remained constant at 78%, supporting the conclusion that the reduction was because of the QI effort and not the result of a national trend.

Although a cost-effectiveness analysis was not performed, a reduction in hospital admission rates could significantly reduce the cost of caring for children with isolated skull fractures.

After the initial 11 guidelines were developed and successfully implemented, ED leadership undertook the development of 14 additional EBGs. All 25 remain in active use.

3.2.4 Standardized Clinical Assessment and Management Plans (SCAMPs) to Produce Value

Standardized Clinical Assessment and Management Plans (SCAMPs) are an exciting innovation proven to improve care and reduce healthcare expenditure across a diverse array of pediatric and adult conditions. Leaders in the cardiovascular program at Boston Children's Hospital developed

* PHIS is a comprehensive pediatric database containing clinical and financial details of millions of patient encounters. PHIS was developed by the Children's Hospital Association (CHA), a business alliance networking 42 leading children's hospitals, to provide a rich data source for administrative data analysis. PHIS has been used by clinician scientists to conduct comparative effectiveness studies on hospitalized children.

SCAMPs, which were subsequently adopted by the hospital as a tool to reduce unnecessary utilization before being widely spread to other areas of the hospital. SCAMPs have been useful in many areas, and the hospital has learned how to optimize them over time.

3.2.4.1 SCAMP Aims

A SCAMP provides clinical decision support to encourage cost-effective healthcare. SCAMPs aim to produce value by (1) reducing practice variability among clinicians, (2) optimizing resource use within care, and (3) improving patient outcomes.

To reduce the cost of care, SCAMPs concentrate on particular types of resource use. For example, outpatient SCAMPs commonly focus on reducing follow-up visits and tests that do not drive clinical decisions, while inpatient SCAMPs tend to focus on reducing length of stay and transitioning care to less resource-intensive settings. Projects in either setting may focus on using less costly alternatives to medications and materials that produce similar, or even better, results.

All SCAMPs aim to optimize current standards of care. Some SCAMPs also focus on outcomes and increasing the safety and efficacy of care by, for example, reducing infection rates, improving survival rates for complex procedures, and stratifying risk for invasive procedures.

3.2.4.2 SCAMP Methodology

A SCAMP guides clinicians through a preferred management pathway for a given patient population with a particular condition—for instance, syncope or Graves' disease. Although the tool recommends standard care, a SCAMP permits providers to leverage their clinical acumen and adapt treatment pathways to address individual patients' needs (Farias et al. 2013).

Each SCAMP collects data about how clinicians follow the pathway and their rationales for diverting from recommended practice. SCAMPs also collect data that may not affect decisions but offer insights into refining the pathway such as patient characteristics, outcomes, and diagnostic test values. This information, combined with frequent data analysis, is used to optimize the SCAMP's care pathway over time in an iterative fashion. This process is illustrated in Figure 3.10.

SCAMPs keep pace with current knowledge through frequent iteration and by incorporating not only knowledge gained from the SCAMP but also knowledge from clinical studies and clinical practice. SCAMPs cycle through four phases—design, pilot, production, and analysis—and are then modified and re-implemented at the point of care, continually improving with each cycle. During redesign, SCAMPs consider data collected in the SCAMP and any recent evidence-based literature. This allows SCAMPs to incorporate and innovate on up-to-date standards.

3.2.4.3 SCAMP Advantages

SCAMPs are a particularly important tool for clinicians uncomfortable with the available evidence, whether they find it inadequate, speculate that it could be improved, or find evidence not directly applicable to their patient population. Therefore, SCAMPs can help to generate additional evidence through robust data collection as patients flow through the care pathway over time. The data collected by the SCAMP methodology help to rapidly test and generate new standards.

SCAMPs also represent a robust tool for engaging clinicians in care optimization. Physician champions play an important role in designing the care pathways and promoting engagement by

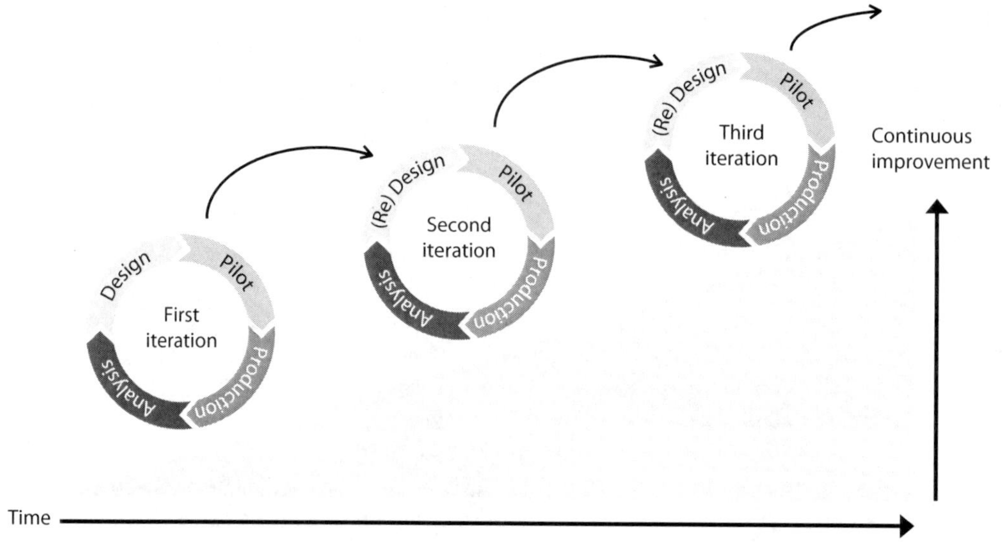

Figure 3.10 Development and improvement methodology for standardized clinical assessment and management plans.

peers in using the SCAMP during care decision-making. Clinicians actively participate through SCAMP production by collecting data on their patients, and most physicians participating in the SCAMP process are engaged and stimulated by the resulting data, not least because it allows them to gain insights into how their peers are assessing and managing their patients with similar conditions and provides information on specific patient populations. Because of the volume of data collected by SCAMPs and the SCAMP structure, the data feedback loop motivates clinicians to remain engaged over time, and SCAMP analysis aggregates treatment decisions, allowing peer comparison of different decision-making processes. Surveys have confirmed that providers have a positive perception of SCAMPs.

3.2.4.4 Success Story: Pediatric Critical Asthma SCAMP

The prevalence of asthma in children has increased in recent years. Despite improved outpatient management, about 10,000 pediatric asthma patients will be hospitalized each year for acute exacerbations of asthma. These hospitalizations are costly, accounting for 36% of asthma-related medical expenses for children (Davis et al. 2011). The use of a standard care pathway has been shown to significantly decrease asthma patients' length of stay (LOS) and, consequently, costs. However, there are limited data for standardizing therapies that contribute to LOS.

The Pediatric Critical Asthma SCAMP was developed to determine how to best reduce LOS for critical asthma patients in the intensive care unit (ICU) and the hospital by standardizing therapeutic regimens. The SCAMP recommends therapies according to exacerbation severity: albuterol (salbutamol) for low severity, heliox for mid severity, and ICU-specific therapies for high severity. The SCAMP intends to reduce the administration of unnecessary ICU-specific therapies by appropriately triaging patients to less resource-intensive therapies. The SCAMP also aims to wean patients off albuterol more quickly because this factors into criteria for discharge from ICU-level care.

SCAMPs allowed clinicians to refine critical asthma care quicker and more flexibly than randomized controlled trials (RCTs). For example, to confirm changes in LOS, an RCT would need to recruit about 400 patients over the course of four years and changes cannot be applied based on the learned experience to improve recommended care pathways. In contrast, the SCAMP has detected significant LOS changes and revised its care pathway twice in four years to produce increasingly positive results.

The SCAMP resulted in more effective weaning of asthma patients from albuterol, which helped to quicken their discharge from the ICU and hospital. The SCAMP reduced average total LOS from 2.7 days at baseline to 2.6 days (5%) in the first iteration, 2.2 days (21%) in the second iteration, and 1.9 days (31%) in the third iteration. Total room and board costs (including nursing time) were reduced by 7% in the first iteration, 19% in the second iteration, and 29% in the third iteration.

3.2.4.5 Success Story: Distal Radius Fracture SCAMP

Distal radius fractures (DRFs) are the most common pediatric fracture. DRFs account for 20% of all pediatric fractures and affect one in a hundred children. Although these fractures are common, several challenges remain with respect to their treatment and management, some of which are related to the need to standardize the care process.

The DRF SCAMP recommends splinting as opposed to casting for certain fracture types. The literature indicates that splints are a safe and effective alternative to casts, but this method had not been adopted into local pediatric care. This change was judged to not only standardize fracture treatment but also to eliminate the need for an additional clinic visit for cast removal and imaging, because splints can be removed by parents at home after three weeks.

The SCAMP successfully changed treatment patterns in physicians. Prior to introduction of the SCAMP, only 1% of patients were splinted, the remaining 99% receiving either a long or short arm cast. After SCAMP implementation, 72% of patients received a wrist splint. The SCAMP reduced the need for follow-up visits because the splints could be removed out of office. For example, the number of torus and Salter-Harris I fracture patients who returned for a follow-up visit decreased from 91% to 80% after SCAMP implementation. Similarly, the number of patients with bicortical or physeal fractures requiring a follow-up after the six-week visit decreased from 44% to 14% and from 39% to 18%, respectively, after SCAMP implementation.

Fewer clinic visits makes it easier for patients and families to adhere to treatment plans and reduces radiographic testing (by 60% in this case), thereby decreasing radiation exposure to patients. The SCAMP also successfully reduced the costs associated with treating DRF, particularly for torus fractures: based on standardized costing analysis, the SCAMP resulted in a 32% reduction in the total cost of all hospital visits and associated tests. This result was independently confirmed through TDABC methods, which showed a 49% reduction in the overall cost of care (Hennrikus et al. 2012).

Healthcare can experience delays when research is performed as part of everyday practice; the DRF SCAMP, however, rapidly bridged the gap between new literature and practice. The SCAMP then collected data to ensure that practice change generated positive effects for the local hospital population. This confirmatory data, combined with a process incorporating input from local orthopedic surgeons, has helped the SCAMP disseminate smoothly into practice.

3.2.4.6 Value Results

Overall, SCAMPs result in improved healthcare value (i.e., better care at a lower cost). Our formal evaluations provided evidence that gains were made without diminishing patient or family satisfaction and while simultaneously maintaining, or even improving, the quality of care.

SCAMPs have produced a number of clinical benefits in addition to those described above, fulfilling their aim to improve patient outcomes. For instance, SCAMPs improved rates of vitamin D repletion in secondary hyperparathyroidism patients by refining decision support for administering particular supplements. SCAMPs also helped more cardiac patients with aortic stenosis to leave the catheterization laboratory ("cath lab") with adequate or ideal outcomes.

Moreover, SCAMPs have helped to decrease complications in medical care and identify factors that may place patients at risk while in hospital. For example, SCAMPs reduced the rate of cytomegalovirus (CMV) infection in organ transplant patients by directing physicians to increase prophylaxis. SCAMPs have also reduced bleeding and clotting complications in critically ill patients receiving extracorporeal membrane oxygenation (ECMO) through improved guidelines for monitoring coagulation activity. SCAMPs also identified asthma as a risk factor for food allergy reactions, helping to ensure appropriate resources for these patients' food challenges.

SCAMPs have also fulfilled goals to standardize care and reduce unnecessary resource utilization. SCAMPs helped fewer unnecessary tests, such as radiographs for patients with distal radius fractures and echocardiograms for patients with chest pain, to be ordered. SCAMPs also reduced the cadence of follow-up visits for several types of patients including those undergoing arterial switch operations, patients with concussion, and patients with distal radius fractures. SCAMPs helped direct care to less intensive care settings when appropriate: as noted above, SCAMPs reduced ICU stays for critical asthma patients and limited the number of resource-intensive visits in the CAT/CR* for food challenge patients.

Reducing resource use saves money. The Critical Asthma SCAMP reduced costs by 25%, the Chest Pain SCAMP decreased costs by 19%, and Distal Radius Fracture costs were reduced by 32%.

Finally, SCAMP efficiency gains have improved patient access. For example, SCAMPs reduced the time from initial visit to first follow-up visit for concussion patients, and SCAMPs identified a need to expand clinic availability for lipid screening and food allergy challenges. Reduced LOS, such as that from the Critical Asthma SCAMP, has improved throughput and ICU access.

3.2.4.7 Network Effects

In the past years, some SCAMPs developed at Boston Children's Hospital have spread to other institutions and provider groups, furthering the reach of optimized care and allowing aggregated data generation for more powerful analyses. SCAMPs are a tool that leverages continuously learning networks that drive better care at lower costs.

* The Center for Ambulatory Treatment and Clinical Research (CAT/CR) is a unique 10-bed ambulatory program for children participating in research. Services include infusion therapies, diagnostic testing, and procedural support.

3.2.5 Engaging Physicians in Quality Improvement (QI)

Physicians play a unique role in healthcare delivery, so actively engaging them is critical to the success of any patient safety and quality program, and, therefore, the success of enterprise high reliability goals. Physicians direct bedside clinical care delivery, develop treatment plans, and carry out specific therapeutic procedures and other interventions. They also uniquely set the tone for internal team dynamics and, individually and collectively, are key players in creating the internal culture of an institution, department, clinic, or practice. Because of the difficulty in establishing practices, licensure, and other issues, physicians often have long tenures in institutions and other practice settings and thus influence the culture over many years.

Successfully engaging physicians begins with successfully engaging physician leaders. In order for quality and safety efforts to gain traction, it is essential that leaders in key positions, such as the chief medical officer, chief quality and safety officer, physician-in-chief, surgeon-in-chief, medical directors, department chairs, and division chiefs, are carefully chosen as individuals who are widely regarded by peers as having a strong reputation for quality and safety in their own practices. These individuals must also embody leadership skills to be able to transfer their personal practice ethics to other physicians under their influence. These individuals must feel accountable for all the clinical activities in their area, not just their own clinical practice. Developing leadership skills in key physicians can help translate a quality and safety agenda into daily practice. As an example, Boston Children's Hospital supported a five-day leadership course for over 80 top leaders in the institution, including many top physician leaders, and also created opportunities for leadership training for physicians chosen to lead quality and safety activities in specific divisions and departments.

Beyond choosing key physician leaders, quality and safety efforts are more likely to succeed if individual physicians are also actively engaged, as these individuals play critical roles in day-to-day clinical activities and set the tone for others in their clinical microsystem. Certain aspects of quality and safety programs are more likely to engage physicians. First, specific initiatives and priorities must be perceived as addressing important clinical problems. Overemphasis of "simple" initiatives that are not viewed as leading directly to important clinical benefit can reduce engagement. An obvious strategy to overcome this problem is setting priorities and initiatives strategically to address physicians' concerns. Another is the careful messaging of priorities to explain why certain initiatives have been selected and having the message reinforced by physician leaders. Giving physicians control of the details of process improvement can also be very useful, as can avoiding "one size fits all" initiatives, as the importance of issues may differ throughout an organization. At Boston Children's Hospital, each department and division creates an annual "Quality Management Plan" for their area, and while the hospital provides direction and sets priorities, the department or division leaders are given ownership and are allowed to customize specific plans to address issues perceived as most important from their perspective.

Another engagement strategy that works, especially with physicians, is making a case for quality improvement through meaningful data collection. Physicians are experts in using quantitative information in their daily practices, and in academic centers they are often well-trained clinical researchers adept at handling and interpreting data. Thus, physicians are highly motivated by compelling data that suggest a potential safety or quality problem or solution. Physicians are often competitive, so data showing how one individual or unit compares with others (or how one department compares with other hospitals) can be especially motivating. At Boston Children's Hospital, physicians actively participate in registries that allow such comparisons and employ data specialists to assess practice. Physician leaders also encourage and support the development of meaningful pediatric practice measures that possess robust statistical properties and risk adjustment and incorporate this information as a key component of quality management plans. In contrast, the use of poor-quality information to guide quality improvement can be demotivating, as physicians often find weaknesses in poor-quality measurements, dispute whether quality concerns are real, or disengage from the entire process. Physician leaders have been careful to align "high stakes" performance measures, such as pay-for-quality programs, with measures that do not have real or perceived weaknesses.

Once physicians are engaged in quality and safety activities, they must be supported. In most practice environments, both academic and nonacademic, physicians juggle many competing priorities for their time and attention. The success of any clinical enterprise depends on physicians spending most of their time doing clinical work. While, culturally, engaging in quality and safety should be considered a required component of professional practice, in reality, efforts are more likely to succeed if physicians have the necessary resources to accomplish quality and safety activities. Examples of resources include quality and safety expertise, computer-based tools, data collection, report generation, project management, and other administrative support. Boston Children's Hospital provides much of this support through expertise housed in a "Program for Patient Safety and Quality" infrastructure but also provides a quality consultant to each department and division to support the clinical leaders.

Another way to support physicians and engagement is by aligning incentives to reduce competing priorities from other activities necessary for professional advancement. In the United States, participating in quality improvement activities is now necessary to maintain professional certification. Specifically, aligning quality and safety projects with opportunities to fulfill certification requirements can encourage physician participation. Many physicians also enjoy networking with other physicians, so collaborative QI projects involving teams from different practices or institutions working toward common quality and safety goals and that allow them to teach and learn from each other can be especially fulfilling. In academic centers, career advancement is often dependent on achieving academic milestones such as writing manuscripts and conducting research. At Boston Children's Hospital, physicians and other stakeholders are engaged via a competitive small grants program and are provided with courses and mentorship in quality and safety research. A Center for Quality and Safety Research within our quality and safety infrastructure was established to facilitate academic career advancement. Increasingly, medical schools are including participation in quality and safety activities as criteria for promotion.

Finally, in order to engage physicians, activities that contribute to physician burnout must be avoided. Physician burnout is an increasing concern in the United States and is reaching alarming proportions in some areas. Major drivers of burnout are increasing demands specific to physicians including production pressure, numerous repetitive documentation requirements, inadequate EMR systems, and concerns about working in an unsupported, punitive environment. It is important to avoid quality and safety activities that are too time-consuming or to implement too many projects simultaneously. It is also critical that complex projects are well designed and supported.

3.2.6 Employee Engagement

Committed, involved, and enthusiastic employees are critical to the success of a highly reliable organization. These employees provide "discretionary effort" to reach other functional areas to improve processes, lower the risk of delivering poor handoffs, and communicate proactively in the service of improving clinical outcomes.

How can this kind of engagement be encouraged? Daniel Pink, author of *Drive* (Pink 2009), identified three questions that employees ask of themselves when deciding the extent to which they should engage in their work: "Do I feel connected to the mission?," "Do I feel as though I am growing/learning?," and "Do I have autonomy in how I do my work?" Employee engagement is consistently below 33% across all sectors in the United States (Gallup 2015). While employee engagement at Boston Children's Hospital is higher than the average, the organization has made a commitment to further increasing employee engagement across the enterprise.

Three strategic goals were identified in the hospital's aim to increase employee engagement: (1) to increase transparency and communication from leadership; (2) to recognize individuals for their work in advancing the values and mission of the organization; and (3) to increase opportunities for professional development at all levels. The hospital embraced a concept called the "five Is," which has driven most of the conversation about employee engagement at Boston Children's Hospital. In this model, employees fall into one of five categories from the least engaged to the most engaged: I feel *Ignored*, I am *Informed*, I am asked to be more *Involved*, my ideas are actually *Incorporated*, and I am *Inspired* (meaning that I believe leadership is supporting possible and positive changes). Unfortunately, most organizations' employees lie between "ignored" and "informed," helping to explain low employee engagement scores. In an attempt to shift employees to "involved," "incorporated," and "inspired," Boston Children's Hospital undertook several multi-year initiatives.

First, a series of retreats was held to engage employees in conversations on how to solve some organizational issues and how to incorporate those ideas into practice. The retreats were then opened up to the hospital's top 300 leaders with the goals of (1) increasing engagement, (2) increasing understanding of organizational strategy, and (3) providing a forum to learn new communication skills to solve organizational issues. The first retreat yielded six task forces that worked for over a year on issues related to improving employee engagement:

- What is the "Children's Way" and how do we reinforce what it means for everyone?
- How do we build the leaders of the future?
- How do we improve transparency and trust?
- How do we deal with controversial issues and create a safe environment?
- How do we use technology to better connect with each other?
- How do we increase employee health and happiness?

These task forces, sponsored by hospital leaders, produced many recommendations. The organization recently conducted its fifth forum, which focused on creating an atmosphere of teamwork through the concept of "psychological safety," as developed by Amy Edmondson from Harvard Business School (Edmondson 1999).

During that session, Boston Children's Hospital leaders participated in a live voting exercise to determine if progress had been made from previous sessions. The results are heartening. There was progress on leadership at all levels, learning from mistakes, and employees felt that support from leadership had increased (Figure 3.11). The leadership's willingness to surface issues of engagement to create a culture of openness and support yielded cultural shifts consistent with increased engagement.

Finally, the hospital has developed a strong commitment to development. Organization leaders have the opportunity to create individual personal development plans and to learn coaching skills necessary to work with employees to create their own development plans. This approach aims to

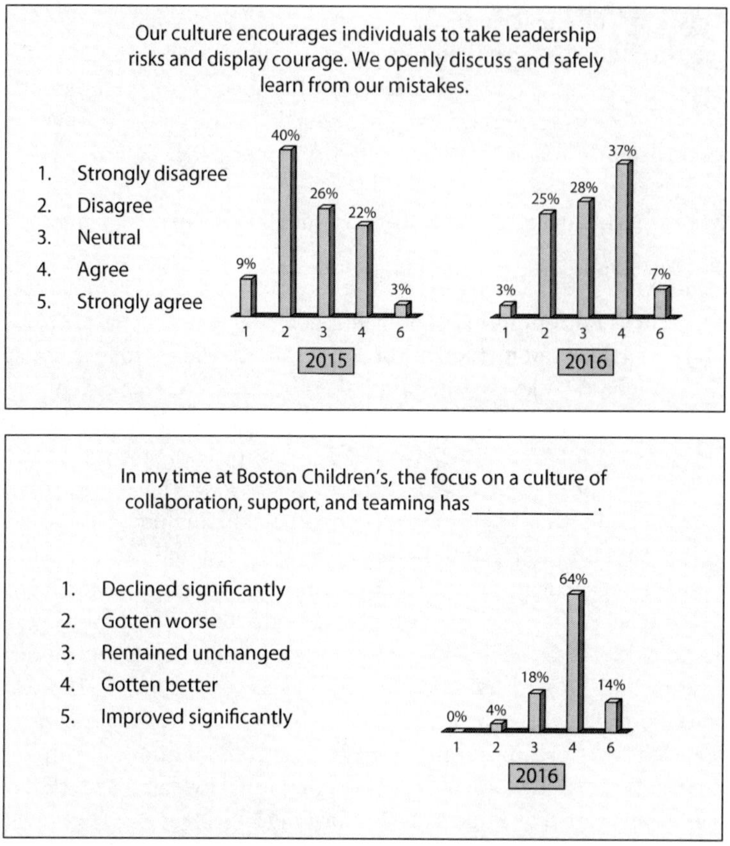

Figure 3.11 Impact of employee engagement initiative at Boston Children's Hospital.

arm all 10,000 employees with high-quality development plans, educational resources, and other professional development tools to motivate employee engagement.

3.2.7 Engaging Pediatric Patients and Their Families

Highly reliable hospitals seek to prevent failures in processes, systems, and people that can lead to mistakes and adverse events, some of which have tragic consequences. Many healthcare systems are adopting concepts used by high reliability industries like aviation and nuclear power (see also Chapter 5) to meet production requirements while reducing accident rates that result in harm. In healthcare, these strategies have been used to reduce adverse patient and employee events by developing highly reliable systems. From our perspective, at the core of highly reliable patient- and family-centered healthcare is the voice and experience of patients and their families.

The Adult Hospital Consumer Assessment of Health Care Providers and Systems (Adult HCAHPS) is a survey tool used throughout the United States to assess patient experiences in adult hospitals in the inpatient setting (CAHPS 2015). For hospitals reimbursed by Medicare*, full payments are distributed only when certain Adult HCAHPS scores are achieved. The Child HCAHPS survey was developed by the Centre of Excellence for Pediatric Quality Measurement (CEPQM) at Boston Children's Hospital to allow parents and guardians to share their experience of their child's inpatient care. Child HCAHPS is now used nationally and addresses several key themes important to patient and family experience including communication with parents, communication with the child, attention to safety and comfort, and the hospital environment, as well as an overall rating of their experience. The data generated by Child HCAHPS are intended to provide actionable information for multiple stakeholders including hospitals, insurers, policy makers, clinicians, and patients and their families.

Boston Children's Hospital uses the data from Child HCAHPS and other experience surveys to inform understanding of its patient and family experience, employee engagement, and patient–family engagement initiatives. These data drive both departmental and hospital-wide changes. Families often express frustration with the long waits for appointments, especially with specialists. The hospital is committed to improving access for patients and has begun improving interactions with their first point of contact on the phone, providing appointment reminders to families through e-mail and text messages, and developing a dynamic dashboard that allows each clinic or department to obtain real-time data on access measures. Small changes can also have a large impact on the patient experience. The hospital has created color-coded role ID badges that hang below the hospital badge for all patient-facing employees. This idea began in the ED in response to a common complaint from patients and families that they "don't know who's who" (i.e., physicians, nurses, clinical assistants, social workers, child life, and administrators). In an already stressful situation, not being able to quickly distinguish a doctor from a social worker adds to families' anxieties. Hospital staff are empowered to recognize improvement opportunities and make changes in their local areas. For instance, Neonatal ICU staff reviewed their Child HCAHPS data and formed a Discharge Work Group after learning that families did not feel as well prepared as expected to care for their children at home. The hospital has made it a priority to make their patient experience data internally transparent to employees and physicians to drive improvement in all areas of the hospital and to actively engage patients and families in ways to improve the experience through advocacy, community engagement, family-to-family mentoring, special projects and committees, and wellness initiatives.

Boston Children's Hospital has a long history of partnering with patients and families and actively engaging them in care. The hospital formed its first Family Advisory Council in the 1970s from grassroots efforts. Since then, the hospital has expanded the Family Advisory Council and formed a Teen Advisory Committee to further strengthen family partnerships and actively address challenges in the patient–family experience. The committees are chaired by family members but are provided with administrative support from hospital staff with commitment and support from hospital leaders (see sidebar for more info on the Family Advisory Committee). Recently, the hospital launched a Virtual Advisors Program so that families can share ideas and give constructive feedback from the comfort of their own homes. Content is posted online for members to review and provide feedback. Families are a key part of our organization; they serve on boards and committees and build meaningful, long-lasting partnerships with hospital leaders.

---

* Medicare is a single-payer national social insurance program that has been administered by the U.S. government since 1966. It provides health insurance for Americans aged 65 and older who have worked and paid into the system through payroll tax.

PATIENT–FAMILY ADVISORY COMMITTEE SIDEBAR

As of June 2017, Boston Children's Hospital had 19 Family Advisory Council members, 20 Teen Advisory Committee members, and 53 Virtual Advisors that have actively worked on well over 98 projects and committees including the enterprise-wide staff high reliability training and sustainment initiatives. In addition, several hospital departments have developed their own Family Advisory Councils to address discipline-specific challenges such as information sharing in the ED. These advisory councils have produced recommendations and projects that help to improve the patient–family experience for all. Some exemplary work by these groups includes the development of a tip sheet to guide employees' interactions with pediatric patients and their families, assessing new technologies and health education materials for family-friendliness, and family-led speaking engagements. Additionally, patient–family speakers participate in new employee hospital orientation to emphasize the importance of patient-centered care. Patient–family speakers have reached over 3,800 employees and have been well received by new employees. Additionally, the Psychiatry Family Advisory Council created a detailed family guide to help families cope and manage during an inpatient stay. This guide provides an overview of what to expect during admission, treatment plans, family coping tips, what to expect going home, and key resources and contacts.

In 2014, the Hale Family Center was built in the hospital's main lobby so that all patients and families could benefit from the services. The Hale Family Center is dedicated to supporting families throughout their experience using a family-centered approach and offers a variety of resources and activities including story hours, wellness classes, scheduled birthday parties, sleeping accommodation, computer access, and quiet rooms. The center is staffed with both Spanish and Arabic interpreters to support our international patients. Child Life Specialists are used throughout the hospital to enhance the patient's stay and engage with the child in a relatable manner. Child Life Specialists help patients adjust to and understand the hospital and their medical situation by taking into account each child's stage of development, background, and culture.

Patient–family engagement is vital to the success of a highly reliable healthcare organization and a superior patient experience as it provides the organization with the opportunity to better understand and address the needs and concerns of those that it cares for. Transparency of quality and experience data, advocacy and community engagement, and active participation from families has allowed Boston Children's Hospital to develop highly reliable initiatives at all system levels.

3.3 Conclusions

Efficient clinical practice is a key feature in the journey toward value-based and high reliability healthcare systems. Boston Children's Hospital exemplifies how efficient clinical practice can be successfully implemented in a complex academic medical center environment using the concept of value-based medicine to improve outcomes and care and by engaging patients, families, and hospital employees in the pursuit of value-based and high reliability practice. Our hope is that lessons learned at Boston Children's Hospital will support global progress in pediatric healthcare practice.

Acknowledgments:

Alyson Cooper, MPH
Michael Doyle
Jonathan Gilman, MBA
Amanda Good, MPH
Ronald R. Heald, MBA
Abigail Kellogg
Jason Miller
Swagoto Mukhopadhyay, MD
Lisa Rubino, MBA
Rachel Yorlets, MPH
Meredith van der Velden, MD
Rachel Yorlets

References

Akenroye, A. T., and A. M. Stack. 2016. The development and evaluation of an evidence-based guideline programme to improve care in a paediatric emergency department. *Emerg Med J* 33 (2): 109–117. doi:10.1136/emermed-2014-204363.

Arnquist, S., J. Rosenberg, and R. Weintraub. 2015. *The Indus Hospital: Building Surgical Capacity in Pakistan (Condensed Version)*. The Lancet Commission on Global Surgery. http://www.lancetglobalsurgery.org/teaching-cases.

Berwick, D. M., T. W. Nolan, and J. Whittington. 2008. The triple aim: Care, health, and cost. *Health Aff (Millwood)* 27 (3): 759–69. doi:10.1377/hlthaff.27.3.759.

CAHPS. 2015. The CAHPS Child Hospital Survey. http://www.ahrq.gov/cahps/surveys-guidance/hospital/about/child_hp_survey.html.

Daniels, K. M., and M. D. Lappi. 2016. Assessing the cost of prophylactic antibiotic use after cleft lip and lip adhesion procedures. *Journal of Healthcare Management* 59 (6): 282–290.

Davis, A. M., M. Benson, D. Cooney, B. Spruell, and J. Orelian. 2011. A matched-cohort evaluation of a bedside asthma intervention for patients hospitalized at a large urban children's hospital. *J Urban Health* 88 (Suppl 1): 49–60.

Edmondson, A. 1999. Psychological safety and learning behavior in work teams. *Administrative Science Quarterly* 44 (2): 350–383.

Farias, M., K. Jenkins, J. LockFriedman, J. Greenberg. 2013. Standardized Clinical Assessment And Management Plans (SCAMPs) provide a better alternative to clinical practice guidelines. *Health Aff (Millwood)* 32 (5): 911–20. doi:10.1377/hlthaff.2012.0667.

Fuchs, V. R. 2013. The gross domestic product and health care spending. *N Engl J Med* 369 (2): 107–9. doi:10.1056/NEJMp1305298.

Gallup. 2015. Employee engagement in U.S. stagnant in 2015. http://www.gallup.com/poll/188144/employee-engagement-stagnant-2015.aspx.

Hanover, J. 2014. *Business Strategy: Getting to Goal – The Role of Cost Accounting in U.S. Health Systems' Transformation*. Framingham, MA: IDC Health Insights.

Hennrikus, W., P. Waters, D. Bae, S. Virk, and A. Shah. 2012. Inside the value revolution at children's hospital boston: Time-driven activity-based costing in orthopaedic surgery. *The Harvard Orthopaedic Journal* (14): 50–7.

Imus, S. 2014. *Healthcare Cost Accounting: 8 Strategies to Streamline Implementation and Quickly Achieve Measureable Results*. Chicago: Becker's Hospital Review.

Institute of Medicine. 2012. *Best Care at Lower Cost: The Path to Continuously Learning Health Care in America*. Washington, DC: National Academies Press.

International Consortium for Health Outcomes Metrics. 2012. http://www.ichom.org/.

International Federation of Accountants. Information Paper: Evaluating the Costing Journey—A Costing Levels Continuum Maturity Framework 2.0. November 2013. http://www.ifac.org.

Kaplan, R. S., and S. R. Anderson. 2003. Time-driven activity-based costing (November 2003). https://ssrn.com/abstract=485443 or http://dx.doi.org/10.2139/ssrn.485443.

Kaplan, R. S., and S. R. Anderson. 2007. *Time-Driven Activity-Based Costing: A Simpler and More Powerful Path to Higher Profits*. Boston: Harvard Business School Press.

Kaplan, R. S., C. H. MacLean, A. Dresner, D. A. Haas, and T. W. Feeley. 2015. *Health Care Providers Need a Value Management Office*. Boston: Harvard Business Review.

Kaplan, R. S., and B. Mistry. 2015. Hopital Universitaire de Mirebalais, Partners In Health in Haiti. *The Lancet Commission on Global Surgery*.

Kaplan, R. S., and M. L. Witkowski. 2012. *Boston Children's Hospital: Measuring Patient Costs (V)*. Boston: Harvard Business School Press.

Kaplan, R. S., and M. L. Witkowski. 2014. Using time-driven activity based costing to identify value improvement opportunities in healthcare. *Journal of Healthcare Management* 59 (6): 399–413.

Lyons, T. W., A. M. Stack, M. C. Monuteaux, S. L. Parver, C. R. Gordon, C. D. Gordon, M. R. Proctor, and L. E. Nigrovic. 2016. A QI initiative to reduce hospitalization for children with isolated skull fractures. *Pediatrics* 137 (6): e1–e9. doi:10.1542/peds.2015-3370.

Moriates, C., V. M. Arora, and N. T. Shah. 2015. *Understanding Value-based Healthcare*. New York: McGraw-Hill Education.

Moriates, C., N. T. Shah, and V. M. Arora. 2013. First, do no (financial) harm. *JAMA* 310 (6): 577–8. doi:10.1001/jama.2013.7516.

Nigrovic, L. E., A. M. Stack, R. C. Mannix, T. W. Lyons, M. Samnaliev, R. G. Bachur, and M. R. Proctor. 2015. Quality improvement effort to reduce cranial CTs for children with minor blunt head trauma. *Pediatrics* 136 (1): e227–33. doi:10.1542/peds.2014-3588.

Pink, D. H. 2009. *Drive: The Surprising Truth about What Motivates Us*. New York, NY: Riverhead Books.

Porter, M. E. 2009. A strategy for health care reform--toward a value-based system. *N Engl J Med* 361 (2): 109–12. doi:10.1056/NEJMp0904131.

Porter, M. E. 2010. What is value in health care? *N Engl J Med* 363 (26): 2477–81. doi:10.1056/NEJMp1011024.

Porter, M. E., S. Larsson, and T. H. Lee. 2016. Standardizing patient outcomes measurement. *N Engl J Med* 374 (6): 504–6. doi:10.1056/NEJMp1511701.

Porter, M. E., and T. H. Lee. 2013. *The Strategy that will Fix Health Care*. Boston: Harvard Business Review.

Porter, M. E., and E. O. Teisberg. 2006. *Redefining Health Care: Creating Value-based Competition on Results*. Boston: Harvard Business School Press.

Woolf, S. H., and L. Y. Aron. 2013. The US health disadvantage relative to other high-income countries: Findings from a National Research Council/Institute of Medicine report. *JAMA* 309 (8): 771–2. doi:10.1001/jama.2013.91.

Chapter 4

Successful Patient Outcomes

Caleb Fan, Sami El-Boghdadly, and Martin A. Makary

Contents

4.1 Introduction ... 71
4.2 Patient Care Committee ... 72
4.3 Infection Control Standards ... 72
4.3.1 Hand Hygiene ... 72
4.3.2 Personal Protective Equipment ... 73
4.3.3 Needlestick and Sharps Injury Prevention ... 73
4.3.4 Cleaning and Disinfection ... 73
4.3.5 Respiratory Hygiene ... 74
4.3.6 Waste Disposal ... 74
4.4 Clinical Outcome Trending ... 74
4.5 Improving Wisely ... 75
4.6 Benchmarking ... 75
4.7 Enhanced Recovery after Surgery ... 77
4.8 Improving Safety Culture ... 79
4.9 Conclusions ... 80
References ... 80

4.1 Introduction

In a 2016 study, medical errors were found to be the third leading cause of death in the United States and an increasingly popular topic in healthcare worldwide (Makary and Daniel 2016). As illustrated in this book, healthcare is turning increasing amounts of attention to the question of how to deliver safer, more reliable medical care. This fundamental question is becoming as important as how to cure disease. In a given year, more lives may be saved through the use of a procedure checklist than the number of lives saved by the newest chemotherapy released in the same year. The problem is great and demands a serious re-review of the way we deliver medical care to patients. In this chapter, we begin by laying a foundation of standards that should be established by individual healthcare organizations. Once standards are determined, clinical outcomes should be measured, trended, and compared both internally and externally. Finally, we explore best practices such as enhanced recovery after surgery (ERAS; also known as *fast-track surgery*, *fast-track programs*, and *enhanced recovery programs*) and the comprehensive unit-based safety program (CUSP), which are tools that can be utilized to provide safer, more reliable medical care.

4.2 Patient Care Committee

The first step is to establish a patient care committee. A patient care committee is an interdisciplinary hospital staff organization whose primary duty is to monitor all patient care practices to ensure that predetermined standards are met. The committee members may include but are not limited to: physicians, nurses, pharmacists, therapists, nutritionists, social workers, and/or technicians. Committees do not only have to monitor patient care practices, but can also be involved in the design, implementation, and analysis of any interventions related to the care of patients in the organization. Potential duties and responsibilities include:

- Recommending practice standards in different patient care settings
- Determining criteria for competence for various job positions in different patient care settings
- Providing recommendations related to staff training and competency
- Recommending clinical policies for approval
- Approving clinical protocols, guidelines, and procedures

In the next section, we establish basic safety standards that may be modified for each unique healthcare organization.

4.3 Infection Control Standards

Healthcare-associated infections (HAIs) remain a major cause of morbidity and mortality in the United States. In 2002, there were an estimated 1.7 million HAIs in U.S. hospitals (Klevens et al. 2007). Infection control standards and precautions are implemented in hospitals to reduce the risk of transmission of pathogens via various mechanisms, including blood, bodily fluids, nonintact skin, and mucous membranes. Infection control standards include but are not limited to: hand hygiene, personal protective equipment (PPE), needlestick and sharps injury prevention, cleaning and disinfection, respiratory hygiene, and waste disposal.

4.3.1 Hand Hygiene

Hand hygiene is one of the most effective methods of preventing the transmission of HAIs, and includes hand rubbing with alcohol gel or handwashing with plain or antibacterial soap and water. Hands should be washed with soap and water if they are visibly soiled. At its simplest, handwashing involves five easy steps: wet, lather, scrub, rinse, and dry. To ensure a thorough technique, after applying soap and water: (1) rub palms together; (2) rub backs of both hands; (3) interface fingers and rub hands together; (4) interlock fingers and rub backs of fingers; (5) rub thumbs in a rotating manner, followed by the area between index finger and thumb; (6) rub fingertips on palms; and

(7) rub both wrists in a rotating manner. If hands are not visibly soiled, alcohol gel is the preferred method of hand hygiene. Hand hygiene procedures should be performed before and after contact with a patient. Healthcare facilities should ensure the availability of handwashing areas with clean running water.

4.3.2 Personal Protective Equipment

PPE includes gowns, masks, eyewear, gloves, and respirators and is designed to protect the skin and mucous membranes of the mouth, eyes, nose, and respiratory tract from infectious materials. The use and type of PPE should be determined by a risk assessment of the extent of contact anticipated with blood and bodily fluids and the likely modes of disease transmission. This assessment should occur prior to proceeding with any healthcare activity. Gowns should be worn if skin or clothing may be exposed to blood or bodily fluids. Masks and protective eyewear should be worn when patient care activities may involve a splash or spray of blood or bodily fluid. Gloves should be worn when touching mucous membranes, blood, bodily fluids, nonintact skin, or other infectious materials to prevent contamination of the provider's hands. After the healthcare activity is concluded, PPE should be removed immediately and hand hygiene procedures should occur. If PPE is saturated with blood or bodily fluids, it should be discarded into a biohazard bag; if not, it may be directly placed into the rubbish bin.

4.3.3 Needlestick and Sharps Injury Prevention

Needlestick and sharps injuries are a serious hazard in the healthcare setting. They may expose healthcare workers to blood-borne pathogens. The risk of needlestick injury is higher when needles: (1) must be taken apart or manipulated after use; (2) need to be manipulated in the client; (3) are being recapped; (4) are used to transfer bodily fluids between containers; (5) are not disposed of in puncture-resistant sharps containers after use. A few safety tips include:

- Avoid using needles whenever safe and effective alternatives are available.
- Activate safety devices on needles and sharps immediately after use.
- Avoid recapping, bending, cutting, or removing needles from the syringe or tube holder.
- Do not overfill sharps containers (stop at full line or when two-thirds full).
- Report needlestick or sharps injuries to employers immediately.

4.3.4 Cleaning and Disinfection

Cleaning and disinfection practices are implemented in patient and common waiting areas and for reusable medical devices. Cleaning is the process of removing foreign material from objects and can be accomplished with water and detergents or enzymatic products. Many disinfectants are not effective when foreign material such as inorganic and organic matter is present. Thus, thorough cleaning is required before disinfection. Cleaning and disinfection procedures should be implemented in patient and common waiting areas. These procedures should utilize Environmental Protection Agency (EPA)-registered disinfectants (or other certified products) following the manufacturer's instructions for amount, dilution, and contact time. Floors and walls do not necessarily need to be disinfected unless they are visibly soiled with blood or bodily fluids. They may be routinely cleaned with only a detergent or disinfectant product.

4.3.5 Respiratory Hygiene

Respiratory hygiene is a method to prevent the spread of respiratory infections from one person to another in a public area. It requires the education of healthcare workers, patients, and visitors to be effective. First, when coughing or sneezing, the nose and mouth should be covered with a tissue or the crook of the elbow to prevent the transmission of respiratory droplets. After contact with respiratory secretions, the hand hygiene techniques described in Section 4.3.1 should be performed immediately. Second, healthcare workers, patients, and visitors should wear a surgical mask when displaying the signs and symptoms of a respiratory illness. Third, common waiting areas should be spacious enough to separate people at least three feet (about a meter) apart. Finally, waiting and common areas should be stocked with alcohol gel devices, surgical masks, tissues, waste receptacles, and respiratory hygiene signs to educate the public.

4.3.6 Waste Disposal

Sharps should be disposed of in a standard-labeled, leak-proof, puncture-resistant sharps container and should be replaced when two-thirds full or filled up to the full line. PPE and disposable items saturated with blood or bodily fluids should be disposed of in biohazard bags (red in the United States; various colors in the United Kingdom depending on the type of biohazard) that are also leak-proof and puncture-resistant. When infectious waste is transported from a healthcare organization, a log must be kept that contains key information: date of disposal, location to which waste is transported, person transporting the waste, and amount and type of waste being transported. Infectious waste can be transported by healthcare organization staff or by an outside organization.

4.4 Clinical Outcome Trending

Clinical outcome trending is essential to continually improve medical practice. The driving force behind healthcare reform in the United States is the healthcare trifecta: achieve better health across populations, control rising costs, and improve the quality of care, which includes patient outcomes and satisfaction.

In a 2009 study, 48% of survey participants reported using standardized outcome measures in physical therapist (physiotherapy) practice (Jette et al. 2009). Of those who used outcomes data, over 90% believed it enhanced communication with their patients and helped direct the plan of care. When practitioners or organizations transition from merely recording results to actually tracking and acting on outcomes, they are empowered to improve patient care, determine best practices, establish care standards and hold staff accountable, influence payment rates, and eliminate practice variation across the profession.

Typical clinical outcomes such as complications and readmissions, mortality and morbidity, and hospital-acquired infections should be measured and trended by each healthcare organization. The patient care committee can help to determine exactly which clinical outcomes to measure. More recently, however, patient-reported outcomes measures (PROMs) have been utilized to determine whether clinicians are improving patient health. Compared with some of the typical clinical outcomes listed, these PROMs may be a better measure of whether an improvement in outcomes actually translates into patients living better, healthier lives. This concept is the driving force behind PROMs.

At the University of Pittsburgh Medical Center (UPMC), PROMs have taken form in the outpatient primary clinic as the SF-36, a 36-question, short-form survey that assesses patients' functional health and well-being. Some of the many benefits of the SF-36 are that it has enabled physicians to more easily identify patients with depression or elderly patients with limited mobility. In addition, PROMs data can potentially help improve the coordination of care in large health systems. Many elderly patients require medical treatment from various specialists. If PROMs data can be standardized and provided to all physicians involved in a patient's care, then physicians will better understand how a patient has responded to various treatments over time.

Unfortunately, new technology always presents complications and challenges. PROMs are not widely utilized in the United States for a number of reasons: (1) physicians cannot bill for the time they spend administering and interpreting PROMs data; (2) collecting and utilizing PROMs data can be disruptive to clinician workflow; (3) PROMs do not necessarily represent a patient's response to medical treatment (e.g., socioeconomic factors can influence PROMs); (4) physicians may not be able to effectively utilize PROMs if not properly trained. Although there are multiple obstacles to overcome before PROMs are widely adopted, there is considerable value in determining whether certain medical interventions truly have positive impacts on patients' lives.

4.5 Improving Wisely

One very successful benchmarking quality improvement (QI) program popular among doctors is "Improving Wisely," which is an approach to the problem of unwarranted practice variation addressed through internal data transparency. In 2016, the American College of Mohs Surgery (an advanced skin cancer treatment) initiated the Improving Wisely National Quality Collaborative as a part of broader multispecialty national QI (funded by the Robert Wood Johnson Foundation and based at Johns Hopkins University). The project uses a physician metric of performance endorsed and developed by the respective specialty association to inform physicians of their individual performance data in a confidential and nonpunitive data report. Improvement among outliers is based on the conceptual model that: (1) outliers may be unaware that they are outliers; (2) no one wants to be an outlier; and (3) a civil, confidential, peer-to-peer data sharing approach in the spirit of improvement is an effective way to engage physicians. Data reports to physicians serve as vehicles for benchmarking QI efforts. Year-to-year changes are similarly measured. Reductions in patient harm and cost savings are calculated among outliers who move toward the mean. Similar improvements have been noted with cost utilization reports to individual doctors for standardized services.

4.6 Benchmarking

Clinical outcomes should not only be compared internally but externally as well. Benchmarking is the process of comparing outcome measures to an external standard. Some equate the external standard with industry averages; however, this is not the case in true benchmarking. The American Society for Quality defines benchmarking as "a technique in which a company measures its performance against that of best in class companies, determines how those companies achieved their performance levels, and uses the information to improve its own performance. Subjects that can be benchmarked include strategies, operations, and processes" (American Society for Quality 2007).

Successful benchmarking depends on the collection of recent and reliable outcomes information. These outcomes measures should be monitored frequently so that they can be compared against those of the best in the business. Benchmarking not only involves comparing outcomes, but also collaborating with other organizations to learn from one another, share information including approaches and/or techniques, and modify best practices to fit an organization's needs. This approach enables organizations to optimize performance and positively impact outcomes.

To simplify the process, Pitarelli and Monnier (Pitarelli and Monnier 2000) describe eight benchmarking stages:

1. Select what to benchmark
2. Identify benchmarking partners (points of reference)
3. Collect and analyze internal data
4. Determine competitive differences by comparing internal with external data
5. Set future performance goals
6. Communicate benchmarking results with the organization
7. Create action plans
8. Take action

Although we have described benchmarking as making comparisons with best practices, industry averages still harness important information. For example, a hospital's QI team can use averages to quickly determine weak areas in need of attention. In addition, averages can be utilized to determine whether or not performance goals are being met, if actions plans are effective, and if any further changes need to be made. However, comparing averages is insufficient; meeting or even beating the national average does not necessarily equal success. Over 250,000 deaths per year were due to medical error in the United States in 2013 (Makary and Daniel 2016); the third biggest cause of death in the United States and approximately 10% of all-cause mortality. A hospital that has a medical error rate resulting in 9% of deaths is better than the national average in 2013. Should the hospital be satisfied, or should it eagerly discover the error rates at the best hospitals and try to learn how those hospitals achieved the lowest medical error rates resulting in death?

Furthermore, performance variation should be studied as closely as average performance. In 2002, an interventional radiology department studied why it had major issues with scheduling delays that resulted in complaints, patient dissatisfaction, and loss of business (Volland 2005). The project team discovered that patients had to make an average of 1.4 calls to schedule an appointment, with a standard deviation of 0.989 and a maximum of seven calls. After the implementation of improvement projects, the average remained unchanged at 1.4 calls, but the standard deviation was reduced to 0.52 with a maximum of three calls. If the department had only compared averages, the improvement in variability would have gone unnoticed. After implementing changes to scheduling, complaints from referring clinics were reduced to zero.

Benchmarking is a continuous process that prevents organizations from stagnating. It enables them to improve by comparing their performance to those that are the best in the industry. Through collaboration and understanding, one organization determines how other organizations achieve their success. Once that is determined, the organization does not simply imitate the more successful organizations, but instead adapts the gathered information to implement it successfully in its unique environment. The final step is to make sure that the changes elicit positive results and to keep repeating the process so that the organization eventually becomes the best in the business.

4.7 Enhanced Recovery after Surgery

One tool that can be utilized to provide safer, more reliable medical care is ERAS.

At its core, ERAS is a multimodal perioperative management pathway that expedites the recovery of surgical patients. Initially, ERAS was developed for colorectal surgery (Bardram et al. 1995), but more recently has been expanded to other surgical subspecialties (Kehlet and Soballe 2010; Kiessling et al. 2013). Surgery leads to physiological responses, including endocrine and metabolic stress reactions that ultimately slow down recovery (Carli 2015). The goal of ERAS is to modify the natural physiological responses that occur during major surgery. ERAS has been associated with reduced length of hospital stay, opiate use, overall complications, and patient costs and increased patient comfort and satisfaction (Thiele et al. 2015).

The physiologic stress response caused by surgery decreases functional status, which is followed by a gradual recovery back to preexisting function. In the preoperative phase of ERAS, the goal is to optimize the patient first. Then, during the intraoperative phase, surgical and anesthetic techniques are used to minimize the surgical stress response. Finally, the postoperative rehabilitation period attempts to accelerate recovery by returning the patient to his or her preexisting functional status more quickly. Interventions in ERAS include but are not limited to:

Preoperative interventions:

- Preadmission counseling and patient education
- Evaluation and optimization of organ function
- Improving physical fitness
- Establishing good nutritional status
- Minimal starvation/no prolonged fasting
- Fluid and carbohydrate loading
- No mechanical bowel preparation
- Thromboprophylaxis

Operative interventions:

- Antibiotic prophylaxis, acid suppression, and prokinetics
- Short-acting anesthetic agents
- Thoracic epidural anesthesia/analgesia
- Elective use of nasogastric decompression, urinary catheterization, and abdominal drainage
- Goal-directed fluid therapy
- Maintenance of normothermia (body warmer/warm IV fluids)
- Minimal tissue handling
- Minimal operative time
- Minimal access surgery
- No drains

Postoperative interventions:

- Preemptive and adequate analgesia (nonopioid)
- Postoperative nausea and vomiting prophylaxis
- Early removal of all drains, tubes, and/or catheters
- Early enteral nutrition
- Early mobilization
- Stimulation of gut motility
- Avoidance of salt and water overload
- Ensuring follow-up after discharge

Many of the ERAS interventions are related to nutrition, because poor nutrition is associated with poor postoperative outcomes (Durkin et al. 1999; van Bokhorst-de van der Schueren et al. 1997) and is a strong predictor of 90-day mortality and poor overall survival (Gregg et al. 2011). Thus, nutritional status should be evaluated in the preoperative period by a nutritionist if possible, and malnutrition should be properly treated. The European Society for Parenteral and Enteral Nutrition defines "severe" nutritional risk as one or more of the following: weight loss greater than 10% in six months, BMI less than 18.5 kg/m2, or a serum albumin of less than 30 g/L (Weimann et al. 2006). Correction of preoperative nutritional deficiency may only require standard nutritional supplements, parenteral nutrition, or a combination of parenteral and enteral nutrition.

Another preoperative ERAS intervention related to the nutrition of the patient is to keep starvation time to a minimum. During surgery, autonomic afferent impulses from surgical trauma stimulate the hypothalamic–pituitary–adrenal axis and mediate the body's endocrine response (Hall 1985). Increased cortisol levels stimulate gluconeogenesis and glyconeogenesis in the liver, proteolysis (Simmons et al. 1984), and lipolysis leading to weight loss and muscle wasting (Desborough 2000). Furthermore, peripheral insulin resistance occurs, which is associated with poor wound healing, increased length of stay, and risk of infective complications (Thorell et al. 1999). Methods to attenuate insulin resistance include adequate pain control (Greisen et al. 2001; Uchida et al. 1988), avoidance of prolonged fasting, and preoperative carbohydrate loading (Scott et al. 2015). A two-hour fast for liquids and a six-hour fast for solids are considered safe and adequate (American Society of Anesthesiologists 2011). Along with minimal starvation, an oral carbohydrate drink is administered two hours before surgery. As an added safety measure, a prokinetic agent can be utilized early in the preoperative period. Furthermore, if postoperative hyperglycemia is controlled, mortality and morbidity can be reduced by almost a half (van den Berghe et al. 2001).

Early postoperative nutrition in the form of enteral nutrition can ameliorate the metabolic response. Gastrointestinal function and tolerability must be assessed prior to starting oral intake. Other ERAS interventions to facilitate this process include postoperative nausea and vomiting prophylaxis, epidural analgesia, and minimal use of drains, tubes, and catheters. Oral or enteral nutrition can be started as early as six to eight hours after surgery (Boelens et al. 2014). Even though early postoperative feeding is safe and recommended (Gustafsson et al. 2012), evidence is weak at best. A 2006 Cochrane review found a nonsignificant direction of effect toward a reduction in complications and mortality rate (Andersen et al. 2006); however, they found no obvious advantage in keeping the patient nil by mouth following gastrointestinal surgery.

ERAS can be an extremely powerful tool. The implementation of ERAS in healthcare systems requires the formation of a multidisciplinary team that should include surgery, anesthesia, nursing, and nutrition. Other members can include therapists and social workers. The fact that ERAS can reduce length of stay and complication rates and increase patient satisfaction (Thiele et al.

2015) has highlighted the importance of perioperative care and the changes that can be made to improve outcomes. All healthcare workers involved in the perioperative care of surgical patients should familiarize themselves with the principles of ERAS.

4.8 Improving Safety Culture

Safety culture is defined as the attitudes, beliefs, and values of all individuals in the workplace. Intuitively, safety culture in the hospital and the operating room (OR) is a driver of quality surgical care. Surgeons have recognized this phenomenon for years; however, an association between safety culture and surgical outcomes has only recently been established (Fan et al. 2016). A healthcare organization with good safety culture should be characterized by staff that are willing to raise safety concerns, responsive management, high patient and employee satisfaction, low nurse turnover rates, and a location that is the hospital of choice for its own employees to receive medical care.

Workplace culture is notoriously difficult to quantify in a methodologically sound and scientifically rigorous way. In 2006, Makary et al. described a validated instrument to measure safety culture in surgery (Makary et al. 2006c). In a study of 60 U.S. hospitals, they determined that the overall hospital safety score varied widely between hospitals, with a range of 20 to 99 out of 100. Since its introduction, 500 U.S. hospitals have utilized the healthcare system survey, and the Agency for Healthcare Research and Quality (AHRQ) has developed a similar survey that measures 12 domains of safety culture. The Joint Commission and other quality organizations have encouraged use of the survey in healthcare to determine the impact of safety interventions after they have been evaluated. An example of a QI program that has been evaluated in this manner is CUSP, which has been implemented in intensive care units (ICUs) and in surgical units (Cooper and Makary 2012; Wick et al. 2012).

In addition to the assessment of safety culture, CUSP focuses on the improvement of teamwork and communication through the surgical checklist. The use of a surgery checklist was first described in 2006 (Makary et al. 2006a), and its impact on reducing mortality rates and complications in noncardiac surgical patients in a global population was described in 2009 (Haynes et al. 2009). The checklist was originally developed and introduced at Johns Hopkins Hospital to deliver safer care by improving safety culture through a civil planning conversation prior to every operation. At the time of checklist development, there was widespread variability in the compliance of evidence-based practices, so another aim of the checklist was to improve compliance of these practices. The lead question of the checklist was designed to promote familiarity of team members and their roles in the OR while anticipating potential hazards. The opening question, "What are the names and roles of the members of the team?" was based on: (1) teamwork successes observed in the surgical team model; (2) studies demonstrating a disconnect between surgeons and nurses, despite perceptions of good teamwork in the OR in roughly half of all operations (Makary et al. 2006b); and (3) studies indicating that over 80% of OR nurses and approximately half of surgeons reported having witnessed disruptive behavior in the workplace within months of being surveyed (Klein and Forni 2011). Today, many QI projects and tools seek to promote a more cordial and civil work environment, as this impact on culture is recognized as contributing to better patient care.

Anonymity among employees in the workplace is a dangerous attribute and can facilitate disruptive behavior. When clinicians and hospitals workers do not know each other's names and specific roles, for example, communication is less civil because it is less personal. Consider e-mail and other anonymous communications; they tend to be more abrasive than in-person conversations due to anonymity. A good QI tool in surgery addresses this issue. A better safety culture has been associated with decreased risk of wrong-site surgery (Makary et al. 2007) and superior patient outcomes in the ICU setting (Huang et al. 2010). Ongoing studies are confirming these findings in other surgical populations.

4.9 Conclusions

Currently, healthcare is focused on the causes and prevention of medical errors in an attempt to improve patient outcomes and deliver safer, more reliable medical care. Given the complexity of the healthcare system, one of the most important ways to improve safety is through systematic protocols, which have been described in this chapter. Beginning with a patient care committee, healthcare organizations should determine their standards and outcome measures and then systematically compare within and between healthcare organizations to target areas that need improvement. Protocols such as ERAS and CUSP have been proven to improve patient outcomes and can be adapted to individual organizations. Once systematic comparisons and protocols become widely implemented, patient outcomes and the quality of healthcare should improve.

References

American Society of Anesthesiologists, Committee. 2011. Practice guidelines for preoperative fasting and the use of pharmacologic agents to reduce the risk of pulmonary aspiration: Application to healthy patients undergoing elective procedures: An updated report by the American Society of Anesthesiologists Committee on Standards and Practice Parameters. *Anesthesiology* 114 (3):495–511. doi:10.1097/ALN.0b013e3181fcbfd9.

Andersen, H. K., S. J. Lewis, and S. Thomas. 2006. Early enteral nutrition within 24h of colorectal surgery versus later commencement of feeding for postoperative complications. *Cochrane Database Syst. Rev.* (4):CD004080. doi:10.1002/14651858.CD004080.pub2.

Bardram, L., P. Funch-Jensen, P. Jensen, M. E. Crawford, and H. Kehlet. 1995. Recovery after laparoscopic colonic surgery with epidural analgesia, and early oral nutrition and mobilisation. *Lancet* 345 (8952):763–764.

Boelens, P. G., F. F. Heesakkers, M. D. Luyer, et al. 2014. Reduction of postoperative ileus by early enteral nutrition in patients undergoing major rectal surgery: Prospective, randomized, controlled trial. *Ann. Surg.* 259 (4):649–655. doi:10.1097/SLA.0000000000000288.

Carli, F. 2015. Physiologic considerations of enhanced recovery after surgery (ERAS) programs: Implications of the stress response. *Can. J. Anaesth.* 62 (2):110–119. doi:10.1007/s12630-014-0264-0.

Cooper, M., and M. A. Makary. 2012. A comprehensive unit-based safety program (CUSP) in surgery: improving quality through transparency. *Surg. Clin. North Am.* 92 (1):51–63. doi:10.1016/j.suc.2011.11.008.

Desborough, J. P. 2000. The stress response to trauma and surgery. *Br. J. Anaesth.* 85 (1):109–117.

Durkin, M. T., K. G. Mercer, M. F. McNulty, et al. 1999. Vascular surgical society of Great Britain and Ireland: Contribution of malnutrition to postoperative morbidity in vascular surgical patients. *Br. J. Surg.* 86 (5):702. doi:10.1046/j.1365-2168.1999.0702a.x.

Fan, C. J., T. M. Pawlik, T. Daniels, et al. 2016. Association of safety culture with surgical site infection outcomes. *J. Am. Coll. Surg.* 222 (2):122–128. doi:10.1016/j.jamcollsurg.2015.11.008.

Gregg, J. R., M. S. Cookson, S. Phillips, et al. 2011. Effect of preoperative nutritional deficiency on mortality after radical cystectomy for bladder cancer. *J. Urol.* 185 (1):90–96. doi:10.1016/j.juro.2010.09.021.

Greisen, J., C. B. Juhl, T. Grofte, et al. 2001. Acute pain induces insulin resistance in humans. *Anesthesiology* 95 (3):578–584.

Gustafsson, U. O., M. J. Scott, W. Schwenk, et al. 2012. Guidelines for perioperative care in elective colonic surgery: Enhanced Recovery After Surgery (ERAS(R)) Society recommendations. *Clin. Nutr.* 31 (6):783–800. doi:10.1016/j.clnu.2012.08.013.

Hall, G. M. 1985. The anaesthetic modification of the endocrine and metabolic response to surgery. *Ann. R. Coll. Surg. Engl.* 67 (1):25–29.

Haynes, A. B., T. G. Weiser, W. R. Berry, et al. 2009. A surgical safety checklist to reduce morbidity and mortality in a global population. *N. Engl. J. Med.* 360 (5):491–499. doi:10.1056/NEJMsa0810119.

Huang, D. T., G. Clermont, L. Kong, et al. 2010. Intensive care unit safety culture and outcomes: A US multicenter study. *Int. J. Qual. Health Care* 22 (3):151–161. doi:10.1093/intqhc/mzq017.

Jette, D. U., J. Halbert, C. Iverson, E. Miceli, and P. Shah. 2009. Use of standardized outcome measures in physical therapist practice: Perceptions and applications. *Phys. Ther.* 89 (2):125–135. doi:10.2522/ptj.20080234.

Kehlet, H., and K. Soballe. 2010. Fast-track hip and knee replacement: What are the issues? *Acta Orthop.* 81 (3):271–272. doi:10.3109/17453674.2010.487237.

Kiessling, A. H., P. Huneke, C. Reyher, et al. 2013. Risk factor analysis for fast track protocol failure. *J. Cardiothorac. Surg.* 8:47. doi:10.1186/1749-8090-8-47.

Klein, A. S., and P. M. Forni. 2011. Barbers of civility. *Arch. Surg.* 146 (7):774–777. doi:10.1001/archsurg.2011.150.

Klevens, R. Monina, Jonathan R. Edwards, Chesley L. Richards Jr., et al. 2007. Estimating health care-associated infections and deaths in US hospitals, 2002 . *Public Health Reports*:160–166.

Makary, M. A., and M. Daniel. 2016. Medical error: The third leading cause of death in the US. *BMJ* 353:i2139. doi:10.1136/bmj.i2139.

Makary, M. A., C. G. Holzmueller, J. B. Sexton, et al. 2006a. Operating room debriefings. *Jt. Comm. J. Qual. Patient Saf.* 32 (7):407–410, 357.

Makary, M. A., A. Mukherjee, J. B. Sexton, et al. 2007. Operating room briefings and wrong-site surgery. *J. Am. Coll. Surg.* 204 (2):236–243. doi:10.1016/j.jamcollsurg.2006.10.018.

Makary, M. A., J. B. Sexton, J. A. Freischlag, et al. 2006b. Operating room teamwork among physicians and nurses: Teamwork in the eye of the beholder. *J. Am. Coll. Surg.* 202 (5):746–752. doi:10.1016/j.jamcollsurg.2006.01.017.

Makary, M. A., J. B. Sexton, J. A. Freischlag, et al. 2006c. Patient safety in surgery. *Ann. Surg.* 243 (5):628–635. https://www.ncbi.nlm.nih.gov/pmc/articles/PMC1570547/.

Pitarelli, E., and E. Monnier. 2000. Benchmarking: The missing link between evaluation and management. 4th ESS Conference, October.

Quality, American Society for. 2007. Quality glossary. http://asq.org/glossary/b.html

Scott, M. J., G. Baldini, K. C. Fearon, et al. 2015. Enhanced recovery after surgery (ERAS) for gastrointestinal surgery, part 1: Pathophysiological considerations. *Acta Anaesthesiol. Scand.* 59 (10):1212–1231.

Simmons, P. S., J. M. Miles, J. E. Gerich, and M. W. Haymond. 1984. Increased proteolysis. An effect of increases in plasma cortisol within the physiologic range. *J. Clin. Invest.* 73 (2):412–420. doi:10.1172/JCI111227.

Thiele, R. H., K. M. Rea, F. E. Turrentine, et al. 2015. Standardization of care: Impact of an enhanced recovery protocol on length of stay, complications, and direct costs after colorectal surgery. *J. Am. Coll. Surg.* 220 (4):430–443. doi:10.1016/j.jamcollsurg.2014.12.042.

Thorell, A., J. Nygren, and O. Ljungqvist. 1999. Insulin resistance: A marker of surgical stress. *Curr. Opin. Clin. Nutr. Metab. Care* 2 (1):69–78.

Uchida, I., T. Asoh, C. Shirasaka, and H. Tsuji. 1988. Effect of epidural analgesia on postoperative insulin resistance as evaluated by insulin clamp technique. *Br. J. Surg.* 75 (6):557–562.

van Bokhorst-de van der Schueren, M. A., P. A. van Leeuwen, H. P. Sauerwein, et al. 1997. Assessment of malnutrition parameters in head and neck cancer and their relation to postoperative complications. *Head Neck* 19 (5):419–425.

van den Berghe, G., P. Wouters, F. Weekers, et al. 2001. Intensive insulin therapy in critically ill patients. *N. Engl. J. Med.* 345 (19):1359–1367. doi:10.1056/NEJMoa011300.

Volland, J. 2005. Quality intervenes at a hospital. *Quality Progress* 38 (2):57.

Weimann, A., M. Braga, L. Harsanyi, et al. 2006. ESPEN guidelines on enteral nutrition: Surgery including organ transplantation. *Clin. Nutr.* 25 (2):224–244.

Wick, E. C., D. B. Hobson, J. L. Bennett, et al. 2012. Implementation of a surgical comprehensive unit-based safety program to reduce surgical site infections. *J. Am. Coll. Surg.* 215 (2):193–200.

Chapter 5

High Reliability Organizations

Frank Federico, Amelia Brooks, and Hanan H. Edrees

Contents

5.1 High Reliability Organizations: A Brief History 84
5.2 General Components of HROs 85
5.3 The Five Principles of an HRO 85
5.3.1 Preoccupation with Failure 85
5.3.2 Reluctance to Oversimplify 86
5.3.3 Sensitivity to Operations 86
5.3.4 Commitment to Resilience 86
5.3.5 Deference to Expertise 87
5.4 Application of HRO Concepts in Healthcare: Advancing toward High Reliability 87
5.4.1 Starting the Journey 87
5.4.2 Leadership Commitment: Role of Senior Leadership/Board/CEO 87
5.4.2.1 Situational Awareness 87
5.4.2.2 Internal Environmental Factors 88
5.4.2.3 External Environmental Factors 89
5.4.3 Leadership Commitment: Role of Middle Managers 89
5.4.4 Standardization and Simplification 90
5.4.5 Measurement 91
5.4.5.1 Are the Data Accurate and Trustworthy? 92
5.4.5.2 Do the Data Add Value? 92
5.4.5.3 Do the Data Speak to Systems and People? 92
5.4.6 Improve and Redesign 92
5.4.7 Improvement Spread and Scale-Up 93
5.4.8 Key Challenges toward Reaching High Reliability and How to Mitigate Them ... 94
5.4.9 Lessons Learned from Strategies toward High Reliability in Healthcare 96
5.4.9.1 Standardization of All Processes and Procedures 96
5.4.9.2 Role of Organizational Leadership in Actively Organizing 96
5.4.9.3 Development of a Culture of Awareness, Improvement, and Trust 96

5.4.9.4 Finding the Right People to Lead These Efforts....... 96
5.4.9.5 Importance of Reeducating Staff on Specific Processes....... 97
5.4.9.6 Importance of Setting Priorities and Targets....... 97
5.4.9.7 Sustaining Culture over Time....... 97
5.5 Conclusions....... 97
Appendix AV.1 Interview with James B. Conway....... 97
AV.1.1 Brief Bio....... 97
AV.1.2 Objectives....... 98
Appendix AV.2 Interview with Dr. David Munch....... 101
AV.2.1 Brief Bio....... 101
AV.2.2 Objectives....... 102
References....... 108

5.1 High Reliability Organizations: A Brief History

Although the ultimate goal is to provide safe hospital care, there is no doubt that patients continue to be harmed. In an effort to keep patients safe, the healthcare industry is moving toward achieving "high reliability"; that is, where healthcare providers function in high-risk environments, learn from their mistakes, and adapt accordingly.

High reliability organizations (HROs) are characterized by complex systems with high workloads and pressures. These organizations have mastered the ability to adapt and respond to unexpected events while delivering reliable and safe outcomes (Rochlin et al. 1998). HROs in nonhealthcare settings such as aviation, manufacturing, nuclear power, and the oil and gas industries have been monitoring and maintaining high levels of safety while operating in hazardous and uncertain situations.

While nonhealthcare industries have successfully adopted a high reliability mind-set, the healthcare industry continues to struggle. This is because healthcare has not traditionally implemented high reliability concepts—which require comprehensive, system-wide approaches—and has yet to fully understand the foundations underpinning high reliability performance (Sutcliffe et al. 2016; Vogus and Hilligoss 2016). In an effort to understand how the fundamental concepts of high reliability apply to healthcare's complex and dynamic environment, it is critical to keep in mind that HROs in healthcare should aim to be harm-free rather than error-free (Sutcliffe et al. 2016).

HROs aim to reduce system failures and inefficiencies while adequately mitigating failures once and if they arise. High reliability organizing is affected by factors related to employees' high-performance work practices, a culture of trust and respect, mindful understanding of how various activities and processes contribute to the entire system, and active organization by organizational leaders (Combs et al. 2006; Flin 2007; Vogus and Sutcliffe 2007a; Weick and Sutcliffe 2015; Sutcliffe et al. 2016). In an effort to provide high-quality care, several hospitals are introducing and applying high reliability concepts within workflows and as part of improvement efforts. High reliability concepts offer an understanding of how individuals and organizations approach and solve quality and patient safety issues in the workplace. In contrast to process improvement projects, where a second project is initiated after successful implementation of the first, actively organizing for a culture of high reliability is continuous and iterative.

There are no step-by-step instructions on how to transform into an HRO. This chapter, therefore, provides a discussion of how organizations can carefully plan, implement, measure, and spread improvements based on their organizational culture, environment, and strategies.

5.2 General Components of HROs

Before exploring the journey to becoming an HRO, it is first important to understand what HROs actually are. In the book *Managing the Unexpected* (Weick and Sutcliffe 2011), Weick and Sutcliffe describe the principles they found in HROs. They define HROs as industries or organizations that have developed certain acts or styles of learning that enable them to manage the unexpected better than other organizations, where "manage the unexpected" is the most important concept. Many events in healthcare such as pressure ulcers, infections, and medication-related events are treated as unexpected, when it has been shown that most are predictable and avoidable. We also know that specific evidence-based practices lower or eliminate some of these events. To achieve HRO status, healthcare settings must reduce the variability that exists and contributes to errors and undesired outcomes. Only then can organizations focus on the unexpected.

HROs eliminate variation by standardizing and simplifying processes while taking human factors into account and monitoring those activities to ensure that they achieve the desired outcomes. These activities include active and engaged leadership, a just and fair culture, transparency, psychological safety alert systems (including an improvement method and a measurement system), and a teamwork culture. Only under these conditions can the characteristics of an HRO begin to take hold.

Why are these principles needed in healthcare? A number of challenges are common to other industries and healthcare (Hines et al. 2008):

- *Hypercomplexity*: The care delivery environment is as complex as any of the "traditional" HROs. There must be effective coordination of the team and the systems that support the delivery of care.
- *Tight coupling*: Teams must work together and coordinate how care is delivered. A failure in one team may have an impact on the actions of other teams involved in care delivery for that patient and other patients.
- *Extreme hierarchical differentiation*: Healthcare continues to possess a rigid hierarchy that makes communication and teamwork difficult. HROs have worked to ensure that members of the team work cohesively independent of rank.
- *Multiple decision-makers in a complex communication network*: Since many individuals are involved in making decisions about a patient, there is a high likelihood of communication and planning failures. Even with the advent of electronic health records (EHRs), there continue to be communication failures.
- *High degree of accountability*: There is a need to understand system versus individual accountability. When a patient who should have gone home dies in the hospital, there must be an investigation to understand what went wrong. Any patient harm should be investigated, and individuals must understand their roles and behaviors and adhere to those expectations.

5.3 The Five Principles of an HRO

5.3.1 Preoccupation with Failure

The first principle of an HRO is preoccupation with failure, enshrined in the principle of "tracking small failures" (Weick and Sutcliffe 2015): HROs focus on tracking small failures, where every defect is an opportunity to learn. In healthcare, we tend to focus only on the events that result in harm. As managers, we must view every near miss and every work-around as indications that the system is not functioning as designed, and we must learn from these situations in order to improve.

Another way to interpret this principle is: We either do not have good processes in place, or we do not believe that current processes are reliable. We will always question the reliability of the steps, even if the outcomes may be good.

5.3.2 Reluctance to Oversimplify

The second principle is the reluctance to oversimplify. In the HRO world, this means that the organization realizes that the world is complex, unknowable, unstable, and unpredictable. HROs put themselves in a position to see the notes as much as possible, welcome diversity, and be prepared to react. However, there is a concern that if no time is taken to step back or if situations are viewed the same as previously and treated in the same way, deeper differences between the events may be masked. For managers and healthcare, this means that when a system fails, we must explore more deeply why the process failed, rather than simply accepting the first finding. Different issues may contribute to the failure.

Another way to interpret this is that HROs do not accept variation as normal. Over time, even the best designed processes may deteriorate or become complex, which translates into a lower likelihood of being followed and greater variation.

5.3.3 Sensitivity to Operations

The third principle is sensitivity to operations, which means that HROs pay attention to where work is completed. Managers must know what happens and where the work is taking place because, at this point, defects can be isolated and addressed before they become part of a cascade of defects. It is important to ensure that people can speak up without fear. One cannot develop a "big picture" of operations if the small contributing components are poorly understood.

Managers and healthcare must consider delivery of care and ensure that the doctors, nurses, and allied health professionals can all speak up when they identify a defect in care at the smallest level. If not addressed, this defect can have a huge negative impact on the rest of the system. Clear and unambiguous language about policy and the intent of what the individuals are trying to achieve is a necessary component. The focus in this principle is for managers and leaders to know exactly where the failure modes or defects are in the system. Systems with less than 80% reliability in standardized processes must understand why their rates are low and begin to address those failures. The intent is to build the system to achieve at least 95% reliability in non-catastrophic processes, and 100% or have multiple redundancies in those processes that must be 100% reliable.

5.3.4 Commitment to Resilience

The fourth principle is commitment to resilience. By developing and maintaining resilience, HROs understand and accept that no system is perfect. For each of our goals, this means that the organization has the ability to recover from or continue to function in the presence of continuous stress. In organizations where there is a lot of variability and chaos, staff are so stressed that they cannot maintain baseline functioning of the system, let alone respond when something is not working.

In healthcare, a ward that does not have standardized, reliable processes places staff under continual stress and, when there is a crisis, the staff cannot respond. In a ward where variation has been eliminated, a patient enters a ward with unique needs and may be in crisis. Since staff do not have to worry about what has been standardized as it is routine, they can more readily focus on the exceptions. To address this variability, leaders and managers must provide timely feedback on performance, with action plans developed with those doing the work. Suboptimal performance must be corrected quickly.

5.3.5 Deference to Expertise

The last principle is deference to expertise. This means that in HROs, the authority to make decisions is placed in the hands of people with the most expertise. This is not necessarily the person with the most experience, but rather the individual who possesses the experience and specific knowledge of the event. Those actually doing the work design the processes.

Healthcare managers must ensure that the hierarchy is flattened, so that someone in authority does not always make decisions but, instead, those who have experience and knowledge about the situation. The person might be any member of the team. There is an expectation that processes are standardized and variation is accepted only when it is in the best interests of the patient and not based on individual autonomy.

5.4 Application of HRO Concepts in Healthcare: Advancing toward High Reliability

5.4.1 Starting the Journey

Initiating the journey to become an HRO is difficult. Applying the concepts of high reliability takes time and requires a strong commitment from leadership at all levels to think about how to transform the organization into a HRO. Training staff on the goals of high reliability thinking and introducing initiatives that allow organizations to adapt and better manage unexpected events are only some of the ways in which HROs operate.

There is no single recipe to guide all hospitals. However, the journey requires building an infrastructure and culture that provide the foundation for the development and application of the principles of HROs to flourish. Each hospital will have its own journey based on its starting point. Organizations may already have some well-established improvement practices in place and should continue to develop those methods. It has usually taken a long time to achieve the systems already in place in most organizations, and it will also take time to change them.

Leaders and managers have the responsibility of setting the strategic direction and then determining what is within their scope or responsibility to contribute to that direction. Individuals at the front line of care depend on managers to interpret what must be accomplished. The frontline staff will then be able to help develop systems and processes to contribute to the goals.

There are leaders at every level of an organization, some with titles and others without. Those with titles should continue in their roles and be role models for desired behavior. Those that do not have titles are the leaders that all look up to and should be respected for the leadership that they provide and be engaged as champions for improvement. No matter an individual's position within an organization, all are needed to achieve the principles of an HRO.

5.4.2 Leadership Commitment: Role of Senior Leadership/Board/CEO

5.4.2.1 Situational Awareness

The journey begins with leadership commitment to achieving zero harm (Chassin and Loeb 2013). Leaders must be aware that various environmental factors will ultimately affect their decision-making and planning of organizational goals and priorities. Therefore, it is essential to carefully assess these internal and external environmental elements as leaders prepare for the adoption of a high reliability mind-set across the organization (Hines et al. 2008). Some organizations identify their internal and external environmental factors by conducting a SWOT analysis, which is a structured planning method that assesses *strengths*, *weaknesses*, *opportunities*, and *threats*.

5.4.2.2 Internal Environmental Factors

Internal environmental factors are organizational components that have an impact on daily operations such as organizational priorities and policies, staff engagement, and resource availability. In an effort to strengthen the internal environment and achieve the goal of high reliability, the following components must be considered.

5.4.2.2.1 Pursuing Strong Senior Leadership Support

Leadership buy-in is essential for the adoption of high reliability as an organizational priority. Successful implementation of this organizational priority involves staff at all levels of the organization. This can be achieved by:

- Encouraging and implementing methods to obtain staff feedback. Some examples include employee engagement surveys, anonymous suggestion boxes, or other forms.
- Rewarding and offering incentives for staff based on desired behaviors and outcomes. When leadership introduces new initiatives, interventions, or policies, it is important to link them with performance incentives; this will motivate staff to participate.

5.4.2.2.2 Establishing a Culture of Transparency, Accountability, and Safety

The role of executive leadership in establishing a high reliability mind-set and increasing awareness is based on creating a strong culture of transparency, accountability, and safety (Hudson 2003). Trust and openness can be embedded by:

- Ensuring a just culture in which accountability is considered. This ensures that staff can report errors and identify system defects in a nonpunitive, blame-free environment. This type of environment promotes a culture that supports continuous learning and improvement.
- Empowering staff to speak up when patient safety is at risk. As a result, there will be an opportunity to prevent unsafe conditions and implement safe practices (Edmondson 2003). For instance, some organizations have established just culture policies to ensure staff protection. Other organizations recognize and incentivize staff for identifying and reporting errors.
- Establishing a positive patient safety culture, where staff openly share their ideas to improve patient care. For instance, sharing new ideas in all-staff meetings or forums fosters an environment where multidisciplinary teams can collectively work together to reach the common goal of safe patient care.

5.4.2.2.3 Building the Business Case for Becoming an HRO (Christianson et al. 2011)

HROs increase employee engagement, which ultimately improves and enhances patient care, satisfaction, and financial performance.

- The journey toward high reliability must involve the chief financial officer (CFO) and the hospital's finance department, given their roles in allocating organizational resources and creating organizational incentive structures (Hines et al. 2008).

- Equipping the CFO with clinical data and the tools necessary to make the business case for quality improvement is essential. Some of these tools may focus on the removal of waste from the system, such as inefficient services, overuse or underuse of medical technology, and reoccurrence of preventable patient harm.

5.4.2.3 External Environmental Factors

In addition to assessing internal environmental factors, leaders should also remember that constantly changing external factors impacts patient care. These elements include but are not limited to external regulations, hospital networks, changing patient populations, and the job market for healthcare professionals (Hines et al. 2008).

5.4.2.3.1 Addressing External Regulations

If senior leaders establish partnerships with leaders in other hospitals to address external regulations and policies, they can recognize that external environmental factors are difficult to tackle alone. These types of collaborations allow hospitals to adapt to or change regulations necessary to achieve the high reliability culture. For instance, hospitals can advise regulators, government, the media, and the public on the significance of reporting medical errors and on the importance of using a just culture and nonpunitive environment to address them.

5.4.2.3.2 Building Collaborations with Local Hospitals

One option is for hospital leaders to establish networks with hospitals in the same geographical locale to address common barriers and challenges such as market share, health emergencies, or disasters.

- Collaborations should focus on specific initiatives rather than all aspects of patient care. For instance, a network might be useful to address local health disasters, where collaborative efforts on preparedness, surveillance, and patient transfers are addressed. Another collaboration might focus on quality and patient safety efforts, where hospitals collectively develop quality indicators to measure performance across hospitals.
- Leaders may also use hospital networks to understand local demographics, the growing patient population, and the changing job market for healthcare professionals—all of which impact healthcare services.
- The networks can be used as a platform to further understand how to standardize processes across hospital settings. By working together, hospitals can exchange healthcare professionals' expertise with the intention of standardizing processes and fostering learning across different institutions.

5.4.3 Leadership Commitment: Role of Middle Managers

Once leadership has set a vision to adopt a high reliability mind-set within their organization, middle managers must guide their staff to achieve this goal. The role of middle management is to establish a culture that defers to insights and recommendations from individuals who are most knowledgeable about the topic or situation, regardless of their position within the organization. In achieving high reliability thinking, middle managers can consider the following:

- Understanding the methods and strategies by which their organization currently identifies, plans, and executes quality and safety initiatives. This information is helpful for identifying barriers and ways to mitigate them in an effort to reduce failure.
- It is essential to elicit ideas from staff on how to integrate quality strategies and measures into existing care processes. Staff from both clinical and nonclinical disciplines should be involved in the planning process, so that they can determine factors influencing the success and potential failure of the projects and initiatives being introduced (Vincent and Amalberti 2016). This also has the purpose of ultimately decreasing resistance from staff. More importantly, this process builds trust in leadership and encourages staff to improve patient outcomes (Vogus and Sutcliffe 2007a).
- Middle managers should identify informal leaders within the organization. While these individuals do not hold formal titles, they should be well known for their seniority, trust, or expertise. Formal and informal leaders help support and establish a strong safety culture.
- When planning improvement initiatives, it is essential for middle managers to simplify systems and integrate their proposed intervention into existing processes and structures. Otherwise, these improvement efforts are unlikely to be sustainable over time and are more likely to fail.
- When introducing a new initiative to staff, it is essential that managers roll out projects incrementally in phases. This allows staff to work together in a supportive culture where redesigning current processes is viewed as a learning experience (Sutcliffe et al. 2016). More importantly, these new initiatives will not be seen as additional tasks that increase workload but as part of daily practice.
- It is important for the organization to offer protected time for staff to work on improvement initiatives, as it is not sustainable for them to participate in such efforts while maintaining their current roles. Therefore, middle managers can work with the leadership and finance department to set priorities about resource allocation.
- Middle managers are responsible for ensuring that improvement initiatives at the local level align with the organizational goals.

Middle managers might also consider a few self-reported assessment tools to measure organizational habits, practices, and culture—all of which are indicators of HROs. For instance, the Safety Organizing Scale (SOS) (Vogus and Sutcliffe 2007b) is a tool used by middle managers to explore safety organizing within their hospitals. The SOS allows behaviors that underlie the safety culture to be identified and the assessment for the potential to improve quality and patient safety.

5.4.4 Standardization and Simplification

It is no surprise that significant variability in the delivery of patient care can lead to errors. Given the diverse backgrounds and experiences of healthcare providers, these clinical and nonclinical processes can become extremely complex—adding unnecessary and unjustified steps or eliminating essential steps. As a result, employees tend to take short cuts to avoid a lengthy care process. While this approach may save time, patients may be harmed if a critical step is overlooked.

The evidence suggests that standardizing and simplifying processes not only reduces errors and saves time, but also enhances patient outcomes and the delivery of care (Hart and

Owen 2005; Runciman et al. 2005; Pronovost et al. 2006). In an effort to standardize and simplify care processes, managers must:

- Understand and assess daily organizational operations and practices. This will help align and compare organizational practices with evidence-based practices and clinical guidelines (Vogus and Sutcliffe 2007a).
- Encourage staff to simplify their work processes to avoid duplication, reduce waste, and decrease the occurrence of errors. Efficient processes utilize fewer resources, including human resources, costs, and time. This can be achieved by mapping out a current process, identifying additional/unnecessary steps, and redesigning the process with the intention of increasing efficiency.
- Provide a supportive environment for staff to openly discuss defects in the care process and suggest alternative methods for standardization and simplification. When management supports well-intentioned staff to standardize their care pathways and clinical processes, patient care is less likely to be compromised (Vogus and Sutcliffe 2007a).
- Encourage staff to implement checklists. The use of checklists is integral to reducing errors and patient harm and increasing adherence to best practices (Hales and Pronovost 2006). In creating and using checklists, multidisciplinary healthcare teams are better able to communicate on how to successfully adopt and implement best practices. In addition to paper-based checklists, electronic checklists are also easy to use and accessible (Hales and Pronovost 2006). Care should be taken to avoid overuse of checklists, which may lead to "checklist-itis" or "checklist fatigue" (Waterson 2014), and may also make healthcare providers dependent on checklists and reluctant to use personal judgment.
- Automate processes if possible. The purpose of automation is to reduce variation and wasted time and to increase efficiency of the services provided.
- Identify and support informal leaders who fully understand and believe in the concepts of standardization and simplification. With middle manager support, these individuals will act as champions in advocating for simple and standard processes across the organization.
- Foster organizational learning and work with staff to share lessons learned from redesigning processes. Effective strategies can be applied to address other system defects.

5.4.5 Measurement

Measurement, in its various forms, should be considered a constant lens through which organizations approach both the journey to high reliability and the long-term sustainability of high reliability as a feature of normal operations. Without continual measurement—both qualitative and quantitative—it is impossible to understand current performance or what will improve reliability in the organization.

Given the amount of data collected in healthcare, one would be forgiven for thinking that data and measurement would not be a challenge for any organization wishing to progress toward high reliability. However, accessing and analyzing good-quality, accurate data to determine reliability is a real challenge for the majority of healthcare organizations. It is true that we collect, store, and report on large quantities of data, but are the data good enough?

When it comes to data and measurement, it is certainly true that quality trumps quantity. Healthcare faces significant challenges, including resources, staffing, finance, patient complexity, integration, and continuity of care, to name but a few. The amount of time that healthcare staff at all levels spend inputting, collecting, analyzing, and reporting on data is, understandably, a source of both concern and frustration. Data must continually be reviewed according to a few core principles to ensure that valuable resources are directed appropriately, that waste is avoided, and that we have the best possible insight into the reality of our own organizations.

5.4.5.1 Are the Data Accurate and Trustworthy?

Inaccurate or untrustworthy data should be a red flag to any organization. Where staff voice concerns over data accuracy, continued efforts to use the same data could result in significant disengagement of the workforce and make any improvement efforts much more challenging. Perhaps more importantly, inaccurate data is a common cause of misdirected resources, as it highlights the wrong focal points and hides real problems. Middle managers play a crucial role in ensuring that all measurements are based on accurate, good-quality data, as they will need access to this information on a daily basis to reach high reliability performance. It is helpful for middle managers to review currently available data with team input to ensure that they are collecting data that truly connect the organization with the patients' experiences of care, the outcomes they achieve, and the performance of the processes that contribute to those outcomes.

5.4.5.2 Do the Data Add Value?

Although continuous, good-quality data are important, organizations must avoid collecting so much data that they lose track of priorities. Many healthcare organizations can be described as "data rich but information poor," that is to say that time and effort are placed in reporting every conceivable metric, leaving little resource to actually drive improvements. It is not uncommon to see monthly performance reports of large hospitals of over 500 pages. Organizations in this position often find it difficult to find focus in their data and end up spreading resources too thinly to drive any real improvement. A good technique here is to examine what is currently being measured and decrease the frequency of collection or reporting where the topic is not a current organizational priority for improvement.

5.4.5.3 Do the Data Speak to Systems and People?

We often speak of measures linking to process and outcomes. These groups of measures are largely, although not exclusively, applied to systems rather than people. The importance of balancing cultural measurement with system measurement cannot be overstated. One does not take precedence over the other; rather, both should be approached with the same enthusiasm and priority. Similarly, quantitative measurement must be balanced with real-life experience. Middle managers must ensure that they spend time with their teams gathering in-person feedback on both culture and systems. This information is helpful for designing improvement interventions, supporting the right type of culture, and determining whether the "hard" data are accurate and provide an honest reflection of the current state.

5.4.6 Improve and Redesign

Healthcare staff are naturally drawn toward improvement, where the vast majority work in the field due to their strong desire to improve the lives and experiences of people requiring care. Consequently, it is not unusual to find that most healthcare staff constantly try many different ways to improve systems and processes, even though they may not necessarily describe it explicitly as "improvement." Middle managers should harness this passion for improvement by applying systematic approaches and methodologies.

Having a consistent approach to improvement helps to reduce wasted efforts and paves the way for accelerated improvement. Reviewing past and present improvement efforts to determine whether their most significant challenges relate to will, ideas, or execution will often result in execution being the largest challenge. Will and ideas come easily to many healthcare staff. Although not always the case, successful improvement relies on a systematic approach to execution that is supported by the organization. Similarly, having a single consistent improvement methodology further supports improvement by creating a common language for staff so that they can easily support each other with improvement efforts.

The HRO characteristic "preoccupation with failure" is a natural partner to systematic improvement. The relentless search for imperfections in systems, processes, and culture provides invaluable learning that helps any HRO to identify and prioritize areas requiring improvement and helps to ensure that the identify/improve cycle is a continuous feature of operations.

5.4.7 Improvement Spread and Scale-Up

Achieving high reliability across an organization is often dependent on being able to spread improvement effectively. Many organizations have pockets of excellence that excel in different types of performance. HROs systematically spread and scale up changes in practice that demonstrate improvement. Successful spread and scale-up requires an understanding of some of the key challenges; therefore, having a systematic framework (Massoud et al. 2006) that supports preparation, development, and execution of spread plans is an excellent way to overcome challenges.

Planning for spread is best started early in an improvement initiative. A well-executed improvement initiative will provide most of the information needed to gain support for spread. For example, the measures collected during the improvement phase will provide excellent evidence of the improvements made and will help to gather support from new teams who may be cautious about adopting ideas from elsewhere. It is important to ensure that the data collected are presented clearly, are easy to understand, and relate to the people that need to be influenced. It can be helpful to include anecdotes or case studies alongside quantitative data, as this very often helps to contextualize why the improvement initiative should be spread.

An aims statement is another aspect of an improvement initiative that transfers effectively to spread planning. Having a clear aims statement for your spread plans provides clarity and purpose when developing the plans and helps to answer the "who," "what," and "where." This provides a strong foundation for more detailed spread plans that should focus on the "how."

The "how" of a detailed spread plan should emphasize sharing and communication. Providing various modes of communication ensures that people can access the information through their preferred mode. For example, it is insufficient simply to e-mail an update and expect that people will feel that they have been communicated with. Time and effort must be invested in two-way communication via multiple modes so that people have clear routes to provide feedback on spread plans and to demonstrate that feedback has been valued. Blogs, vlogs, newsletters, e-mails, in-person visits, and social media all provide great platforms for communicating spread plans and are transparent. A measurement plan must also be included alongside the spread plan since, in the same way that measurement provides objective feedback on an improvement initiative, it allows you to gauge whether your plan is helping to achieve the expected spread.

Ensuring that organizational leaders who value the subject of improvement efforts as supporting strategic priorities are supportive can facilitate the execution of a spread plan. Having clear leadership support and an executive sponsor can be as helpful in the spread phase as during the improvement phase. Leaders should provide public support for the efforts while working to remove any barriers to spread experienced by the operational team and linking the topics back to organizational priorities.

5.4.8 Key Challenges toward Reaching High Reliability and How to Mitigate Them

Many of the challenges faced when attempting to drive systemic change in healthcare organizations are similar, if not identical; the journey to high reliability is no different. Tackling these challenges successfully requires an appreciation of the balance between generalizable principles and local customization.

Despite an eagerness to focus on delivering improvement as early as possible in any given activity, time spent understanding the nature, scope, and scale of the likely challenges is an essential and value-added first step in any journey to high reliability. It is helpful if this step is informed by the broad challenges of high reliability and organizational change, but the focus should be on interpreting potential challenges in the context of the local environment. It may be helpful to think of this phase as *diagnostic*, the aim being to understand what aspects of the local environment, system, and culture are likely to present challenges so that mitigation can be developed. The following activities may be helpful in the diagnostic phase:

- Spending time talking to people who have previously attempted change, improvement, or reliability work in the organization and asking them about their experiences and challenges and how these were tackled. Unsuccessful changes should not be excluded, since they offer a wealth of learning from experiences from an outcomes perspective. Gathering information about opinion leaders, unofficial leaders, and communication channels that can help drive engagement is also useful.
- Focusing on testing and analyzing the data and information about the system whose reliability needs to be improved. Checking that data are accurate, provide the whole story, and are easily accessed can also provide information about where to look for potential challenges and to focus attention on more detailed investigations as to why a particular challenge exists.
- Deeper analyses of particular challenges can be helpful in determining cause and effect and thus help to construct mitigation strategies that are more likely to be successful. Root cause analysis is one approach that, if used cautiously, can help to answer questions as to why a challenge exists.

While the specific challenges experienced during the journey to high reliability will depend on the working context and the individual characteristics of the organization, very few challenges will be completely unique. The second step in predicting and mitigating challenges is to seek and learn from lessons from elsewhere and apply these lessons to the local context. Accessing learning can be considered from a couple of different perspectives:

- Lessons specific to high reliability very often require research into fields external to healthcare, such as nuclear power, aviation, Formula One, and the oil industry, which are all highly regarded for their commitment to high reliability. They provide a wealth of information on experiences, journeys, and lessons. Although it is common in healthcare to find that medics, in particular, dismiss lessons from other industries, there is in fact much to learn, and engaging in this process can save large amounts of time and effort.

- Learning can also be specific to the system, topic, or field that is being worked on. Successes and failures from previous work within and external to the organization can be a rich source of information on what does and does not work to improve reliability and outcomes relevant to the specific field of focus.

As a caution, both of these approaches and, indeed, any attempt to access and apply learning from elsewhere can easily provoke a "not invented here" reaction from teams who feel that they have nothing to learn from others or who are defensive of their way of doing things. This is a natural human response to change and can be mitigated by making use of broad engagement and tests of change prior to implementation. For example, allowing staff to study, visit, experience, and learn first hand about the way that others tackle similar problems can be an important first step, but it will not be possible to provide every individual with that opportunity. Designating small groups to access the learning and bring it back to the local team (who then review and test ways in which it can be applied to the local context) is helpful for boosting engagement, accessing learning, and developing custom solutions.

This approach is also useful for generating belief that high reliability, as a general principle, can be achieved within the healthcare environment. Some individuals may hold the view that high reliability cannot be achieved in an environment where such extreme variation exists. While this is a significant challenge to high reliability in and of itself, it does not render high reliability an impossible goal, but it does mean that it is important to generate enthusiasm and belief along the way. Accessing learning, both internal and external, provides evidence that high reliability is a realistic goal. Similarly, both formal and informal leaders can play a vital role in preventing some of the likely cultural challenges to high reliability by publicly demonstrating support and enthusiasm for the approach.

Challenge and mitigation are continuous features of any change effort and will feature both proactive and reactive elements. The strategies detailed here largely focus on proactively planning for challenges and developing mitigation strategies. However, no matter how much time is invested in planning, new challenges will always arise along the journey to high reliability, and it is important to know how to face these challenges individually and as a team as they arise.

The first step is to make sure new challenges are recognized as quickly as possible. Effective two-way communication channels are needed to access that information and to create an environment of psychological safety, such that people feel able to share the challenges and issues with management and the team. Once new challenges are recognized, the strategies detailed here can be applied in much the same way. A diagnostic exercise may be required to fully understand the challenge, and the team will need to engage in developing and testing solutions.

The journey to high reliability will almost certainly feature significant challenges. By planning for challenges that can be predicted and planning methods to address challenges that cannot, each challenge can be viewed as a positive step toward achieving high reliability and not as an indicator of potential failure.

5.4.9 Lessons Learned from Strategies toward High Reliability in Healthcare

5.4.9.1 Standardization of All Processes and Procedures

To create reliable processes that yield consistent results, standardization must be an organizational priority. Multiple methods used to conduct a specific process, procedure, or practice increase variation and leave room for errors and, as a consequence, a lack of consistency in patient outcomes. Standardization happens when collaborative knowledge from multidisciplinary teams is used to map out both existing and ideal processes. After the process is mapped, these teams can make decisions based on the most efficient and practical steps to improve quality and reduce costs.

5.4.9.2 Role of Organizational Leadership in Actively Organizing

Leaders who actively organize are aware of how current operations and new initiatives affect the organization. Leadership engagement in executive walk-arounds, such as the IHI *Patient Safety Leadership WalkRounds*™, allows senior leaders to visit clinical units and departments to identify and trend operational, clinical, and patient safety problems.

5.4.9.3 Development of a Culture of Awareness, Improvement, and Trust

Leaders must also establish a culture of transparency, where employees are willing and able to identify system defects and openly suggest and recommend changes. Transparency in sharing data relevant to staff is key. Involving staff at all organizational levels (whereby each individual has the potential and power to identify and make changes that will positively impact patient care) will ensure a culture of high reliability. This ultimately conveys the message that quality improvement and patient safety are everyone's responsibility, not only the responsibility of leadership and management.

5.4.9.4 Finding the Right People to Lead These Efforts

It is essential to engage formal and informal leaders—individuals who influence the decision of others based on their expertise and experience in ways other than formal authority and power—in the journey toward high reliability. These active leaders will help to identify what is working well and what is not. After identifying a problem, they ask questions to determine the root cause of the issue rather than jump to conclusions. Additionally, these individuals always engage staff and ask about their prior experiences with other healthcare organizations. These individuals also challenge current organizational beliefs and question staff's explanations on existing problems by asking:

- "How can this be done differently?"
- "What have other organizations done to address a similar problem?"
- "In your previous working experience, what were the recommendations on how to improve this situation?"
- "If this problem persists, what would this mean for us as an organization?"

5.4.9.5 Importance of Reeducating Staff on Specific Processes

Reeducating staff on specific practices and processes being conducted in the organization is important to ensure sustainability of quality and patient safety efforts, encourage employees to question existing practices, and identify sources of potential failure. Middle managers should also educate staff on how to respond to challenges and continuously search for ways to implement promising solutions; this will drive shared learning throughout the organization.

5.4.9.6 Importance of Setting Priorities and Targets

Efforts by leadership and middle management must be collaborative to ensure that organizational priorities are set and targets are clear. Ensuring that staff are aware of specified targets allows them to work toward achieving them. Furthermore, these organizational priorities and targets must be manageable and not overburden staff with additional work, instead incorporating targets and measures relevant to existing practices.

5.4.9.7 Sustaining Culture over Time

Achieving high reliability is an ongoing process that should include continuous evaluation and improvement of current processes, procedures, and practices.

5.5 Conclusions

The journey toward high reliability takes time and requires commitment from leadership and staff at all levels. While no step-by-step instructions exist on how to become an HRO, the strategies outlined in this chapter offer guidance on how to plan, implement, measure, and spread improvements throughout the organization. It is important to remember that each healthcare provider has the potential and opportunity to identify areas for improvement. Finally, with strong leadership commitment, these healthcare providers can work as a team to achieve safe and reliable care.

Appendix AV.1 Interview with James B. Conway

AV.1.1 Brief Bio

James B. Conway has extensive experience in engaging senior leadership on the journey toward high reliability. He was the former Senior Vice President at the Institute for Healthcare Improvement from 2006 to 2009, the Chief Operating Officer at the Dana-Farber Cancer Institute from 1995 to 2005, and was the Assistant Hospital Director at Boston Children's Hospital for 27 years. Mr. Conway is an adjunct professor at the Harvard School of Public Health. He interacted with thousands of trustees through his work in *Get Boards on Board* (5 Million Lives Campaign 2008; Conway 2008) with the Institute for Healthcare Improvement (IHI), and serves on the Boards of Lahey Health and Winchester Hospital.

AV.1.2 Objectives

- Understand how to engage the board and C-suite to lead the organization on its journey to high reliability
- Discuss the challenges faced on the journey
- Describe ways to overcome those challenges

1. ***In your previous role as chief operating officer (COO), you have helped lead the Dana-Farber Cancer Institute through its quality improvement journey and to achieving high reliability. May you share your experience on how this journey started and how it progressed?***

   The journey began back in February 1995 with the discovery of a horrible tragedy, when Dana-Farber killed a cancer patient—*The Boston Globe* healthcare journalist and wife of a Dana-Farber staff member. Betsy received an overdose of chemotherapy and died in December 1994. At time of death, the case was reviewed, and nothing was found. A few months later a clerk was entering Betsy's medication information into a computer program, noticed the largest dose of chemotherapy in this patient in this type of protocol that they have ever seen. And when she talked, the institution then became devastated.

   All the regulatory agencies moved and issued all of their findings. The findings weren't new news to frontline staff because that was the world they lived in every day. But they were new to the governing board and leadership.

   Arrogance of excellence is the risk of any great hospital. You can spend every moment talking about the good stuff—care, caring, hope, discovery—and forget to create a space to confront the suffering, harm, tragedy, waste, and death.

   The trustees of Dana-Farber felt they have been duped. They didn't understand the realities of practice. They became immediately engaged, and felt they had a moral and ethical responsibility to disclose. At that time, most organizations did not disclose; they said stuff happened. But again Dana-Farber's board and CEO said that we have a moral and ethical obligation to disclose, and we did.

   This is how the journey started....

2. ***In your experience, what is the role of senior leadership and the board in leading the journey to high reliability?***

   We set an aim of never again, and within the three years that we would be recognized measurably as the safest cancer program in the United States. The governing board support us and held us accountable to that. This would be a transparent journey with the board, leadership, staff, the community, the patients and families, the agencies, and the public health department. And we would be in partnership with them.

   Betsy Lehman felt she was having an atypical response and tried to get our attention. We didn't listen to her or honor her voice. In moving forward we said that patients and families with partner with us in all aspects of care, and they did. Dana-Farber brought in outside consultants to inform our journey forward; many of them were from outside healthcare. We admitted we didn't know everything. Consultants from Massachusetts Institute of Technology (MIT) introduced us to the role of culture in the workplace. We built a fair and just culture, which was essential, and we also made a commitment to staff to support them. In our mind, Betsy's death was the failure of systems, not people and we implemented system based design and positioned our staff to work in this type of design. Dana-Farber wrote articles and case studies on what we learned; we wanted to share the story of Betsy's death (Conway et al. 2006) and people across the world were interested (there but for the grace of God, go I).

3. ***How did you engage the board?***

   We were transparent. The CEO and leadership told the board what happened and they were outraged. In every hospital, these serious cases happen—and when the board or leadership is told about these incidents, they also would be outraged.

   But in many parts of the healthcare system, we don't have transparency. So we set specific goals and set specific aims. Aims that "we will never do this." Aims of zero harm—so that these aims were recognized in our minds and in our data in front of other organizations and in front of the nation.

   And then we had a commitment that we would never again discuss care without the patients and families as partners as well as recipients of the care. We were one of first adult hospitals in country to have a Patient–Family Advisory Committee. All these were triggered by the board and approved by the board at the highest levels. It wasn't an "if discussion" but it's a "when" and "how" discussion. This had clear elements of high reliability. Then, the journey with the board continued, turning into a true partnership for continuous improvement and excellence. We had set quarterly metrics with aims/goals (do what, by when, measured how). The board would applaud if we achieved them. If we didn't, there were questions around "why not and what's being done." We were held accountable and given three months to take care of this—so clear goals with accountability.

   The board studied high reliability, and many of the board members were invited into conversations of learning. We had people in the chemical industry, the president of *Legal Seafood*, industrial safety experts, and many more. And we invited in various individuals who had perspectives of high reliability. For example, one of our root-cause-analyses was done through the aviation industry.

4. ***How did you engage other C-Suite leaders?***

   Each of us was the leader of the organization with individual as well as shared responsibilities for outcomes. Compensation was linked to outcomes. There was a clear expectation that we had a collaborative, collective responsibility for clinical, financial, service, and experience outcomes. The C-suite also went to school. They were sent off to courses with the Institute for Healthcare Improvement (IHI) and others. People were just discovering this field in the 1990s—no one had discovered patient safety outside of anesthesia. Then, these tools and techniques, became the way we did all the work. Not only the way we did quality and safety, but the way in which we did work across the organization.

5. ***HROs require staff at all levels within the organization to be engaged in actively organizing for safety. How did you engage, empower and include staff in the process?***

   We stared out with a devastated staff, and everyone talked about what happened under their watch. We talked about and built a nonpunitive culture. And in addition to the patients and families being harmed, we talked about and supported the staff being harmed. We talked about transparency. We opened town hall meetings with the staff, and they were intensely involved. We got specific recognition from the Joint Commission for our approach and gave a copy of that to every staff member involved. Leadership was very visible, in the workspace. Five times a year, we invited over 100 people to sit in a large conference room in the organization and ask them: what was frustrating them in the clinical, the research, and the administrative areas. We shared what we learned in these sessions, and then shared this in the hospital newsletter. There was lots of shame and blame, and then we worked on the notion of a fair and just culture. And we talked about how individuals would not be accountable for broken systems. We set behavioral expectations. People were told: "I don't care how much money you generate for the organization. If you don't treat patients respectfully then you don't belong here." We did executive rounds where we were seeing the staff, patients and families; we had a partnership to develop a common set of goals and achieve our mission.

6 ***What are some of the challenges and barriers you and your team experienced in moving toward high reliability? How were these mitigated?***

One of the biggest challenges is most change fails—anywhere from 60% to 80% of change fails. We couldn't afford to allow this to happen. McKinsey said that the single largest reason for failing is failure to engage people who are closest to the work. In second place was the failure of leaders to follow the behaviors necessary to support the change moving forward. We needed to focus and prioritize. If you try to do everything, then you accomplish nothing. People were overwhelmed. We had to agree to put things in the parking lot. It had to be systematic; it couldn't be doing a little bit of this or a little bit of that.

Then, we have to set and monitor indicators. Every good idea, and there are lots of those, had to fit into the stated theory of the work. We were very specific with the management and training they had. And this is where the governing board came in—the outcomes needed to be on track to achieve the aims.

Change is hard.

The second thing was culture. We had a difficult culture. Over time I've learned that "crappy" culture produces crappy results. High performance teams can accomplish anything. Teamwork in a fair and just culture, gives people the opportunity to open up and speak. All of this is essential, and it will move the journey of continuous improvement forward. We had to change the culture to give people the courage to speak up, to learn, and then we would mitigate the chances of these things from happening again.

We engaged the patients. I spent 27 years in Boston Children's. I learned that if we listen to the parents, patients, and families, they will teach us a lot of things. We had to push to get people to begin this. Then, once we began this, we learned things they didn't learn before. And as always, the challenge was spread and sustainability. And how to do this work across the organization requires a relentless focus on systematic improvement using frameworks espoused by groups like the Institute for Healthcare Improvement, Baldrige, Six Sigma, etc.

7 ***Thank you for sharing your rich experience. What advice do you have for healthcare leaders as they are moving through the process of actively organizing for safety?***

I was involved with the *Getting Boards on Board* IHI report in 2005, where there were six important elements to consider in working with boards (based on work that was done with thousands of trustees).

First, is to set aims. If you don't know where you're going, you won't get there. Aims need to be strategic. Then you build the foundation with people, cultures, education, structures, and processes. We are going to school over and over. After that comes the building of will. At a hospital where I am a board member, we start every meeting speaking about the patients we hurt since the last board meeting or we start a story with something that went well or something that failed. This is the power of transparency. We get so caught up with the every day. And the big problem is that the governing board is being overwhelmed with data. This is followed by ideas, the theory of the work forward, followed by execution and accountability for results.

In many organizations, there is no accountability. When you miss it [a targeted measure], then it's ok; you almost got it. I have been teaching *Getting Boards on Board* since 2005 with IHI. I am a trustee for the Lahey Health System. And last Thursday, we had over 100 board members meet to focus on quality. We had outside experts who took the journey, shared it with us, and inspired us. But the journey doesn't end there with "spray and pray." Now we are meeting to take it to the next step.

It's hard work. Even though I and many others have been teaching and sharing in this area since 2005, quality improvement is still moving forward slowly. I have an expression called "projectitis." Today there are so many projects with no common foundation or no common language. This is nothing like the journey a high reliability organization would take.

I worked with a hospital on the west coast of the United States, where the board asked IHI to come in and see if the organization was as good as they thought they were. We engaged with board, the leadership, and staff. And when I met with a staff nurse, I asked her two questions "what did she love about her practice" and "what keeps that from happening every day?" To the first she almost brought me to tears when she talked about the care and caring. For the second she said: "I come to work every day and sit at the bottom of the waterfall, and the stuff keeps coming and coming. I'm drowning. I don't know how I'm surviving." The leadership needs to set very specific aims, position them for success through partnership, and hold them accountable.

When we were asked the question: "Who killed Betsy Lehman?" We said: "Executives and leaders because we failed to put in place systems into support safe practice." Boards expect healthcare providers, who suffer from being human, to be perfect 100% of the time. Boards and Leadership must put in place systems that mitigate the chances that their humanness will prevent harm from reaching the patient.

An American Society of Clinical Oncology article summarized our journey at Dana-Farber in three words: burden (we all carry the burden for the patients harmed and do), responsibility (we have a responsibly to fix it, to prevent it from happening again), and power (using the tragedy to drive exceptional improvement). And as tragic as these events are, if you have the courage you can bring profound change in the aftermath. Peter Senge, author of *The Fifth Discipline*, talked about the notion of creative tension, where we set a bold aims against the reality of practice. The tragic event, appropriately managed, will be a gift to drive the most amazing movement forward. Today, Dana-Farber is a widely respected organization; it is still striving for continuous learning and improvement for those we are privilege to partner with and serve.

Appendix AV.2 Interview with Dr. David Munch

AV.2.1 Brief Bio

Dr. Dave Munch is a Senior Principal at Healthcare Performance Partners and has led Lean production applications that have resulted in improvements in both clinical and non clinical processes. He is the former Chief Clinical and Operations Officer at Exempla Lutheran Medical

Center. Dr. Munch served on the Agency for Healthcare Research and Quality's High Reliability Advisory Group. He is also a faculty member for the Belmont University Lean Healthcare Certificate Program.

AV.2.2 Objectives

- Discuss how to apply Lean thinking in clinical and nonclinical processes
- Understand how to engage clinicians and middle managers to toward high reliability organizing
- Discuss the importance of measurement

1. ***In your previous role as a Chief Clinical and Quality Officer at Exempla Lutheran Medical Center, you have applied Lean thinking in clinical and nonclinical processes, which ultimately led to significant improvements. Kindly share your experience on how this evolved.***

   I am an Internist by training and practice. And I did that for 20 years—in both inpatient and outpatient settings. I'm old enough in that as an emergency physician in the first year or two, I saw the environment in different settings (inpatient and outpatient). And over the course of time, I got frustrated with the silos and systems. I worked in a community hospital in the suburbs in Denver then became the chief medical officer of Columbia HCA HealthONE. Three years later I accepted a job as the Chief Clinical and Operating Officer of Exempla Lutheran Medical Center. Our strategic plan was that we would be in the top decile in all publically reported quality indicators within five years. This was our strategic plan: let's make sure we provide the best quality first, before anything else. We were working wonderfully hard. And the CEO said that we were working too hard and that this is not sustainable; we were focusing on some things and not others. We fundamentally had to redesign care to make the right work easier to do.

   Also, operations needed to own improvement as a core responsibility. We used Lean methods and principles as the foundation of this strategy and were able to achieve our quality goals in 3½ years while increasing our operating margins! So, if done right, higher quality is going to cost less as long as you have correct processes in place. We learned about a different way to lead. The first line of defense is the frontline staff, nurse, supervisor, or director. These are the people that see the issues from their teams. Middle managers play a critical role in how care is delivered. They are also the most overburdened employees in the healthcare system. Taking a good nurse and promoting him/her into a management role requires training and support in being a manager and we often don't provide that. Management is a skill set that isn't taught in nursing or medical school. I think this is a blind spot for our industry and there is a paucity of literature on this subject. I often tell people that I've had the privilege of making thousands of mistakes. I think we can do a better job developing managers and the management systems such that we don't make nearly as many mistakes as I did in my journey.

   We live in very complex systems and there are methods of leadership that work in complex systems and those that don't. W. Edwards Deming defines a system as an interdependent group of items, people and processes with a common aim. The key words to his definition are interdependency and aim especially the interdependencies of front line staff with middle managers, and middle managers with executives. Let me use a Stephen Covey tool to describe this; *begin with the end in mind.* In the ideal state of a hospital with respect to quality and reliability what are the staff doing? They are doing the standard work because good efficient effective work has been designed for them that doesn't waste their time. We live in complex systems where errors will happen. Not only is it safe for front line staff to surface errors, it is rewarded. That is a significant opportunity with respect to many organizations. Also, in the ideal state, the front line staff have the skills themselves to problem solve effectively using methods that solve the problems to root cause such that they stay solved.

So, who is responsible for creating this environment? It is the people they report to, that ever so important supervisor or middle managers. Therefore, what do they need to do to create this environment of safety? Middle managers need to have enough time to participate in quality and safety which most of them currently don't have. So you have to reform their job. They also have to have knowledge in problem solving skills. To continually develop their team, they have to turn into coaches rather than experts. In addition, they also need to establish a *sensitivity to operations*, being able to measure their current performance, do basic run charts, Pareto analysis and team huddles so that everyone knows what is going on and what needs to be addressed.

So, who is responsible for creating the management systems activities described above? It is the people those managers report to, the executive. Therefore, what does the executive need to do to create and support the management systems at the middle? They need to align everyone toward "true north" (i.e., the aim) and provide the support and coaching for the middle manager in their development to be able to do so. They need to provide the systems and support structures for the management and address barriers, one of which is overburden. So the executive turns into a coach of the middle manager. The middle manager turns into a coach of their front line team. This is the fundamental change in leadership method that has to occur at all levels.

Most U.S. organizations are not effective at deploying Lean [methods] because they only use the tools, not the management systems to deploy and sustain the processes effectively. Without this, you will not be able to sustain change. Entropy is real in health systems. System-ness needs to be achieved.

We need to provide a foundation for reliability where middle managers are measuring the most important parameters in their team over time. And when they do a Pareto analysis, they are orchestrating improvements around this. Again, we have to redesign the managers work. We can't add more tasks to manager's jobs. We need to dive in and challenge the efficiency of their work environment starting with all of those meetings they attend.

I will go through each of the characteristics of high reliability organizations:

a. *Sensitivity to Operations:* Within these systems, I can walk on every unit and look at their [quality] boards and determine the status of their performance based on the daily responsibilities, daily metrics (e.g., hand hygiene rates), or other indicators (e.g., are we meeting our goals with patient transfers of 30 minutes from the emergency department to the ward?). These performance measures can also be established as longer term metrics, such as elimination of preventable mortality. This is one aspect of sensitivity to operations. Another one is around the TeamSTEPPS, daily huddles and debriefings where metrics from the board are reviewed at the beginning of each shift. We solicit solutions to close the gap as quickly as possible and assign a single person to oversee the task and take the responsibility for its closure; single point accountability (SPA). In doing so, we as their supervisor agree to give them the support needed to be able to assume the responsibility reasonably. That is the only way to fairly hold team members accountable.

b. *Reluctance to Simplify*—or oversimplify: If you do an A3 [structured problem solving method in Lean management and first used in Toyota] properly, it is a more effective form of the common PDSA [plan-do-study-act]. To do an A3 properly, it starts with a deep understanding of the current state. It is intimated in the "P" of PDSA but commonly overlooked. It involves baseline metrics, how deeply we understand the current situation, interviews, and people's knowledge about the situation. This is current state analysis where we study and know the problem deeply. So after this, you are in a much better position to understand the cause of the problem in the current state by doing a fishbone diagram, 5 Whys exercise or other approach. What is critical to proper performance of A3 is to use the tollgate process. Don't go to the next step until you've fully vetted the previous step. If you do each of these properly before you move to the next step, then the solutions can be more easily discovered. The standard IHI Model for Improvement is very synergistic with the use of A3 problem solving. By reflecting on the first two questions of:
   i. What are we trying to accomplish?
   ii. How will we know that a change is an improvement?

      We orient our problem solving to the highest priorities and establish the measures that determine our success. We can then use A3 approach to PDSA to address the third question:
   iii. What change can we make that will result in improvement?

c. *Preoccupation with Failure*: Team huddles need to shift the thinking from reactive to proactive and anticipate what could go wrong. Consider changing your morning safety question from: *What problems happened today?* to *What is the next patient safety issue we will experience based on risks you see currently?* This necessitates a deeper level of thinking around risk management. It serves to uncover the "*Latent Errors*" as James Reason describes, before they can cause harm to patients. Once these are identified, you can use A3 problem solving or other technique to address the risks, advancing the reliability of your care systems.

d. *Commitment to resilience:* Do you have a process to deal with unanticipated situations. How quickly are issues identified and how quickly are they addressed? Mitigation is a very important aspect of reliability; recognizing problems when they occur and responding to them immediately. Think of Toyota. First of all, problems are easily identified because the work is standardized significantly which makes it easier to see problems (a variation from the standard). Once that occurs, there is immediate attention given to the issue by the team leader or supervisor such that the defect is not passed down the assembly line and into the car. A good example in healthcare is the Rapid Response Team (RRT). The standard work is the stable patient, stable vitals, mental status etc. When the vital signs deteriorate that is the signal of a problem and a team of people responds immediately. Question: In an environment of high variation with few standards, how does one tell the difference between a variation and a problem? It may be very difficult until the bad outcome informs you. Therefore, unnecessary variation needs to be engineered and managed out of the care processes if you hope to achieve high reliability. The middle manager plays a very important role in establishing resilience by reinforcing standard work, encouraging the surfacing of problems and responding timely. It can be supported by the right metrics and vigorous team communication.

e. *Deference to Expertise*: The closer you are to the front line, the more knowledge you have as to what is broken and what needs to be done. Expertise lies at the frontline. Our roles as managers and executives therefore need to shift to genuine listening to those who report to us and use that information to inform solutions. This is the cornerstone of engagement. The Toyota model believes that value comes from frontline [staff]. And as an executive, I need to support the frontline. If you follow the Toyota model carefully, then you can get to high reliability.

2. ***How did you incorporate Lean management systems/thinking into the daily practice of healthcare providers?***

a. *How did you engage physicians in the process?*

There are a few ways to engage them. The engagement of any human requires relationship and trust. And so engaging physicians requires those pieces. I go into organizations and had the privilege in the last seven years to work with management system groups and Lean systems. I worked with over 150 hospital systems, and I see what works well and what doesn't. Physicians are not one single amorphous mass. There are layers of physicians:

i. Frontline physicians
ii. Administrative physicians (C-suite or VPMAs)
iii. Official physician leaders (department chairs or medical staff)
iv. Unofficial physician leaders (individuals who have been there for a while, are well respected, and may have had formal position in the past)

We need to engage physicians into the different roles they can bring to the table. And we have to understand what responsibility lies in which bucket. From the frontline physician, we need insights and participation on how to fix problems. From the administrative/chief physicians, we need to bring systems and structures to support this. If there are contracting and equipment issues, then need to get these things supported. From the official physician leaders, they will be able to communicate back and forth, to and from physicians, advocate for them, and help with change management. And this is the same with unofficial physician leaders. Then, you set a plan based on the activities identified, talk with them ahead of time, and ask for the necessary support. It's important to nurture and develop various physicians at various levels:

i. *Find common ground*: What are the issues that are important to physicians, the team, the board, and the hospital in general? Find out what is important to the physicians that are also aligned with the strategic plan. This should be the highest priority because incentives are aligned.

ii. *Establish a mutual exchange of value*: What is important to the physicians that may not necessarily be aligned to the strategic plan? If you are willing to work on these, the physicians will be more likely to cooperate with your strategic initiatives whether or not they are important to the physician. This is a partnership, meeting each other's needs. If you work on these issues for the physicians, then they are going to be more willing to work on your issues. Create a mutual exchange of value.

iii. *Respectful transparency*: Transparency is important but it should not be a "Gotcha." It needs to be rolled out in a respectful manner. So for physicians who are having difficulty on their specific indicators, we can ask them: "How can we help you look better in this profile?" Because three months from now, everyone's name will be published. So we need to give people an opportunity to perform and improve before/during the "quiet period."

iv. *Respect physicians' time*: Meetings at 10 a.m. are very disruptive to physicians' other obligations even if it may be most convenient for you. You need to consider their other responsibilities and ask them: "What time works for you?"

v. *Give physicians a voice*: Engage physicians early in the strategic planning; listen to their ideas and issues. Use these insights to inform your strategies. Don't just inform them after the fact. Get physician input as broadly as possible by establishing a dialogue. Recruit physicians as part of the system of leadership.

The goal is to establish a long-term partnership based on trust and mutual respect. It will take time and effort and you'll never be done working on it. It is, however, critically important to your success long term.

b. *How did you engage middle managers in the process?*

Redesign their work, and give them back some time. Engage them in improvement. As you work on their unit, engage them in participating in the value stream mapping or other improvement efforts. You need them to take responsibility of the [quality] boards and huddles which will happen if we redesign their work and give them the coaching they need for the changes. Support their development in all of the tools, such as A3, TeamSTEPPS, and others, and give them the time to do it. Help them develop their "management standard work," the things they do reliably daily, weekly, monthly, and annually around these systems. If they are struggling, deal with it. Understand the barriers and developmental needs and invest in them. They and you will need coaching in management systems.

Establish a cadence of review. Executives need to go monthly (at least) to where the work is being done on the units [i.e., inpatient wards and outpatient settings] and ask specific questions during every visit. Mini-operational reviews should happen, that is, in 15 minutes, asking:

i. "How's it going? Let's review your metrics."

ii. "What is working well?" "Where are you getting advancements?" "Who to acknowledge?"

iii. "What are you having difficulty with?" At the early stages, people will be too scared to speak. As a leader, you can't blame people and need to help them understand the process.

iv. "What are you doing about it?" "What is your plan?" And each of these questions is an opportunity for coaching and mentoring.

v. "What do you need from me?" Executive needs to Lean in to help solve problems. Questions should end in "What? By when? And who will take lead?" Executives should leave the clinical area with an agreement. And that [the agreement] becomes the executive's first query the next time he/she shows up on that unit.

The executive is responsible for establishing and maintaining the management systems that allow well-intentioned managers to participate in quality improvement. If the executive doesn't do their part, then the management systems will predictively fall apart. So there is only one failure mode of this system and that lies at the feet of the executive. If they don't do their part then the system of reliability deteriorates over time. So, the executive needs to develop their own standard work; the tasks they perform reliably daily, weekly, monthly and annually.

Who does this for executives?

Everyone, at all levels, needs coaching in these skills and behaviors; *all levels* including the executive. Decide who will take on those coaching roles and allow those people to be frank with you: Truth over Harmony as CEO Jack Barto from New Hanover Regional Medical Center would say.

How do you start this conversation with the executives?

To have the coaching conversation with executives, you need to establish what the goals are for this transformation to high reliability. You then need to explore what it will take both personally for the CEO, and organizationally. This is hard work that takes commitment and it is best to come to agreement with everyone's eyes open than to go down a path that fails over time. You need to establish coaching at all levels for the development and respect of the people who work there. As issues come up, you need to deal with them. "What are we doing to address this?" You must be able to describe the current leadership work and surface the issues to create *constructive* tension that forces you to work through them. Coaching sessions need to occur at least monthly, if not weekly with a discipline of reviewing leadership standard work and dealing with gaps in a supportive and transparent manner. The biggest challenge is getting the executive willing to be challenged. You could start with mini steps (one-on-one) and pick small tasks first. One colleague told me: "Don't change anything. Pilot everything." A great use of the scientific method. And if you put together a plan, then you need to give the people the ability to fix and address, but you have to give them an opportunity to do this. Have your organization set up some principles everyone agrees to—for instance, "No problems remain hidden," or "listen first." Toyota Production System is based on a set of principles. The standard work in the factory in Japan may be different than that in the U.S., but adherence to the 14 Toyota principles is carefully followed and practiced.

3. ***As organizations are moving toward high reliability, what are some of the benefits associated with measurement? How were these incorporated into practice?***

Measurement is absolutely foundational to improvement, reliability and assurance. The struggle with organizations is that they sometimes don't have the right measures or are too dependent on measures that require data systems and delays. Many useful measures can just be done using graph paper and a pencil. For example, assign a nurse on a unit to observe hand washing every day in her ward for 45 minutes (no specific time), and post that information on the unit (information gathered using a pencil). Or document the time of request and time of arrival of every patient who comes up from the emergency department. There are many processes and measurements that help the people doing the work. There is a balance between the process and outcomes measures that needs to be established. Hospitals many times do not generate the process measures needed to make the outcomes reliable. High reliability requires knowing your process measures and acting on them. This makes the outcomes more reliable.

Data should drive action. A useful question for your organization is to ask "What are you doing about the gaps you've identified in your data?" If there is no clear response then you should ask: "Then why are you expending the resources to measure it?" If you're not taking action on your data you're wasting precious resources and fooling yourself. Take these measures off your plate and replace them with those you act on.

In summary, a balance of process and outcomes measures is important. Acting on them is even more important. Many very useful measures can be performed with graph paper and a pencil and take a few seconds to record. You don't need fancy analytics for everything. Get creative with how you measure your work.

4. ***Thank you for sharing your rich experience. What advice do you have for organizations as they are moving through the process of actively organizing for safety?***

   My advice is: understand that no systems get better without attention. No person improves without coaching. The deeper you get into this journey, the more you realize you develop the systems that give you high-quality results, so with time these will merge.

- *Phase 1: Discovery*. What is going on? We need to know what is going on now to understand the current state, or organizational assessment.
- *Phase 2: Design*. This is where tools of Lean, PDSA, model for improvement, and others can be effective. We must design good standard work, which is waste-free and effective.
- *Phase 3: Deployment of standard work*. Provide enough instruction where people get it and coaching where the new standard work becomes a habit.
- *Phase 4: Systems for sustaining performance*. The management systems themselves. The managers must own the sustainment of performance. If this is delegated to the quality office, you will not have sustainable change. The quality officer can be the coach and can help with periodic inspections, but management needs to own it.

This is all about changing the culture and establishing the management systems to drive improvement.

References

5 Million Lives Campaign. 2008. Getting started kit: Governance leadership "Boards on Board" how-to guide. Cambridge, MA: Institute for Healthcare Improvement.

Chassin, M. R., and J. M. Loeb. 2013. High-reliability health care: Getting there from here. *Milbank Q.* 91 (3):459–490.

Christianson, M. K., K. M. Sutcliffe, M. A. Miller, and T. J. Iwashyna. 2011. Becoming a high reliability organization. *Crit. Care* 15 (6):314. doi:10.1186/cc10360.

Combs, J., Y. Liu, A. Hall, and D. Ketchen. 2006. How much do high-performance work practices matter? A meta-analysis of their effects on organizational performance. *Pers. Psychol.* 59 (3):501–528.

Conway, J. 2008. Getting boards on board: Engaging governing boards in quality and safety. *Jt Comm J Qual Patient Saf.* 34 (4):214–220.

Conway, J., D. Nathan, E. Benz, L. N. Shulman, S. E. Sallan, P. Reid Ponte, S. B. Bartel, S. B. Bartel, M. Connor, D. Puhy, and S. Weingart. 2006. Key learning from the Dana-Farber Cancer Institute's 10-year patient safety journey. In *American Society of Clinical Oncology*, pp. 2–6.

Edmondson, A. C. 2003. Speaking up in the operating room: How team leaders promote learning in interdisciplinary action teams. *J. Manag. Stud.* 40 (6):1419–1452.

Flin, R. 2007. Measuring safety culture in healthcare: A case for accurate diagnosis. *Saf. Sci.* 45 (6):653–667.

Hales, B. M., and P. J. Pronovost. 2006. The checklist: A tool for error management and performance improvement. *J. Crit. Care* 21 (3):231–235. doi:10.1016/j.jcrc.2006.06.002.

Hart, E. M., and H. Owen. 2005. Errors and omissions in anesthesia: A pilot study using a pilot's checklist. *Anesth. Analg.* 101 (1):246–250, table of contents. doi:10.1213/01.ANE.0000156567.24800.0B.

Hines, S., K. Luna, J. Lofthus, M. Marquardt, and D. Stelmokas. 2008. *Becoming a High Reliability Organization: Operational Advice for Hospital Leaders*. Agency for Healthcare Research and Quality (AHRQ). AHRQ Publication (08-0022).

Hudson, P. 2003. Applying the lessons of high risk industries to health care. *Qual. Saf. Health Care* 12 (Suppl. 1):i7–i12.

Massoud, M. R., G. A. Nielsen, K. Nolan, M. W. Schall, and C. Sevin. 2006. A framework for spread: From local improvements to system-wide change. IHI Innovation Series White Paper. Cambridge, MA: Institute for Healthcare Improvement.

Pronovost, P., D. Needham, S. Berenholtz, et al. 2006. An intervention to decrease catheter-related bloodstream infections in the ICU. *N. Engl. J. Med.* 355 (26):2725–2732. doi:10.1056/NEJMoa061115.

Rochlin, G. I., T. R. La Porte, and K. H. Roberts. 1998. The self-designing high-reliability organization: Aircraft carrier flight operations at sea. *Naval War College Review* 51 (3):97.

Runciman, W. B., M. T. Kluger, R. W. Morris, et al. 2005. Crisis management during anaesthesia: The development of an anaesthetic crisis management manual. *Qual. Saf. Health Care* 14 (3):e1. doi:10.1136/qshc.2002.004101.

Sutcliffe, K. M., L. Paine, and P. J. Pronovost. 2016. Re-examining high reliability: Actively organising for safety. *BMJ Qual. Saf.* 26 (3): 246–251. doi:10.1136/bmjqs-2015-004698.

Vincent, C., and R. Amalberti. 2016. *Safer Healthcare*. New York: Springer.

Vogus, T. J., and B. Hilligoss. 2016. The underappreciated role of habit in highly reliable healthcare. *BMJ Qual. Saf.* 25 (3):141–146. doi:10.1136/bmjqs-2015-004512.

Vogus, T. J., and K. M. Sutcliffe. 2007a. The impact of safety organizing, trusted leadership, and care pathways on reported medication errors in hospital nursing units. *Med. Care* 45 (10): 997–1002. doi:10.1097/MLR.0b013e318053674f.

Vogus, T. J., and K. M. Sutcliffe. 2007b. The safety organizing scale: Development and validation of a behavioral measure of safety culture in hospital nursing units. *Med. Care* 45 (1):46–54. doi:10.1097/01.mlr.0000244635.61178.7a.

Waterson, P. 2014. *Patient Safety Culture: Theory, Methods and Application*. United Kingdom: Ashgate Publishing.

Weick, K. E., and K. M. Sutcliffe. 2011. *Managing the Unexpected: Resilient Performance in an Age of Uncertainty*, Vol. 8. San Francisco: John Wiley & Sons.

Weick, K. E., and K. M. Sutcliffe. 2015. *Managing the Unexpected: Sustained Performance in a Complex World*. Hoboken, NJ: John Wiley & Sons.

Chapter 6

Information Technology: A Neural Network for Reliable Healthcare

Hee Hwang

Contents

6.1 Introduction 111
6.2 The Evolution of Health Information Technology 112
6.3 Electronic Health Records 113
6.4 Interoperability as an Innovation Accelerator 116
6.5 Patient Safety Using Radio-Frequency Identification and Barcode Technology 118
6.6 Patient Engagement and Experiences 119
6.7 Conclusions 120
References 121

6.1 Introduction

Health information technology (IT) functions like a neural network to connect digital health stakeholders and foster transparency for reliable healthcare. It is a key enabler of healthcare's triple aims of improving the patient experience (including quality and satisfaction), improving population health, and reducing the per capita healthcare costs. In this chapter, we discuss technological advances and trends in health IT over recent years that are expected to affect future healthcare delivery and power new models of value-based care. Specifically, we discuss the adoption of the electronic health record (EHR) as core health IT, the importance of interoperability as an innovation accelerator, the use of radio-frequency identification (RFID) and barcodes to ensure patient safety, and patient engagement and experience technology.

6.2 The Evolution of Health Information Technology

Health IT describes the set of tools needed to facilitate electronic documentation and management of healthcare delivery. It is crucial to multiple stakeholders in medicine, including patients, physicians, nurses, public agencies, payers, researchers, and vendors. Advances in IT have provided new opportunities to pursue the triple aims of improving the patient care experience, improving the health of the population, and reducing per capita healthcare costs (Berwick, et al. 2008). Health IT enables the capture and analysis of various large clinical data sets, which represent an enormous resource to improve the quality and efficiency of healthcare systems. These data are central to advancing medical knowledge and driving continual improvement in healthcare delivery (Goodby et al. 2011). They are also an essential tool for enabling the transition from the fee-for-service to the fee-for-value model, the latter prioritizing the improvement of quality, safety, efficiency, patient engagement, and population health.

Clinical and administrative data are captured at the point of care through delivery processes or while conducting research. These data include: (1) structured data such as medication orders and sensors; (2) unstructured data such as medical images and videos; and (3) semi-structured data such as medical records. The commonly used types of administrative and clinical information systems are described in Table 6.1. Administrative applications generally support the management and operation of the healthcare organization, whereas clinical applications contain clinical or health-related information used by healthcare providers as part of patient care (Wager et al. 2013). The use of increasingly sophisticated health IT is improving the timely availability of clinical data critical for real-time population surveillance and is valuable for high-quality clinical care (Bardach et al. 2009).

Advances in health IT and the continued adoption and meaningful use of EHRs, the health information exchange (HIE), personal health records (PHRs), telehealth, mobile health applications, and other health IT systems are expected to continue to improve patient-centered care.

Table 6.1 Common Administrative and Clinical Information Systems

Administrative Applications	Clinical Applications
Patient administration systems • Admission, discharge, transfer (ADT) • Patient registration • Patient scheduling • Patient billing • Utilization management *Other administrative and financial systems* • Accounts payable • General ledger • Personnel management • Materials management • Payroll • Staff scheduling • Revenue cycle management	*Ancillary information systems* • Laboratory information system • Radiology information system • Pharmacy information system (PhIS) *Other clinical information systems* • Nursing documentation • Physician documentation (electronic health record; EHR) • Computerized provider order entry • Clinical decision support system • Telemedicine and telehealth • Rehabilitation service documentation • Medication administration system • Electronic prescribing • Health information exchange

Source: Summarized and modified from Table 4.1 in Wager, K.A. et al., *Health Care Information Systems*, 3rd edn, San Francisco: Wiley, 2013.

These systems facilitate and accelerate coordinated care between different healthcare organizations and patient engagement to self-manage their health.

As examples, the following represent some of the most promising and innovative emerging technologies and trends that are likely to be considered and adopted by healthcare organizations:

- *Cloud computing*: Cloud computing provides easy, scalable access to computing resources and IT services. The cloud enables data aggregation and integration across the enterprise and better decision-making, especially when combined with new technologies such as artificial intelligence (AI).
- *Artificial intelligence*: AI, cognitive computing, and medical image analysis are expected to become more clinically meaningful as health-related data sources and computer processing power grow rapidly. These technologies unlock the value of "big" healthcare data, help providers to pursue personalized medicine approaches to diagnosis, treatment, and monitoring; for example, personalized cancer treatment, disease progression tracking, and early detection of eye disease. In the clinical setting, AI and clinical decision support provide opportunities to augment traditional, human-centered diagnosis and treatment paradigms with more scientific, data-driven healthcare delivery models.
- *Social networking or social media*: Social networking or social media refers to a variety of technologies that support and/or mediate communication between organizations, communities, and individuals, notable and popular examples being Facebook, Twitter, YouTube, and personal blogs. The widespread public adoption of social media has provided a tremendous opportunity and power to connect with patients and strengthen and preserve the doctor–patient relationship (Impact Advisors 2014). These technologies, especially in combination with the use of PHRs, will be valuable in monitoring chronic disease and for public health research.
- *Mobile health*: Mobile health (mHealth) helps to introduce new technologies to healthcare and provides new ways to interact with stakeholders and deliver healthcare (Impact Advisors 2014). Smartphones and the growing number of medical devices connected to them can be used to seamlessly provide information and new capabilities to patients and their families, thereby empowering self-care. In addition, wearable sensor technology, which continuously captures and collects physiological data, can be used in the management of chronic diseases and to monitor patients after discharge from hospital. As the line between consumer health wearables and medical devices begins to blur, these devices will increasingly be used to monitor a range of medical risk factors and assist self-diagnosis and behavioral change (Piwek et al. 2016).

Patient-empowered technology and information integration have started to and will continue to personalize medicine. It is now possible to envision a future in which treatments are specifically tailored to an individual's genetics, prescriptions are analyzed for likely effectiveness, and researchers study clinical data in real time to more rapidly learn what is and is not effective (West 2011).

6.3 Electronic Health Records

A variety of terms have been used to describe EHR-related IT systems, including electronic medical records (EMRs), computerized medical records (CMRs), electronic clinical information systems (ECIS), and computerized patient records (CPRs) (Hoyt and Yoshihashi 2014). In 2008, the

National Alliance for Health Information Technology released standard definitions for the EMR, the EHR, and the PHR (Horowitz et al. 2008):

- *Electronic medical record (EMR)*: An electronic record of health-related information on an individual that can be created, gathered, managed, and consulted by authorized clinicians and staff within one healthcare organization.
- *Electronic health record (EHR)*: An electronic record of health-related information on an individual that conforms to nationally recognized interoperability standards and that can be created, managed, and consulted by authorized clinicians and staff across more than one healthcare organization.
- *Personal health record (PHR)*: An electronic record of health-related information on an individual that conforms to nationally recognized interoperability standards and that can be drawn from multiple sources while being managed, shared, and controlled by the individual.

The adoption of an EHR does not necessarily indicate that the end user is using the advanced capabilities of an EHR (Hoyt and Yoshihashi 2014). According to HIMSS Analytics (Chicago, Illinois), a commercial provider of healthcare IT analytics, even as of 2015 there continued to be low use of advanced EHR capabilities according to the EMR adoption model, which assesses the IT adoption level of hospitals using an eight-step scale of cumulative capabilities (Table 6.2; HIMSS Analytics 2016). In 2006, no hospital had a complete EHR capable of data warehousing and standard-based HIE, and, in 2015, only 4.2% of hospitals surveyed had a complete EHR. It is notable that it takes a long time to achieve significant national adoption of health IT in the United States.

In 2009 in the United States, as part of the American Recovery and Reinvestment Act (ARRA), about $20 billion–$30 billion was set aside for a program called the Health Information Technology for Economic and Clinical Health (HITECH) Act to provide financial incentives for clinicians and hospitals to promote the adoption of certified EHRs. HITECH proposed the meaningful use of interoperable EHRs throughout the U.S. healthcare delivery system as a critical national goal. In this context, "meaningful use" was defined as the use of certified EHR technology in a meaningful manner (e.g., electronic prescribing) and ensured that the certified EHR technology was connected in a manner that provided for the electronic exchange of health information to improve the quality of care. Furthermore, HITECH dictated that in using certified EHR technology, the provider must submit to the Secretary of Health & Human Services (HHS) information on quality of care and other measures (CDC 2016). The concept of meaningful use in health IT prioritized the following policies:

- Improving quality, safety, and efficiency and reducing health disparities
- Engaging patients and families in their health
- Improving care coordination
- Improving public and population health
- Ensuring adequate privacy and security protection for personal health information

Programs prompting the use of EHR systems (including for meaningful use) and EHR certification and incentive programs increased the adoption of certified EHR systems in the United States. By 2015, nearly all reporting hospitals (96%) possessed certified EHR technology, and 40% of hospitals had adopted comprehensive EHR systems with advanced levels of functionality (ONC 2016). As EHR adoption is now widespread at the state level, federal governmental efforts

Table 6.2 Cross-Regional EMR Adoption Model Score Distribution, 2015

Stage	*Cumulative Capabilities*	*Asia Pacific:* N = *770 (%)*	*Middle East:* N = *142 (%)*	*United States:* N = *5,460 (%)*	*Canada:* N = *641 (%)*	*Europe:* N = *2,395 (%)*
Stage 7	Complete EMR, data analytics to improve care	0.5	0.0	4.2	0.2	0.1
Stage 6	Physician documentation (templates), full CDSS, CLMA	3.9	11.3	27.1	0.9	4.6
Stage 5	Full R-PACS	7.4	21.1	35.9	3.4	17.5
Stage 4	CPOE, clinical decision support (clinical protocols)	1.7	3.5	10.1	1.6	5.5
Stage 3	Clinical documentation, CDSS (error checking)	0.6	19.0	16.4	31.2	3.2
Stage 2	CDR, controlled medication vocabulary, CDS, HIE-capable	32.7	19.0	2.6	31.5	30.2
Stage 1	Ancillaries—lab, rad, pharmacy—all installed	4.9	9.9	1.7	13.9	14.2
Stage 0	All three ancillaries not installed	48.2	16.2	2.1	17.3	24.1

Source: Courtesy of HIMSS Analytics. *Note:* EMR: electronic medical record; CDSS: clinical decision support system, CLMA: closed-loop medication administration; R-PACS: radiology-picture archiving and communication system; CPOE: computerized physician order entry; CDR: clinical data repository; CDS: commissioning data set; HIE: health information exchange.

focusing on EHR adoption are shifting to interoperability of health information and the use of health IT to support care delivery system reform (ONC 2016).

Regarding the value of health IT, HIMSS provides the Health IT value suite, which highlights hundreds of examples of healthcare organizations in five categories: satisfaction, treatment/clinical, electronic secure data, patient engagement and population management, and savings. Electronic clinical indicators can also be used to monitor and measure quality of care and patient safety through the use of health IT. For example, the administration rate of preventive antibiotics, length of hospital stay, and thrombolytic treatment time after acute myocardial infarction patients' arrivals were used to demonstrate the value of health IT in a Stage 7 hospital (Yoo et al. 2014).

The EHR mainly serves as a source of information and documentation for individual patient care, clinical research, and population health. Effective EHR system use enables innovation to achieve highly reliable healthcare and improved clinical outcomes. The HIMSS Analytics EMR adoption model can be used as a good reference for a healthcare organization to plan strategies and roadmap for IT investment. Beyond Stage 7, innovative applications for patient engagement, population health, and precision medicine using mobile and advanced analytics technologies will be able to be considered for healthcare organizations.

6.4 Interoperability as an Innovation Accelerator

Interoperability describes the ability of different IT systems and software applications to communicate, exchange data, and use the exchanged information (HIMSS 2013). In an interoperable health IT ecosystem, (1) all individuals, their families, and healthcare providers should be able to send, receive, find, and use EHRs in an appropriate, secure, timely, and reliable manner; (2) critical public health functions including real-time case reporting, disease surveillance, and disaster responses should be supported; and (3) there is support for data aggregation for research purposes, which can lead to improved clinical guidelines and practice (ONC 2015).

Three levels of health IT interoperability exist:

- *Foundational interoperability*: Allows data exchange from one IT system to another and does not require the receiving information technology system to interpret the data.
- *Structural interoperability*: Is an intermediate level that defines the data exchange structure or format (i.e., message format standards). It ensures that data exchange between IT systems can be interpreted at the data field level.
- *Semantic interoperability*: Provides interoperability at the highest level, that is, the ability of two or more systems or elements to exchange information and to use the information that has been exchanged (IEEE 2010).

Interoperability requires appropriate standards to exchange and share information between health IT systems in a secure and reliable way. The number of links needed to connect n different systems increases by $n \times (n - 1)/2$ as a combinatorial explosion. For example, linking six nodes requires 15 interfaces, as indicated in the schematic, with the center of the star in the figure on the right indicating a single standard being used to link six nodes (Benson and Grieve 2016).

Healthcare data interoperability includes standards for: (1) data for medication (e.g., RxNorm, UMLS), diagnosis (e.g., ICD-10), laboratory tests/clinical observations (e.g., LOINC), and comprehensive clinical terminology (e.g., SNOMED CT); (2) messages (e.g., HL7 messages); (3) documents (e.g., CCR, CDA, and CCDA); and (4) other areas such as clinical decision support (e.g., ARDEN) and clinical information models (e.g., CIMI).

HL7 International is the leading standards development organization (SDO) for healthcare interoperability. As a new approach and after implementation and experience of the other HL7 standards, HL7 developed another form of interoperability called an *application program interface* (API) (Benson and Grieve 2016). An API is widely used in IT and is a set of services provided by a programming library that can be used by another program to achieve its own goal. The new API-based approach, named *Fast Healthcare Interoperability Resources* (FHIR, pronounced "fire"), was first published as a draft standard for trial use in February 2014 and is expected to be a normative edition of the standard in 2018. FHIR is a standard framework that leverages web standards and applies a tight focus on implementation, promoting access and delivery of data while offering enormous flexibility. Its versatility and modular structure means that patients and providers can apply it to mobile devices, web-based applications, cloud communications, and EHR data sharing.

FHIR describes data formats and elements (known as *resources*) and an API to exchange EHRs (Wikipedia 2016). Open-source implementations of FHIR data structures, servers, clients, and tools include HL7 reference implementations in a variety of languages, SMART on FHIR, and HAPI-FHIR in Java (Wikipedia 2016).

The vision of SMART on FHIR is to enable medical applications to run on diverse EHR systems at the point of care as simply as apps work on a smartphone. SMART on FHIR provides a framework to integrate applications using FHIR and is suitable for use in many contexts where FHIR is used (Wikipedia 2016, Andrews 2016, SMART 2016). An ecosystem that uses API-enabled EHRs, which compares a classic EHR with ecosystem apps supported by a uniform public API for health data, where a third-party app written once can run anywhere and be reused on multiple EHRs (Mandl et al. 2015). The end user can select apps from a gallery, just as on a smartphone.

There are now a number of examples illustrating the success of SMART on FHIR applications in EHRs with regard to extensions, patients, and research (Raths 2016):

- Boston Children's Hospital is building an open-source pharmacogenomics decision support service to provide medication dosage guidance at the point of care.
- Intermountain Healthcare has enhanced the Pediatric Growth Chart SMART on FHIR app developed by Boston Children's Hospital to be able to move the standard growth curves to external files and add tabular data to curve printouts for parents.
- Wolters Kluwer's UpToDate uses FHIR to make their applications contextual to patients when launched from EHRs.
- ClinicalTrialsMatch matches patients to clinical trials via a web service that applies eligibility criteria to patient characteristics.
- The POCRnet Patient-Powered Research Networks (PPRNs) is developing an app that will enable a participant to retrieve their common clinical data set from the provider and redirect the FHIR resources to a chosen PPRN URL, where the data will be translated, integrated, and made available to researchers as specified by the participant.
- In a breast cancer pilot, Boston Children's Hospital, Dana-Farber Cancer Institute, Intermountain Health, Massachusetts General Hospital, and Sysbiochem are collaborating to develop services to deploy predictive clinical models using FHIR.
- The SMART on FHIR Genomics server builds on FHIR Genomics to enable clinicogenomics apps to run with features such as authentication, patient scoping, and authorization.

- Vanderbilt-Ingram Cancer Center investigators have developed the SMART Precision Cancer Medicine app to aid cancer care by enabling clinicians to find contextual information about a patient's cancer genome in the clinical setting (Vanderbilt 2016).

In the era of precision medicine, IT and interoperability must be supported in a manner that is both compatible with the clinician's clinical workflow and economically feasible to deploy in modern healthcare environments (Sanders and Rehm 2015). To accelerate precision medicine approaches, fundamental changes are needed in the infrastructure and mechanisms for data collection, storage, and sharing. In this context, a precision medicine ecosystem is now developing and starting to link clinicians, laboratories, researchers, patients, and EHR vendors (Sanders and Rehm 2015). The new precision medicine ecosystem building blocks, which shows the infrastructure that supports the precision medicine ecosystem, connects multiple stakeholders, and integrates the flow of materials, knowledge, and data needed to generate, validate, store, refine, and apply clinical interpretations. The ecosystem can include biobanks, research databases, case-level databases, clinical knowledge-sharing networks, clinical laboratories and their information systems, EHRs and associated clinical decision support tools, and the patient-facing infrastructure or portal. Genetic information and clinical decision support are often impossible to visualize without robust access to the patient's genetics results, and reports require standard interfaces between the EHR vendors and laboratories (Sanders and Rehm 2015). Several groups, including DIGITizE AC and NHGRI, are working to promote interoperability of genetic information between multiple stakeholders.

However, clinical information in EHRs is inherently complex. Interoperability is difficult to achieve and takes a long time, due to several barriers including technical, financial, organizational, legal, and cultural factors that affect information sharing (Edmunds et al. 2016). Various healthcare stakeholders' interests in and continuous efforts for interoperability are expected to lead to innovation and transformation of healthcare systems.

6.5 Patient Safety Using Radio-Frequency Identification and Barcode Technology

RFID, a wireless system that uses radio-frequency electromagnetic fields to obtain data to track and identify items, is now being incorporated into healthcare organizations in various areas. RFID tags enable items or devices to be scanned so that their contents, location, manufacture date, order numbers, and shipping data can be transmitted to the correct person for use within the organization (Slack 2013). For example, pharmaceutical companies use RFID to track counterfeit products and prescriptions for clinical trials and to manage inventories. In hospitals, RFID is used to track expensive medical equipment, patients, staff, blood, and inventories (Reiner and Sullivan 2005).

Real-time documentation and cross-checking of care practices in the EHR using RFID and barcode technology have the potential to ensure patient safety, increase work efficiency, and improve care processes. It can also be used to reduce administrative workloads for nurses, allowing them more face-to-face time with patients and thus increasing patient satisfaction. The delivery or transfer of specimens and materials could be tracked real-time, resulting in improved quality of care, prevention of medical errors, and efficient use of resources by emphasizing accountability (Yoo et al. 2016).

To ensure patient safety, the closed-loop medication administration (CLMA) system with RFID and barcode technology can be implemented in several areas, including but not limited to drug delivery, medication administration, blood products, human milk, and infusion pumps.

An example of the use of CLMA for tracking and monitoring medication infusion pumps. First, a physician's order(s) can be transmitted to a smart pump server after being approved by the pharmacy. The nurse at the bedside uses a scanner on the smart pump (or a third-party scanner) to scan the patient's armband, the medication label, and his/her nursing badge (in the case where a third-party scanner is used, the nurse would also scan the smart pump). This information is then sent wirelessly from the smart pump to the pump server. The pump server, which is electronically linked to the computerized physician order entry (CPOE), the pharmacy information system (PhIS), the positive patient identification (PPID), and/or the electronic medication administration record (eMAR), tethers the administration to the medication order. If the scanned information matches the physician's order, the pump server populates the smart pump's parameters according to the stored doctor's orders. The nurse then reviews the entries and starts the infusion. The automated system transmits the infusion with the associated clinician and patient IDs to the eMAR (Trbovich et al. 2009).

The use of RFID technology is also broadening to smart-room systems when used in conjunction with ultrasound-based real-time location systems (RTLS), workflow software, bedside computer terminals, and EHR systems (Wasserman 2010; Berkowitz and McCarthy 2012). The smart-room system recognizes the staff before they enter a patient's room and then displays the information on a monitor in a room. Caregivers can use the system to view the patient's health information and physicians can check medical information in real time. Wi-Fi RFID tags equipped with temperature and humidity sensors could be embedded in smart-room technology to customize the environment and improve patient comfort (Wasserman 2010).

6.6 Patient Engagement and Experiences

The patient is the most underutilized healthcare resource (Garrido et al. 2016), but recognition of the importance of patient engagement is increasing in health delivery. There is a need to tap the benefits of health technologies to better manage patients and improve their outcomes using patient-empowered tools. In addition, with the ever-increasing amount of patient-generated data from connected medical devices, apps, and sensors, engaging patients via these devices seems like an obvious progression for the healthcare industry.

Health information technologies such as EHR, patient portals, patient engagement platforms, and remote monitoring tools have the greatest potential to empower and enable patients with their own clinical information and self-care for long-term management.

Patient portals represent a gateway to patient engagement and are key to connecting providers and patients outside the office. Patient portals can enhance patient–provider communication and enable patients to check test results, refill prescriptions, review their medical records, and view educational materials. Patient portals can also be used to streamline administrative tasks such as registration, appointment scheduling, and patient reminders (athenahealth 2014). A study from Kaiser Permanente and the National Institute of Health (Sarkar et al. 2014) suggested that patients who used patient portals for prescription refills experienced greater medication adherence and improved outcomes and, in one specific case, patients with diabetes who used an online patient portal to refill medications experienced increased adherence and their cholesterol levels improved. As medication nonadherence is one of the main contributors to healthcare costs, Internet-based patient portals look set to play an important role in healthcare delivery. Kaiser Permanente also offered four key lessons from 10 years of experience with patient portals (Garrido et al. 2016):

- Secure e-mail between patients and physicians supports improved outcomes and patient-centered care.
- Patient portal use positively impacts patient loyalty to the health plan and member satisfaction.
- Evidence of a relationship between secure e-mail and other kinds of utilization is mixed.
- Even with the best intentions, e-health disparities can emerge. Members with the highest rate of registration and use of the portal are between 60 and 68 years old, white (non-Hispanic), and educated to postgraduate level.

The use of mobile technology has the potential to reduce or even eliminate discontinuity in patient care and engagement due to lack of access to other types of technology, such as a computer with Internet connectivity (Heath 2015). Recently, researchers from Stanford University illustrated the feasibility of large-scale smartphone-based data collection (McConnell et al. 2016), which allowed for rapid, large-scale, and detailed assessment of physician activity, fitness, and sleep. However, sustained engagement remained a challenge due to a significant drop in engagement for many participants over the course of the study. Balancing engagement, data feedback, and study design were clear areas for further research, and ideas for improving engagement included EHR integration, more personalization, earlier participant feedback, and an element of "gamification."

The convergence of social and healthcare data and AI technology is likely to spur new and even obvious products such as exercise apps that not only propose exercise schedules, but also the best time to do it and, in turn, coaching to stick to that schedule (Stone et al. 2016). For care of the elderly, in-home health monitoring and health information access will be able to detect changes in mood or behavior and alert caregivers. Personalized rehabilitation and in-home therapy will reduce the need for hospital or care facility stays (Stone et al. 2016)

6.7 Conclusions

With advances in IT, data from EHR, PHR, HIE, personal health devices, and mobile apps are key innovation enablers. Enhanced interoperability between different stakeholders fosters healthcare innovation. Meaningful use of health data and IT systems can achieve the triple aims of healthcare, namely, improving the patient experience, advancing population health, and reducing per capita costs. Also, the growing contribution of health IT will have potential in the delivery and assessment of future healthcare provision and individual patient care.

A health IT system implemented to help promote and ensure patient safety must also cause no harm (Wager et al. 2013). As EHR, PHR, and other health IT systems become more widely deployed and used, it will be critical to develop best practices based on high-level evidence and ongoing quality improvement (Wager et al. 2013).

References

Andrews, J. 2016. Precision medicine: Analytics, data science and EHRs in the new age. *Healthcare IT News*, August 15. Available from: http://www.healthcareitnews.com/news/precision-medicine-analytics-data-science-and-ehrs-new-age.

Aronson, S. J. and H. L. Rehm. 2015. Building the foundation for genomics in precision medicine. *Nature* 526 (7573): 336–342.

Athenahealth. 2014. 5 elements of a successful patient engagement strategy. Available from: https://www.athenahealth.com/whitepapers/patient-engagement-strategies.

Bardach, N. S., J. Huang, R. Brand, and J. Hsu. 2009. Evolving health information technology and the timely availability of visit diagnoses from ambulatory visits: A natural experiment in an integrated delivery system. *BMC Medical Informatics and Decision Making* 9 (1): 1.

Benson, T., and G. Grieve. 2016. *Principles of Health Interoperability: SNOMED CT, HL7 and FHIR*. London: Springer.

Berkowitz, L. and C. McCarthy. 2012. *Innovation with Information Technologies in Healthcare*. New York: Springer Science & Business Media.

Berwick, D. M., T. W. Nolan, and J. Whittington. 2008. The triple aim: Care, health, and cost. *Health Affairs* 27 (3):759–769.

CDC. 2016. Meaningful Use. From Daniels, J. H. Healthcare it adoption, function, value & beyond. December 22. Available from: http://www.himssconference.org/sites/himssconference/files/pdf/VCS3.pdf.

Davis, A.M., M. Benson, D. Cooney, B. Spruell, and J. Orelian. 2011. A matched-cohort evaluation of a bedside asthma intervention for patients hospitalized at a large urban children's hospital. *J. Urban Health* 88 (Suppl. 1):49–60.

Edmunds, M., D. Peddicord, and M. E. Frisse. 2016. Ten reasons why interoperability is difficult. In Charlotte A. Weaver, Marion J. Ball, George R. Kim, Joan M. Kiel (eds) *Healthcare Information Management Systems*, 127–137. Switzerland: Springer.

Garrido, T., B. Raymond, and B. Wheatley. 2016. Lessons from more than a decade in patient portals. Available from: http://healthaffairs.org/blog/2016/04/07/lessons-from-more-than-a-decade-in-patient-portals/.

Goodby, A. W., L. Olsen, and M. McGinnis. 2011. Clinical data as the basic staple of health learning: Creating and protecting a public good: Workshop summary. Washington, DC: National Academies Press.

Heath, S. 2015. Effective patient engagement strategies using health IT. *EHR Intelligence*. Available from: https://ehrintelligence.com/news/effective-patient-engagement-strategies-using-health-it.

HIMSS. 2013. What is interoperability? December 18. Available from: http://www.himss.org/library/interoperability-standards/what-is-interoperability.

Horowitz, J., D. Mon, B. Bernstein, and K. Bell. 2008. Defining key health information technology terms. Washington, DC: Department of Health and Human Services, Office of the National Coordinator for Health Information Technology.

Hoyt, R. E., and A. K. Yoshihashi. 2014. *Health Informatics: Practical Guide for Healthcare and Information Technology Professionals*. San Bernardino, CA: Informatics Education.

IEEE. 2010. Standards Glossary. December 18, 2016. Available from: http://www.ieee.org/education_careers/education/standards/standards_glossary.html.

Impact Advisors. 2014. Emerging technologies in healthcare: A white paper. Naperville, IL: Impact Advisors LLC.

Mandl, K. D., J. C. Mandel, and I. S. Kohane. 2015. Driving innovation in health systems through an apps-based information economy. *Cell Systems* 1 (1):8–13.

McConnell, M. V., A. Shcherbina, A. Pavlovic, et al. 2016. Feasibility of obtaining measures of lifestyle from a smartphone app: The MyHeart counts cardiovascular health study. *JAMA Cardiology*:67–76. doi:10.1001/jamacardio.2016.4395.

ONC. 2015. Connecting health and care for the nation: A shared nationwide interoperability roadmap version 1.0. The Office of the National Coordinator for Health Information Technology.

ONC. 2016. Adoption of electronic health record systems among U.S. non-federal acute care hospitals: 2008–2015. December 23. Available from: https://dashboard.healthit.gov/evaluations/data-briefs/non-federal-acute-care-hospital-ehr-adoption-2008-2015.php.

Piwek, L., D. A. Ellis, S. Andrews, and A. Joinson. 2016. The rise of consumer health wearables: Promises and barriers. *PLoS Medicine* 13 (2):e1001953.
Raths, D. 2016. Mix of applications at showcase to demonstrate FHIR's potential. Available from: http://www.healthcare-informatics.com/blogs/david-raths/mix-applications-showcase-demonstrate-fhir-s-potential.
Reiner, J., and M. Sullivan. 2005. RFID in healthcare: A panacea for the regulations and issues affecting the industry. *Healthcare Purchasing News* 29 (6):74–76.
Sarkar, U., C. R. Lyles, M. M. Parker, et al. 2014. Use of the refill function through an online patient portal is associated with improved adherence to statins in an integrated health system. *Medical Care* 52 (3):194.
Slack, C. 2013. Impact of radio-frequency identification (RFID) technologies on the hospital supply chain: A literature review. *Perspectives in Health Information Management* 10:1.
SMART. 2016. Something new and powerful: SMART on FHIR®. December 17. Available from: http://smarthealthit.org/smart-on-fhir/.
Stone, P., R. Brooks, E. Brynjolfsson, et al. 2016. *Artificial Intelligence and Life in 2030: One Hundred Year Study on Artificial Intelligence: Report of the 2015–2016 Study Panel*. Stanford, CA: Stanford University.
Trbovich, P. L., J. Jeon, and A. Easty. 2009. *Smart Medication Delivery Systems: Infusion Pumps*. Toronto, ON: University Health Network.
Vanderbilt. 2016. SMART precision cancer medicine. December 17, 2016; Available from: http://www.vicc.org/smart-pcm/.
Wager, K. A., F. Wickham Lee, and J. P. Glaser. 2013. *Health Care Information Systems: A Practical Approach for Health Care Management*, 3rd edn. San Francisco, CA: Jossey-Bass.
Wasserman, E. 2010. Health-care facilities embrace RFID. *RFID Journal* 1–7.
West, D. M. 2011. *Enabling Personalized Medicine through Health Information Technology*. Washington, DC: Center for Technology Innovation at Brookings.
Wikipedia. 2016. Fast healthcare interoperability resources. December 17. Available from: https://en.wikipedia.org/wiki/Fast_Healthcare_Interoperability_Resources.
Yoo, S., H. Hwang, and S. Jheon. 2016. Hospital information systems: Experience at the fully digitized Seoul National University Bundang Hospital. *Journal of Thoracic Disease* 8:S637.

Chapter 7

Healthcare Education and Training to Support a Responsive Healthcare System: Canadian Perspectives

Steve Slade, Tanya Horsley, and Andrew Padmos*

Contents

7.1 Introduction 123
7.2 Medical Education Is Rooted in Social Accountability and the Broad Determinants of Health 124
7.3 Regionalization and Academic Health Centers 125
7.4 Interprofessional Healthcare Delivery through Teams 127
7.5 Research, Clinical Investigation, and Data in Education and Training 129
7.6 Leadership, Management, and Governance 130
7.7 Technology-Enabled Learning and Competence-Based Medical Education 130
7.8 Professional Learning and Development, Skills-Upgrading, and Talent Acquisition and Management 131
References 133

7.1 Introduction

Canada's medical care system is a multisector, multiorganization enterprise that establishes and maintains standards of education and healthcare delivery across jurisdictions. Provincial governments are responsible for delivering Canadian healthcare, including oversight of education and training institutions that prepare the health workforce for clinical practice. Although there are

* Please note that the authors comments, observations, opinions, and other expressions are theirs alone; they do not necessarily reflect those of their employers and/or affiliated institutions.

gaps in areas such as pharmacare and dental services, Canadians have the benefit of publicly funded, comprehensive, and universally accessible medical services.

In Canada, physicians are largely remunerated through health insurance plans that are administered by provincial/territorial governments. Governments defer licensing responsibility to profession-led provincial/territorial medical regulatory authorities (MRAs) that are autonomous within their jurisdictions. MRAs, in turn, base licensing decisions on the physician's acquisition of credentials conferred by recognized certifying bodies. Put simply, provincial/territorial governments pay for insured medical services delivered by physicians who are licensed by MRAs. While governments and MRAs bear administrative authority for medical services, other agencies are responsible for developing the education, training, and credentialing system that prepares physicians for practice. The role and function of these latter agencies are the focus of this chapter.

We outline our strengths and weaknesses in building an education and training infrastructure that supports a responsive healthcare system from a Canadian perspective. An overview of the complimentary and converging roles of key organizations and sectors is given. Evolving pedagogies, strategies, and initiatives are explored along the learning continuum from undergraduate and postgraduate medical education to ongoing continuing professional development (CPD). Some common challenges are highlighted, including Canada's lack of progress in implementing models of interprofessional education, supporting the careers of clinician scientists, and systematically planning and gauging the outcomes of health education and training. We start by examining the premise that medical education and training are guided by an overarching commitment to social accountability.

7.2 Medical Education Is Rooted in Social Accountability and the Broad Determinants of Health

The discourse on social accountability in medical education is as active today as it was a century ago. As part of his 1910 study of medical schools in the United States and Canada, Abraham Flexner wrote that "the physician's function is fast becoming social and preventive ... upon him society relies to ascertain, and through measures essentially educational to enforce, the conditions that prevent disease and make positively for physical and moral well-being" (Flexner 1910). More recently, social accountability has crystallized as the cornerstone of medical education. Writing for the World Health Organization in 1995, Charles Boelen and Jeffery Heck defined medical school social accountability as "the obligation to direct their education, research and service activities toward addressing the priority health concerns of the community, region and/or nation they have a mandate to serve" (Boelen and Heck 1995). With the words of Flexner and Boelen and Heck echoing through the twentieth and early twenty-first centuries, social accountability now underpins medical education.

In Canada, new consensus statements on undergraduate and postgraduate medical education identify social accountability as a core value. Medical schools are urged to "respond to the diverse needs of individuals and communities" (Association of Faculties of Medicine of Canada 2010). This overarching goal translates into a number of specific action areas. The review of postgraduate medical education identified the need to "ensure the right mix, distribution, and number of physicians to meet societal needs" (Association of Faculties of Medicine of Canada 2012). Medical schools and government funders have the authority and means to respond by adjusting the number of medical students as well as the allocation of training positions across specialties. Indeed, pan-Canadian and jurisdiction-specific efforts are underway to generate better data and a more coordinated approach to physician workforce planning. These efforts are timely, as numerous signs suggest that Canada has not yet trained the right number and types of physicians.

Canada's history is marked by a cyclical waxing and waning of medical workforce supply. In response to perceived population need, we will, for a time, allow medical class sizes to grow while continuing to recruit international medical graduates (IMGs) into residency training programs as well as directly into fully licensed medical practice. Canada's first-year medical class size doubled between 1997 and 2015 (Association of Faculties of Medicine of Canada 2016a), far outpacing population growth. At the same time, there was a sixfold increase in the number of IMGs entering residency training (Canadian Post-M.D. Education Registry 2016a). Whether or not population healthcare needs are adequately met, periods of physician workforce growth have been slowed or halted for a variety of reasons, including concern about rising healthcare costs and competing social priorities.

Too often, Canadians are perplexed by metrics that juxtapose increased health expenditure and medical workforce growth against poor access to family doctors, excessive surgical wait times, and physician underemployment. If social accountability is linked to getting the physician workforce right in terms of size and specialty mix, then the evidence suggests Canada has room for improvement.

Canada's recent review of medical education and training makes further links between social accountability and the broad determinants of health (Association of Faculties of Medicine of Canada 2012). Patient-centered care demands an understanding and appreciation of patients in their socioeconomic context, including personal characteristics related to education, employment, culture, gender, housing, income, and social status. Healthcare providers are increasingly aware of the importance of cultural competence in providing care to indigenous peoples, immigrant populations, the homeless, and other distinct patient populations. Initial education and training may provide insufficient opportunity to acquire the cognitive and empathic communication skills required to competently care for the diverse patients who will be encountered in future day-to-day practice. These competencies are often acquired on the job after formal training, certification, and licensing. As a result, Canada's medical leaders continue to call for greater "integration of prevention and public health competencies in the MD education curriculum" (Association of Faculties of Medicine of Canada 2010).

Of course, efforts to build a patient-centered workforce are not solely focused on physicians. Other health professions are reflecting on what needs to be done to ensure their training fosters caregivers who meet patient needs. For example, nursing schools see the need to produce graduates "who possess the depth and the breadth of knowledge, skills, and attitudes necessary for an increasingly demanding role" while fostering evidence-based practice to optimize patient outcomes (Canadian Association of Nursing Schools 2010). Pharmacists are calling for educational programs to enable them to support their evolving professional role, one that moves "away from a focus on dispensing medications to one emphasising the provision of patient-centred, outcomes-focused care" (Canadian Pharmacists Association 2016). In this way, health professions see their training programs as the foundation of reliable, socially accountable healthcare that strives to build a steady and adequate supply of highly qualified, highly motivated, and high-potential personnel to serve patients.

7.3 Regionalization and Academic Health Centers

Given Canada's sparsely distributed population, and only a handful of larger towns and cities, it is perhaps not surprising that healthcare delivery has become highly regionalized. As noted in Section 7.1, provincial/territorial governments bear responsibility for publicly funded healthcare services. Responsibility is further delegated to regional health authorities (RHAs) that oversee healthcare delivery within subprovincial geographic areas. RHAs may transfer operational authority to facilities and service providers that focus on local needs such as hospital-based care, long-term care, emergency services, or home care services. In general, RHAs are responsible for the efficient use of public funds in the delivery of healthcare services that respond to local needs.

Medical educators are aware of the challenges faced by regions, and the consensus view is that social accountability can be cultivated through diverse learning and work environment experiences (Association of Faculties of Medicine of Canada 2012). New distributed medical education models are making important inroads into Canada's rural regions. Recent increases in medical school enrolment have been realized, in part, through the creation of regional medical campuses. Affiliated with existing medical schools in large cities, regional campuses are typically situated in smaller centers surrounded by less densely populated areas but with the necessary infrastructure to deliver the full curriculum associated with an undergraduate medical degree. The "necessary" infrastructure includes academic faculty to provide basic science teaching and clinical learning opportunities, administrative staff and university facilities, and the student support services that make regional education and training experiences equivalent to those at the main campuses in large urban centers.

Distributed medical education has advanced rapidly in Canada. In 2005, only two universities had regional medical campuses, the University of Montreal and the University of British Columbia (Association of Faculties of Medicine of Canada 2013). By 2015, eight universities were operating 12 regional campuses in five provinces. Some medical schools have taken a different approach to training physicians for rural healthcare. Established in 2005, the Northern Ontario School of Medicine (NOSM) is designed to deliver a "distinctive model of distributed, community-engaged, and socially accountable medical education" (NOSM 2016a). NOSM is a freestanding medical school (not a regional campus) affiliated with Lakehead University in Thunder Bay and Laurentian University in Sudbury. Having created a network of 70 community partners, NOSM offers an "innovative model of community-engaged medical education and research" (NOSM 2016b). The MD program at Newfoundland and Labrador's Memorial University also features a large rural medical education network that supports the program's commitment to train "physicians with exemplary skills for rural and regional practice" (Memorial University 2016). These educational models produce medical graduates who are more likely to practice in rural and small town communities (Canadian Post-M.D. Education Registry 2016b), and set the stage to look more fully at how distributed education affects rural population health.

Communication technologies are essential in distributed education. NOSM relies on sophisticated videoconferencing technology to connect its network of teaching and healthcare delivery sites. Similarly, the University of British Columbia relies on its videoconferencing bridge to join several medical campuses situated throughout the province. With over 108 programs offered electronically, nursing schools use distance learning technologies that combine

> … print-based modules, interactive web-based learning, and audio- and video-conferencing to provide education closer to home. For students, this means having the support of their family and friends along with the encouragement to stay and work in their communities.
>
> **(Canadian Nurses Association 2013)**

Here again, we see multiple health professions adapting their educational approaches to produce an adequate supply of highly qualified, highly motivated, and high-potential personnel to serve patients in diverse communities.

Academic health centers (AHCs) are inextricably linked to regionalized healthcare and medical education in Canada. A 2010 report defines the AHCs tripartite mission as (1) being focused on timely access to advanced patient care services, (2) training the next generation of healthcare professionals, and (3) conducting cutting-edge research (Brimacombe 2010). For many regions, AHCs function as a hub, referral center, and administrative headquarters for a broad range of healthcare services overseen by RHAs. Medical residents play an important role providing hospital-based care, illustrating the interdependency of regional AHCs and medical faculties. Technologies such as telecare, teletriage, and electronic health records (EHRs) are commonplace in AHCs and give distant communities access to specialty services that, in the past, were only available in large urban centers. Populations benefit from direct patient care and, with an estimated 3.5% of Canada's gross domestic product attributable to medical schools and their affiliated academic centers, much broader social impacts accrue from AHCs (Association of Faculties of Medicine of Canada 2014).

7.4 Interprofessional Healthcare Delivery through Teams

The patient experience of healthcare is multidisciplinary. For a single medical problem, a patient may visit their family doctor for initial diagnosis, followed by referral to one or more specialists; therapeutic treatments may be given by physiotherapists, occupational therapists, or others; pharmacists and social workers may be involved; and the patient may receive ongoing care and monitoring by a nurse practitioner. Recent Canadian studies have looked at how interprofessional collaborative teams and new healthcare delivery models optimize scopes of practice and improve patient-centred care (Canadian Health Services Research Foundation 2012; Canadian Academy of Health Sciences 2014; Minister of Health, Government of Canada, 2015). This area of research will grow as healthcare provider roles continue to evolve.

While the patient experience is multidisciplinary, systems are not necessarily designed to support interprofessional healthcare delivery through teams. Strong forces keep healthcare professions fragmented and siloed in Canada. At the highest level, the Canada Health Act places particular emphasis on medical services provided by physicians in hospitals. The act has little or nothing to say about nurses, psychologists, pharmacists, physiotherapists, and other healthcare providers. As guiding legislation, the Canada Health Act sets the tone for provincial/territorial healthcare systems that concentrate funding on physicians and hospitals. Routine dental services are not covered through public healthcare, and prescription drugs are only covered for senior citizens; these services, and others such as physiotherapy and cognitive behavioral therapy, are paid for out of pocket or by private health insurance or are not accessed at all. The publicly funded healthcare system is not legislated (and likely not adequately resourced) to provide the personal aid and extended home care services that would help Canadians remain in their homes as they age and require escalating levels of healthcare. In this milieu, it is challenging indeed to advance interprofessional, team-based healthcare.

Nevertheless, interprofessional, team-based care is embraced by healthcare providers and health system leaders. For example, the College of Family Physicians of Canada (CFPC) advocates for its "Patient's Medical Home." This is an interprofessional model

> … where a team or network of caregivers, including nurses, physician assistants, and other health professionals—located in the same physical site or linked virtually from different practice sites throughout the local or extended community—work together with the patient's personal family physician to provide and coordinate a comprehensive range of medical and health care services required by each person. It is where

> patient–doctor, patient–nurse, and other therapeutic relationships are developed and strengthened over time, enabling the best possible health outcomes for each person, the practice population, and the community being served.
>
> **(College of Family Physicians of Canada 2016)**

Ontario Family Health Teams (2016) aim to bring together family physicians, nurse practitioners, registered nurses, social workers, dieticians, and other professionals to care for patients through group funding arrangements. Alberta funds primary care networks that bring together physicians and other health providers such as nurses, dieticians, and pharmacists to provide primary healthcare to patients (Alberta Health 2016). Funded by the federal government, the Canadian Partnership Against Cancer is perhaps one the most comprehensive, sustained, and interprofessional efforts to address a specific health condition. These and other interprofessional healthcare efforts are encouraging and could, in time, help to reshape how healthcare is routinely funded and delivered in Canada.

Should interprofessional teams become the prevailing healthcare funding model in Canada, considerable effort would have to be put into restructuring healthcare education and training. At present, healthcare professions are trained in relative isolation of one another. Some Canadian universities have created integrated faculties of health science that administer most or all healthcare programs through a single deanery. It is more common, however, to find faculties of medicine, nursing, and health sciences operating more or less independently. It is difficult to conceive that collaborative, interprofessional healthcare education can occur in an environment where faculties and departments compete for the same resources, yet this is the norm in Canada.

As with frontline healthcare teams, university-based interprofessional health education and training is being fostered in a number of quarters. The University of Manitoba (2017) has created an Office of Interprofessional Collaboration that connects the faculties of dentistry, medicine, nursing, pharmacy, and rehabilitation sciences. Queen's University (2017) has developed instructional resources that provide medical, nursing, and rehabilitation therapy content for interprofessional teaching, learning, and practice. As part of its preceptor e-learning course, Dalhousie University (2017) has developed a module that fosters interprofessional learning. More formally, the University of Laval has implemented mandatory interprofessional training courses. According to the university,

> These inter-faculty courses are under the joint responsibility of the Faculties of Medicine, Nursing Sciences, and Social Sciences. Medical students are paired with colleagues from other health and social science disciplines. In addition, the students must complete an integration project for the Physician, Medicine and Society IV course, supervised by a long-term care nurse. Moreover, the program is given in an integrated complex housing three health science faculties (medicine, pharmacy and nursing sciences) and the Faculty of Medicine includes a Vice-Deanship dedicated to rehabilitation studies.
>
> **(FMEC MD 2015)**

The preceding commentary on AHCs and interprofessional education fits into a broader discourse on the role of learning organizations. Given the matrixed systems in which we work and negotiate decisions, and the rapidly evolving body of evidence on which decisions are based, now, more than ever, organizations need to embody the ethos of being learning organizations. While multiple definitions exist, learning organizations are often seen as places "where people continually expand their capacities to create the results they truly desire, where new and expansive patterns of thinking are nurtured, where collective aspiration is set free, and where people are continually learning how to learn together" (Senge 2006). In realizing this role, learning organizations foster interprofessional care and work to produce a highly qualified and highly motivated workforce to serve patients.

7.5 Research, Clinical Investigation, and Data in Education and Training

Canada prides itself as being a leader in research and innovation across the full spectrum of health and life sciences, including advances in drug and health technologies and health workforce and systems. Its active response to the severe acute respiratory syndrome (SARS) outbreak in 2003 showcased the excellence of Canadian scientists who, in only 11 weeks, sequenced the SARS genome and expedited the development of vaccines and a treatment in unprecedented time. Canada reaffirmed its role as a world leader through the role played by Canadian scientists in developing antibodies to treat Ebola in the 2016 outbreak. These achievements are exemplars of Canada's scientist community and underscore the importance of partnerships between the Canadian government—namely, the Canadian Institutes of Health Research (CIHR) and the Public Health Agency of Canada (PHAC)—and researchers from across Canada.

Academic institutions have historically been the main beneficiaries of health research funding; however, funding, particularly from the funding Councils, has remained stagnate with no increases announced for 2017. The impacts of decreased funding have been consequential and, while the issues are complex and stem from multiple impediments, downstream effects include fewer researchers, particularly physician scientists. Physician scientists provide a unique and invaluable lens through which biomedical research questions can be raised and researched. Historically, they have also played an irreplaceable role in translating research into practice to the benefit of patient health outcomes.

The translation of theory and data from biomedical research has demonstrable and quantifiable impacts on healthcare and delivery and can take many forms and approaches (Shojania et al. 2002). Research translation materializes into behaviors that can significantly reduce clinical variation and addresses important sources of cognitive error through evidence-informed practices. Beyond the carefully curated data provided through research, there is an increased expectation to use patient data available to physicians through EHRs as a means of re-shaping clinical practice and directing continuous learning. This is, however, challenging, and requires multiple competencies and perspectives (across healthcare professionals) to both interpret and apply findings. Will our education and healthcare systems be able to fully realize functional and operational changes necessary to support the new clinician as data analyst? With so many competing priorities placed on curricula and the faculty who are entrusted to ensure its delivery, how do we nurture clinicians who can expertly interpret predictive algorithms generated from their practice?

The chronic challenges associated with Canada's national funding infrastructure, and specifically the removal of funding support for the MD/PhD Awards Program (2015), has raised concerns at the highest levels of government, catalyzing a number of initiatives to explore and address issues. Led by Dr. David Naylor, Canada launched a review of its research enterprise, including the nation's primary granting councils (CIHR, the Natural Sciences and Engineering Research Council [NSERC], the Social Sciences Health Research Council [SSHRC]) and the Canada Foundation for Innovation (CFI), Canada Research Chairs, and Genome Canada. The Naylor report outlines 35 key recommendations including new coordinating mechanisms of the four major research funding bodies as well as a phased increase to the federal budget for research related activities totaling 1.3 billion dollars (Advisory Panel for the Review of Federal Support for Fundamental Science, 2017).

Another battleground is the future of biomedical researcher education and training. The Association of Faculties of Medicine of Canada (AFMC) has expressed concern related to training and education for the next generation of health researchers in Canada (Association of Faculties of Medicine of Canada 2016b). Issues related to funding, training, collaboration, and engagement are echoed by the Canadian Consensus Conference for Clinician Scientists, a consortium of the AFMC, the College of Family Physicians of Canada, and the Royal College of Physicians and Surgeons of Canada (RCPSC). These national organizations align deeply in their shared vision of education and training excellence across the medical education continuum. Shared success between these organizations could realize a successful strategy for attracting, training, and sustaining a substantive pipeline of career clinician scientists.

7.6 Leadership, Management, and Governance

As outlined throughout this chapter, Canada's healthcare system may be described as one of locally provided healthcare services overseen by regionalized health authorities accountable to the public via a civil service bureaucracy that is answerable to political leaders.

Many would argue that Canada does not have a healthcare system per se, but rather a patchwork of local, regional, and provincial authorities responsible for healthcare delivery. Pointing to the weaknesses of a federated system, some would argue that competing interests vie for recognition and funding, operating without coherent and cohesive programs to manage the perspectives and interests of health profession, patient, and other advocacy groups. It is difficult to effect change and drive down costs through process engineering reforms such as using less expensive staff, due to the barriers of professional training, certification, and licensure. In this line of argument we see failings of management and governance in the healthcare system; we also see in it the leadership challenges facing Canada.

Nevertheless, there are signs of change in response to population and patient needs. In 2016, the newly elected prime minister of Canada issued a very public mandate letter to the federal minister of health calling for increased effort to advance home care, pharmacare, and mental healthcare. Partially in response to the burden of increased health expenditure, and recognizing overlapping provider roles, there is a growing expectation of standardized clinical services and supports to enable the introduction of clinical assistants and extenders (e.g., nurse practitioners, paramedics, and anesthesiology technicians) who will provide more and improved services at lower cost with better outcomes. There are also early indications that medical authorities are looking critically at the system of privileging physicians as quasi-autonomous members of medical staff. Some health system leaders and managers would move medical staff toward employment contracts, which take physicians away from traditional fee-for-service compensation models. The pros and cons of these changes are oft debated, but it is certain that an active dialog is underway in Canada.

7.7 Technology-Enabled Learning and Competence-Based Medical Education

Canada is a leader in competency-based medical education. Founded on CanMEDS roles, the RCPSC leads efforts to implement "Competence by Design" (CBD), a vision of learning and practice that spans medical careers from residency to retirement. CBD begins with mapping out learning milestones and entrustable professional acts (EPAs) that uniquely define specialty and subspecialty training. A CBD approach to residency education entails the development of a curriculum that centers on the attainment of specialty-specific milestones and EPAs, as developed by national specialty committees and leaders within each specialty and subspecialty discipline. Canada's transition to CBD is the largest and most comprehensive pedagogical change undertaken by medical educators since the change ignited by Abraham Flexner over a century ago.

The University of Toronto's Division of Orthopaedic Surgery served as a pilot project for competency-based residency training. Prompted in part by reduced training opportunities for residents, the University of Toronto's program is based on a number of competency principles including "progression through training based on demonstration of competency rather than a time based approach; early development of technical skills; frequent and rigorous assessment and feedback and elimination of non-productive educational time" (University of Toronto 2017). These principles feature prominently in the broader evolution toward competency-based residency training.

Broad success will depend in part on technologies to support CBD implementation. To this end, the RCPSC has developed the e-Portfolio, an electronic tool that allows learners, preceptors, and administrators to track learning progress. Tracking is centered on milestones and EPAs, and the tool standardizes evaluation metrics while allowing open-ended feedback on performance and learning objectives. While initial development of the e-Portfolio focuses on residency training, the technology is being developed to support and guide lifelong learning.

A thorough review of the diverse technologies that support today's residency training is well beyond the scope of this brief chapter; however, something must be said about the role of simulation in medical education. Simulation takes many forms, and traditional standardized patient and role-playing approaches have evolved to reflect greater medical and situational complexity. The props that are used in simulation—instruments, models, mannequins, and the like—have become increasingly sophisticated. The artificial intelligence, adaptability, and graphical renderings of computer-based learning tools continue to become more lifelike. Learning technology has come a long way indeed.

In Canada, simulation tools have become an essential part of undergraduate and postgraduate medical education. The doubling of medical class sizes has had a predictable impact on learning opportunities for medical students and patients. A growing number of learners vie for increasingly sparse opportunities to experience the clinical scenarios they will face in future practice. Simulation provides content for that experiential gap. Moreover, simulation brings greater uniformity and standardization to the learning experience in terms of instructional content, as well as to the assessment data and feedback given to learners. It is difficult to imagine medical education without the simulation aids we now rely on.

7.8 Professional Learning and Development, Skills-Upgrading, and Talent Acquisition and Management

As of 2012, the Canadian Institute for Health Information maintained workforce information for 27 health profession groups (Canadian Institute for Health Information 2012). Each of these groups is regulated in one or more Canadian jurisdictions, and all are supported by one or more professional healthcare organizations. Due, perhaps, to the breadth of care they provide and the risk/benefit they pose to population health, physicians are the health profession for which most information is available. As with the preceding sections of this chapter, this final piece focuses on what we know about the medical workforce.

Medical regulators typically require physicians to participate in the CPD programs of the College of Family Physicians of Canada, the RCPSC, or the Collége des Médecins du Québec. The maintenance of certification (MoC) program of the RCPSC supports lifelong learning and enhancement of professional competence, covering activities such as: (1) knowledge management, (2) learning with practice data, and (3) professional contributions. The first of these activities—knowledge management—has been the focus of traditional CPD programming. Quite rightly, this area acknowledges the rapid evolution of science and technology as applied to professional practice and the consequent imperative of "keeping up" and "staying ahead." From the patient and regulatory perspective, knowledge management and medical expertise are paramount.

The latter two CPD activities—learning with practice data and professional contributions—are at a more aspirational stage of development within CPD support programs. As part of its competency-based CPD initiative, the RCPSC is beginning to look at how clinical practice data can prompt new insights and drive quality improvement. Multisource feedback, patient satisfaction surveys, patient and population outcomes data, and electronic medical records (EMRs) are among the many resources that are being studied and developed as supports for practice excellence. Consideration of professional contributions and probity become increasingly important as the course of medical careers becomes better understood. As per the earlier reflection on healthcare management and governance, physicians make important contributions to the health of their disciplines, be it through teaching, research, or other nonclinical activities. Participation in national specialty societies, professional colleges, RHAs, and the like reflect a commitment to stewardship and probity. These laudable activities are part of CPD and underpin the privilege of professional autonomy.

The agencies, programs, and technologies that monitor medical CPD are part of a complex system that aims to produce a steady and adequate supply of highly qualified, highly motivated, and high-potential personnel to serve patients. CPD programs like the RCPSC's MoC program can and will be enhanced to support physicians in the pursuit of competency-based practice. At the same time, the instructional content of lifelong learning—CPD offerings themselves—will need to be brought into greater alignment with physicians' learning needs, which, in a competency-based model, are inextricably linked to patient and population health needs. Such an undertaking will require the coordinated efforts of CPD providers, government funders, researchers, and other health system stakeholders.

This last reflection on the need for a coordinated effort among broad stakeholders brings us full circle. Social accountability is accepted as the foundation and *raison d'être* of health professionals' education. A common sense of purpose and commitment to patients, to society, and to science and learning is key to ensuring education and training to support a responsive healthcare system. Where change is necessary, it will be necessary to overcome the weight of legislation, entrenched practices, risk intolerance, vested interests, and inertia. We have argued that change can be leveraged through strategies and initiatives that foster interprofessional education; competency-based learning and practice; research and the careers of clinician scientists; and improved data and evidence to evaluate the outcomes of medical education and training. Canada is at various stages in moving each of these areas forward, and sustained attention and effort will be necessary to ensure we continue to do so.

References

Advisory Panel for the Review of Federal Support for Fundamental Science. 2017. Investing in Canada's future: Strengthening the foundations of Canadian research. http://www.sciencereview.ca/eic/site/059.nsf/vwapj/ScienceReview_April2017-rv.pdf/$file/ScienceReview_April2017-rv.pdf.

Alberta Health. 2016. Primary care networks review. http://www.health.alberta.ca/documents/PCN-Review-2016.pdf

Association of Faculties of Medicine of Canada. 2010. *The Future of Medical Education in Canada (FMEC): A Collective Vision for MD Education*. Ottowa, Canada: Association of Faculties of Medicine of Canada (AFMC).

Association of Faculties of Medicine of Canada. 2012. *Future of Medical Education in Canada Postgraduate Project: Public Report*. Ottawa, Canada: Association of Faculties of Medicine of Canada.

Association of Faculties of Medicine of Canada. 2013. Canadian medical education statistics. https://afmc.ca/sites/default/files/documents/en/Publications/CMES/Archives/CMES2013Vol35.pdf

Association of Faculties of Medicine of Canada. 2014. The economic impact of Canada's faculties of medicine and health science centres. https://afmc.ca/pdf/Economic_Impact_Study_Report_FINAL_EN.pdf

Association of Faculties of Medicine of Canada. 2016a. Canadian medical education statistics. https://afmc.ca/sites/default/files/CMES2016-reduced.pdf

Association of Faculties of Medicine of Canada. 2016b. A re-envisioning of health research in Canada. https://afmc.ca/sites/default/files/documents/AFMC_Research_Position_Paper_EN.pdf

Boelen, C., and J. E. Heck. 1995. *Defining and Measuring the Social Accountability of Medical Schools*. Geneva, Switzerland: World Health Organization.

Brimacombe, G. 2010. Three missions one future: Optimizing the performance of Canada's academic health sciences centres. A report from the National Task Force on the future of Canada's academic health sciences centres. Available from: ahscntf. org/docs/AHSCs/NTF% 20Report/Final% 20Report/05.30-NTF-EN-FINAL.pdf. Accessed November 8, 2013.

Canadian Association of Nursing Schools. 2010. The case for healthier Canadians: Nursing workforce education for the 21st century. http://casn.ca/wp-content/uploads/2014/12/CASN2010draftJune1.pdf

Canadian Health Services Research Foundation. 2012. http://www.cfhi-fcass.ca/Libraries/Commissioned_Research_Reports/Virani-Interprofessional-EN.sflb.ashx

Canadian Institute for Health Information. 2012. Canada's health care providers, 1997 to 2011: A reference guide. https://secure.cihi.ca/estore/productSeries.htm?locale=en&pc=PCC56

Canadian Nurses Association. 2013. Meeting future healthcare needs through innovations in nursing education. Policy brief #2. https://www.cna-aiic.ca/~/media/cna/files/en/hhr_policy_brief2_e.pdf?la=en

Canadian Pharmacists Association. 2016. Toward an optimal future: Priorities for action. http://www.pharmacists.ca/cpha-ca/assets/File/pharmacy-in-canada/Thought%20Leadership%20Summit%20Research%20Report_01.pdf

Canadian Post-M.D. Education Registry. 2016a. Annual census of post-M.D. trainees (Table F-1 in reports from 1997/98 to 2015/16). https://caper.ca/en/post-graduate-medical-education/annual-census/

Canadian Post-M.D. Education Registry. 2016b. Fact sheet: Initial practice locations. https://caper.ca/~assets/FactSheetonInitialPracticeLocationB.pdf

College of Family Physicians of Canada. 2016. A vision for Canada: Family practice, the patient's medical home. http://www.cfpc.ca/uploadedFiles/Resources/Resource_Items/PMH_A_Vision_for_Canada.pdf

Dalhousie University. 2017. Preceptor eLearning Course. Module 5: Fostering interprofessional learning. http://preceptor.healthprofessions.dal.ca/?page_id=1608

Flexner, A. 1910. *Medical Education in the United States and Canada: A Report Submitted to the Carnegie Foundation for the Advancement of Teaching*. New York: The Carnegie Foundation for the Advancement of Teaching.

FMEC MD. 2015. Five years of innovations at Canadian medical schools. https://afmc.ca/pdf/fmec/FMEC-MD-2015.pdf

Northern Ontario School of Medicine. 2016a. About NOSM. http://www.nosm.ca/about_us/default.aspx

Northern Ontario School of Medicine. 2016b. Innovative education and research for a healthier North". http://www.nosm.ca/about_us/default.aspx

Memorial University. 2016. Rural medical education network. https://www.med.mun.ca/RMEN/Home.aspx

Minister of Health, Government of Canada. 2015. Unleashing innovation: Excellent healthcare for Canada. Report of the Advisory Panel on Healthcare Innovation. http://healthycanadians.gc.ca/publications/health-system-systeme-sante/report-healthcare-innovation-rapport-soins/alt/report-healthcare-innovation-rapport-soins-eng.pdf.

Ontario Family Health Teams. 2016. Family health teams. http://www.health.gov.on.ca/en/pro/programs/fht/

Queen's University. 2017. Interprofessional education resources. http://healthsci.queensu.ca/education/oipep/

Senge, P. M. 2006. *The Fifth Discipline: The Art and Practice of the Learning Organization*. New York: Currency Doubleday.

Shojania, K. G., B. W. Duncan, K. M. McDonald, and R. M. Wachter. 2002. Safe but sound: Patient safety meets evidence-based medicine. *JAMA* 288 (4):508–513.

University of Manitoba. 2017. Interprofessional collaboration. http://umanitoba.ca/faculties/health_sciences/education/ipc/about_ipc.html

University of Toronto. 2017. Message from the program director. http://orthopaedics.utoronto.ca/about/program_director.htm

Chapter 8

Integration of Primary Healthcare and Hospitals

F.D. Richard Hobbs and Clare J. Taylor

Contents

8.1 What Is Primary Care? ... 136
8.2 Acute Illness Care ... 137
8.2.1 Chronic Disease Prevention and Management ... 138
8.3 Chronic Disease Management Case Studies in Cardiovascular Disease ... 139
8.3.1 Case Study 1: Cardiovascular Disease Prevention ... 139
8.3.1.1 Scale of Cardiovascular Disease ... 139
8.3.1.2 Role of Primary Care in CVD Prevention ... 140
8.3.2 Case Study 2: Stroke Prevention in Atrial Fibrillation ... 141
8.3.2.1 Scale of Atrial Fibrillation-Related Stroke ... 141
8.3.2.2 Role of Primary Care in AF Stroke Prevention ... 141
8.4 Multimorbidity ... 142
8.5 Women's Health ... 143
8.5.1 Contraception ... 144
8.5.2 Abnormal Uterine Bleeding and Pelvic Pain ... 144
8.5.3 Infertility ... 144
8.5.4 Obstetric Care ... 145
8.5.5 Menopause ... 145
8.5.6 Suspected Gynecological Cancers ... 145
8.6 Child Health ... 146
8.6.1 Routine Surveillance and Vaccinations ... 147
8.6.2 Child Protection ... 147
8.6.3 Serious Illness ... 148
8.6.4 Chronic Diseases in Children ... 148

8.6.5 Mental Health 148
8.6.6 Summary 149
8.7 Academic Primary Care 149
8.8 Acknowledgments 149
References 149

8.1 What Is Primary Care?

Definitions of primary care vary across health systems. Primary care is sometimes misleadingly referred to as the first point of contact healthcare, whether Accident and Emergency (A&E; the Emergency Department [ED]) in tertiary care hospitals or the assistance of a birthing care worker in remote communities. Such first-contact care does not, in isolation, meet a modern definition of primary care, which requires a number of elements in addition to the first point of contact: local accessibility for a definable community, continuity of care over time, coordination of care with social agencies and hospitals, a focus on population health as well as individual care, and, crucially, a focus on prevention as much as treatment. In many highly developed healthcare systems, primary care is also the gatekeeper to accessing hospital care and the access point to some medically determined social benefits. A&E may provide urgent or rescue-first care, but this does not constitute primary care.

Provision of at least some of these elements of care is important to health systems, since there is evidence that the greater the measurable delivery of primary care, the better the health outcomes and the lower the health system costs. In many parts of the world, primary care development has been accompanied by investment in multidisciplinary teams (such as with doctors, nurses, pharmacists, or counselors) working together within the community and sometimes in the same building. Within primary care, the medical role (primary care physician or general practitioner [GP] in the United Kingdom) varies by system but is mostly designated *general practice* or *family medicine*, though some would argue that internal medicine partially meets the definition, as do some community-based specialists. The skill sets needed to provide primary care have evolved the medical role such that most generalist medicine is now the domain of primary, not hospital, care. This generalist shift has secondarily enabled superspecialization in hospitals, by releasing the burden of major illness identification and follow-up from hospitals and releasing clinical time for the extraordinary technical advances in personal healthcare seen today.

However, systematically managing more complex disease in the community and diagnosing important illness earlier and more accurately requires an important interface with hospitals. This is not just in relation to referral to specialist services, but also open (unrestricted) access to laboratory and imaging tests to better phenotype illness and avoid the risks associated with diagnoses being made on purely clinical signs and symptoms. Access to hospital investigations for primary care is best accompanied by health system guidelines on what circumstances or types of presentation should prompt testing, to limit the risks of overinvestigation and, indeed, underinvestigation. Both extremes pose risks for patients and costs to health systems. Examples of such diagnostic algorithms include the Wells score (Wells et al. 2003) (see Figure 8.1) for those in whom pulmonary thromboembolism may need excluding, or the Ottawa (ankle) rule for imaging a painful ankle after trauma (Stiell et al. 1992), where algorithm validation on patients in the setting in which it is to be applied is essential (Stiell et al. 1993).

This interdependency of healthcare elements between primary, secondary (hospital), tertiary (superspecialist), and indeed social care requires balance and integration. This is an increasing challenge for most health systems, as the costs of providing ever more advanced specialist care for a

Clinical feature	*Points*
Active cancer (treatment ongoing, within six months, or palliative	1
Paralysis, paresis, or recent plaster immobilization of the lower extremities	1
Recently bedridden for three days or more or major surgery within 12 weeks requiring general or regional anesthesia	1
Localized tenderness along the distribution of the deep venous system	1
Entire leg swollen	1
Calf swelling at least 3 cm larger than asymptomatic side	1
Pitting edema confined to the symptomatic leg	1
Collateral superficial veins (non-varicose)	1
Previously documented DVT	1
An alternative diagnosis is at least as likely as DVT	−2
Clinical probability simplified score	
DVT likely	**2 points or more**
DVT unlikely	**1 points or less**

Figure 8.1 Example of a validated clinical decision rule: the two-level DVT Wells score. (Adapted with permission from Wells PS, et al. Evaluation of D-dimer in the diagnosis of suspected deep-vein thrombosis, *N Engl J Med.* 2003;349(13):1227–35.)

minority of the population has eroded the proportion of healthcare expenditure available to focus on disease prevention and illness management for the majority. Unfortunately, coupled with the perceived lower status of primary care as a career choice in many countries, there is an undersupply of primary care physicians at a time of rising service demand and pressure on hospitals. This is exacerbated by the rapidly rising social needs of increasingly comorbid, elderly populations, leading to difficulties in discharging patients. It has never been more important to integrate health and social service provision at every level.

8.2 Acute Illness Care

The need for well-trained generalists is exemplified by the diagnostic challenges of managing presentations of acute illness in primary care. The commonest presentations are for musculoskeletal problems, other painful conditions (especially headache), and acute infections. The principal diagnostic challenges are similar: to separate the serious from the manageable against the characteristics of the presentation with the epidemiologically driven prior probabilities of more important but rarer causes of acute illness. Investigating every headache with imaging might, for example, identify all tumors early but at huge cost to the health system, the environment, and the overinvestigated people who may have unrelated artifacts identified that either do not require management or that no one knows how to manage.

For musculoskeletal diseases, primary care can relieve symptoms and promote recovery through advice as well as medication, and sometimes via access to specialist services such as physiotherapy. Further investigation of acute injuries or chronic joint degeneration acts as an important gatekeeper to limit imaging or referral to patients whose symptoms either do not resolve in an expected timescale or worsen. However, early detection and specialist treatment of acute inflammatory disease also mandates that primary care can differentiate signs and provides early diagnostic work-up in such cases.

Attempting to differentiate viral from bacterial illness is a critical new priority for health systems, due to the need to reduce antibiotic resistance, and requires much more careful use of antibiotics (and a complete ban on their use in animals as growth promoters). This must be implemented in primary care, where most infections present and where the use of rapid diagnostics can help (where available) (Bisno et al. 2002), where time for resolution and review is easier for patients (Little et al. 2014), and where diagnostic skills can be augmented by experience or validated symptom scores (Fine et al. 2012; Little et al. 2013; Hay et al. 2016). However, primary care is equally crucial for the recognition of rare devastating illness such as bacterial meningitis in children, where detection at the earliest possible opportunity may be key to survival. Clinical acumen remains a critical skill for the generalist.

Of course, a further health system priority in managing infection risk is better prevention, especially through immunization programs. In many countries, this represents a population role integrated into a surveillance activity in primary care, such as influenza vaccination alongside elderly health checks or childhood immunization schedules alongside child development clinics. In addition to such routine clinic prevention, primary care must also provide systematic mechanisms to ensure full population coverage of immunization programs. This generally requires some method of identifying the target population (such as asthmatic patients eligible for annual influenza vaccination) and then the use of a call and recall system to invite the patient and remind those nonresponding. Such mechanisms, when integrated into primary care with a registered patient list, offer effective and efficient population-level prevention, whether for immunization or disease screening (such as cervical cancer cytology). Some systems will provide such prevention through school-based clinics or national advertisement programs, but coverage for all population prevention activities will be greatest and cheapest when integrated with well-organized primary care.

8.2.1 Chronic Disease Prevention and Management

Since the 1980s, the greatest change for primary care roles has been in chronic disease prevention and diagnosis, and it is this focus that has most enabled superspecialization in hospitals. Most of the diagnoses and subsequent management of major diseases that afflict patients and cost health systems are now possible in primary care, including hypertension, asthma, chronic obstructive pulmonary disease (COPD), diabetes, skin disorders, and heart failure.

Such chronic diseases have become more prevalent as causes of early mortality have declined and as populations adopt unhealthier lifestyles. Indeed, the World Health Organization (WHO) has shifted its primary focus from communicable disease, malnutrition, and unsanitary conditions to noncommunicable diseases (NCDs), since these disorders are now the globally dominant preventable causes of disease. The primary prevention of these most disabling (and therefore costly) events through the identification and treatment of disease risk factors is a key primary care role alongside the secondary prevention of decline or subsequent events in those unfortunate enough to suffer disease end points. This is best illustrated by case studies of primary care systems, and we have selected prevention of cardiovascular disease (CVD) as an example, given that the WHO has identified CVD outcomes as the most important NCD globally. The 10 leading diseases and risk factors are shown in Figure 8.2.

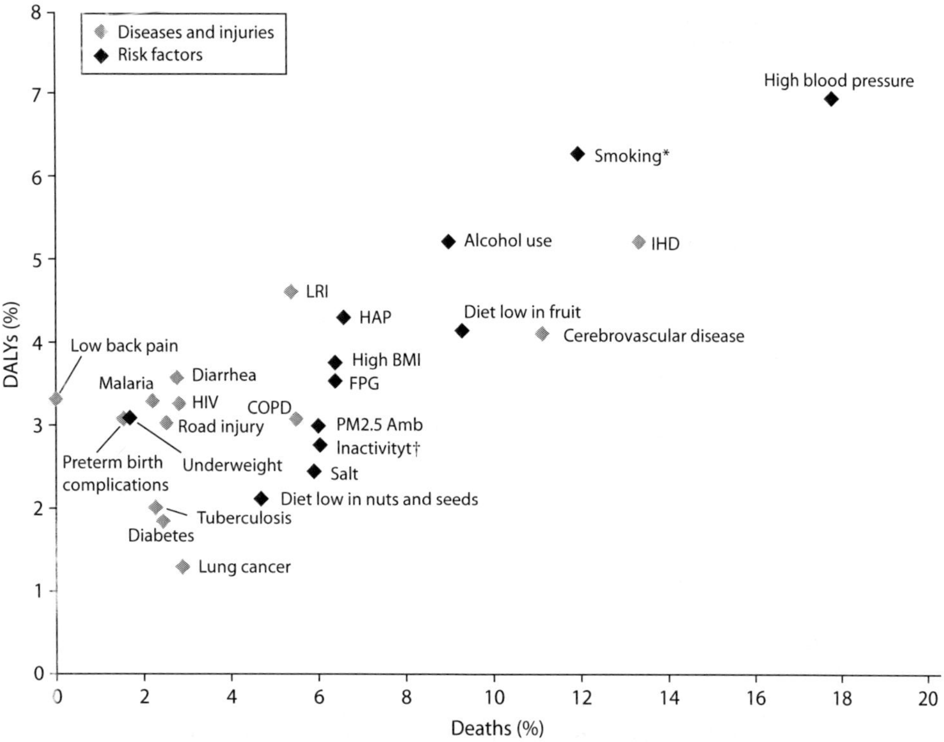

Figure 8.2 Comparison of leading diseases/injuries and leading risk factors on percentage of deaths/disability-adjusted life years (DALYs). (From Lozano et al., *Lancet* 380, 9,859, 2013.)

8.3 Chronic Disease Management Case Studies in Cardiovascular Disease

8.3.1 Case Study 1: Cardiovascular Disease Prevention

8.3.1.1 Scale of Cardiovascular Disease

- CVD remains the leading cause of global morbidity and mortality (Mortality and Causes of Death Collaborators 2015). The risk factors of abnormal lipids, smoking, hypertension, diabetes, abdominal obesity, poor diet and irregular physical exercise account for more than 90% of the CVD risk in epidemiological studies (Yusuf et al. 2004).
- The commonest risk factor for CVD is hypertension, with a global prevalence estimated at 26.4% (972 million adults) in 2000 and a predicted rise of 60% to a total of 1.56 billion adults (29.2%) by 2025 (Kearney et al. 2005). A major predictor of coronary heart disease (CHD) and stroke (Kannel 1996; Lewington et al. 2002), international guidelines highlight the management of hypertension (Mancia et al. 2013; James et al. 2014) based on huge clinical trial data sets (Turnbull et al. 2005) showing that a net blood pressure (BP) reduction of 10–12 mmHg systolic BP and 5–6 mmHg diastolic BP reduces stroke incidence by 38% and CHD by 16% (Mortality and Causes of Death Collaborators 2015). In absolute terms, treating 1,000 patients in four five-year CV risk groups observed in the placebo arms of trials (five-year risks of <11%, 11%–15%, 15%–21%, >21%) with BP-lowering treatment for

five years would prevent 14 (95% confidence intervals (CI) 8–21), 20 (8–31), 24 (8–40), and 38 (16–61) cardiovascular events, respectively ($p = 0.04$ for trend) (Blood Pressure Lowering Treatment Trialists et al. 2014).

- Interventions that lower low-density lipoprotein (LDL)-C concentrations are also proven to significantly reduce the incidence of CHD and other major vascular events in a wide range of individuals. A meta-analysis of 14 statin trials showed that for every 40 mg/dL (1 mmol/L) decrease in LDL-C, a 21% decrease in CHD risk after one year of treatment was achieved (Cholesterol Treatment Trialists et al. 2010). These data are incorporated into clinical guidance such as the American Heart Association/American College of Cardiology (AHA/ACC) (Stone et al. 2014) and National Cholesterol Education Program (NCEP) Adult Treatment Panel (ATP) III guidelines in the United States (Grundy et al. 2004), the Joint Task Force of European Societies guidelines in Europe (Piepoli et al. 2016), and the National Institute for Health and Care Excellence (NICE) in the United Kingdom, which all recognize the importance of dyslipidemia, as well as hypertension and smoking, as the main risk factors for CVD. They also provide practical tools (Framingham, SCORE, and QRisk 10-year CVD risk algorithms, respectively) to assist short-term risk estimation in individuals without prior cardiovascular disease, though there remain many barriers to guideline implementation in routine clinical practice (Graham et al. 2006).

8.3.1.2 Role of Primary Care in CVD Prevention

- Primary care is critical to the implementation and success of CVD prevention programs, identifying those without established CVD, and assessing their eligibility for intervention based on their risk profile.
- This necessitates case finding of CV risk factors, such as through opportunistic measurement of BP during consultations for other problems or asking about smoking or weight at the end of consultations. All adults should have occasional BP checks, enquiries about lifestyle, and at least one screening lipid check from age 40 onward.
- Earlier surveillance should occur in anyone with a family history of premature vascular disease (before 55 in men or 60 in women), those with diabetes, or smokers.
- Anyone with risk factors should be risk assessed using any validated CVD risk score such as Framingham, SCORE, or QRisk. Thresholds for instigating preventive therapy vary by country. Assessment of high-risk patients may be performed using preexisting clinic population data, generating a list of individuals ranked in terms of their likelihood to score highly on a formal vascular risk assessment, and enabling physicians to reduce costs by calling in the most appropriate patients first.
- This approach requires a robust electronic patient database and needs significant financial support; however, it is inclusive of all patients and provides a rational approach to identifying patients most likely to derive benefit from treatment in a priority sequence.
- Embedded CVD risk calculators can automatically provide a CVD risk score based on data extracted from the patient's electronic record. For example: (1) in New Zealand, system improvements in primary care practice software were highly successful, increasing the CVD risk assessment screening rate from 4.7% to 53.5% over 12 months ($n = 6{,}570$) (Sinclair and Kerr 2006); and (2) integration of a web-based decision support system (PREDICT-CVD) with primary care electronic medical record software improved CVD risk documentation fourfold in a primary care practice of 3,564 patients (Wells et al. 2008).

- Although general practice will, in most countries, have a unique role in screening or identifying those patients eligible for CVD primary prevention, primary care also has an essential role in better monitoring and follow-up of those patients identified at high risk and warranting interventions. The implementation strategies for better uptake of lifestyle advice and therapeutic interventions are common across primary and secondary care.
- Following initiation of CVD preventive therapies and advice on smoking cessation, weight control, and increased exercise, primary care has a key role in monitoring risk factor control and therapy compliance, which is best achieved through structured follow-up clinics.

8.3.2 Case Study 2: Stroke Prevention in Atrial Fibrillation

8.3.2.1 Scale of Atrial Fibrillation-Related Stroke

- In terms of stroke prevention, alongside detection and management of hypertension and other vascular risks, the most important strategy is the diagnosis and stroke risk stratification and management of atrial fibrillation (AF).
- AF is the commonest cardiac arrhythmia, with about 1%–2% of the general population estimated to be affected (Camm et al. 2012). It is a particularly common disorder in the elderly, with over 5% over the age of 65 and 10% of people over the age of 75 suffering from AF (Hobbs et al. 2005; Heeringa et al. 2006), with the prevalence predicted to rise (Fuster et al. 2011; Rahman et al. 2016).
- Patients with AF are at an almost fivefold higher risk of stroke compared with age-matched individuals in normal sinus rhythm (Wolf et al. 1991), as well as at twice as high risk of all-cause mortality and heart failure. About 20% of all ischemic strokes are attributable to embolism as a result of AF (Albers et al. 2004).
- Not only do patients with AF have more strokes, they also develop more recurrent and severe strokes regardless of age (Jorgensen et al. 1996) and are more likely to be left with long-term disability and require long-term care (Lin et al. 1996; Lamassa et al. 2001).
- Preventing stroke should be one of the most important priorities of any healthcare system. It is a devastating outcome for patients and their families, second only to cancer in terms of what patients most want to avoid (or at least after surviving a stroke). Managing stroke and its sequelae has huge cost implications for health and social care systems.

8.3.2.2 Role of Primary Care in AF Stroke Prevention

- Fortunately, there are very effective treatment options to significantly attenuate this AF stroke risk, with recent guideline updates in the United States, Europe, and the United Kingdom converging over the evidence guiding their recommendations.
- However, repeated audits in these same countries continue to show underdiagnosis of AF and undermanagement of stroke risk, despite the huge evidence base. Most variation occurs in general practice, where there is often less understanding of the evidence base, differing perceptions on the generalizability of the evidence base compared with specialists, or greater concerns over the risks of treatments than the benefits.
- The European Primary Care Cardiovascular Society (EPCCS) has published practical guidance on how to implement the largely specialist-derived guidelines in stroke prevention in AF (SPAF) in primary care (Hobbs et al. 2016b). These make recommendations based on the trade-off between the benefits and harms of any intervention, taking into account the

quality of the underpinning evidence, and therefore denote the certainty with which the statements are made. They also stress the importance of discussion with the patient about the risks and benefits of the interventions and, critically, their values and preferences.

- SPAF defines six areas for policy development for primary care: (1) how to identify patients with AF; (2) how to determine their stroke risk (a validated clinical risk score is shown in Figure 8.3); (3) whether to recommend modification of this risk; (4) what management options are available, with practical recommendations on maximizing benefit; (5) minimizing risk if anticoagulation is recommended (see the anticoagulation risk score in Figure 8.4); and (6) the reasons why antiplatelet therapy is no longer recommended.
- The full guidance is available on the EPCCS website (http://www.epccs.eu), which provides downloads, highlights the summary recommendations, and indicates where the position taken is clearly evidence-based (green) and where it is more inferred and consensus-based (blue). It also specifies studies carried out in primary care settings and, therefore, the most relevant evidence to primary care.

8.4 Multimorbidity

In terms of chronic disease management, multimorbidity is an immediate and expanding challenge for many health systems. This can be defined as the coexistence of several chronic diseases or medical conditions in one person. It is increasingly common among older people, as effective interventions reduce fatal events but increase the prevalent disease population and life expectancy of the general population continues to rise. As a result, multimorbidity is now a fundamental care issue that presents a number of complex challenges for health systems, patients, and clinicians.

$CHADS_2$	Score	CHA_2DS_2-VASc	Score
Congestive heart failure	1	Congestive heart failure/left ventricular dysfunction	1
Hypertension	1	Hypertension	1
Aged ≥75 years	1	**Aged ≥75 years**	**2**
Diabetes mellitus	1	Diabetes mellitus	1
Stroke/TIA/TE	2	Stroke/TIA/TE	2
Maximum score	6	**Vascular disease (prior MI, PAD, or aortic plaque)**	1
		Aged 65–74 years	1
		Sex category (i.e., female gender)	1
		Maximum score	**9**

CHA_2DS_2-VASc

- In patients with a $CHADS_2$ score of 0–1, or
- When a more detailed stroke risk assessment is indicated

Figure 8.3 Example of a validated clinical risk score: the CHADS2-VASc estimation of stroke risk in AF. (European Heart Rhythm Association et al., *Eur. Heart J.* 31, 19, 2010.)

Letter	Clinical characteristic*	Points awarded
H	Hyperternsion	1
A	Abnornmal renal and liver function (1 point each)	1 or 2
S	Stroke	1
B	Bleeding	1
L	Labile INRs	1
E	Elderly (e.g., age > 65 years)	1
D	Drugs or alchol (1 point each)	1 or 2
		Maximum 9 points

*Hypertension is defined as systolic blood pressure > 160 mmHg.
INR = internatlonal normalized ratio.

Figure 8.4 Example of a validated medical risk score: the HAS-BLED bleeding risk score for anticoagulation. (European Heart Rhythm Association et al., *Eur. Heart J.* 31, 19, 2010.)

In the United Kingdom, almost one in three people, or 15 million individuals, currently have a long-term condition (LTC), and half the population over 60 has an LTC. LTCs account for half of all GP appointments and 70% of inpatient bed days. It is estimated that the treatment and care of these patients accounts for 70% of the acute care budget in England; over two-thirds of NHS expenditure for one-third of the population. Those with LTCs are also likely to have a lower quality of life (Department of Health 2016).

Currently, primary and hospital care health systems often invite patients to clinics for individual conditions, or clusters of conditions, and deliver structured care for that specific disease; for example, diabetes. However, in practice, many people do not have one LTC but several conditions, either concordant (linked problems, often with similar interventions advocated), discordant (unrelated problems), or both. Multimorbid patients, therefore, find themselves attending multiple distinct clinics, which may be inconvenient and inefficient for themselves and for practices. They may receive conflicting advice and/or prescribed drugs from different practitioners, and may also feel that the things that matter most to them—the problems that directly affect their quality of life—are not necessarily the highest priority for each doctor or nurse consulted. Existing systems that address circumscribed conditions were never designed to manage the levels of multimorbidity now present in 50% of patients over the age of 75 (Salisbury et al. 2011) and increasingly prevalent within deprived communities (Barnett et al. 2012). This is a key area that needs much better coordination in primary care and at the interface with secondary care. Furthermore, since guidelines recommend explicit management targets for specific conditions, care is often determined by individual target metrics or a tick-box application of guidelines that sustains a disease-by-disease approach to treating patients, rather than necessarily prioritizing treatments that directly affect their quality of life. Multimorbidity also drives a considerable burden of treatment (Mair and May 2014), a major area for better healthcare integration to reduce the costs and risks of polypharmacy.

8.5 Women's Health

Primary care can provide a holistic approach to managing a woman's health throughout her lifetime. Gynecological and obstetric issues are often just one part of the medical history, and a longitudinal relationship with primary care can ensure that all conditions are managed appropriately

(Howe 2012). The hospital's role is dependent on the nature of the condition and the expertise available within primary care. Some women's health complaints, such as suspected gynecological cancer, require urgent referral to secondary care for specialist input, while for other conditions contact with a hospital is rarely required.

8.5.1 Contraception

Contraception is an important consideration for most women from their teenage years through to the menopause. It must be easily accessible and, ideally, free of charge, to ensure women have control over their reproductive health and to avoid unwanted pregnancy. The provision of contraceptive services varies widely. Primary care is ideally placed to provide information about contraceptive choices, both to women who present to discuss the topic and to those attending for another reason. Oral contraceptives, such as the combined and progesterone-only pill, can be prescribed in primary care with the full medical history available, which can be searched to identify any relative or absolute contraindications (Percy 2016). Long-acting reversible contraceptives (LARCs) such as subcutaneous implants and intrauterine coils can be provided within a primary care setting, if clinicians, usually GPs, are trained on how to insert and remove devices. More invasive techniques such as female tubal ligation require hospital referral, but represent a small proportion of the overall contraceptive workload.

8.5.2 Abnormal Uterine Bleeding and Pelvic Pain

The normal menstrual cycle lasts around 28 days, and includes a period (menstruation) at the start of each cycle, which typically lasts around five to seven days. Any bleeding outside of this time, such as between periods or after intercourse, or particularly heavy menstrual bleeding, is considered abnormal uterine bleeding (AUB). A wide range of conditions can cause AUB, including polyps, fibroids, infection, and gynecological cancers. An initial assessment can be carried out in primary care and should include a thorough history, including sexual history, and clinical examination including vaginal and speculum examination. A pregnancy test should be carried out, swabs taken to check for evidence of infection, and blood tests may be considered to assess hormone levels and for signs of anemia. Pelvic ultrasound can also be arranged in primary care to examine particularly for uterine (e.g., fibroids) and ovarian (e.g., cysts and tumors) pathology. If more invasive investigations and treatment are required such as diagnostic hysteroscopy, polyp removal, or hysterectomy, referral to hospital is necessary (van Dongen et al. 2007).

Pelvic pain is abnormal, and also requires initial assessment. The causes of pelvic pain may include gynecological and gastrointestinal causes. If pelvic inflammatory disease is suspected with infection as a possible cause, empirical treatment with antibiotics in primary care may help to reduce the risk of future complications. Endometriosis is also a cause of chronic pelvic pain and can often go undiagnosed. Referral to specialist services and investigation via laparoscopy are required to confirm the diagnosis and to guide treatment.

8.5.3 Infertility

Infertility affects one in seven heterosexual couples in the United Kingdom (Balen and Rutherford 2007). The WHO reported global trends in infertility prevalence from 1990 to 2010 and found 48.5 million couples were unable to have a child after five years of trying

(Mascarenhas et al. 2012). Primary care may be the first port of call for couples struggling to conceive and can provide general advice, such as the importance of taking folic acid each day to reduce the risk of birth defects and the importance of regular intercourse over a period of time (usually at least one year) before a label of infertility is considered. When appropriate, initial investigations for both male and female factors may also be carried out, including hormone tests, pelvic ultrasound, and semen analysis. Once the results of these tests are available, referral to hospital care is usually required for confirmation of the cause of infertility and discussion of available management options.

8.5.4 Obstetric Care

Pregnancy is not pathological, although complications can occur. In most countries, women are monitored at intervals during their pregnancy to detect any abnormality at an early stage. Management of women at low risk can usually be carried out in primary care, led by a midwife, with referral to a hospital-based obstetrician if problems arise.

The location of childbirth is highly variable across the world. A balance between management strategies that minimize the risk of maternal and fetal complications and excessive or unnecessary obstetric intervention can be difficult to achieve. The availability of an experienced obstetrician and pediatrician is important in high-risk deliveries to ensure that any complications can be dealt with quickly and safely. However, there is an increasing caesarean section rate, particularly in developed countries, which can be associated with complications for both mother (slower recovery time, risk of ectopic pregnancy, or stillbirth in subsequent pregnancies) and baby (neonatal respiratory distress syndrome, link to allergies).

Midwife-led care for women at low risk of obstetric complications can reduce caesarean section rates without any harmful outcomes for mother or baby (McLachlan et al. 2012). It can also improve satisfaction rates for women. In a randomized controlled trial of 2314 low-risk women pregnant women in Melbourne, Australia, women receiving midwife-led care were more positive about their overall birth experience, felt more in control during labor, were less anxious, and had more manageable pain (McLachlan et al. 2016).

8.5.5 Menopause

The menopause occurs in the late 40s to mid-50s for most women, with an average age of 51 in the industrialized world. For many women, the menopause represents a time of transition and can be associated with physical and mental health symptoms. Primary care clinicians can both identify symptoms and discuss management options with patients, including hormone replacement therapy (HRT), without the need for hospital involvement (Johnston 2011). Specialist clinics may be helpful in patients who are unable to take first-line therapies or when initial treatments have failed to control symptoms (Stute et al. 2016).

8.5.6 Suspected Gynecological Cancers

Patients with symptoms suggestive of gynecological malignancy require urgent referral to hospital for further investigation. Postcoital bleeding may suggest cervical cancer, and investigation with colposcopy and biopsy is required to confirm or rule out the diagnosis. Patients presenting with postmenopausal bleeding should be assessed with hysteroscopy and biopsy to look for endometrial cancer. Patients with nonspecific symptoms such as bloating, early satiety, and pelvic pain may have ovarian cancer. Investigations such as serum CA125 (cancer biomarker) levels and pelvic ultrasound may be initiated in primary care, but should not prevent referral when the index of suspicion for a potential ovarian malignancy is high (Møller et al. 2015).

Cervical screening programs operate in many countries around the world. Screening for disease should only be instituted for diseases that are judged to meet certain WHO criteria, as shown in Figure 8.5. Primary care often has a role in carrying out smear tests, which can be performed by practice nurses. This represents a large workload that is best carried out in a primary care setting to ensure the wide population coverage required for screening to be effective.

8.6 Child Health

The relationship between primary care and hospitals is particularly important for child health. Children and young people are frequent users of healthcare services, and they need to be seen at the right time by the right healthcare professional to ensure that their condition, whether acute or chronic, is diagnosed and managed in a timely way.

Children, particularly very young children from birth to four years of age, frequently need to see a healthcare professional (Hobbs et al. 2016a), most often for developmental checks, vaccinations, or minor illnesses, which are particularly prevalent in children. Older children may present with diseases of adolescence such as acne and are increasingly consulting with mental health problems. In the United Kingdom, consultations with children and young people account for more than 20% of workload; however, the configuration of children's health services varies hugely around the world, with some being purely hospital based.

In countries where GPs are trained in the care of children and work as part of a multidisciplinary team including practice nurses, health visitors, and social workers, primary care is well placed to address most healthcare needs of children and young people (Royal College of General

Knowledge of disease:

The condition should be important

There must be a recognizable latent or early symptomatic stage

The natural course of the condition, including development from latent to declared disease, should be adequately understood

Knowledge of test:

Suitable test or examination

Test acceptable to population

Case finding should be continuous (not just a "once and for all" project)

Treatment for disease:

Accepted treatment for patients with recognized disease

Facilities for diagnosis and treatment available

Agreed policy concerning whom to treat as patient

Cost considerations:

Costs of case finding (including diagnosis and treatment of patients diagnosed) economically balanced in relation to possible expenditures on medical care as a whole

Figure 8.5 Recommended screening criteria according to the WHO. (From Wilson, J. M. G. and Jungner, G., Principles and practice of screening for disease, World Health Organization Public Health Paper, 34, 1968.)

Practitioners 2010). GPs' offices in the community are often convenient for parents who need to attend appointments on a regular basis, and familiarity with the child and other family members can help the primary care team to spot problems early. Clear pathways between primary and secondary care are crucial to ensure holistic care. Timely referral to a hospital specialist is important for serious, life-threatening illness and for chronic disease management where specialist expertise is needed.

8.6.1 Routine Surveillance and Vaccinations

Vaccines save more lives than virtually any other healthcare intervention (Ozawa et al. 2016). The vaccination schedules in many countries include diseases that were fatal no more than a generation ago. Primary care is located in the community, so provides parents with easy access and a familiar environment in which to have their child vaccinated. As technologies have developed, new vaccines have been added to the schedule. In the United Kingdom, the nasal influenza vaccine is now offered to children aged two, three, and four every autumn to protect them against the potentially serious complications of influenza. Practice nurses carry out the majority of immunizations, with GP advice where needed, and can efficiently vaccinate children within the practice population at a low overall cost to the healthcare system.

Routine surveillance programs help to identify childhood problems in which intervention can significantly improve clinical outcomes at an early stage. Height and weight are key measures that are regularly checked by health visitors and monitored on universal growth charts. In addition, periodic developmental checks help to identify children who may have physical or sensory needs. Developmental milestones are, within a normal range, similar for most children. Failing to hit these key time points can indicate serious underlying illness and/or environmental factors. Detection at an early stage is important to trigger input from appropriate health professionals such as hearing specialists, speech and language therapists, or learning disabilities teams.

8.6.2 Child Protection

Primary care teams based in the community see children and their families on a regular basis and are, therefore, well placed to spot when something might be wrong. Looking after the whole family allows a unique perspective into the household rather than just the individual child. If a patient with young children is drinking to excess or there is a history of domestic violence, the primary care team may be able to piece things together and identify problems at an earlier stage than if the child were seen in a hospital. A bruise that is inconsistent with the mechanism of injury described by the parent, a child who seems unnecessarily frightened, or a parent shouting aggressively at a child in the waiting room are all instances that might raise the possibility of that child being actively harmed or at risk of harm. Identifying child abuse at an early stage provides a window for children and their families to receive support and intervention. In the most serious cases, this may be lifesaving.

Pediatricians, both community and hospital based, with expertise in child protection are often part of the child protection team needed to deal with abuse. Other healthcare professionals such as social workers, school nurses, and health visitors are also important members of the team. Child protection is everyone's business, and excellent communication and information sharing is required to ensure harm to children is stopped.

8.6.3 Serious Illness

Children experience many minor illnesses, particularly in the early years of life. These are usually self-limiting and do not require intervention. However, it is vital for healthcare professionals in first contact with young patients to be able to spot the signs of serious illness. In children, sepsis is of particular concern (Dellinger et al. 2013). Learning how to spot the signs of a sick child and experience in a secondary care setting where seriously ill children are more likely to present are both important aspects of generalist training. For primary care, thorough examination and appropriate safety netting are vital to ensure safe care. Children can change very quickly—often improving after a dose of paracetamol (acetaminophen)—but, similarly, they can deteriorate quickly and lack the physiological reserve that in adults allows for a more gradual deterioration.

Illnesses like bacterial meningitis, pneumonia, and septicemia require intravenous antibiotics, fluids, and close monitoring that can only be delivered in hospital. Children with severe sepsis may require respiratory and circulatory support only available through pediatric intensive care units. Triaging patients to ensure that children who are seriously unwell are seen is a challenge for any healthcare system. The role of primary care is to differentiate self-limiting minor illness from more serious conditions that require referral to hospital for specialist input.

8.6.4 Chronic Diseases in Children

Children may initially present to primary care with chronic conditions. In particular, patients with learning disabilities require timely and appropriate care, and this is sometimes lacking in healthcare systems. Patients may not explain their symptoms in the most likely way or may be unable to communicate the cause of their distress. It is important for GPs to identify symptoms suggestive of chronic disease and refer appropriately.

Ongoing management of these patients and their families often involves a relationship with their clinicians in both primary and secondary care. A hospital specialist usually leads the management of LTCs such as epilepsy, congenital heart disease, or cystic fibrosis, particularly around the time of diagnosis. However, these patients may develop other common childhood illnesses that require management in the same way as other children but with their chronic disease also in mind. For example, conditions such as conjunctivitis, eczema, or head lice are not normally treated by a hospital specialist and can be safely managed in primary care.

8.6.5 Mental Health

The incidence of mental health problems in children has increased significantly over the past decade. Child and adolescent mental health services in the United Kingdom are simply overwhelmed with long waiting times, meaning that children and their families can struggle for long periods before getting the help they need (Callaghan et al. 2017). Primary care has a role in the initial assessment of these patients. GPs can identify those who need to be seen urgently—for example, a teenager with depression and suicidal ideation—and ensure they obtain timely help. Primary care teams may also identify young people who require mental health intervention but do not recognize it themselves. For example, a young patient may be noted to have a low weight during a routine check-up, and further discussion may reveal an abnormal relationship with food and the possibility of anorexia nervosa. Eating disorders can be particularly challenging to diagnose and treat and often require input from specialist psychiatrists. The young person may hide their symptoms from family and friends as part of their illness.

GPs may also be able to assess situations in which other health professionals, rather than child and adolescent mental health services, may be more appropriate to help with the child's needs. For example, for a child brought to their GP by a parent concerned about reading or writing skills, an educational psychologist (accessed via the school system) may be best placed to diagnose dyslexia and provide appropriate support.

8.6.6 Summary

Primary care expertise is crucial for the safe management of children and young people. Most young children have a significant number of often minor illnesses, but spotting potentially life-threatening disease is important. A hospital attendance for every child with a minor illness would be unsustainable in most healthcare systems. Primary care is well placed to assess and manage the majority of children. This is often more convenient for parents and can avoid secondary care services becoming overwhelmed with children who do not need to be there, in turn ensuring that acute hospitals have the capacity to treat seriously ill patients.

8.7 Academic Primary Care

A key function for all health systems is to invest in an academic base to support the delivery of high-quality primary care. This needs to encompass the development of undergraduate teaching and understanding of the importance of primary care (Smith 2011) to health systems and how this integrates with hospital care, postgraduate training programs on the specialist career track for primary care physicians (Taylor et al. 2013), and clinical research.

Primary care-led/based research has been very influential in changing international clinical guidelines in areas such as better disease management (Mant et al. 2007; Sullivan et al. 2007), promoting innovation in self-management (Fitzmaurice et al. 2005; Farmer et al. 2007; McManus et al. 2010), and on risk assessment (Hippisley-Cox et al. 2008; Little et al. 2013) and better diagnosis (Thompson et al. 2006; Hamilton et al. 2009; Mant et al. 2009) among many other areas. This is a key primary care function.

8.8 Acknowledgments

FDRH is part funded by NIHR SPCR, NIHR CLAHRC Oxford, and NIHR Oxford BRC, and is a professorial fellow at Harris Manchester College. CJT is a National Institute for Health Research (NIHR) academic clinical lecturer.

References

Albers, G. W., P. Amarenco, J. D. Easton, R. L. Sacco, and P. Teal. 2004. Antithrombotic and thrombolytic therapy for ischemic stroke: The Seventh ACCP Conference on Antithrombotic and Thrombolytic Therapy. *Chest* 126 (3 Suppl.):483S–512S. doi:10.1378/chest.126.3_suppl.483S.

Balen, A. H., and A. J. Rutherford. 2007. Management of infertility. *Br. Med. J.* 7620:608.

Barnett, K., S. W. Mercer, M. Norbury, G. Watt, S. Wyke, and B. Guthrie. 2012. Epidemiology of multimorbidity and implications for health care, research, and medical education: a cross-sectional study. *Lancet* 380 (9836):37–43.

Bisno, A. L., M. A. Gerber, J. M. Gwaltney, Jr., E. L. Kaplan, and R.H. Schwartz. 2002. Practice guidelines for the diagnosis and management of group A streptococcal pharyngitis: Infectious Diseases Society of America. *Clin. Infect. Dis.* 35 (2):113–125. doi:10.1086/340949.

Blood Pressure Lowering Treatment Trialists Collaboration, J. Sundstrom, H. Arima, et al. 2014. Blood pressure-lowering treatment based on cardiovascular risk: A meta-analysis of individual patient data. *Lancet* 384 (9943):591–598. doi:10.1016/S0140-6736(14)61212-5.

Callaghan, J. E., L. C. Fellin, and F. Warner-Gale. 2017. A critical analysis of child and adolescent mental health services policy in England. *Clin. Child Psychol. Psychiatry* 22 (1):109–127. doi:10.1177/1359104516640318.

Camm, A. J., G. Y. Lip, R. De Caterina, I. Savelieva, D. Atar, S. H. Hohnloser, G. Hindricks, and P. Kirchhof. 2012. 2012 focused update of the ESC Guidelines for the management of atrial fibrillation: An update of the 2010 ESC Guidelines for the management of atrial fibrillation. Developed with the special contribution of the European Heart Rhythm Association. *Eur. Heart J.* 33 (21):2719–2747. doi:10.1093/eurheartj/ehs253.

Cholesterol Treatment Trialists Collaboration, C. Baigent, L. Blackwell, J. Emberson, L. E. Holland, C. Reith, N. Bhala, R. Peto, E. H. Barnes, A. Keech, J. Simes, and R. Collins 2010. Efficacy and safety of more intensive lowering of LDL cholesterol: A meta-analysis of data from 170,000 participants in 26 randomised trials. *Lancet* 376 (9753):1670–1681. doi:10.1016/S0140-6736(10)61350-5.

Dellinger, R. P., M. M. Levy, A. Rhodes, D. Annane, H. Gerlach, S. M. Opal, J. E. Sevransky, C. L. Sprung, I. S. Douglas, R. Jaeschke, T. M. Osborn, M. E. Nunnally, S. R. Townsend, K. Reinhart, R. M. Kleinpell, D. C. Angus, C. S. Deutschman, F. R. Machado, G. D. Rubenfeld, S. A. Webb, R. J. Bearle, J. L. Vincent, and R. Moreno. 2013. Surviving sepsis campaign: International guidelines for management of severe sepsis and septic shock, 2012. *Intensive Care Med.* 39 (2):165–228.

Department of Health. 2016. Ten things you need to know about long-term conditions. http://webarchive.nationalarchives.gov.uk/20130107105354/http://www.dh.gov.uk/en/Healthcare/Longtermconditions/tenthingsyouneedtoknow/index.htm

European Heart Rhythm Association, European Association for Cardio-Thoracic Surgery, A. J. Camm, P. Kirchhof, G. Y. Lip, U. Schotten, I. Savelieva, S. Ernst, I. C. Van Gelder, N. Al-Attar, G. Hindricks, B. Prendergast, H. Heidbuchel, O. Alfieri, A. Angelini, D. Atar, P. Colonna, R. De Caterina, J. De Sutter, A. Goette, B. Gorenek, M. Heldal, S. H. Hohloser, P. Kolh, J. Y. Le Heuzey, P. Ponikowski, and F. H. Rutten 2010. Guidelines for the management of atrial fibrillation: The Task Force for the Management of Atrial Fibrillation of the European Society of Cardiology (ESC). *Eur. Heart J.* 31 (19):2369–2429. doi:10.1093/eurheartj/ehq278.

Farmer, A., A. Wade, E. Goyder, P. Yudkin, D. French, A. Craven, R. Holman, A. Kinmonth, and A. Neil. 2007. Impact of self monitoring of blood glucose in the management of patients with non-insulin treated diabetes: Open parallel group randomised trial. *BMJ* 335 (7611):132. doi:10.1136/bmj.39247.447431.BE.

Fine, A. M., V. Nizet, and K. D. Mandl. 2012. Large-scale validation of the Centor and McIsaac scores to predict group A streptococcal pharyngitis. *Arch. Intern. Med.* 172 (11):847–852. doi:10.1001/archinternmed.2012.950.

Fitzmaurice, D. A., E. T. Murray, D. McCahon, R. Holder, J. P. Raftery, S. Hussain, H. Sandhar, and F. D. R. Hobbs. 2005. Self management of oral anticoagulation: Randomised trial. *BMJ* 331 (7524):1057. doi:10.1136/bmj.38618.580903.AE.

Fuster, V., L. E. Ryden, D. S. Cannom, et al. 2011. 2011 ACCF/AHA/HRS focused updates incorporated into the ACC/AHA/ESC 2006 guidelines for the management of patients with atrial fibrillation: a report of the American College of Cardiology Foundation/American Heart Association Task Force on practice guidelines. *Circulation* 123 (10):e269–e367. doi:10.1161/CIR.0b013e318214876d.

Graham, I. M., M. Stewart, M. G. Hertog, and Force Cardiovascular Round Table Task. 2006. Factors impeding the implementation of cardiovascular prevention guidelines: findings from a survey conducted by the European Society of Cardiology. *Eur. J. Cardiovasc. Prev. Rehabil.* 13 (5):839–845. doi:10.1097/01.hjr.0000219112.02544.24.

Grundy, S. M., J. I. Cleeman, C. N. Merz, H. B. Brewer Jr, L. T. Clark, D. B. Hunninghake, R. C. Pasternak, S. C. Smith Jr, and N. J. Stone. 2004. Implications of recent clinical trials for the National Cholesterol Education Program Adult Treatment Panel III guidelines. *Circulation* 110 (2):227–239. doi:10.1161/01.CIR.0000133317.49796.0E.

Hamilton, W., T. J. Peters, C. Bankhead, and D. Sharp. 2009. Risk of ovarian cancer in women with symptoms in primary care: Population based case-control study. *BMJ* 339:b2998. doi:10.1136/bmj.b2998.

Hay, A. D., N. M. Redmond, S. Turnbull, H. Christensen, H. Thornton, P. Little, M. Thompson, B. Delaney, A. Lovering, P. Muir, J. Leeming, B. Vipond, B. Stuart, T. Peters, and P. Blair. 2016. Development and internal validation of a clinical rule to improve antibiotic use in children presenting to primary care with acute respiratory tract infection and cough: A prognostic cohort study. *Lancet Respir. Med.* 4 (11):902–910. doi:10.1016/S2213-2600(16)30223-5.

Heeringa, J., D. A. van der Kuip, A. Hofman, J. A. Kors, G. van Herpen, B. H. Stricker, T. Stijnen, G. Y. Lip, and J. C. Witteman. 2006. Prevalence, incidence and lifetime risk of atrial fibrillation: The Rotterdam study. *Eur. Heart. J.* 27 (8):949–953. doi:10.1093/eurheartj/ehi825.

Hippisley-Cox, J., C. Coupland, Y. Vinogradova, J. Robson, R. Minhas, A. Sheikh, and P. Brindle. 2008. Predicting cardiovascular risk in England and Wales: Prospective derivation and validation of QRISK2. *BMJ* 336 (7659):1475–1482. doi:10.1136/bmj.39609.449676.25.

Hobbs, F. D., C. Bankhead, T. Mukhtar, S. Stevens, R. Perera-Salazar, T. Holt, and C. Salisbury. 2016a. Clinical workload in UK primary care: a retrospective analysis of 100 million consultations in England, 2007–14. *Lancet* 387 (10035):2323–2330. doi:10.1016/S0140-6736(16)00620-6.

Hobbs, F. D., D. A. Fitzmaurice, J. Mant, E. Murray, S. Jowett, S. Bryan, J. Raftery, M. Davies, and G. Lip. 2005. A randomised controlled trial and cost-effectiveness study of systematic screening (targeted and total population screening) versus routine practice for the detection of atrial fibrillation in people aged 65 and over. The SAFE study. *Health Technol. Assess.* 9 (40):iii–iv, ix–x, 1–74.

Hobbs, F. R., C. J. Taylor, G. Jan Geersing, F. H. Rutten, and J. R. Brouwer. 2016b. European Primary Care Cardiovascular Society (EPCCS) consensus guidance on stroke prevention in atrial fibrillation (SPAF) in primary care. *Eur. J. Prev. Cardiol.* 23 (5):460–473. doi:10.1177/2047487315571890.

Howe, A. 2012. What's special about medical generalism? The RCGP's response to the independent Commission on Generalism. *Br. J. Gen. Pract.* 62 (600):342–343. doi:10.3399/bjgp12X652175.

James, P. A., S. Oparil, B. L. Carter, W. C. Cushman, C. Dennison-Himmelfarb, J. Handler, D. T. Lackland, M. L. LeFevre, T. D. MacKenzie, O. Ogedegbe, S. C. Smith Jr, L. P. Svetkey, S. J. Taler, R. R. Townsend, J. T. Wright Jr, A. S. Narva, and E. Ortiz. 2014. 2014 Evidence-based guideline for the management of high blood pressure in adults: report from the panel members appointed to the Eighth Joint National Committee (JNC 8). *JAMA* 311 (5):507–520. doi:10.1001/jama.2013.284427.

Johnston, J. 2011. Managing the menopause: Practical choices faced in primary care. *Climacteric* 14 (Suppl. 2):8–12. doi:10.3109/13697137.2011.626616.

Jorgensen, H. S., H. Nakayama, J. Reith, H. O. Raaschou, and T. S. Olsen. 1996. Acute stroke with atrial fibrillation. The Copenhagen stroke study. *Stroke* 27 (10):1765–1769.

Kannel, W. B. 1996. Blood pressure as a cardiovascular risk factor: Prevention and treatment. *JAMA* 275 (20):1571–1576.

Kearney, P. M., M. Whelton, K. Reynolds, P. Muntner, P. K. Whelton, and J. He. 2005. Global burden of hypertension: Analysis of worldwide data. *Lancet* 365 (9455):217–223. doi:10.1016/S0140-6736(05)17741-1.

Lamassa, M., A. Di Carlo, G. Pracucci, A. M. Basile, G. Trefoloni, P. Vanni, S. Spolveri, M. C. Baruffi, G. Landini, A. Ghetti, C. D. Wolfe, and D. Inzitari. 2001. Characteristics, outcome, and care of stroke associated with atrial fibrillation in Europe: Data from a multicenter multinational hospital-based registry (the European Community stroke project). *Stroke* 32 (2):392–398.

Lewington, S., R. Clarke, N. Qizilbash, R. Peto, and R. Collins. 2002. Age-specific relevance of usual blood pressure to vascular mortality: A meta-analysis of individual data for one million adults in 61 prospective studies. *Lancet* 360 (9349):1903–1913.

Lin, H. J., P. A. Wolf, M. Kelly-Hayes, A. S. Beiser, C. S. Kase, E. J. Benjamin, and R. B. D'Agostino. 1996. Stroke severity in atrial fibrillation. The Framingham study. *Stroke* 27 (10):1760–1764.

Little, P., B. Stuart, F. D. Hobbs, C. C. Butler, A. D. Hay, J. Campbell, B. Delaney, S. Broomfield, P. Barratt, K. Hood, H. Everitt, M. Mullee, I. Williamson, D. Mant, and M. Moore. 2013. Predictors of suppurative complications for acute sore throat in primary care: Prospective clinical cohort study. *BMJ* 347:f6867. doi:10.1136/bmj.f6867.

Little, P., M. Moore, J. Kelly, I. Williamson, G. Leydon, L. McDermott, M. Mullee, and B. Stuart. 2014. Delayed antibiotic prescribing strategies for respiratory tract infections in primary care: Pragmatic, factorial, randomised controlled trial. *BMJ* 348:g1606. doi:10.1136/bmj.g1606.

Lozano, R., M. Naghavi, K. Foreman, et al. 2013. Global and regional mortality from 235 causes of death for 20 age groups in 1990 and 2010: A systematic analysis for the Global Burden of Disease Study 2010. *Lancet* 380 (9859):2095–2128.

Mair, F. S., and C. R. May. 2014. Thinking about the burden of treatment. *BMJ* 349:g6680. doi:10.1136/bmj.g6680.

Mancia, G., R. Fagard, K. Narkiewicz, J. Redón, A. Zanchetti, M. Böhm, T. Christiaens, R. Cifkova, G. De Backer, A. Dominiczak, M. Galderisi, D. E. Grobbee, T. Jaarsma, P. Kirchhof, S. E. Kjeldsen, S. Laurent, A. J. Manolis, P. M. Nilsson, L. M. Ruilope, R. E. Schmieder, P. A. Sirnes, P. Sleight, M. Viigimaa, B. Waeber, and F. Zannad. 2013. 2013 ESH/ESC guidelines for the management of arterial hypertension: The Task Force for the Management of Arterial Hypertension of the European Society of Hypertension (ESH) and of the European Society of Cardiology (ESC). *Eur. Heart J.* 34 (28):2159–2219. doi:10.1093/eurheartj/eht151.

Mant, J., F. D. Hobbs, K. Fletcher, A. Roalfe, D. Fitzmaurice, G. Y. Lip, and E. Murray. 2007. Warfarin versus aspirin for stroke prevention in an elderly community population with atrial fibrillation (the Birmingham Atrial Fibrillation Treatment of the Aged Study, BAFTA): A randomised controlled trial. *Lancet* 370 (9586):493–503. doi:10.1016/S0140-6736(07)61233-1.

Mant, J., J. Doust, A. Roalfe, P. Barton, M. R. Cowie, P. Glasziou, D. Mant, R. J. McManus, R. Holder, J. Deeks, K. Fletcher, M. Qume, S. Sohanpal, S. Sanders, and F. D. R. Hobbs. 2009. Systematic review and individual patient data meta-analysis of diagnosis of heart failure, with modelling of implications of different diagnostic strategies in primary care. *Health Technol. Assess.* 13 (32):1–207, iii. doi:10.3310/hta13320.

Mascarenhas, M. N., S. R. Flaxman, T. Boerma, S. Vanderpoel, and G. A. Stevens. 2012. National, regional, and global trends in infertility prevalence since 1990: A systematic analysis of 277 health surveys. *PLoS Med.* 9 (12):e1001356. doi:10.1371/journal.pmed.1001356.

McLachlan, H. L., D. A. Forster, M. A. T. Farrell, L. Gold, M. A. Biro, L. Albers, M. Flood, J. Oats, and U. Waldenstrom. 2012. Effects of continuity of care by a primary midwife (caseload midwifery) on caesarean section rates in women of low obstetric risk: The COSMOS randomised controlled trial. *BJOG* 119 (12):1483–1492. doi:10.1111/j.1471-0528.2012.03446.x.

McLachlan, H. L., D. A. Forster, M. A. Davey, T. Farrell, M. Flood, T. Shafiei, and U. Waldenstrom. 2016. The effect of primary midwife-led care on women's experience of childbirth: Results from the COSMOS randomised controlled trial. *BJOG* 123 (3):465–474. doi:10.1111/1471-0528.13713.

McManus, R. J., J. Mant, E. P. Bray, R. Holder, M. I. Jones, S. Greenfield, B. Kaambwa, M. Banting, S. Bryan, P. Little, B. Williams, and F. D. R. Hobbs. 2010. Telemonitoring and self-management in the control of hypertension (TASMINH2): A randomised controlled trial. *Lancet* 376 (9736):163–172. doi:10.1016/S0140-6736(10)60964-6.

Møller, H., C. Gildea, D. Meechan, G. Rubin, T. Round, and P. Vedsted. 2015. Use of the English urgent referral pathway for suspected cancer and mortality in patients with cancer: Cohort study. *BMJ* 351:h5102.

GBD 2013 Mortality and Causes of Death Collaborators. 2015. Global, regional, and national age-sex specific all-cause and cause-specific mortality for 240 causes of death, 1990–2013: A systematic analysis for the Global Burden of Disease Study 2013. *Lancet* 385 (9963):117–171. doi:10.1016/S0140-6736(14)61682-2.

Ozawa, S., A. Portnoy, H. Getaneh, S. Clark, M. Knoll, D. Bishal, H. K. Yang, and P. D. Patwardhan. 2016. Modeling the economic burden of adult vaccine-preventable diseases in the United States. *Health Affairs* 35 (11):2124–2132.

Percy, L. 2016. The new UK Medical Eligibility Criteria (UKMEC): What has changed? *J. Fam. Plann. Reprod. Health Care* 42 (2):81–82. doi:10.1136/jfprhc-2016-101488.

Piepoli, M. F., A. W. Hoes, S. Agewall, C. Albus, C. Brotons, A. L. Catapano, M. T. Cooney, U. Corrà, B. Cosyns, C. Deaton, I. Graham, M. S. Hall, F. D. Hobbs, M. L. Løchen, H. Löllgen, P. Marques-Vidal, J. Perk, E. Prescott, J. Redon, D. J. Richter, N. Sattar, Y. Smulders, M. Tiberi, H. B. van der Worp, I. van Dis, and W. M. Verschuren. 2016. 2016 European Guidelines on cardiovascular disease prevention in clinical practice: The Sixth Joint Task Force of the European Society of Cardiology and other societies on cardiovascular disease prevention in clinical practice (constituted by representatives of 10 societies and by invited experts) developed with the special contribution of the European Association for Cardiovascular Prevention & Rehabilitation (EACPR). *Eur. Heart J.* 37 (29):2315–2381. doi:10.1093/eurheartj/ehw106.

Rahman, F., G. F. Kwan, and E. J. Benjamin. 2016. Global epidemiology of atrial fibrillation. *Nat. Rev. Cardiol.* 13 (8):501. doi:10.1038/nrcardio.2016.114.

Royal College of General Practitioners. 2010. *RCGP Child Health Strategy 2010–2015*. London, UK: Royal College of General Practitioners.

Salisbury, C., L. Johnson, S. Purdy, J. M. Valderas, and A. A. Montgomery. 2011. Epidemiology and impact of multimorbidity in primary care: A retrospective cohort study. *Br. J. Gen. Pract.* 61 (582):e12–e21.

Sinclair, G., and A. Kerr. 2006. The Bold Promise project: A system change in primary care to support cardiovascular risk screening. *N. Z. Med. J.* 119 (1245):U2312.

Smith, S. R. 2011. A recipe for medical schools to produce primary care physicians. *N. Engl. J. Med.* 364 (6):496–497. doi:10.1056/NEJMp1012495.

Stiell, I. G., G. H. Greenberg, R. D. McKnight, R. C. Nair, I. McDowell, and J. R. Worthington. 1992. A study to develop clinical decision rules for the use of radiography in acute ankle injuries. *Ann. Emerg. Med.* 21 (4):384–390.

Stiell, I. G., G. H. Greenberg, R. D. McKnight, R. C. Nair, I. McDowell, M. Reardon, J. P. Stewart, and J. Maloney. 1993. Decision rules for the use of radiography in acute ankle injuries: Refinement and prospective validation. *JAMA* 269 (9):1127–1132.

Stone, N. J., J. G. Robinson, A. H. Lichtenstein, C. N. Bairey Merz, D. M. Lloyd-Jones, C. B. Blum, R. H. Eckel, A. C. Goldberg, D. Gordon, D. Levy, D. M. Lloyd-Jones, P. McBride, J. S. Schwartz, S. T. Shero, S. C. Smith Jr, K. Watson, and P. W. Wilson. 2014. 2013 ACC/AHA guideline on the treatment of blood cholesterol to reduce atherosclerotic cardiovascular risk in adults: a report of the American College of Cardiology/American Heart Association Task Force on Practice Guidelines. *Circulation* 129 (25 Suppl. 2):S1–S45. doi:10.1161/01.cir.0000437738.63853.7a.

Stute, P., I. Ceausu, H. Depypere, I. Lambrinoudaki, A. Mueck, F. R. Perez-Lopez, Y. T. van der Schouw, L. M. Senturk, T. Simoncini, J. C. Stevenson, and M. Rees. 2016. A model of care for healthy menopause and ageing: EMAS position statement. *Maturitas* 92:1–6. doi:10.1016/j.maturitas.2016.06.018.

Sullivan, F. M., I. R. Swan, P. T. Donnan, J. M. Morrison, B. H. Smith, B. McKinstry, R. J. Davenport, L. D. Vale, J. E. Clarkson, V. Hammersley, S. Hayavi, A. McAteer, K. Stewart, and F. Daly. 2007. Early treatment with prednisolone or acyclovir in Bell's palsy. *N. Engl. J. Med.* 357 (16):1598–1607. doi:10.1056/NEJMoa072006.

Taylor, C. J., T. Bailey, and M. Wilkinson. 2013. Academic general practitioner training: developing an essential workforce. *Educ. Prim. Care* 24 (6):401–403.

Thompson, M. J., N. Ninis, R. Perera, R. Mayon-White, C. Phillips, L. Bailey, A. Harnden, D. Mant, and M. Levin. 2006. Clinical recognition of meningococcal disease in children and adolescents. *Lancet* 367 (9508):397–403. doi:10.1016/S0140-6736(06)67932-4.

Turnbull, F., B. Neal, C. Algert, J. Chalmers, N. Chapman, J. Cutler, M. Woodward, and S. MacMahon. 2005. Effects of different blood pressure-lowering regimens on major cardiovascular events in individuals with and without diabetes mellitus: Results of prospectively designed overviews of randomized trials. *Arch. Intern. Med.* 165 (12):1410–1419. doi:10.1001/archinte.165.12.1410.

van Dongen, H., C. D. de Kroon, C. E. Jacobi, J. B. Trimbos, and F. W. Jansen. 2007. Diagnostic hysteroscopy in abnormal uterine bleeding: a systematic review and meta-analysis. *BJOG* 114 (6):664–675. doi:10.1111/j.1471-0528.2007.01326.x.

Wells, P. S., D. R. Anderson, M. Rodger, et al. 2003. Evaluation of D-dimer in the diagnosis of suspected deep-vein thrombosis. *N. Engl. J. Med.* 349 (13):1227–1235. doi:10.1056/NEJMoa023153.

Wells, S., S. Furness, N. Rafter, et al. 2008. Integrated electronic decision support increases cardiovascular disease risk assessment four fold in routine primary care practice. *Eur. J. Cardiovasc. Prev. Rehabil.* 15 (2):173–178.

Wilson, J. M. G., and G. Jungner. 1968. Principles and practice of screening for disease. World Health Organization Public Health Paper, p. 34.

Wolf, P. A., R. D. Abbott, and W. B. Kannel. 1991. Atrial fibrillation as an independent risk factor for stroke: The Framingham study. *Stroke* 22 (8):983–988.

Yusuf, S., S. Hawken, S. Ounpuu, et al. 2004. Effect of potentially modifiable risk factors associated with myocardial infarction in 52 countries (the INTERHEART study): Case-control study. *Lancet* 364 (9438):937–952. doi:10.1016/S0140-6736(04)17018-9.

Chapter 9

Performance Parameters

Jules Martin, Alison Alsbury, and Will Reynolds

Contents

9.1 The Contemporary Performance Challenge: New Care Models in the United Kingdom..... 156
9.1.1 Why Is Maturity the Third "M"? 157
9.1.2 Understanding the Three M's 157
9.2 What Performance Is Key? Measuring Patient Outcomes 158
9.2.1 Defining Clinical Quality 158
9.2.2 Measuring Clinical Quality through Patient Outcomes 160
9.2.2.1 Example of a "Sentinel" Care Quality Indicator: The UK NHS "Never Event" Definition 161
9.2.3 Qualitative and Quantitative Approaches and When to Use Them 163
9.2.4 Using Key Performance Indicators (KPIs) to Measure and Manage Delivery of a Health Pathway 164
9.2.5 Summary 167
9.3 What Performance Is Key? Staff 167
9.3.1 Summary 169
9.4 What Performance Is Key? Contracts 169
9.4.1 Measurement of Value 169
9.4.4.1 Example: Central London Clinical Commissioning Group (CCG) Best Value Contract Review Approach 169
9.4.2 Measuring Return on Investment 171
9.4.3 Learning from Applying Best Value Criteria during Contract Reviews 172
9.4.4 Summary 173
9.5 What Performance Is Key? Reward 173
9.5.1 Summary 174
9.6 How Do We Know the Whole System Is Performing? Business Intelligence Indicators .. 174
9.6.1 Why Involve Business Intelligence? 174
9.6.1.1 Commissioning Case Study: Neurology 175
9.6.1.2 Commissioning Case Study: Fecal Calprotectin 175
9.6.2 Ensuring Robust Service Management 176

9.6.3 Using BI Wisely ... 177
9.6.4 Summary ... 177
9.7 How Do We Learn by Doing? Continuous Improvement, Governance, and Data ... 177
9.7.1 How Performance Metrics Enable Whole System Management ... 177
9.7.2 How Performance Metrics Can Drive Good Planning ... 178
9.7.3 How Performance Metrics Can Support Good Decision-Making ... 179
9.7.4 Summary ... 181
9.8 How Is the Care System Performing? The Importance of Benchmarking ... 183
9.8.1 Spending the Tax Payer's Money Wisely ... 183
9.8.2 Ensuring High-Quality, Cost-Effective Health Services—The Provider Challenge ... 183
9.8.3 Practical Tips for Meaningful Benchmarking ... 184
9.8.4 Summary ... 185
9.9 Conclusion: Using the Three Ms to Enable Whole System Management ... 185
9.9.1 Measurement ... 186
9.9.2 Methodology ... 186
9.9.3 Maturity ... 186
References ... 186

9.1 The Contemporary Performance Challenge: New Care Models in the United Kingdom

National Health Service (NHS) England's strategic Five Year Forward View (NHS England 2014) depends on the creation of new care models to face current financial and performance challenges. The policy framework was developed to promote accountable care partnerships and networks, encourage collaboration, and improve integration between health and social care. The NHS in the United Kingdom is currently trialing new contractual arrangements in shadow form as 50 "Vanguard" sites, 27 "Integration Pioneers," and 17 "Primary Care Home" pilots. Each looks at different elements of the new care models, and the learning is shared across these pilot sites and with wider communities through the new care models program run by NHS England.

New contractual options include the Multispecialty Community Provider—a framework-accountable care network contract that enables "groups of general practitioners (GPs) to combine with nurses, other community health services, hospital specialists, and perhaps mental health and social care to create integrated out-of-hospital care."

A further new option will be the integrated hospital and primary care provider (Primary and Acute Care Systems), "combining for the first time general practice and hospital services, similar to the Accountable Care Organisations now developing in other countries too." Other options include Urgent and Emergency Care Networks, Acute Care Collaboratives, and a framework for providing Enhanced Care in Care Homes.

The Five Year Forward View defines the contemporary challenge clearly:

The challenges facing the NHS are shared with those of all other industrialized countries' health systems:

- Changes in patients' health needs and personal preferences: people wish to be informed and involved in their own care in an era when long-term conditions take 70% of the health service budget.

- Changes in treatments, technologies and care delivery: although uptake of new technologies is variable, this is causing substantial transformation in the NHS's ability to predict, diagnose, and treat disease.
- Changes in health services funding growth. Given the after-effects of the global recession, most western countries will continue to experience budget pressures over the next few years. During this period the NHS financial assumption has to be "flat cash," rather than the 6%–7% real annual increases in funding seen in the first decade of this century.

Long-term conditions are now a central task of the NHS; caring for these needs requires a partnership with patients over the long term rather than providing single, unconnected "episodes" of care. As a result there is now quite wide consensus on the direction we will be taking:

- Increasingly we need to manage systems—networks of care—not just organizations.
- Out-of-hospital care needs to become a much larger part of what the NHS does.
- Services need to be integrated around the patient.

The driver for new care models is, therefore, these three critical elements of a multifaceted challenge. Performance parameters shift dramatically in these new arrangements. All new care models are based on shared objectives across commissioner and provider, and all are based on creating accountable care systems. The actual forms (Integrated Care Organization, Accountable Care Network, Accountable Care Partnership, etc.) all become secondary to the main driver—care system integration.

This chapter seeks to explore how traditional performance parameters might need to change to face this challenge. To understand how they might change, we will be examining the three M's—measurement, methodology, and maturity—deliberately looking at each main theme through a lens that reflects the changing role of all partners in the system and how the form and utilization of performance parameters has and continues to evolve.

9.1.1 Why Is Maturity the Third "M"?

Traditional performance management approaches have concentrated on measurement and methodology without necessarily concentrating on maturity (of the organization, collaborative or joint working, or of the functioning of the care system). The speed and complexity of change have now provided a much greater imperative to implement a whole system approach, essentially requiring both commissioners and providers to create rapidly developing communities of practice. Key to this is leadership, accountability, relationships, and communication. Without some reflection on the maturity of these key elements in performance frameworks, the ability to create effective communities of practice cannot be tested.

9.1.2 Understanding the Three M's

This chapter therefore examines the three M's in some detail:

- *Measurement*: What performance is key? We provide an overview of the best ways to measure four key elements of healthcare delivery—patient outcomes, staff, contracts, and rewards.
- *Methodology*: How do commissioners and providers achieve value for money and ensure that they deliver appropriate outputs and outcomes?
- *Maturity*: How far can commissioners and providers distill their shared commitment and learning into a truly integrated system?

9.2 What Performance Is Key? Measuring Patient Outcomes

Different healthcare systems throughout the world are developing a shared interest in the systematic assessment and international benchmarking of quality of care provided in different healthcare systems. This will only be possible if universally acceptable quality indicators can be identified to enable the effective measurement of patient outcomes.

Yet, despite the challenges of cross-national data comparisons, there is now a considerable body of data that allows comparisons of healthcare quality in selected areas of care. Some important comparisons have been made from existing indicators collected by most national healthcare systems; for example, avoidable mortality and cancer survival. These demonstrate both the potential power of cross-national comparisons and some of the difficulties in drawing valid interpretations from the data (e.g., there are different national definitions for avoidable mortality).

The three quality domains identified as important by High Quality Care for All: NHS Next Stage Review (Department of Health 2009), namely effectiveness of care, patient safety, and patient experience are proving to have international currency but do not link quality and cost-effectiveness. They remain key clinical quality domains in the United Kingdom, but performance quality criteria are now being framed more clearly by the triple aim of the Five Year Forward View:

- A radical upgrade in prevention: To reduce the health and well-being gap
- New care models: To reduce the care and quality gap
- Efficiency and investment: To reduce the financial and resource gap

Therefore, the key challenge is to identify quality performance parameters that address all three gaps using clinical quality as the driver of prevention and efficiency.

9.2.1 Defining Clinical Quality

Defining healthcare quality is multidimensional, complex, and can be defined in different ways depending on whether you are speaking to a patient, a clinician, a commissioner, a provider, or a central regulator. Different stakeholders within the system will always have different motivations and incentives to measure, prioritize, and accentuate different elements of "quality."

For example, a clinician might prioritize achieving the right clinical diagnosis and following best practice referral pathways. In contrast, a patient may take this element of care for granted and instead may emphasize the importance of good communication skills. What is clear is that, even among patients, there is no consensus on the best way to define "quality." Patients with chronic conditions may have different priorities than adults with acute minor ailments. Continuity of care tends to be a higher priority among older people and those who feel vulnerable (Nutting et al. 2003), but ease and speed of access are often emphasized by younger patients without chronic illnesses. Irrespective of these different viewpoints, in recent years the measurement of one dimension of quality has consistently been given primacy by stakeholders: patient experience.

The 2008 Darzi NHS Next Stage Review (Darzi 2008) defined quality in the NHS as being related to three core areas:

- Patient safety: *Primum non nocere*—"first do no harm"—has been a central pillar of healthcare provision since Hippocrates developed the notion in the fifth century BC. As health delivery approaches evolve and change, it is the system leaders' responsibility to ensure a safe environment and reduce avoidable harm.

- Clinical effectiveness: Effectiveness of care means understanding success rates from different treatments for different conditions and making decisions that are always evidence-based and scientifically robust. Assessing clinical effectiveness includes clinical measures such as mortality or survival rates, complication rates, and measures of clinical improvement.
- The patient experience: Quality of care includes quality of caring. This means how personal care is—the compassion, dignity, and respect with which service users are treated, which can only be improved by analyzing and understanding service user satisfaction with their own experiences. This extends to the positive experiences of patients' carers and families.

Before 2008, policymakers primarily defined health service and system performance in the United Kingdom as achieving productivity targets, activity volumes, waiting times targets, and service outputs (Raleigh and Foot 2010). These activity and output measurements are often proxies for outcomes and can help to build a picture of quality and system efficiency. However, they cannot—and should not—replace patient outcome measures.

The NHS attempted to codify this focus on outcomes in the NHS Outcomes Framework in 2010 (Figure 9.1). By clearly setting out the whole system's definition of outcomes, the NHS aimed to introduce a uniform approach to the measurement of patient outcomes across the system.

Lohr and Schroeder (1990) developed an alternative way to express patient-focused quality indicators as "The Five Ds":

- Death: a bad outcome if untimely
- Disease: symptoms, physical signs, and laboratory abnormalities
- Discomfort: symptoms such as pain, nausea, or dyspnea
- Disability: impaired ability connected to usual activities at home, at work, or in recreation
- Dissatisfaction: emotional reactions to disease and its care, such as sadness and anger

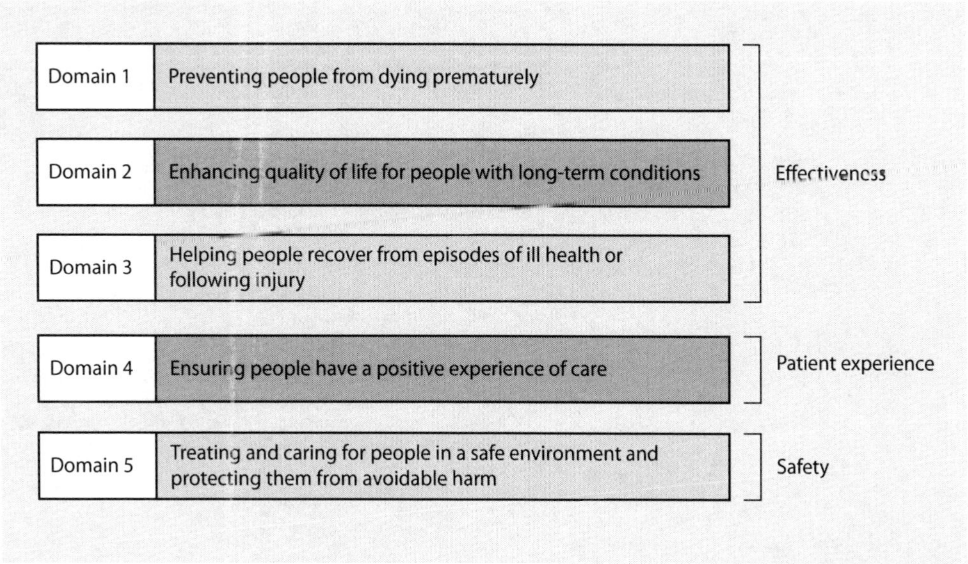

Figure 9.1 The five "outcome domains" of the NHS Outcomes Framework. (Source: Whole Systems Integrated care module working group Central London CCG, North West London collaboration of Clinical commissioning.)

Other outcomes frameworks attempt to contextualize outcomes in an integrated way and encompass all of the support that patients can receive (i.e., including social care and charity services as well as health service delivery) and how all of this support contributes to deliver holistic patient outcome benefits. The model in Figure 9.2 attempts to illustrate how data can be collected to reflect integrated care delivery.

Whichever definition of quality a health system uses, it must focus on patient care by tracking and measuring clinical outcomes. In the words of the Berwick Report, "the quality of patient care should come before all other considerations in the leadership and conduct of the NHS, and that patient safety is the keystone dimension of quality, the pursuit of continually improving safety should permeate every action and level in the NHS" (McKee 2013).

9.2.2 Measuring Clinical Quality through Patient Outcomes

The key measurement of success within a health system is clinical outcomes, and these can only be measured by using robust, evidence-based clinical quality indicators that are designed, defined, and implemented with scientific rigor. Good clinical indicators create a framework to monitor safety and quality as well as to drive clinical improvement. These indicators also help managers to prioritize scarce clinical and management resources within the healthcare system. Consequently, designing and calibrating these indicators correctly is essential to the delivery of a safe health system that has the ability to drive continuous clinical improvement and swiftly identify and tackle underperformance.

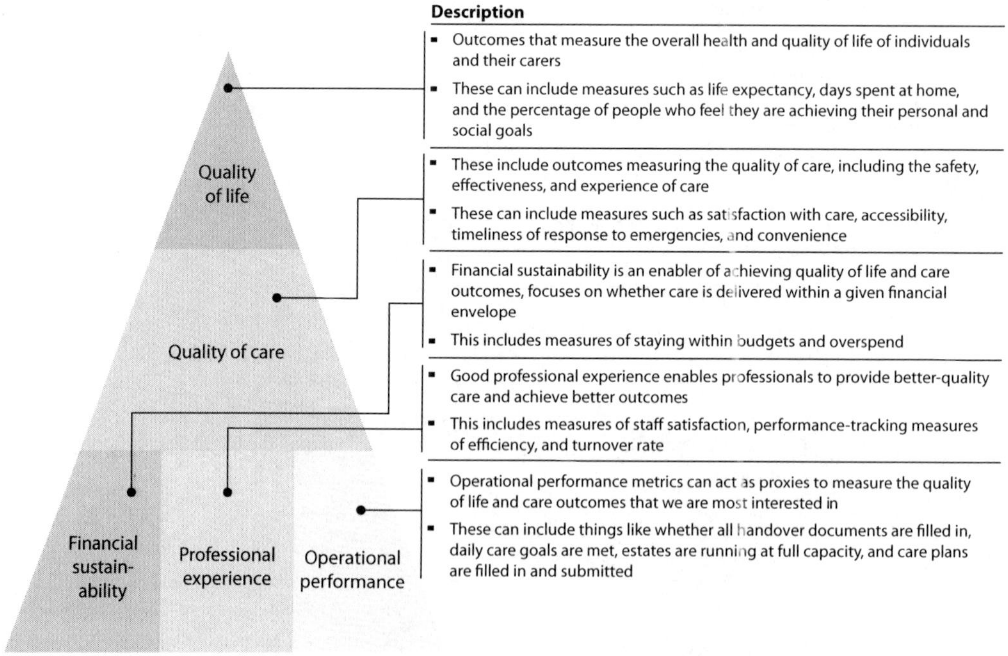

Figure 9.2 An example of an integrated outcomes matrix. (Source: Whole Systems Integrated Care module working group, Central London CCG, North West London Collaboration of Clinical Commissioning.)

Clinical quality indicators can take the form of "sentinel" indicators, which identify individual care incidents that trigger further investigation. "Sentinel events" represent extreme examples of poor performance and are generally used as part of a risk management approach by automatically triggering an investigation when such an event occurs. One example of a sentinel indicator in the United Kingdom is the NHS's "Never Event" indicator (see Section 9.2.2.1), which is a method of identifying individual incidents which should never occur as a proxy of how well a health system manages risk and has developed mechanisms to avoid episodes of care that should never occur.

9.2.2.1 Example of a "Sentinel" Care Quality Indicator: The UK NHS "Never Event" Definition

NHS England defines "Never Events" as follows (NHS England 2016a):

> "Never Events" are serious incidents that are wholly preventable as guidance or safety recommendations that provide strong systemic protective barriers are available at a national level and should have been implemented by all healthcare providers. Each Never Event type has the potential to cause serious patient harm or death. However, serious harm or death is not required to have happened as a result of a specific incident occurrence for that incident to be categorised as a Never Event.

Never Events include incidents such as

- Wrong surgical site
- Instrument retained post-surgery
- Wrong administration route for chemotherapy

Clinical quality indicators can also take the form of "rate-based" indicators. These indicators use data about frequently occurring events that can be expressed as numbers, rates, mean values, ratios, or proportions (i.e., proportions within a given time period) for a sample population. Rate-based indicators permit comparisons between providers or health systems over time. Rate-based indicators need both a numerator and a denominator specifying the population at risk for an event and the period of time over which the event may take place.

Donabedian (1988) argued that the most important consequences and markers of high-quality care were care outcomes but that these outcomes were more likely to be realized if structural arrangements and processes of care met quality standards. "Sentinel" and "rate-based" indicators are used to monitor how well an organization is performing in terms of delivery of the structures and processes that scientific evidence has proven to be causally linked to the delivery of excellent patient outcomes. In addition, and self-evidently, organizations also monitor the patient's actual clinical outcomes (using short- and long-term rate-based and sentinel indicators). In this way, these three types of indicator (*structure*, *process*, and *outcome* measures) provide a holistic picture of the extent to which a health organization or system is delivering high-quality care as well as providing the ability to specify *how* that quality of care has been delivered.

9.2.2.1.1 Structure Indicators

"Structure" indicators describe health system characteristics that affect the system's ability to meet the healthcare needs of individual patients or a community. Structure indicators include physical equipment and facilities and describe the type and amount of resources used by a health system to deliver services. They can relate to the number of staff delivering a service, staff mix, beds, buildings, or supplies. Categories of structure indicators include

- Facilities
- Equipment
- Personnel
- Administration
- Protocols

Examples of structure indicators include

- Staff mix (i.e., the proportion of specialists to other doctors, or of doctors to nurses)
- Access to specific technologies (i.e., diagnostics)
- Access to specific units (i.e., stroke units)

9.2.2.1.2 Process Indicators

Process indicators assess what the healthcare provider did for the patient and how well it was done. Processes are a series of interrelated activities undertaken to achieve objectives. Process indicators measure the activities and tasks in episodes of patient care. Categories of process indicators include

- Management
- Records
- Diagnosis
- Treatment plan
- Sequencing

Examples of process indicators include

- Proportion of patients attending an Accident and Emergency (A&E) department who are seen, treated, admitted, or discharged in under four hours
- Proportion of patients treated according to agreed clinical guidelines and pathways
- Proportion of patients with diabetes given regular foot care

9.2.2.1.3 Outcome Indicators

As a rule of thumb, structure and process indicators are easier to measure, but outcome indicators are more important. Outcome indicators describe the patient's health status following a care episode or episodes. Outcome indicators are more challenging to collect than other types of indicator but give the richest understanding of whether the healthcare intervention has delivered its intended benefits. An ideal outcome indicator would capture the effect of healthcare processes on the health and well-being of patients, their families, and the wider population. Because of the difficulty in measuring end result outcome indicators (as these end results can often take years to come to fruition, such as five-year cancer survival), intermediate outcome indicators are often used. Intermediate outcomes are important as they allow leaders to track progress toward an end outcome, assess what difference they are making in the short to medium term, and assess cost-effectiveness by direct or indirect means. Intermediate outcome measures reflect changes in physiological status that affect subsequent health outcomes, and in this way these intermediate measures can act as proxies that highlight health components that are scientifically proven to be statistically associated with improved end health outcomes. Categories of outcome indicators include

- Patient satisfaction
- Health status
- Completion of treatment
- Readmission pattern
- Needs of readmission

Examples of outcome indicators include

- Intermediate outcomes
  - HbA1c results for diabetics
  - Blood pressure results for hypertensive patients
  - Cortisol levels for immunology patients
- End outcomes
  - Quality of life
  - Mortality
  - Morbidity
  - Work status
  - Patient satisfaction
  - Friends and family satisfaction (e.g., the Friends and Family Test)

One example of an effective outcome measure developed by the NHS is the "Friends and Family Test" (FFT; NHS England 2014). The FFT is based on the principle that the most powerful measure of good care is if the patient would recommend the service to their closest acquaintances. Since 2013, most NHS providers have been required to ask patients whether they would recommend the service to their friends or family. Since its launch, the FFT has produced around 25 million pieces of patient feedback (with this figure increasing by one million responses a month), making it the biggest source of patient opinion in the world. Scores so far have told health system managers that over 90% of patients served within the NHS would recommend it to their loved ones. Patient comments have also identified areas where improvements can be made so that providers can enhance their services. Since 2014, it has also been a requirement for all NHS providers to ask their staff whether they would recommend the service that they work within to their friends and family. The FFT is a simple but powerful example of an end outcome measure.

9.2.3 Qualitative and Quantitative Approaches and When to Use Them

While many quality indicators can be collected "quantitatively" (i.e., counted and defined in terms of rate-based or sentinel indicators), quality information lies on a continuum and requires a number of different data collection approaches. Some "hard to measure" aspects of care quality can only be assessed through qualitative measures such as patient feedback, clinical audit, interviews, or peer review.

When designing a system's quality performance parameters, quantitative quality measurement initiatives should be combined with locally developed qualitative measures of performance to provide a rich and nuanced picture of health outcomes. This better enables thoughtful reflection by system leaders on how patient care can be improved.

9.2.4 Using Key Performance Indicators (KPIs) to Measure and Manage Delivery of a Health Pathway

A key performance indicator (KPI) is a metric used to evaluate factors that are crucial to the success of an organization and to demonstrate how effectively an organization is achieving key objectives. Using KPIs to monitor healthcare pathways is one of the most effective ways to assess system performance. Health organizations and systems should measure against four key performance domains:

- *Timeliness of intervention*: This measure collects information about whether the healthcare intervention (i.e., diagnosis or a management intervention) came at the most appropriate time; for example, whether an illness or condition was diagnosed and treated at the earliest reasonable juncture to enable optimization of patient outcomes. Another example might be measuring whether deterioration in a condition was managed at the earliest possible stage.
- *Outputs*: Health output KPIs provide information on the quantity of goods and services provided by healthcare systems and a measure of productivity or efficiency in healthcare delivery. While output KPIs indicate the activities and processes delivered by the organization, output measures do not directly address the patient value or outcome derived from the intervention. Outputs can help to build a picture of whether the system is delivering the types of activity that are causally linked to outcomes, but they can only ever act as a proxy for patient outcomes.
- *Efficiency of processes*: Measurements of the efficiency of processes within a health system express the extent to which the various parts of the system interact seamlessly, minimizing the effort (resources) required to deliver the best patient outcome in the most cost-effective way. One of the key measurements of efficiency is establishing how smoothly transitions between the different activities and processes provided by the health system are delivered.
- *Outcomes*: Health outcome KPIs, as discussed above, describe the patient's health status following a care episode or episodes and can either be intermediate outcomes or end outcomes. Monitoring pathways' KPIs can provide rich information on proxy indictors that are causally linked to good patient outcomes but do not provide direct evidence on patient outcomes themselves. These patient outcome KPIs must be collected in alternative ways by tracking patient experiences and clinical outcomes using patient-level data analysis.

The timeliness of an intervention can often be measured by how early in the pathway assessment, monitoring, or treatment occurs. An example of a healthcare activity that ensures timely intervention is regular blood pressure or glucometer checks for type 1 diabetes patients to avert crisis.

Once the patient has entered the system, one of the most powerful ways to measure outputs and process efficiency is by tracking patient flow (and changes in patient flow over time) down predetermined clinical pathways using well-designed KPIs. Figure 9.3 illustrates examples of acute and community clinical pathways running in parallel:

- Activity flows from left to right.
- The top half of the diagram, shown by the red box, is a (high-level) indicative acute pathway.

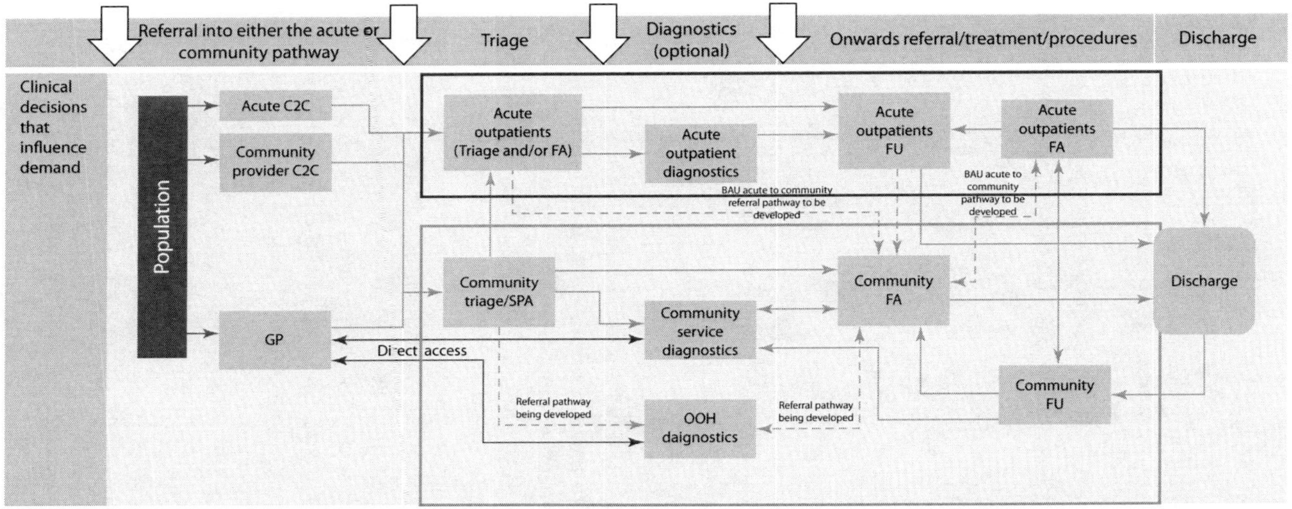

Figure 9.3 Indicative acute and community pathway.

- The bottom half of the diagram, shown by the green box, is a high-level community pathway.
- The blue boxes within the pathways are "points of delivery" within the system.
- In this case, the flow that commissioners (i.e., budget holders) want to see, where clinically appropriate, is downward (i.e., shifting acute activity into more cost-effective community services).
- At each stage of the pathway, clinicians have an opportunity to affect demand by making clinical decisions that determine how the patient flows down the pathways (decision points are indicated by the white arrows).
- For example, a general practitioner (GP) could make a decision to refer to a community service.
- The community service clinician then decides to refer the patient for a diagnostic test and, following a first appointment (FA) and a follow-up appointment, the patient is discharged.

By using KPIs to measure outputs at various points during delivery in the system, a manager can gain a good understanding of how well the system is operating and how well a provider is performing. For example, a KPI mandating that a provider delivers a minimum number of FAs per month can be used to measure whether the provider is delivering as contracted.

KPIs can also be used to measure the time that elapses between different points of delivery and to test whether the provider is delivering care within agreed tolerances. One way of doing this is to use a "Referral to Treatment Time" (RTT) KPI, which mandates and monitors the maximum time that can elapse between initial referral and the patient's appointment. If the provider is breaching the RTT KPI threshold, this might indicate that the provider is either not delivering enough activity to meet demand or that there are inefficiencies within the provider's processes that are delaying the efficient delivery of the service.

The data collected from pathway KPIs also enable commissioners to track whether the system is being delivered as cost-effectively as possible. As already noted, in this indicative system, acute care is more expensive than community care. The commissioner, therefore, wants to encourage clinically appropriate referrals that mean that all patients that can be seen in the less expensive community service are seen in that setting (and that no one who could be seen in the community service is seen in the more expensive acute setting). Commissioners can use activity KPIs to show whether the total number of patients and the proportional split of patients between acute and community services is as expected. If this is not the case, the commissioner can then use other performance measurement tools such as clinical audit to establish whether demand is being wrongly directed by referring clinicians and can work with the provider to intervene and improve system demand management through improved referral behavior.

In this way, pathway KPIs enable system monitoring so that poor performance can be quickly identified and mitigated. For this reason, pathway KPIs are powerful management tools, but they are limited to describing how well the system components are being delivered rather than how well patient end outcomes have been achieved as a result of the delivery of those components.

Individual pathway KPIs can act as powerful output measures that enable leaders to track benefits. However, individual KPIs can also be misleading when viewed in isolation. Furthermore, to create effective new care models in a complex system, baskets of interrelated variables provide a much more compelling description of system dynamics than individual metrics alone.

This point is best illustrated by a worked example. A commissioner creates a new dermatology community service designed to pull activity out of an acute dermatology service and to re-provide this service at a lower price point in a more convenient location for the patient. This service model should, therefore, deliver a transactional saving to the commissioner through the differential unit cost of the community service compared with the acute service. When monitoring this service, the commissioner may be pleased to see acute activity falling and community service activity ramping up. As a result, the commissioner may leave this service to continue delivering "savings" without taking a closer look to validate their assumption. However, unbeknown to the commissioner, the RTT has increased significantly within the acute setting as the secondary care service is experiencing a shortage of clinical capacity caused by an unfilled vacancy exacerbated by staff annual leave. As a result, the acute waiting list is growing, and patients are left unseen.

Had the commissioner included the acute RTT metric within a dashboard examining the performance of both the acute service (where reductions in activity are being targeted) and the community service (where the activity is intended to flow to), the commissioner would quickly spot this false positive and work with the acute service to address the problem, which may also present a clinical risk because of increasing patient waiting times. This example shows how baskets of interrelated data, presented in a dashboard, can make entire pathway management much easier. Too often, commissioners restrict their KPI analysis and monitoring activity to individual metrics that provide a simplified, binary worldview. Instead, commissioners must develop their own picture that reflects the complexity of the system that they are managing.

9.2.5 Summary

Patient outcome measurement is the cornerstone of the development and monitoring of good clinical practice across a health organization or system. In order to measure patient outcomes effectively, managers and clinicians must

- Agree a clear and shared definition of clinical quality, expressed in the language of patient outcomes, that then underpins everything that the organization or system does
- Design indicators and metrics that collect information that enable clinical leaders to track patient outcomes and to understand the process by which those outcomes were delivered
- Create a mixture of qualitative and quantitative measurement approaches that enable the system to measure all elements of the patient experience
- Develop and deploy a range of KPIs that enable system leaders to forensically manage a health pathway and track the way that benefits are delivered

9.3 What Performance Is Key? Staff

NHS England has set a series of specific performance targets to reduce avoidable harm. Perhaps the most familiar is the A&E four-hour target: the regulator requires that at least 95% of patients attending an A&E department must be seen, treated, admitted, or discharged in under four hours.

Meeting this target requires a hospital to work most efficiently in its busiest department but also requires productive, efficient, and Lean processes from much of the rest of the acute facility. This target was introduced in 2004 and the system failed to meet this target in year one. The King's Fund (2017) analyzed the main reasons for the system's failure to meet this target in 2004/2005 and found that

- There were not enough inpatient beds
- There were delayed discharges
- There were delays in accessing specialist opinions

- There were not enough nurses
- There were not enough middle-grade doctors
- Departments were too small
- There were delays in accessing diagnostic services

With the exception of capacity challenges (beds and the physical size of the department), all of these performance challenges related to people and the processes and systems within which they worked.

The performance parameters for recovery of the A&E four-hour target vividly show how efficiency, Lean processes, and productivity need to be embedded in the management of the wider system. The length of time spent by patients in A&E depends on the type of A&E unit they visit. Minor A&Es (types 2 and 3, such as urgent care centers or minor injury units) nearly always treat people in less than four hours, but major A&Es (i.e., type 1 emergency departments, which are consultant-led 24-hour services with full resuscitation facilities and designated accommodation to receive A&E patients) deal with higher numbers of attendees and more serious cases, meaning they find it harder to achieve the four-hour target.

In this example, A&E target recovery requires a clear diagnostic both of the end-to-end emergency pathway and of that pathway's place in the wider care system in order to understand where removal of inefficiencies can improve speed of treatment, admission, or discharge. This includes

- Analysis of bed usage and length of stay throughout the hospital to ensure adequate flexibility in bed occupancy
- Analysis of discharge planning and speed of discharge once patients are deemed medically fit
- Analysis of four-hour breaches according to specialty to understand each specialty's response time
- Analysis of staffing levels and roles and responsibilities (nurses, junior doctors, middle-grade doctors, consultants, technicians, support staff) to ensure speedy triage and the most effective use of each member of the team
- Analysis of speed of access to diagnostic services and of how much point of care testing can be introduced into A&E

A recovery trajectory is always built around improvements in flow including improved access for "blue light" emergencies, introducing an ambulance liaison to improve the reception of ambulances at the hospital, optimizing the patient flow within the emergency department, addressing contingent and contributory flows within the hospital, and developing seamless transitions between the hospital and community or domiciliary care. Most care systems set performance parameters and protocols for shared responsibilities such as integrated discharge (examples include the requirement for patients and carers to be informed of their discharge plan within 24 hours of admission, a low or zero numerator on delayed transfers of care, etc.).

However, the most important critical success factor for any sustained recovery in A&E performance is less visible and quantifiable. The requirements of the revised, streamlined four-hour target processes for each individual within the emergency department team and for the wider medical and non-medical clinical workforce within the hospital need to be embedded in objectives and appraisals and need to become "the way we work." Critically, they also need to transfer "from ward to board"; that is, to be embedded in the culture of the entire hospital, with the most senior leadership actively modeling the behaviors and expectations of effective, productive, and timely clinical interventions.

9.3.1 Summary

Staff performance is key to providing a high-quality experience for patients during care and delivering high-quality patient intermediate and end outcomes. The framework within which staff work is the key success factor for staff performance. Developing a framework that supports staff and enables them to optimize their performance should be a priority for clinical leaders, and this can only be achieved by closely measuring staff performance and activity flow within the framework in which staff work.

9.4 What Performance Is Key? Contracts

9.4.1 Measurement of Value

As noted above, KPIs are a crucial tool for measuring the absolute and comparative value delivered by a service to an organization, its patients, and its staff. Another approach that an organization can deploy to ensure that it is effectively measuring the value delivered by the services that it provides (or have commissioned) is by carrying out a Best Value Service or Contract Review. Such a review enables an assessment of existing services and is particularly useful when making an assessment about the relative value of a number of different services or contracts that are being provided or commissioned by an organization. This process then provides the information required by organizational leaders to make decisions about where to remove costs by decommissioning services or where to focus improvement program to increase the efficiency of services that deliver comparatively less value to patients, staff, or the taxpayer (for those health systems that are publicly funded).

9.4.4.1 Example: Central London Clinical Commissioning Group (CCG) Best Value Contract Review Approach

Central London CCG's Best Value Contract Review began in August 2016 following ratification of the process by the Turnaround Board in July 2016. Contracts were grouped into three tranches:

- Tranche 1: Nonclinical or highly discretionary contracts
- Tranche 2: Priority clinical contracts (based on a matrix scoring contracts against value, geography, and complexity of decommissioning)
- Tranche 3: All remaining contracts

The approach outlined in Figure 9.4 illustrates the basis for prioritization of Tranche 2 and was used during Central London CCG's Best Value Contract Review.

Once contracts had been prioritized, best value was measured by applying a "logic model." By completing a "logic model" like the one set out in Figure 9.5 for each service being reviewed, the reviewer could fully understand the scheme/service under review and establish how the components of the commissioned scheme/service were intended to fit together and interrelate to deliver the desired service.

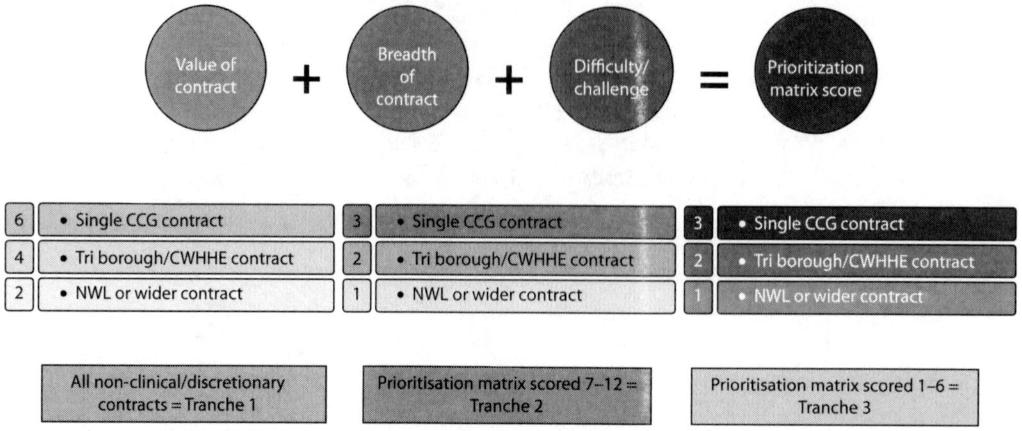

Figure 9.4 Central London CCG's Best Value Contract Review prioritization criteria.

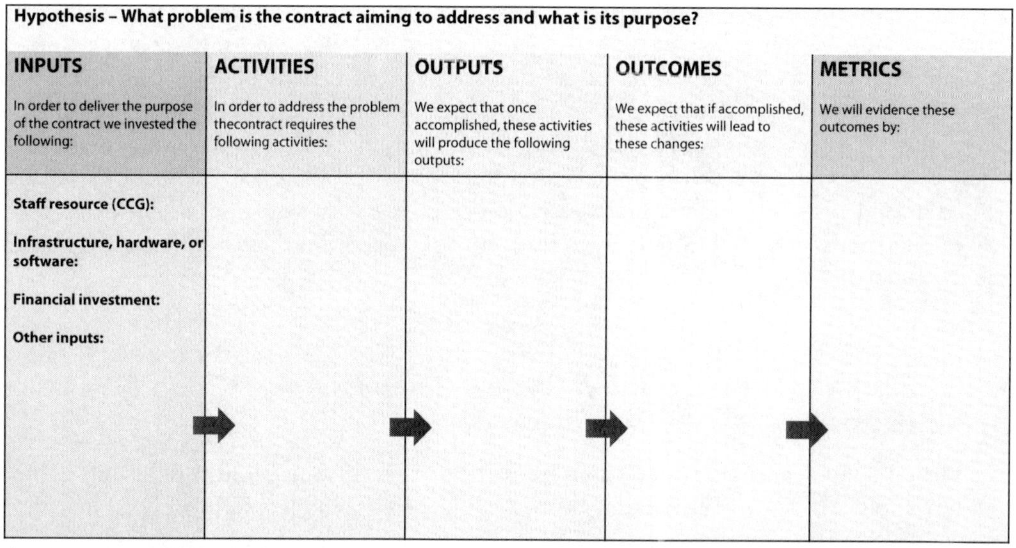

Figure 9.5 Example logic model framework.

This process enables the reviewer to identify any flaws in the service's design *in principle* (i.e., gaps in the service design, service specification, and/or contract outcome-focused KPIs methodology) as well as any shortfalls in delivery *in practice* (i.e., failure to hit KPIs, breaching of tolerances on quality indicators, or a failure to mobilize elements of the commissioned service within agreed timeframes). Any identified gaps can then be explored further by analyzing whether they are

- Hampering the delivery of benefits
- Frustrating the tracking of benefits
- Preventing the service from delivering additional benefits
- Stopping the service from delivering the same level of benefit more cost-effectively or efficiently

This logic model fits into a wider review process. The overall review process for a Best Value Review is set out in Figure 9.6, which shows where the logic model fits into the process. The logic model is the foundation of the whole review, as it provides the framework for the reviewer to explore how well value is being delivered (and where the service may be underperforming since it also steers the reviewer toward explanations about why the service may not be delivering). Figure 9.6 shows the decision tree that the reviewer must follow to obtain to a decision on the reviewed service's future.

What is crucial about the Best Value process is the taking into account of a range of "value" measures in order to deliver a balanced view of comparative value of that service when compared with other services within the organization's portfolio. Ultimately, each organization's definition of value will be determined by that organization's priorities, the statutory framework in which it works, and the financial circumstances experienced by the organization.

9.4.2 Measuring Return on Investment

One of the key ways to measure the delivery of financial value or value for money (VFM) is through a Return on Investment (ROI) analysis. An ROI assessment is often a simple "£ made or £ saved versus £ spent" equation. An ROI approach can be used as part of a mixture of other indicators or factors (such as service quality; efficiency; clinical outcomes; the comparative cost,

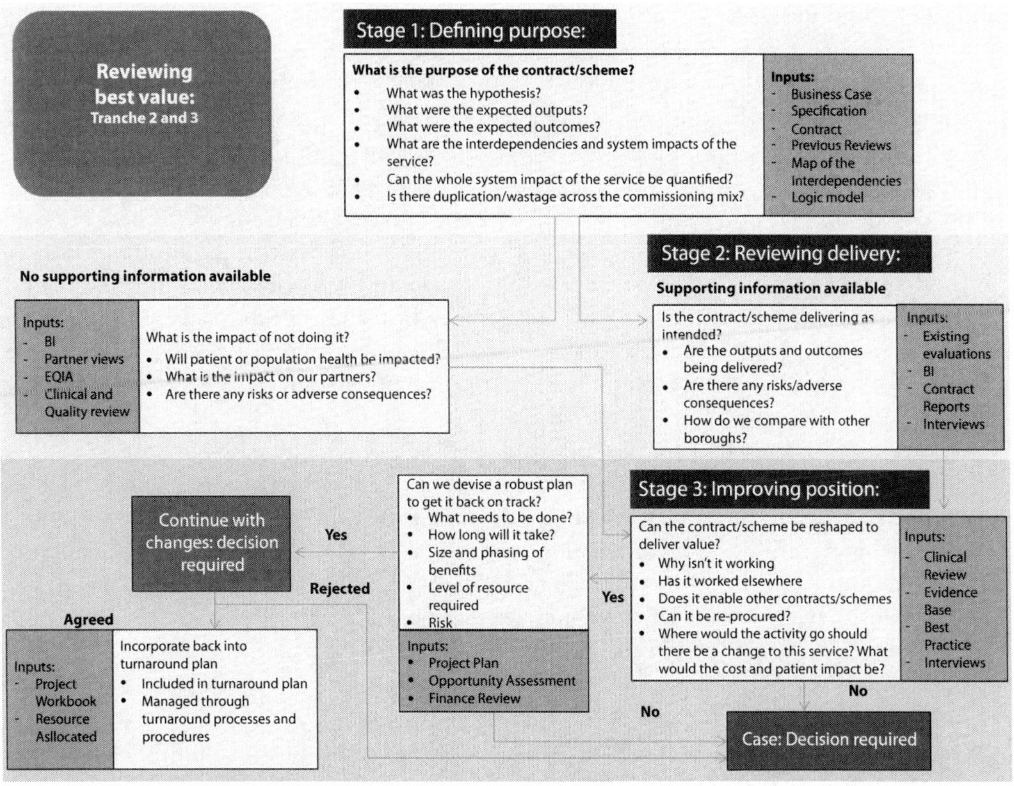

Figure 9.6 Central London CCG's Best Value Contract Review decision tree.

quality, or productivity of similar services in neighboring areas, etc.; or the impact of removing a service on the patients or staff affected) that can be weighed up in order to help a reviewer establish whether an existing service is delivering best financial value.

A useful rule of thumb when assessing whether a service is delivering a satisfactory ROI is to calculate whether a service is delivering three times the financial return from an investment (i.e., for every £1 spent a service is delivering £3 worth of savings).

9.4.3 Learning from Applying Best Value Criteria during Contract Reviews

From the above case study, several key performance-related themes emerged and have been echoed in other Best Value Contract Reviews:

- Align internal processes: It is important to ensure that the commissioning and decommissioning decisions taken by any commissioner are fully reflected within the CCG contracts team, finance team, and the central contracts team.
- Stock takes matter: Review contract registers every six months to ensure that they align with local commissioning arrangements and the Central London CCG budget.
- Create and deploy KPIs that track outcomes effectively: NHS contracts often include little information on the outcomes that the contract is designed to deliver, which will make accountability within new care models impossible to track.
- Tie KPIs to ROI: Any investment or commissioning decision is supported by a set of draft KPIs and metrics that include a clear understanding of activity and how it relates to outputs and outcomes.
- Avoid duplication: In a complex care system, map all other services with similar outcomes so that commissioning leadership can take decisions with an understanding of wider provision.
- Good metrics do not compensate for poor service design. Returning to the example of the community dermatology service, commissioners may have devised the right metrics, data collection, data collation, and reporting mechanisms for a new service but not necessarily in the full context and dynamics of the pathway that they are managing across acute and community services. However, if commissioners have not developed contractual levers to drive demand out of the acute into the community service, the metrics will provide a good picture of a failed approach.
- Ensuring that contractual levers are in place is one, if not the most, important factor in delivering benefits, and this should be as much of a priority for managers when designing services as the metrics that they want to use to measure benefit realization.
- Less is more: Managers often fall into the trap of developing information schedules that include large numbers of metrics. Commissioners must think carefully about the use they are going to make of each indicator and whether this indicator is essential. It is preferable to have a smaller basket of high-quality outcome-focused KPIs that are well recorded by health professionals and that the provider reliably reports against than to have a long list of indicators that are not well recorded or reported against.
- When devising information schedules, commissioners must think carefully about the KPIs that are required to track benefits and assess the service's value to commissioners. This means challenging themselves to distill a small number of interrelated and well-calibrated

indicators that place the minimum burden on providers but still satisfy the statutory and informational requirements of the commissioner.
- Standardize KPIs where possible: It is important that individual project KPIs are standardized across the system to enable the metrics from a large number of projects and programs to be aggregated into meaningful whole system summary metrics. Without standardization, it is difficult, if not impossible, to create useful thematic summaries of performance that enable whole system management.

9.4.4 Summary

The measurement of the absolute and comparative value of the services that an organization delivers is crucial to enable managers to prioritize and phase service provision. This section has discussed several approaches that enable the effective measurement of the financial value of services or contracts:

- Measurement of value through Best Value Contract Review: Logic models can help to clearly break a service down into its constituent components to enable analysis and measurement of the value delivered by a service and to equip managers with the information needed to ensure continuous improvement. This measurement of "value" includes both patient and financial outcomes.
- Measuring ROI: The benchmark for the measurement of financial value is using an ROI calculation and establishing whether a service is providing a satisfactory financial return on financial investment. ROI must always be balanced against patient value and should not be used in isolation to measure the "value" of a service to the wider system or the patients it serves.
- Learning from applying best value criteria during contract reviews: Measurement of value can only be achieved by taking a well-informed investment, having a good map of the whole health and care system before making a change, communicating any changes adequately, ensuring that services are designed well, tracking benefits through a small number of well-designed KPIs, and embedding and applying contract controls rigorously. Measurement is just one part of a wider commissioning process that must be delivered effectively to achieve good patient outcomes.

9.5 What Performance Is Key? Reward

The way the NHS currently pays for healthcare can support or hinder health and social care organizations from working as an effective, aligned system to meet patient and population needs. However, patient-centered, networked care is emerging in the United Kingdom, and the challenge for both commissioner and provider is to find an appropriate method of measuring and incentivizing performance.

The NHS currently rewards acute providers using an activity-based payment approach, which arguably incentivizes increased activity. Integrated out-of-hospital care can reduce acute activity, but there is rarely a commensurate and immediate reduction in acute costs. Block payments for community and mental health services also provide no clear incentive to reduce the overall costs of activity or engage proactively in prevention.

A multilateral risk-and-gain share approach changes the payment model but is deeply reliant on a common vision, clear whole system redesign, and design of a payment mechanism that matches the desired patient outcomes. The two key components of a multilateral gain/loss sharing mechanism are

- That it covers multiple providers and one or more commissioners
- That financial gains/losses are identified and distributed based on system financial performance and/or other metrics such as quality and outcome performance

NHS Improvement's (one of the key UK regulators, previously Monitor) guidance reads: "The gain/loss sharing mechanism works by comparing the expected commissioner spend (associated with delivering care) with the actual outturn. The difference between the expected spend and actual outturn forms the gains/losses pool" (Monitor 2015).

In practice, this means that commissioners can bring together payments for multiple providers and that both commissioners and providers can contribute to system-wide change while reducing individual organizational risk. Monitor guidance describes various models that can be adapted to reflect the maturity of joint commissioning and of collaborative agreements within the care system.

In reality, long before a risk-and-gain share is undertaken, most communities of practice usually enter into bi- or trilateral joint venture arrangements, either with shared business goals or framed by a memorandum of understanding. Mature system relationships take time to develop, and most changes in contractual arrangements that enable gradual progress toward the end goal are incremental rather than the immediate complex framing of a long-term alliance contract.

9.5.1 Summary

Designing reward mechanisms well is crucial to incentivizing the behaviors of all actors in an organization or system. Outcome measurement underpins this approach by enabling the tracking of performance and reward (or sanction) of system actors based upon their delivered outcomes.

Having discussed what performance is key and how that performance should be measured, we now consider the methodologies deployed by health commissioners and providers to achieve value for money and ensure that they deliver appropriate outputs and outcomes.

9.6 How Do We Know the Whole System Is Performing? Business Intelligence Indicators

Establishing a robust business intelligence (BI) function within a health organization or system is fundamental to the delivery of good outcomes, because getting BI methodology right enables leaders to track delivery against their performance parameter measurements.

9.6.1 Why Involve Business Intelligence?

Key performance indicators are often designed in isolation without involving business analytics or seeking detailed business information. Yet, within a complex care system, it is never too early to involve BI to ensure performance.

Effective BI teams in both commissioners and providers adopt the theory that they are there

- To dig out anomalies and investigate
- To scope out opportunities and issues through more thorough care system analysis
- To interpret benchmarking data as a useful starting point for a deep dive to fully establish the scale and scope of any savings opportunities

BI works best for both provider and commissioner when accompanied by clinical audit. This ensures that any business cases consider the appropriateness of the proposed performance and productivity actions and enable teams to fully understand the clinical drivers. We present two case studies that bring the importance of BI and analytics to life.

9.6.1.1 Commissioning Case Study: Neurology

In January 2016, a CCG Commissioning for Value pack produced as part of the RightCare program identified CCG "A" as being an outlier for neurological spend when compared with ten similar CCGs. The pack suggested that CCG A could potentially save up to £150 thousand per year if it reduced its neurological spend to the same level as the five best comparable CCGs. This launched a scoping exercise to identify how to realize the potential savings.

An existing community headache service within another CCG (CCG "B") was identified as a model to replicate, so CCG A sourced the business plan and savings assumptions used for CCG B's community headache service and applied them to CCG A.

The projected benefits and savings for the community service were based on

- Cheaper tariff in the community (£86 vs. £93 for CCG B)
- Reduced diagnostics (MRI scans reduced by 50% when patients are managed in a community setting)
- Reduced A&E attendances, acute outpatient appointments, and inpatient admissions for neurological-related conditions
- Removing the current high levels of patient dissatisfaction

When the BI team ran the savings assumptions against CCG A's spend on patients with headaches, the savings were not deemed high enough to make it economical to commission the community headache clinic based on the CCG B model.

9.6.1.2 Commissioning Case Study: Fecal Calprotectin

Fecal calprotectin (FC) tests are a standard pathology test available to all GPs that can be used to distinguish inflammatory bowel disease (IBD, a serious condition) from irritable bowel syndrome (IBS, an uncomfortable but not life-threatening condition). This is a useful tool in routine patients because IBD requires diagnostic confirmation and treatment whereas IBS can be managed by GPs and may have other causes such as stress or recent lifestyle changes.

In the three CCGs considered, the data suggested that GPs were not using routine FC tests, with 2016/2017 forecast growth in these three CCGs for diagnostic colonoscopy in excess of 44% year-on-year. A diagnostic colonoscopy costs £600 and an FC test around £35.

BI teams provided the following support services to ensure value-for-money commissioner spend:

- Further analysis including a detailed look at FC tests undertaken by GP practices alongside the number of diagnostics by practice to highlight inconsistencies (via pathology data from providers, where available).
- "Searches" conducted to find out if other CCGs already have a process and/or GP education in place and key learning (a neighboring CCG possibly has a process in place as year-on-year growth is −2%).
- Scoping a clinical audit to be undertaken in key trusts to ascertain the proportion of routine activity for IBS/IBD as opposed to standard screening and other reasons.
- BI analysis to support the business case, defining the headline activity and the potential savings opportunity (£150–£300 thousand recurrent savings).
- A plan implemented to include a more standardized approach to FC testing in primary care via GP education.
- A Quality, Innovation, Productivity, and Prevention (QIPP)-able process defined to monitor pathology and GP referral activity as well as diagnostic colonoscopy allowing targets/trajectories to be put in place.
- A process to implement the addition of a new Planned Procedure with a limited Threshold (PPwT) documentation requirement on providers (for IBD/IBS pathway patients) to ensure that when they receive a referral, the GP has included the results of the pathology test, with referrals being rejected for patients who have not had an FC test or where the result of the test suggests that the patient will not benefit from diagnostic colonoscopy.

9.6.2 Ensuring Robust Service Management

Business analysis and informatics are clearly key to commissioner performance, but they play an equally important role in provider performance by analyzing processes and then ensuring adherence to Lean service redesign.

As well as ensuring that the correct Lean indicators are in place, the right processes must also be in place to support robust service management. These include

- Clarity on the organization's expectations about when project and program managers need to involve BI during the project cycle, and what input is required from BI into regular monitoring and horizon scanning.
- Ensuring that financial and activity reporting is fully aligned so that the organization can track delivery of its plan, support strong governance and accountability, and take any remedial action required at pace.
- Setting up regular reporting and data discussion meetings to ensure that monitoring takes place. Where relevant, this includes mandating regular meetings with external contractors to ensure that performance data are received and reviewed on a regular basis.

Organizations may also want to create internal tolerances and thresholds within which activity and spending would be expected to fall and processes that, if thresholds are breached, would trigger escalation and risk management processes to ensure that risks are visible, well managed, and automatically identified.

9.6.3 *Using BI Wisely*

In contrast to traditional data collection approaches, which tended to collate and report metrics to summarize service performance over a discrete historical time period (i.e., monthly reporting), modern technology now offers opportunities to collect and report these data in real time. The more up to date the data, the more applications these data can offer organizations. Real-time data flows, for example, offer the potential for data to be used for dynamic resource management and planning rather than just the monitoring and scrutiny of past performance, which has traditionally been the way that health economies have used performance data.

For instance, by using real-time data flows to manage beds, hospitals can significantly improve bed utilization by minimizing "down time," speeding up transitions, and reducing the time elapsed between a patient being discharged and a new patient being transferred into the bed. Real-time data also speed up the identification of risks and can therefore help organizations mitigate them before they develop into issues. They also enable nimble decision-making that can fix issues quickly instead of only becoming aware of them months later. The benefits to clinical quality of this real-time feedback loop are self-evident. Algorithms that utilize real-time data could even be used in future to identify "never events" as they are unfolding and to raise an alarm to prevent them occurring: a real and meaningful clinical and organizational benefit.

9.6.4 *Summary*

Getting BI methodology right enables managers to track performance parameters, escalate risks and issues, and manage change safely and efficiently. Good BI systems also help to identify opportunities for service improvement and can support the delivery of better patient and financial value. Once BI methodology is agreed on, the next step is to ensure that these BI processes and resources fit into an effective governance framework to drive good decision-making and therefore continuous improvement across organizations and systems.

9.7 How Do We Learn by Doing? Continuous Improvement, Governance, and Data

9.7.1 *How Performance Metrics Enable Whole System Management*

Performance metrics are tools that enable scrutiny, oversight, measurement, and monitoring of the services and schemes being delivered by an organization. Ultimately, these performance-monitoring tools should feed into processes that serve a robust governance framework and enable leadership to monitor and manage risk effectively and plan in an informed way.

Having a nimble BI team that pulls well-designed KPI data through effective reporting mechanisms (contractual or otherwise) and then presents this information in an accessible and meaningful way is vital to supporting good decision-making within an organization. Organizations must give thought to each stage of the data flow, specifically:

- Data recording
- Data collection
- Data collation
- Data reporting

The outputs from these data management mechanisms should feed into frameworks of regular monitoring meetings for each service, which in turn report upward into departmental or directorate, organizational, and system management meetings served by summary datasets and "dashboards" at each step (i.e., project metrics are summarized into program metrics and program metrics into directorate metrics, etc.) (Figures 9.7 through 9.10).

As meetings rise through the governance process, metrics should become more thematic (i.e., summarizing an entire population segment's care model) to enable monitoring and oversight of system segments and eventually the whole system at scale. It is important to remember that the goal is to understand the whole system, so the development of individual metrics at a project level must reflect the need for that metric to flow upward and fit into a wider framework that explains the whole system. This is only possible if key metrics are standardized and where this is applied across all services. If standardization does not happen, it become very difficult to aggregate data and analyze it in a consistent way.

9.7.2 How Performance Metrics Can Drive Good Planning

As well as being integral to the monitoring of current service delivery and improving the way that organizations manage their scarce and expensive resources, high-quality data reporting and analysis are essential when planning service transformation and when developing new services. To enable good planning, BI must be embedded in project and program teams from project inception. These multidisciplinary teams must also include designated clinical, finance, procurement, and contracting leads (if required) as well as project team members. Creating this core team from project inception has the following benefits:

- *Methodology*: Input from all relevant specialties helps to ensure that the correct methodologies and thinking are embedded within the team's approach from the outset.

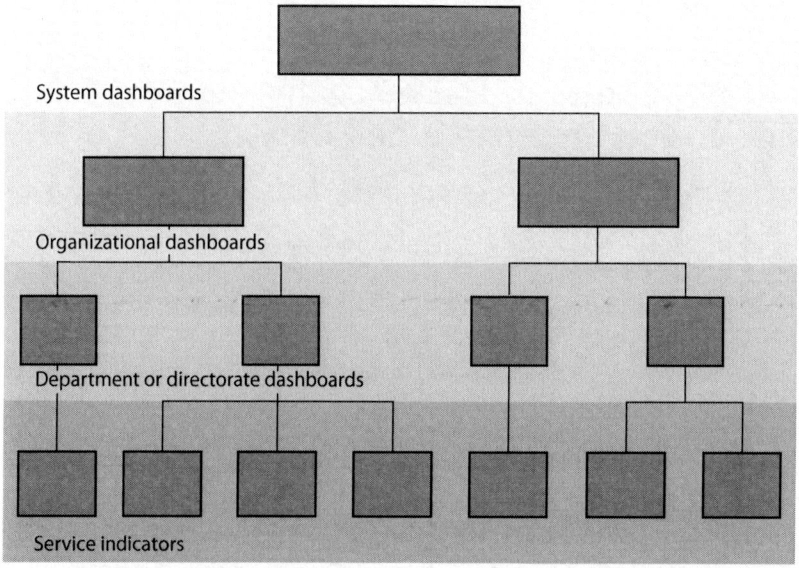

Figure 9.7 Example of upward data flow, beginning with service-level indicators and eventually contributing to a whole system view.

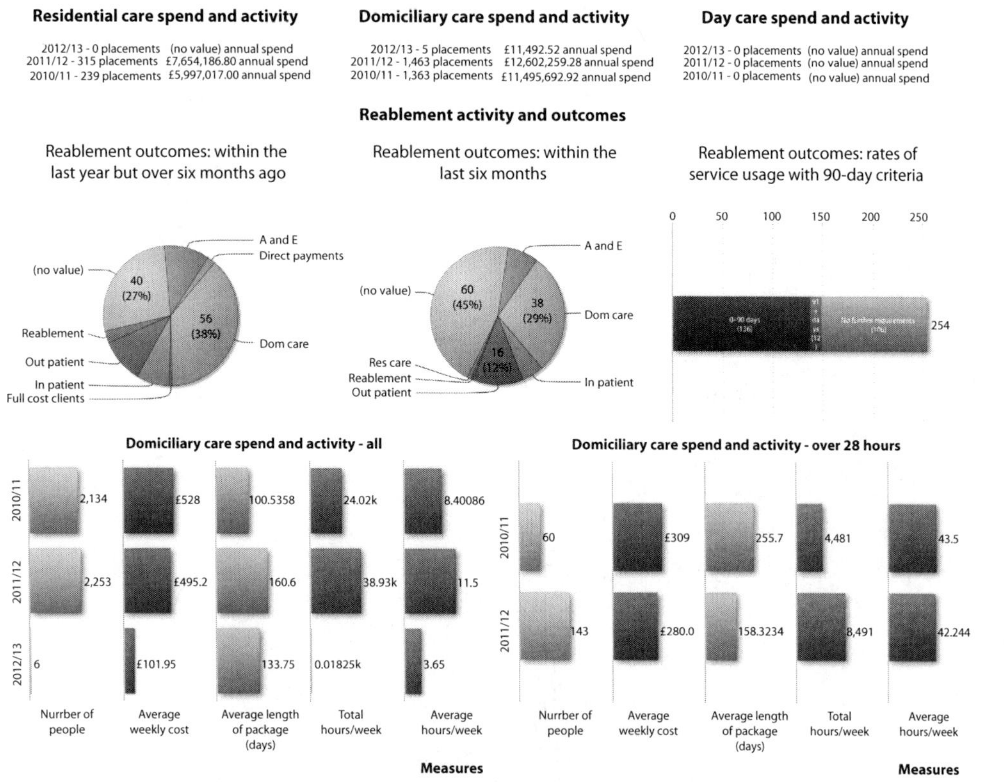

Figure 9.8 Example of a social care organizational dashboard.

- *Resource management*: If their intensive support is not required initially, plans can be made about the appropriate times to reengage with each specialty to ensure that resources are available when needed during the project's lifespan.
- *Assurance*: Group discussion and joint planning will clarify the various project stages that other specialist teams are expecting to be consulted on to provide assurance that plans are robust.
- *Governance compliance*: In relation to the above, this will enable the project manager to include related governance checkpoints and gateways in their plan that are required during the project's lifespan to enable robust planning and avoid delays in progressing the agreed plan.
- *Role and responsibilities are clearly defined*: Roles and responsibilities can be clarified at the start of the project to ensure that no false assumptions are made about other parts of the business picking up elements of the work. This will ensure nothing is missed from the plan and that the critical path elements are clearly delineated and related tasks distributed between teams and team members.

9.7.3 How Performance Metrics Can Support Good Decision-Making

Once the team structure and data flow have been optimized, it is crucial that organizations and systems create strong and streamlined decision-making processes to (1) enable the correct decisions to be made, and (2) use performance data to drive the appropriate prioritization of resources and phasing of work. Best practice suggests that good decisions can be made with two or three decision-making layers. The NHS England RightCare team has recently developed a healthcare reform process map

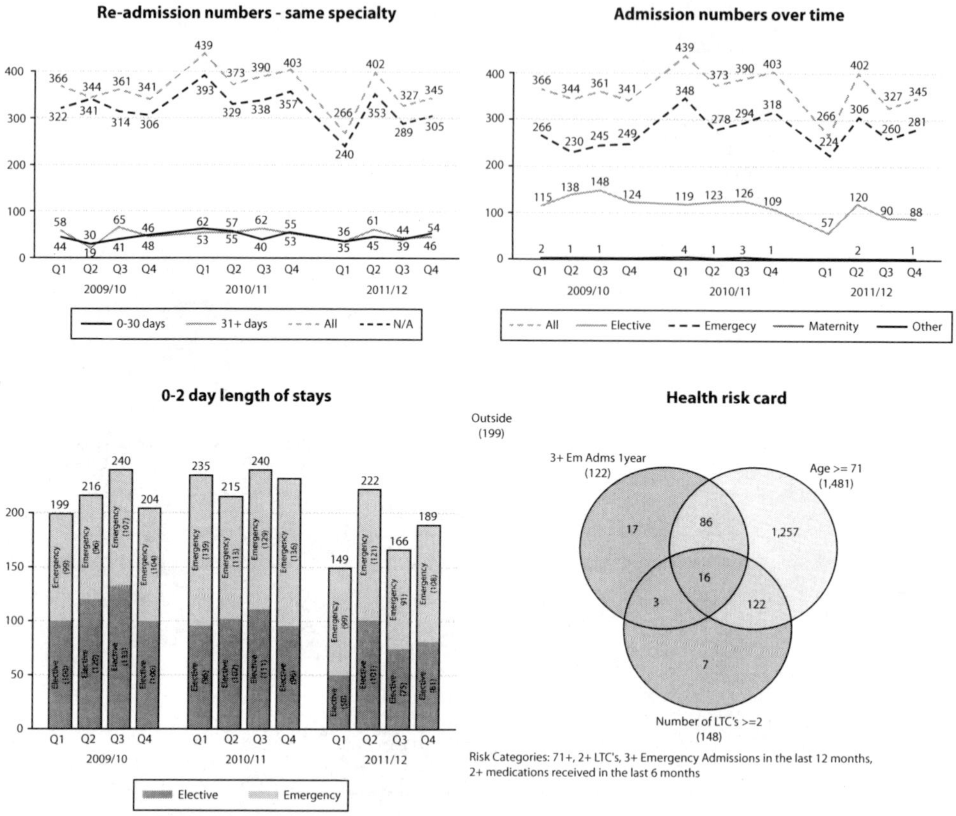

Figure 9.9 Example of a health organizational dashboard.

that neatly summarizes the steps required to bring about high-quality service and system improvement (Figure 9.11). The reform map delineates three elements: mechanisms, processes, and decisions. High-quality informatics and performance and quality metrics are fundamental processes that underpin and support the mechanisms that lead to consensus and therefore decision-making.

High-quality data presented in a meaningful way can lead to swift and correct decisions. Data must support good system reform decisions by enabling managers to answer three fundamental "deal-breaker" questions:

- Does the proposed approach improve or maintain health outcomes?
- Does the proposal save money?
- Are we confident there is an evidence base for change?

Once a proposal has passed these three "deal-breaker" tests, the following three questions can be used to prioritize and determine the delivery order of the schemes an organization or system has chosen to deliver:

- Is it quick and easy?
- How much does it save?
- What is the rate of return?

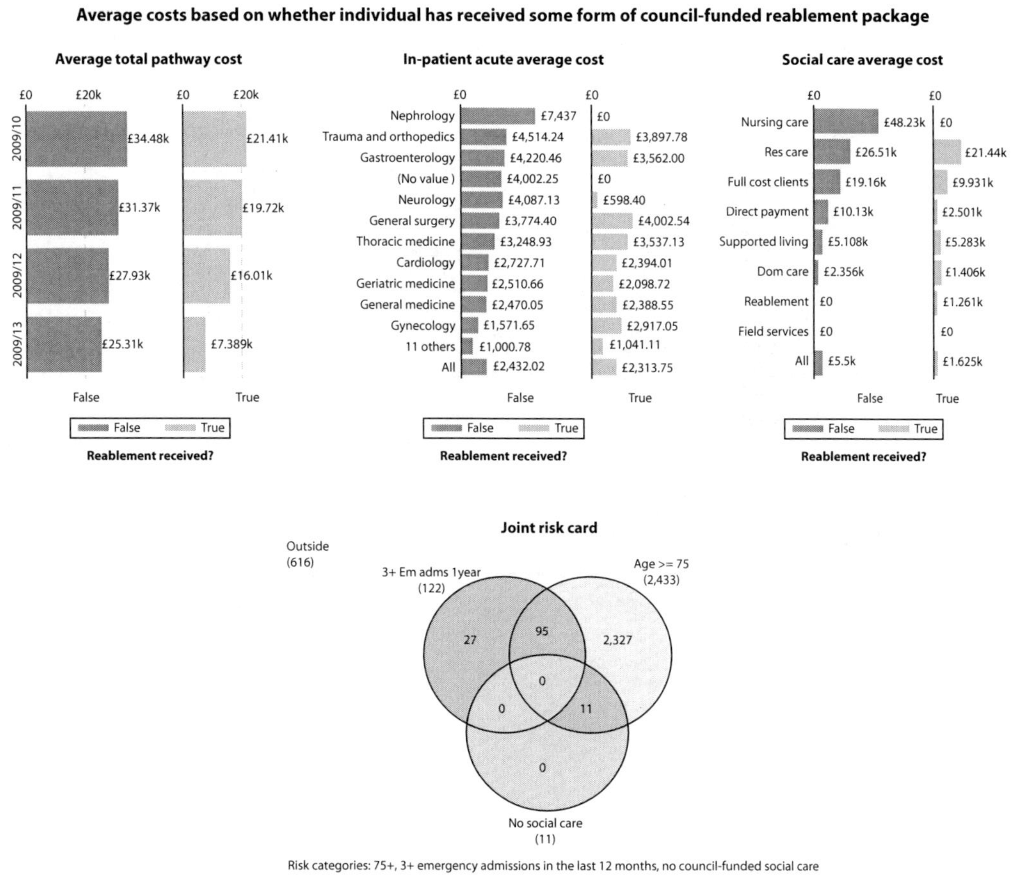

Figure 9.10 Example of a joint health and social care system dashboard.

Decision trees can feed into and support this decision-making process. The example below is from the Blackpool CCG, who developed this approach and then reevaluated all of the schemes that they were working on (Figure 9.12). As a result of applying their own decision-making criteria, the CCG took the decision to deprioritize or stop a large amount of their current work and to prioritize a host of other schemes. This lesson shows that good performance parameters are not enough on their own, and that robust decision-making processes and strong governance consistently applied are also required to ensure that performance parameters lead to performance improvement.

9.7.4 Summary

One of the key enablers of good decision-making in any health organization or system is for clinical leaders to have an up-to-date, whole system view of performance. This whole system view can only be created by having consistent, standardized performance metrics that feed into a coherent network of data recording, collection, collation, analysis, and reporting.

However, accurate information alone is insufficient to enable good decision-making. Robust performance metrics and reporting must be combined with a well-designed and policed governance framework supported by logically consistent decision-making processes. This marriage of

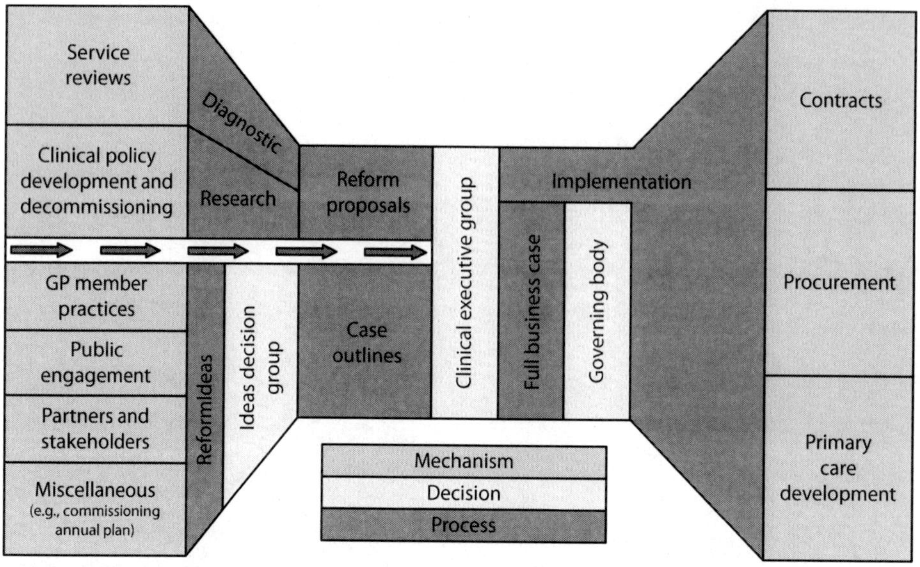

Figure 9.11 NHS RightCare healthcare reform process map (NHS England 2016b).

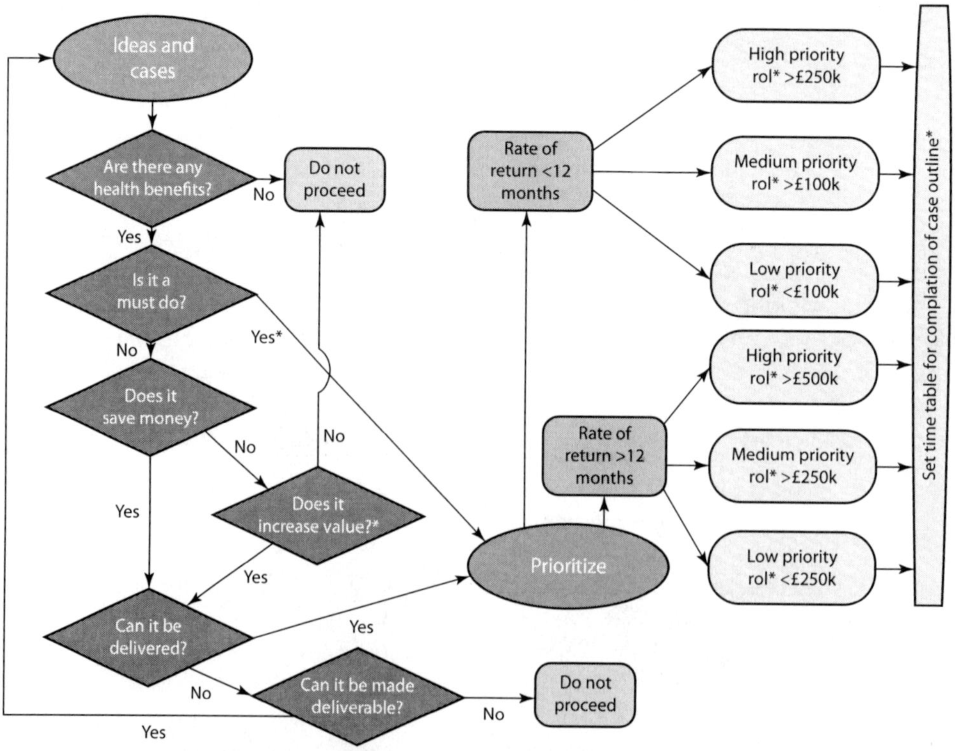

Figure 9.12 Blackpool CCG Decision Tree for prioritizing reform proposals.

good data and robust governance enables high-quality decision-making, which in turn drives continuous improvement of system value and patient outcomes.

Once internal system monitoring and decision-making methodologies have been optimized in this way, leaders can then look beyond their own system and enhance their understanding of "what good looks like" by comparing their own system with external health and care systems. The final methodology to support high performance is benchmarking.

9.8 How Is the Care System Performing? The Importance of Benchmarking

Before taking any whole system actions to improve performance, it is critical to lift heads above normal horizons and undertake both commissioner and provider benchmarking.

9.8.1 Spending the Tax Payer's Money Wisely

In the United Kingdom, three main commissioners are relevant to the new care models: NHS England for specialist commissioning and primary care; CCGs for each local health economy; and local authorities for public health and health-related social care, education, and housing spend. In commissioner terms, benchmarking means understanding the public funding spend and activity profile of the care system at a whole population level and then by population health segment and care model.

Interrogating spend enables a commissioning organization's leaders to focus on the areas where it is a performance outlier. By undertaking diagnostics of spend and activity profiles across the health sectors that impact it (i.e., acute sector, community sector, mental health, and primary care) and comparing this spend and activity against other organizations who operate within the same or comparable systems, an organization can identify where it is experiencing negative variation in financial and non-financial outcomes.

Within the NHS, there is a wealth of benchmarking information and studies to provide viable comparisons. Professional bodies, consultancies, and the NHS Benchmarking Network have all published specific studies, with particularly relevant examples to the new care models challenge being "The National Audit of Intermediate Care" (2015); and the "Older People's Care in Acute Settings" (2016).

At a more granular level, to benchmark spend on specific points of delivery or pathways, commissioning organizations can also access "off-the-shelf" benchmarking tools and resources (so, for example, a CCG could use the NHS England Commissioning for Value packs and NHS RightCare data) to build on a whole care system diagnostic and create a detailed understanding of where they could do more to reduce spend and activity. Deep dives into areas where unwarranted variation has been identified can then help an organization to better understand capacity, demand, and spend and identify areas where they can take immediate action.

9.8.2 Ensuring High-Quality, Cost-Effective Health Services—The Provider Challenge

On February 2, 2016, the final report and recommendations of the Carter review into NHS acute services was published (Department of Health 2015). Entitled "Operational Productivity and Performance in English NHS Acute Hospitals: Unwarranted Variations," it has 15 overall recommendations based on the use of benchmarking comparisons throughout the sector. The report also created the concept of a "model hospital," identifying nine practices that are key elements in developing a successful organization. Carter claims that implementing model hospital practices could save the NHS £5 billion.

The Carter review illustrates well how many performance elements contribute to high-quality, cost-effective services. His recommendations are grouped into three domains: (1) optimizing clinical resources, (2) optimizing nonclinical resources, and (3) quality and efficiency across the patient pathway. These three domains are potentially applicable in a wider context than removal of variation in the acute setting. The ultimate aim of benchmarking, irrespective of whether it is viewed through the commissioner or provider lens, is to identify and remove unwarranted variation in resource use and duplication of patient pathways.

9.8.3 Practical Tips for Meaningful Benchmarking

Some key steps need to be followed to enable successful and meaningful benchmarking, including the following:

- Data standardization must take place to ensure that data are comparable. On the commissioner side, the performance challenge is to ensure value for money spent and resource allocation against population health need. One way to do this is by using "weighted populations," which take variances in a population's age and sex distribution into account along with the varying acuity of a specific population.
- The time period is also important. Many population health needs can only be fully understood by examining the full annual cycle of need, that is, the full year effect of data. Seasonality is a factor in fluctuations in healthcare demand (crudely put, in the United Kingdom, demand goes up in winter and down in summer, but this is not always the case, depending on the specific weather that year) as are other factors such as industrial action or any other major events such as epidemics or freak weather events that may impact demand.
- Comparing organizations with similarly structured health economies (by geography and demography) is also important. For example, comparing a central London healthcare system with a rural model may create "false positives" by identifying areas of variation in spend or activity that are more a function of geography than system efficiency. Crudely contrasting systems may throw up starkly contrasting benchmarking outputs that can be confusing to decipher.
- Getting the right balance between "indicative data" and "evidential data." Benchmarking provides indicative data, which provides comparisons between comparable health systems (usually by demography). These indicative data can help managers to identify broad areas of opportunity and "where to look." However, these data alone cannot provide an understanding of the "how." Local systems must look at local, evidential data (i.e., public health data, patient-level data, clinical audits, and quality impact assessments) to understand exactly how their system can be improved. Getting the balance right between indicative benchmarking data, which shows where to look, and evidential data, which shows how to bring about change, is crucial to delivering improved outcomes.

For both provider and commissioner benchmarking, it is also important to examine the dynamics that shape the entire system by including all key indicators in an analysis. Looking at just one or a small number of indicators without understanding the wider context can be misleading; high demand in one area is not necessarily an indicator of excess demand but may be more of a reflection of the way that the system is calibrated. For example, a system that has relatively high elective admissions must be understood in the context of other interrelated variables. For instance, the care system may have lower than average nonelective admissions. Viewing system segments in isolation without understanding the wider context can lead to misunderstanding.

Wider "sizing" of the system can also be useful to understanding whether monthly spend (also called "run rate") is in line with current budget and income as well as affordable in terms of future allocation of funding. Modeling demand forward against expected income is vital to identify and manage future financial risk and to make adjustments to deal with forecast reductions or increases in budget.

The ultimate goal for a really mature system is to be able to benchmark not just cost and quality but also the appropriateness of the patient journey. The NHS "Year of Care" pilot (2011) began by benchmarking each site's performance against national performance benchmarks but increasingly found that benchmarking system change activity (i.e., care planning) within a learning set enabled them to more quickly identify the characteristics of a rapidly maturing system. They then developed a series of long-term condition-specific or population health need-specific comparators within their particular action learning sets. This approach shows how partners can practically use benchmarking data to help their systems develop faster through peer engagement, review, and challenge.

9.8.4 Summary

Benchmarking is the final piece of the jigsaw. It enables system leaders to look "beyond their noses" by understanding how other systems operate and how differences in system delivery dynamics can alter patient and financial outcomes. However, comparing systems through benchmarking can be fraught with difficulty if managers are unaware of how inherent differences in system characteristics (such as demography, geography, or system maturity) shape outcomes. Benchmarking can highlight useful comparisons through indicative data, but evidential data and detailed analysis must follow. If these steps are followed, then benchmarking can equip organizations and systems to mature in ways that may not have been possible by looking at internal performance parameters alone.

9.9 Conclusion: Using the Three Ms to Enable Whole System Management

The key challenge facing modern health and care systems is that most systems are struggling to operate as mature integrated care systems. Substantial progress has been made in governance and accountability, particularly in areas that are seeking devolution of powers and funding. However, genuine integration cannot be achieved without a shared understanding by all contributing organizations of what good care looks like.

The unifying currency that enables a system of national and local commissioners, providers, and regulators to ascertain the value provided to patients is measuring and monitoring patient outcomes. The unifying currency for joint commissioners is value for money.

Several performance parameters are required to enable system leaders to monitor patient outcomes. As each system is different, the key choices for system leaders are to decide what tools and frameworks most enable achievement of shared objectives. By getting performance indicators and protocols right and then reporting performance through a well-designed management information system and governance framework, system leaders can ensure they have the information and processes at their disposal to make good decisions.

9.9.1 Measurement

This chapter has set out the four priority areas for performance parameters to measure: patient outcomes, staff and use of resources, appropriateness of and compliance with contracts, and the system of sanctions and rewards for healthcare providers. Defining and measuring good patient outcomes is the critical success factor for any health and social care system. It is only when a system can agree on common objectives and shared outcomes that allocation of staffing and resources, contracts, and reward mechanisms can be defined and measured.

9.9.2 Methodology

Once common goals have been defined and success measures agreed, clearly defined methodologies enable the rapid development of effective collaborative care. Well-structured BI processes are required to feed into streamlined governance and accountability frameworks. This provides the foundation for good decision-making, especially when supported by best practice system reform processes such as decision trees and the use of whole system benchmarking.

9.9.3 Maturity

The level of challenge facing the NHS in a period of financial austerity and spending restraint requires care systems to develop in both pace and scale. Developing appropriate measurements and methodologies are often the first key steps in maturing collaborative relationships by focusing organizations on common goals. Fundamentally, where collaboration starts is less important than understanding the level of system maturity. True maturity only comes when performance parameters are aligned to achieve shared goals across the health and care system.

References

Darzi, A. 2008. *NHS Next Stage Review: Leading Local Change*. London: Department of Health.

Donabedian, A. 1988. The quality of care. How can it be assessed? *JAMA* 260 (12):1743–1748.

Department of Health. 2009. High Quality Care for All. http://webarchive.nationalarchives.gov.uk/+/www.dh.gov.uk/en/Healthcare/Highqualitycareforall/index.htm

Department of Health. 2014. The NHS Outcomes Framework 2015/16. https://www.gov.uk/government/uploads/system/uploads/attachment_data/file/385749/NHS_Outcomes_Framework.pdf

Department of Health. 2015. Productivity in NHS Hospitals. https://www.gov.uk/government/publications/productivity-in-nhs-hospitals

The King's Fund. 2017. What's going on in A&E? The key questions answered. https://www.kingsfund.org.uk/projects/urgent-emergency-care/urgent-and-emergency-care-mythbusters.

Lohr, K. N., and S. A. Schroeder. 1990. A strategy for quality assurance in medicare. *N Engl J Med* 322 (10):707–712.

McKee, M. 2013. Improving the safety of patients in England. *BMJ* 347:f5038.

Monitor. 2015. Multilateral Gain/Loss Sharing to Support New Models of Care: An Introduction. https://www.gov.uk/government/publications/multilateral-gainloss-sharing-an-introduction

NHS Benchmarking Network. 2015. National Audit of Intermediate Care Summary Report 2015. http://www.nhsbenchmarking.nhs.uk/CubeCore/.uploads/NAIC/Reports/NAICReport2015FINALA4printableversion.pdf

NHS Benchmarking Network. 2016. Older People's Care in Acute Settings.

NHS England. 2014. The Friends and Family Test. *Publications Gateway Ref* (01787).

NHS England. 2016a. Never Events. https://www.england.nhs.uk/patientsafety/never-events/

NHS England. 2016b. NHS RightCare. https://www.england.nhs.uk/rightcare/

NHS England and Care Quality Commission. 2014. *NHS Five Year Forward View* pp. 16–16. London: NHS England.

Nutting, P. A., M. A. Goodwin, S. A. Flocke, S. J. Zyzanski, and K. C. Stange. 2003. Continuity of primary care: To whom does it matter and when? *Ann Fam Med* 1 (3):149–155.

Raleigh, V., and C. Foot. 2010. Getting the measure of quality. *Opportunities and Challenges*.

Year of Care Programme Board. 2011. Year of Care: Report of ndings from the pilot programme. http://www.yearofcare.co.uk/sites/default/files/images/YOC_Report%20-%20correct.pdf

Chapter 10

Quality and Cost in Healthcare: Improving Performance

Bruno Holthof

Contents

10.1 Introduction ... 189
10.2 Five Strategies for Success ... 190
 10.2.1 Creating Scale in Clinical and Administrative Support Systems ... 191
 10.2.2 Forming Clinical Teams to Treat High Volumes of Patients ... 192
 10.2.3 Using Minimally Invasive Techniques ... 193
 10.2.4 Involving Patients in Self-Managing Their Health ... 195
 10.2.5 Target Interventions to Patients Most Likely to Benefit ... 197
10.3 Implications for Decision-Making ... 198
10.4 Circle of Improvement: Better Outcomes, Reduced Footprint, More Cash ... 199
 10.4.1 Outcome ... 200
 10.4.2 Footprint ... 200
 10.4.3 Cash ... 201
 10.4.4 Productivity ... 201
10.5 Conclusions ... 202
References ... 202

10.1 Introduction

Healthcare services are the largest economic activity in developed countries. The percentage of gross domestic product (GDP) spent on healthcare services in 2014 ranged from 17% in the United States to 9% in the United Kingdom, with per capita differences between the two countries even more pronounced. The United States spent $9,400 per person on healthcare in 2014 compared with $3,400 in the United Kingdom, including public spending of 48% in the United States and 83% in the United Kingdom (World Bank 2016).

Despite the rising proportion of GDP spent on private and public healthcare, every healthcare provider is constantly faced with the dual need to improve patient outcomes and reduce costs. This performance challenge applies not only to public healthcare organizations but also private healthcare organizations.

In this chapter, we provide pragmatic advice for healthcare leaders who want to improve performance and ensure that in doing so they improve patient outcomes (see also Chapter 9) and healthcare system productivity.

We first describe five strategies with proven effectiveness if executed well: (1) create scale in clinical and administrative support services; (2) form clinical teams that treat a high volume of patients; (3) use minimally invasive techniques that reduce length of hospital stay or—even better—allow same-day treatment without an overnight stay; (4) involve patients in self-managing their health; and (5) target interventions to patients who are most likely to benefit.

Although healthcare is very complex, there are only a few decisions that healthcare leaders must get right: the first is to recruit and develop the right people and skill sets, and the second is to make the right investment decisions related to equipment, information technology (IT), and infrastructure. We go on to provide advice on how healthcare leaders can successfully execute the proposed strategies by ensuring that they make the right decisions with respect to staff and investments.

Clinical leadership and engagement are key to achieving expected performance improvements. Finally, we describe the circle of improvement, which is composed of better patient outcomes, reduced footprint, and more cash to invest. This powerful improvement circle engages clinicians and generates the cash required to invest in new technologies and infrastructure.

10.2 Five Strategies for Success

Healthcare systems are organized and financed in very different ways across the developed world, with large variations even within the same country. Therefore, the overall environment in which healthcare leaders operate varies significantly and can be subdivided into four sub-environments according to the type of health financing (a private market or a public service) and the provider payment system (a fee-for-service system or a capitated system).

A single healthcare organization often operates in these four sub-environments simultaneously. Healthcare trusts in the United Kingdom, for example, offer public services based on a fee-for-service tariff. They can offer public services with a capitated payment for specific patients' groups (e.g., the frail elderly, musculoskeletal conditions) or for entire local populations. They also offer services to private patients in the United Kingdom or coming from abroad and in return receive fee-for-service or capitated payments. In this section, we describe five generic strategies proven to improve outcomes for patients within any of the sub-environments mentioned above and at the same time increase healthcare system productivity.

All of these strategies, however, require the use of digital technology for implementation. Some of these technologies are described in more detail in Chapter 12. In many other sectors, products and services have already been redesigned using digital technology. The Fourth Industrial Revolution refers to the fusion of technologies across the physical, digital, and biological worlds, which is creating entirely new capabilities and dramatic impacts on political, social, and economic systems. The Fourth Industrial Revolution will also significantly transform the way healthcare is delivered. The strategies in this section are described in decreasing order of maturity of the digital technology required to transform how healthcare is provided.

Creating scale in clinical and administrative support systems requires significant investment in mature IT systems such as enterprise resource planning systems and data warehouse systems. Furthermore, forming clinical teams that treat a high volume of patients requires investment in integrated electronic patient records (see Chapter 6) across the referral network.

Using minimally invasive techniques that reduce length of hospital stay or, even better, allow same-day treatment without an overnight stay requires investment in state-of-the-art treatment rooms supported by digital-enabled diagnostic and interventional equipment/devices leveraging breakthroughs in nanotechnology.

Involving patients in self-managing their health requires investment in digital applications and services that sit on top of the above-mentioned integrated patient records.

Targeting interventions to patients most likely to benefit requires investment in high-throughput gene sequencing equipment. The genomic data need to be combined with data from the integrated patient record and from the patient digital applications. The combined genotype and phenotype can then be analyzed in "big data" centers. This will lead to better definition of diseases and therefore more targeted therapies, also known as "precision" or "personalized" therapy.

10.2.1 Creating Scale in Clinical and Administrative Support Systems

The scale of healthcare provider organizations remains small and most operate regionally. Consolidation and globalization in healthcare services are slower than in other industries. In the future, healthcare providers are expected to further consolidate within healthcare systems (e.g., Hospital Corporation of America) but increasingly also across healthcare systems (e.g., Ramsay Health Care).

My experience at the Antwerp Hospital Network illustrates that even small-scale consolidation can drive significant productivity gains. In 2004, three smaller hospital groups were merged into one larger group to operate healthcare facilities on seven sites in the Antwerp region with a turnover of €460 million. Before the merger, each hospital had its own board, management team, and administrative services (human resources [HR], finance, IT, and procurement). Each hospital also had its own clinical support services such as pharmacy, sterilization services, and clinical laboratories. The merger provided the opportunity to consolidate the payroll, accounting, invoicing, purchasing, logistics, and software development functions. In addition, pharmacy, sterilization, and clinical laboratories were centralized. The consolidation and centralization in itself led to a significant productivity increase through a reduction in head count. More importantly, however, the merger and centralization required a redesign of all involved processes leading to automation where possible. Automation subsequently enabled upgrading of the skill mix in these departments.

For example, the order-to-payment process was completely redesigned and automated. Before the redesign, orders were telephoned, faxed, and/or e-mailed to suppliers, while the paper-based approval process running in parallel regularly lagged behind and often approved the order after it had already been sent to the supplier. The supplier delivered the product/service, requesting paper confirmation of delivery to be signed by the department, and subsequently sent a paper invoice to the accounting department. Accounting needed paper copies of the order, the delivery confirmation, and the invoice before making a manual payment to the supplier and a manual entry into the general ledger. An automated three-way matching process in the enterprise resource planning

(ERP) system eliminated many steps in this process, minimized the number of manual human interventions, and increased the quality and speed of the order-to-payment process.

In order to support this automation of the administrative processes, the Antwerp Hospital Network had to implement an ERP system. This involved a multi-million euro investment and a multi-year change. The resulting productivity increase in the administrative functions, however, was significant.

Another benefit of the consolidation, redesign, and automation of the administrative processes was that the Antwerp Hospital Network could develop a powerful management information system that provided the basis for benchmarking similar clinical services within the group and comparing them with national benchmarks. By shifting more patients to outpatient services and reducing length of hospital stay using internal and external benchmarks, the Antwerp Hospital Network closed over 15% of the inpatient capacity and at the same time treated more patients with this reduced capacity, which also led to significant productivity increases in the clinical departments.

The additional investment required in data warehousing and business intelligence (BI) software was limited compared with the investment in ERP implementation. Nevertheless, the investment in mature digital technologies and the resulting productivity increases explain the significant increase in revenues of the Antwerp Hospital Network to €640 million in 2015, and the Earnings Before Interest Tax Depreciation and Amortization (EBITDA—a good indicator of profitability and cash generated) increased to 10% of revenues in 2015.

10.2.2 Forming Clinical Teams to Treat High Volumes of Patients

Surgical innovation has a huge impact on improving human health, particularly for cancer treatment and the replacement of diseased organs by transplantation or with prosthetic devices. In the United Kingdom, every person will on average undergo seven surgical procedures during his or her lifetime (Royal College of Surgeons 2016).

For several cancer, cardiovascular, and musculoskeletal interventions, there is a clear correlation between volume and outcome. Hospitals that perform a greater number of interventions have better patient outcomes and surgeons that perform a greater number of interventions have better outcomes (Jain et al. 2004; Davies and Lawton 2016; De la Garza-Ramos et al. 2016). This evidence is increasingly being used to concentrate interventions in "centers of excellence" or "focused clinics," because higher volumes not only lead to better outcomes but also to higher productivity.

A UK Monitor report in 2015 showed that elective care accounts for 34% of the activity of acute hospitals and around 30% of spending (Monitor 2015). The report aimed to identify productive elective pathways in the United Kingdom and internationally and to understand the practices driving higher productivity with a focus on best practice found in two elective care pathways: eye surgery and orthopedic surgery. High-volume providers can implement the best practices identified more easily than providers with low volumes can. Due to the high volume of patients treated each day, these providers can invest in dedicated processes, people, and infrastructure to ensure a fast and smooth flow of patients through the system. At the same time, they have the opportunity to achieve a high capacity of staff, equipment, and facility utilization.

For example, a high-volume provider can invest in a digital preadmission process, a "one-stop-shop" outpatient preadmission clinic, dedicated theatre sessions with clinical staff present and trained to perform more procedures per day than in less focused providers, introduce rapid recovery practices by dedicated allied health professional teams, and provide digital follow-up of uncomplicated patients.

Likewise, high-volume providers can employ several surgeons to perform the same procedures and recruit, train, and develop nurses and allied health professionals dedicated to the patient pathway. The high patient volume sustains the creation of large multidisciplinary teams where clinical leaders have sufficient time and exposure to develop and update standardized pathways and protocols, standardize the use of medical and other supplies, and negotiate better prices with suppliers. High volume and focus also encourage the use of simple but effective performance management systems. The clinical team is large enough to devote time to analyze and discuss real-time outcomes and productivity metrics, engage in peer review, and focus on continuously improving the pathway. These clinical teams are also large enough to engage with patients and families in their care throughout the pathway. Patients in these high-volume clinics benefit from the reduction in readmission rates, shorter lengths of hospital stay, and reduced surgical site infection rates.

Several case reports on successful high-volume-focused clinics have been published. In a 2011 publication, the INSEAD Business School analyzed Coxa Hospital in Finland (INSEAD 2011), a focused joint-replacement hospital, and in 2012, the Harvard Business School published the case of the Hospital for Special Surgery (Harvard Business School 2012). Both cases provide examples of focused clinics in musculoskeletal disorders and describe how these clinics have implemented the above best practices.

Other providers are creating large referral networks to ensure that sufficient patients are referred to their center of excellence. The evidence demonstrates that some healthcare services benefit if provision is focused on fewer sites rather than spreading it thinly across many sites (Keogh 2013). Many of these advantages accrue from the concentration of expensive clinical teams, equipment, and infrastructure on one site serving a demand large enough to ensure high levels of facility use. Clinicians working in these facilities undertake greater volumes of procedures, enabling them to develop and maintain their skill set more easily than in low volume centers. The presence of a large group of clinicians also creates the opportunity for shared learning, and centralization facilitates the co-location of certain interdependent services. Percutaneous coronary intervention, interventional radiology, major trauma, hyperacute stroke, and vascular surgery are good examples of specialized services requiring large catchment areas.

These clinical networks require significant investments in electronic patient records (EPRs; see also Chapter 6) and the development of interfaces between EPRs of different providers. Large EPR providers are emerging, but the development and implementation of middleware and/or interfaces to connect different EPRs is still at an early phase.

In order to create centers of excellence or focused clinics, healthcare leaders must make choices. This is one of the most difficult strategies to execute within existing healthcare provider organizations, because clinical staff tend to try to keep services within their own organization.

10.2.3 Using Minimally Invasive Techniques

Laparoscopic surgery ("keyhole surgery") reduces length of hospital stay or even allows same-day treatment without an overnight stay for many abdominal procedures. Keyhole surgery has subsequently been applied to thoracic surgery and at other sites. Academic medical centers and life sciences companies are innovating in robotic surgery, organ reconditioning, gene therapy, nanotechnology, and image-guided diagnostic and surgical techniques. All these innovations will make further reductions in length of stay or more same-day treatments possible.

In 2012, Life Sciences Partners, a European private equity fund dedicated to funding human life sciences companies, launched its Health Economics Fund. This has a unique focus on investing in medical devices, diagnostics, and digital health companies developing and commercializing products that simultaneously improve patient outcomes and reduce the cost of care. Sequana Medical, one of its portfolio companies, has developed the Alfapump, a medical device that improves the quality of life of liver disease patients and has the potential to reduce the cost of treating patients with refractory ascites.

Liver cirrhosis is a growing medical problem and can be caused by alcohol misuse, viral hepatitis, and many other causes. Approximately 60% of cirrhotic patients will develop ascites in the 10 years following diagnosis, a condition associated with significantly increased morbidity and mortality (D'amico et al. 1995). A large volume of ascites in the abdominal cavity increases abdominal pressure, causes respiratory discomfort, and reduces appetite and mobility. First-line treatment is large-volume paracentesis (LVP), an invasive procedure that aims to aspirate ascitic fluid from the abdomen using a needle and tube system. Typically, patients will simultaneously receive intravenous albumin to prevent paracentesis-induced circulatory dysfunction and, depending on disease severity, LVP will be performed once, twice, or three times per month. This invokes frequent hospital visits and places a significant burden on patients, their environment, and the hospitals. In between hospital visits, the ascites rapidly reaccumulates, resulting in the reappearance of all complications.

The Alfapump is a small, battery-powered pump that pumps ascites from the abdominal cavity into the bladder where it is excreted via urination. The Alfapump is implanted subcutaneously by a minimally invasive procedure under general or local anesthetic. Two catheters are connected to the pump: one located in the intraperitoneal cavity, the other connecting the pump to the bladder. The daily volume of transferred ascites can be adapted on a patient-specific basis, and the pump can be wirelessly charged through the skin and pump data transferred online to follow pump performance remotely.

Based on current data, the Alfapump has a very positive impact on quality of life; it improves mobility and nutritional state, reduces the time spent visiting hospital, helps as a bridge to liver transplant and, in specific cases, helps to cure liver disease. The results of a randomized controlled trial will be published in 2017.

As well as offering clinical benefits, the Alfapump has economic benefits. In a detailed analysis for the German market, there were annual cost savings for patients undergoing two or three LVP/month of €40,000 and €80,000, respectively. This is a good example of how a minimally invasive technique can offer simultaneous benefits to patients and healthcare system productivity.

Unfortunately, the investments needed to provide these minimally invasive treatments are rising. Robotic surgery, image-guided diagnostics, and keyhole interventions require large investments in state-of-the-art treatment rooms with expensive imaging and surgical equipment. An extreme example is a proton beam therapy center. Proton beam therapy is a type of radiation treatment that uses protons rather than X-rays to treat cancer and allows for higher radiation doses to the tumor while sparing the healthy tissues surrounding the tumor. A single treatment room for proton therapy, however, requires an investment of about €30 million–40 million. At these costs, healthcare leaders must carefully assess any increase in productivity that can be achieved by investing in new technologies.

The development and adoption of such technologies rapidly decreases the need for hospital beds and implies that technology investments need to be concentrated in fewer locations for quality and affordability reasons. Many healthcare providers, however, are too slow to adapt their bed capacity according to the new technologies being adopted. One reason is that most healthcare systems are confronted with an aging population. The number of patients aged 75 years or older is rapidly increasing, and the current models of care often lead to admissions of frail, elderly patients. These patients occupy the beds that become available after the introduction of minimally invasive techniques. This is despite the evidence showing that many patients, in particular frail, elderly people, have better outcomes when a hospital stay is avoided and when they are treated as an outpatient, as a day case patient, or through outreach directly into the patients' own homes (Future Hospital Commission 2013). A responsive and rapid assessment of frail, elderly patients followed by treatment, supportive care, and rehabilitation closer to or in patients' homes is associated with lower mortality, greater independence, and a reduced need for long-term care.

This approach does not require new technologies but it does require a different clinical mindset with the following characteristics:

- "Ambulatory by default": the principle to minimize overnight hospital admission
- "Assess to admit": capable clinical assessment, often multidisciplinary, before a decision to admit to hospital is made
- "Enhanced recovery": the principle to de-escalate care rapidly as the patient improves, thus minimizing iatrogenic or hospital-induced illness and the "post-hospital syndrome" of physical and mental debility
- "Discharge to assess": an early move from the hospital to a facility closer to home to deliver enabling care and determine ongoing care needs in close coordination with social care services

In November 2015, Oxfordshire health and social care providers agreed to work together to develop a joint plan to enable patients no longer needing acute medical care to move from the hospital setting into either a nursing home or their own home. In order to coordinate and manage the needs of the patients being transferred to nursing homes or their own homes, a multiagency Liaison Hub, located in the John Radcliffe hospital, was established in December 2015. The hub currently operates a virtual ward of all frail, elderly patients, provides day-to-day support to nursing homes, social workers, therapists, general practitioners (GPs) and hospital clinicians, and manages communication with patients and families.

The Liaison Hub's multidisciplinary team consists of qualified nurses with acute medical experience and expertise in complex discharge planning working alongside discharge planners. The hub works closely with staff from adult social care, therapy staff, consultant geriatricians, and senior interface physicians.

As a consequence of these changes, the Oxford University Hospitals Trust was able to close acute beds that were no longer needed. Outcomes for frail, elderly patients improved because they became less dependent on acute care. The productivity of the healthcare system increased because similar services could be provided with less bed capacity.

10.2.4 Involving Patients in Self-Managing Their Health

One in three adults in the United Kingdom has a long-term condition (LTC), and they account for half of GP appointments, 70% of inpatient bed days, and 70% of the acute care budget, that is, over two-thirds of NHS expenditure for one-third of the population. Because of increasingly effective interventions that can reduce fatal events, the prevalence of these chronic diseases is rising, as is overall life expectancy. As a consequence, multimorbidity, defined as the co-occurrence of more than one long-term condition in an individual, is increasing and becoming a major challenge for many health systems (see also Chapter 9).

Since lifestyle choices are a major reason for the rise in chronic diseases, promoting healthy lifestyles is the most important strategy to improve the health status of a population. The role of the government and society at large in promoting healthy lifestyles is crucial. Education, employers, "big food," the media, and other organizations all play major roles. In the Kingdom of Saudi Arabia (KSA), for example, over 70% of the population is obese or overweight.

Healthcare providers can use every patient contact to promote healthy lifestyles, focus on early detection of complications (e.g., diabetes in obese patients), treat complications at home rather than in a hospital, and use digital technology to prevent patients with LTCs from deteriorating and needing costly interventions. We elaborate on the latter two strategies: hospital@home and digital health.

The hospital@home concept offered by Oxford University Hospitals is a service that provides acute care in patients' homes for a defined time period. This is achieved either by assessing the patient in their home using point-of-care testing or by transferring them to the hospital only for assessment but continuing to provide care/treatment in the patient's home as long as is feasible.

This service has two main goals: to avoid hospital admissions and to support the safe transfer of patients from secondary care to the patient's own home where care can be safely continued. This includes patients who require ongoing treatment, monitoring, nursing care, and therapy support but who would remain in hospital without this provision.

Patients with pneumonia, cellulitis, volume depletion/dehydration, urinary tract infections/urosepsis, deep vein thrombosis, pulmonary embolism, and acute decompensating heart failure are examples of patient groups that might benefit from a hospital@home service. The types of treatments delivered by hospital@home include the administration of parenteral therapy, intravenous medications and/or fluids, antibiotics, oxygen via an appropriate delivery device, and palliative/pain medication. The teams delivering this service consist of senior registered nurses supported by clinical support workers, therapists, pharmacists, and gerontologists.

Currently, most patients with LTCs present to their GP or hospital services when they deteriorate. These reactive approaches lead to more frequent use of emergency hospital services and often result in poor outcomes and inefficient healthcare use. The development of technologies such as wearable devices, smartphones, computer tablets, and machine learning provide an unprecedented opportunity to apply the benefits of digital technologies to healthcare.

As an example, Oxford University Hospitals have developed and implemented an electronic application that can be used by nurses to input vital signs (blood oxygen saturation, pulse rate, respiratory rate, and blood pressure) on a tablet. The application has been carefully developed and tested to ensure that the time needed to register vital signs using the tablet is less than by using a paper-based system. Adoption has, therefore, been very fast across all hospital sites. Based on the collected data, an evidence-based risk score for every hospitalized patient is calculated that enables early intervention before patients deteriorate. Oxford University Hospitals are now developing a comparable self-management application for patients at home. If patients adopt the self-management application, algorithms can be developed to estimate personalized risk scores throughout the pathway so that patient care becomes agnostic to the patient's location. Patients and their caregivers will be guided toward preventative management, thereby minimizing the likelihood of severe episodes and emergency hospital admissions. In the future, contactless vital sign collection will be possible via webcam sensors. Proof-of-concept studies have already been completed in neonates and dialysis patients (Villarroel et al. 2014, 2017). As indicated above, these digital technologies are still very much in the research phase and will be further developed over the next five years as part of a large UK government grant.

10.2.5 Target Interventions to Patients Most Likely to Benefit

In 1944, Lewis wrote in *The Lancet:* "We clearly understand a phenomenon here and there; those we think we understand become our pride and bulk largely in our consciousness; those we do not understand are conveniently ignored, or, more often, we give them names and deceive ourselves that we then understand them." We are now in 2016, but these reflections remain very relevant.

Many diseases are poorly defined. Disease taxonomy is based on symptoms (e.g., irritable bowel syndrome), histology (e.g., inflammatory bowel disease), physiology (e.g., hypertension), an eponym (e.g., Alzheimer's disease), or an organ (e.g., breast cancer, heart failure). A better understanding of the genotype and phenotype of patients will lead to better disease definitions in the future. Cancer illustrates this well; today, most cancers are defined by the organ in which they arise but genotypic and phenotypic data will underpin increasingly better definitions of individual cancers.

Fifty per cent of the UK population will suffer from cancer at some stage in their lives. Major challenges in cancer management are late diagnosis and resistance to therapy. The cost of chemotherapy used to treat late-stage cancer creates a huge burden on healthcare systems, only improves survival by a few months or years, and reduces quality of life as a consequence of chemotherapy side-effects.

Next-generation sequencing (NGS) will enable scientists and clinicians to stratify patients into subgroups based on tumor mutations. By sequencing the genome of circulating tumor cells, the diagnosis of cancer can be made much earlier. Early diagnosis; stratification of patients according to tumor mutations; and early treatment with precision surgery, radiotherapy, and chemotherapy will create new possibilities to cure cancers rather than simply prolong life by a few months or years. This will transform the outcomes achieved for patients and significantly improve the productivity of the healthcare system.

Gene sequencing will also provide evidence to clinicians to stop using certain treatments. For example, in 2009 the UK National Institute for Health and Care Excellence (NICE) issued its guideline for using rituximab as a possible first treatment for patients with chronic lymphocytic leukemia (CLL) in combination with fludarabine and cyclophosphamide (NICE 2009). However, the German CLL8 study published in 2014 indicated that rituximab does not benefit patients with mutations in the PEST (a peptide sequence that is rich in proline [P], glutamic acid [E], serine [S], and threonine [T]) domain of *NOTCH1* (Stilgenbauer et al. 2014). In the same way, more evidence is being generated on the efficacy of treatments in particular patient groups.

In the future, the boundary between diagnostics, drugs, devices, and digital products will blur. For example, a "smart" pill is a device that contains a pharmaceutical drug with a chip. Is this a drug, a device, or a digital product or service? The use of smart pills can track patient compliance and, in combination with patient reminders in case of noncompliance, can contribute to better outcomes.

Diagnostics, drugs, and devices are likely to be combined with digital products that generate data to trigger a service to improve health outcomes for patients. These new products/services allow the continuous generation of real-world data before and after approval by regulatory agencies, thereby complementing the evidence base of the randomized clinical trials required for approval.

Comparable to the strategic choices needed to execute forming clinical teams to treat high volumes of patients, it is very difficult for healthcare leaders to take the decision to eliminate products or services where the cost is too high compared with the gain in patient outcomes. The clinicians currently providing these services will resist this strategy and defend their own role and budgets.

10.3 Implications for Decision-Making

To successfully implement the five described strategies, healthcare leaders must clearly understand the implications of these strategies on how they should take key decisions in their organization. In essence, healthcare providers need to take only two key decisions: investment decisions related to technology and estates, and decisions related to recruitment and development of professional staff.

Almost the entire annual investment budget of healthcare providers is allocated to estates, equipment, and IT investments. The above strategies have a profound impact on how to prioritize the investment budget. Providers need to spend less on building patient wards, because the number of beds required in the future will decrease significantly. They need to spend more on high-tech treatment rooms and much more on digital transformation.

The case of the new hospital of the Antwerp Hospital Network in Belgium illustrates the importance of making the right decisions related to new infrastructure. The Antwerp Hospital Network in Belgium is still operating a hospital, ZNA Stuivenberg, which opened in 1884. At the time, the design and construction of ZNA Stuivenberg were state-of-the-art and was based on Pasteur's new insights into infectious diseases. Long corridors connected inpatient wards and a "sophisticated" ventilation system was used to avoid the spread of infectious diseases. Of course, ZNA Stuivenberg is now completely outdated. In 2009, the Antwerp Hospital Network asked a renowned architect to design and build a brand-new facility in the center of Antwerp, which will be called ZNA Cadiz.

The Belgian healthcare system, however, has over twice the number of hospital beds per capita (6.5 beds per 1,000 people) than the United Kingdom and the United States (2.9 beds per 1,000 people) (World Bank 2016). Given the overcapacity of beds in Belgium, but even more so in Antwerp, the investment in a new hospital would not be justified if the ambition was to build a large new inpatient facility.

Therefore, the Antwerp Network Hospital made the decision to build a very flexible building in which patient rooms could be converted into outpatient treatment rooms and where the "hot floor" with operating rooms and intensive care units could be expanded. Within the basic concrete grid of the hospital, a patient room, a treatment room, and an operating room can be designed and constructed so that future changes in light of the introduction of new technologies can be made without touching the main concrete structure of the new hospital.

To justify the investment, two hospitals will be taken out of service, thereby reducing inpatient capacity. The new building will incorporate the latest technology such as automatic guided vehicles for logistics, reduced energy consumption, minimized traveling distances for personnel by optimizing patient flows, and a need for fewer shifts in the evenings and weekends through intelligent department design. In summary, the operation of this new facility will be more efficient, thereby ensuring a return on investment.

This example illustrates that investment decisions on estates have a long-term impact on capacity and the flexibility to adjust capacity. In the extreme case of ZNA Stuivenberg, the hospital will have been in operation for almost 130 years when its successor ZNA Cadiz opens in 2019. Most hospitals, however, have a long lifetime and, with technology constantly changing, healthcare leaders will need to invest less in buildings, and if new buildings are constructed, the design should allow for flexible use of the building over its lifespan.

The five strategies described also require increased investment in digital technology. So far, enterprise resource systems and EPRs are already a reality in most healthcare systems. However, the digital support needed to engage patients in self-management and to target treatments to individual patients still requires additional investment and functionalities.

Clinicians will use paper-free digital information at the point of care to improve delivery, outcomes, and patient safety, sharing care plans across all care settings. Clinical decision support is likely to be embedded in clinical workflows, reflecting best practice and the latest guidelines. The information system may provide alerts to identify potential risks such as sepsis, thereby reducing the need for emergency/acute intervention. Multidisciplinary teams will provide patient care supported by integrated messaging, workflow, screen sharing, and conferencing. A major effort will be necessary to reconcile terminology across care settings including those for medication, problems, diagnoses, and allergies. Longitudinal patient records are needed for shared proactive care in the management of LTCs. This will enable pathway planning informed by high-quality data on resource usage, availability, and outcomes.

Patients may be empowered with access to an integrated record, relevant advice and information, and the opportunity to contribute data. They are likely to engage with online support for appointments, consultations, care plans, and preferences. They will be enabled to use web, mobile, and sensor technologies for self-management and to receive information relevant to their condition. The use of digital technologies will deliver high-quality care in the most appropriate setting, closer to home and ambulatory by default.

As healthcare providers invest more in robotics and machine learning, the required skills and the mix of skills on the work floor need to change significantly. To successfully implement the five strategies, providers have to make the right recruitment and development decisions. Traditional healthcare recruitment hires GPs, specialist doctors, nurses, advanced nursing, allied health professionals, and administrative/logistical staff. However, many administrative activities will be taken over by the patients themselves. Similar to the banking or airline sector, patients are likely to get used to providing medical history information, making their own appointments, and downloading test results online.

Other skills are necessary to accomplish this transformation. As large electronic datasets become available, statisticians, mathematicians, and engineers will be needed to analyze data and develop algorithms to support clinical decision-making and intervention. These statisticians, mathematicians, and engineers will work in multidisciplinary teams alongside clinical professionals. Even the training of clinicians needs to adapt to interact with new technologies and provide a human interface with patients at the same time.

For example, the vision of Oxford University's Life Sciences campus in Headington is a significant reduction in the square meters required for current hospital activities. Older parts of the estate will be demolished, and the out- and inpatient capacity concentrated in the recently constructed hospital buildings. The Big Data Institute opened in 2017, housing newly recruited clinicians, statisticians, and engineers. Future investments are planned for a Precision Medicine Institute to provide high-tech treatment rooms for proton beam therapy and robotic and image-guided surgery.

10.4 Circle of Improvement: Better Outcomes, Reduced Footprint, More Cash

Besides making decisions that prepare healthcare organizations for future technologies, healthcare leaders will also need to engage clinicians in the significant changes required by the five strategies. Too often, executives in healthcare organizations focus only on cost reduction, thus creating tension with clinicians who want to focus on improving patient outcomes. All five strategies can help healthcare providers deal with this balance of outcomes versus cost. All five strategies maintain or increase outcomes for patients, permit providers to reduce the resources needed to deliver these outcomes, and therefore generate cash to invest in the organization.

It may be helpful to first agree on the definitions of the terms that are used. Creating a common language and ensuring that every staff member understands what each word means is an important first step in the change program.

Michael Watkin emphasizes this need for a common language in his book *The First 90 Days* (Watkins 2003):

> "Suppose you wanted to introduce the transition acceleration framework in your organisation. How might you best do it? The starting point is to introduce a new vocabulary for talking about transitions. This probably is the single most important step your organisation can take to institutionalise transition acceleration. A common language makes discussions of these issues dramatically more efficient. Perhaps more important, it means that conversations will happen that wouldn't have happened otherwise."

In this section, the words outcome, footprint, cash, and productivity are defined.

10.4.1 Outcome

Outcome is the result of a treatment. The outcome can be measured either as a clinically defined outcome (e.g., five-year survival rate after cancer treatment) or a patient-reported outcome (e.g., ability to perform daily living activities). There are several possible outcome measures: survival rates, recovery times, pain levels, range of movement, complication rates, well-being, and so on, and clinicians must define what is clinically most relevant for their patients and patients have to report what is most valuable to them (see also Chapter 9).

To compare outcomes between providers, these measures have to be adjusted for the underlying risk of the patient population treated. In 1993, Holthof and Prins (1993) described a way of measuring perinatal outcomes using a logistic regression approach so that expected perinatal mortality could be compared with actual perinatal mortality performance in maternity centers. This was an early example of a risk-adjusted outcome measure.

Many clinicians and patients confuse good outcomes with good quality. Good quality does not always mean a good outcome and a good outcome does not always mean good quality.

Assume a clinician performs a high-quality procedure but there is evidence that this procedure does not lead to improved outcomes or, even worse, it may even harm the patient. In this case, the service provided is of high quality but the outcome is poor.

Quality can also be defined in other ways than by good outcome. For example, patients may experience long waiting times and find that the quality of care provided is poor but they may report good outcomes or there may be clinical evidence that the outcome of the treatment was excellent.

10.4.2 Footprint

Delivery of healthcare services requires resources: staff members, supplies, and space (as a proxy for capital invested in buildings and equipment). All the strategies described will reduce the need for staff and/or supplies and/or space. This is referred to as a reduction in footprint. For example, bed capacity reduction was mentioned in many of the strategies. Fewer beds means less staff, catering, and medical supplies, and less space needed. Although healthcare organizations are very complex, their cost structure is very simple. Between 55% and 60% of costs are spent on staff salaries, 25%–30% on supplier invoices, and 10%–20% on depreciation/interest for investments made in buildings and equipment. A physical reduction in footprint will therefore reduce costs.

10.4.3 Cash

Although you may expect this definition to be trivial, many health economic arguments and hence pricing, reimbursement, and investment decisions are made on the concept that new technologies will improve the efficiency of the healthcare system. It will be argued, for example, that a diagnostic, drug, device, digital product, or service will reduce length of stay and therefore save the system costs. Therefore, the return on investment of this technology will be positive and it should be adopted widely in the healthcare system. As indicated above, costs are only saved if the footprint is physically reduced. Only then will the cost structure of the provider change and cash be released.

Without a physical reduction in footprint, more specifically a reduction in the number of full-time equivalent (FTE) staff employed, a reduction in the spending on suppliers, and/or a reduction in the square meters of space used, the cost structure of healthcare providers will not change and no cash will be released.

10.4.4 Productivity

Productivity is measured by dividing the rate of output per unit of input. In this chapter, output has been defined as health outcomes. Productivity is thus defined as health outcomes produced (e.g., healthy living years) divided by resources used (personnel, supplies, and capital). In his book *Redefining Health Care*, Michael Porter defines value as the health outcomes achieved per dollar of cost compared with peers (Porter 2010). This illustrates how important a common language is. Why is it important to define productivity in the same way as Michael Porter defines value? If output is defined by using activity levels (e.g., number of surgeries performed divided by the resources used or number of scans performed divided by the resources used), providers could focus on increasing productivity and performing additional activity that does not lead to improved outcomes or could even harm patients. In the end, patients and society are not interested in undergoing more operations or scans. They want a healthy life.

The performance circle of improving outcomes, reducing footprint, and generating cash, which together improve the productivity of the healthcare system, requires a clear understanding of the words used, significant clinical leadership, and executional discipline throughout the organization.

The starting point for engaging clinicians is the common goal: to improve patient outcomes and give patients more healthy life years. The five strategies described improve or at least maintain the outcomes delivered for patients. All five will certainly reduce the footprint or the use of resources and therefore increase productivity (or create value as defined by Michael Porter).

The trick is to make sure that clinicians have the discipline to release the cash. Reduction in footprint means that existing structures have to be changed. For example, a medical specialty may have an entire ward for inpatients, but when length of stay is reduced and some procedures can even be performed without an overnight stay, this ward may have to be shared with another specialty. This may induce resistance from doctors and nurses who have worked on the same ward for many years.

To drive this circle of improvement and keep it going, it is useful to develop top-down targets on the resources available for the different patient pathways and departments. These targets can be set using benchmarks of how much of a resource (FTE staff, number of beds, number of operating theatre sessions, etc.) is required by best practice healthcare providers. Healthcare leaders need to discuss these targets and benchmarks with clinicians in order to get buy-in. Top-down targets will guide clinical leaders on how to achieve the final phase in the improvement process: the release of cash.

The reward of engaging clinicians and overcoming resistance is that more cash will be generated for investment in IT, equipment, or infrastructure.

10.5 Conclusions

Innovation and digital transformation of care delivery will significantly improve patient outcomes and at the same time improve the productivity of healthcare systems. Hospitals of the future are likely to have fewer beds and more high-tech treatment rooms. Provider teams will not only consist of doctors, nurses, and other health professionals but also contain engineers, statisticians, and mathematicians. They will provide treatments where diagnostics, drugs, and devices are integrated with digital technology so that data can be collected. By analyzing the data, treatments will be targeted to the right patients at the right time who are enabled to increasingly self-manage their health. Patients and society are likely to benefit from improved health outcomes and a reduction in the resources needed to achieve these outcomes.

References

D'amico, G., L. Pagliaro, and J. Bosch. 1995. The treatment of portal hypertension: A meta-analytic review. *Hepatology* 22 (1):332–354.

Davies, J. M., and M. T. Lawton. 2017. Improved outcomes for patients with cerebrovascular malformations at high-volume centers: The impact of surgeon and hospital volume in the United States, 2000–2009. *J Neurosurg* 127 (1):69–80.

De la Garza-Ramos, R., N. B. Abt, P. Kerezoudis, W. Krauss, and M. Bydon. 2016. Provider volume and short-term outcomes following surgery for spinal metastases. *J Clin Neurosci* 24:43–46. doi:10.1016/j.jocn.2015.08.008.

Future Hospital Commission. 2013. *Future Hospital: Caring for Medical Patients*. Royal College of Physicians. https://www.rcplondon.ac.uk/projects/outputs/future-hospital-commission

Harvard Business School. 2012. Hospital for Special Surgery. http://www.hbs.edu/faculty/Pages/item.aspx?num=47956

Holthof, B., and P. Prins. 1993. Comparing hospital perinatal mortality rates: a quality improvement instrument. *Med Care* 31 (9):801–807.

INSEAD. 2011. Coxa Hospital, Finland. http://www.reform.uk/wp-content/uploads/2014/11/Coxa_Hospital.pdf

Jain, N., R. Pietrobon, S. Hocker, et al. 2004. The relationship between surgeon and hospital volume and outcomes for shoulder arthroplasty. *J Bone Joint Surg Am* 86-A (3):496–505.

Keogh, B. 2013. Review into the quality of care and treatment provided by 14 hospital trusts in England: Overview report. NHS. https://www.nhs.uk/nhsengland/bruce-keogh-review/documents/outcomes/keogh-review-final-report.pdf

Monitor. 2015. Multilateral Gain/Loss Sharing to Support New Models of Care: An Introduction. https://www.gov.uk/government/publications/multilateral-gainloss-sharing-an-introduction

National Institute for Health and Care Excellence. 2009. Rituximab for the First-Line Treatment of Chronic Lymphocytic Leukaemia. https://www.nice.org.uk/guidance/TA174

Porter, M. E. 2010. What is value in health care? *N Engl J Med* 363 (26):2477–2481.

Royal College of Surgeons. 2016. https://www.rcseng.ac.uk

Stilgenbauer, S., A. Schnaiter, P. Paschka, et al. 2014. Gene mutations and treatment outcome in chronic lymphocytic leukemia: results from the CLL8 trial. *Blood* 123 (21):3247–3254. doi:10.1182/blood-2014-01-546150.

Villarroel, M., A. Guazzi, J. Jorge, S. Davis, P. Watkinson, G. Green, A. Shenvi, K. McCormick, and L. Tarassenko. 2014. Continuous non-contact vital sign monitoring in neonatal intensive care unit. *Healthc Technol Lett* 1 (3):87–91.

Villarroel, M., J. Jorge, C. Pugh, and L. Tarassenko. 2017. Non-contact vital sign monitoring in the clinic. IEEE 12th International Conference on Automatic Face & Gesture Recognition. *IEEE Computer Society*.

Watkins, M. 2003. *The First 90 Days*. Boston: Harvard Business School Press.

World Bank. 2016. Health expenditure per capita (current US$) [Internet]. The World Bank. 2016 [cited 13 October 2016]. Available from: http://data.worldbank.org/indicator/SH.XPD.PCAP?view=chart

Chapter 11

Leadership through Crisis

Bandar Al Knawy

Contents

11.1 Introduction 205
  11.1.1 Context 205
  11.1.2 What Is Crisis? 206
  11.1.3 Causes of Crises 206
  11.1.4 Types of Crisis 207
11.2 Managing Crisis 207
  11.2.1 Types of Organizational Responses to Crises 207
  11.2.2 Stages of Crisis 208
11.3 Roles of Leaders in Managing Crisis 208
  11.3.1 Leaders' Roles in Pre-Crisis Stages 211
  11.3.2 Leaders' Roles in the Emergency Response Stage 211
  11.3.3 Leaders' Roles in Building Resilience 212
  11.3.4 Leaders' Roles in the Excellence Stage 212
11.4 Crisis Management Plan 213
  11.4.1 Stakeholder Involvement 214
References 214

11.1 Introduction

11.1.1 Context

Following an outbreak of Middle East Respiratory Syndrome Corona Virus (MERS–CoV) in the Emergency Department (ED; Accident and Emergency, A&E) in August 2015, the leadership at the King Abdulaziz Medical City in Riyadh, Saudi Arabia (KAMC-R) decided to close the hospital. It was a difficult decision, since the King Abdulaziz Medical City ED is one of the busiest in the Middle East, and the hospital provides care to thousands of patients. Therefore, hospital closure affected patients and the wider community, particularly as the outbreak coincided with Hajj, during which time two million pilgrims travel to Saudi Arabia. Furthermore, the event coincided with the start of the academic term, interrupting the education of thousands of students and the training of many healthcare professionals.

Over the following weeks, the leadership managed not only to control the outbreak and recommission the services, but also to launch a journey of transformation to excellence. In this chapter, I reflect on this experience and describe the lessons learned and the roles of leaders in managing crisis.

11.1.2 What Is Crisis?

An organizational crisis is a critical event that may pose a threat to the organizations' existence or its ability to perform its core functions properly. Crises have different causes, severities, impacts, patterns, and outcomes. Although crises differ in many aspects, they share two common features: they create uncertainty and threaten the well-being of the organization. For example, a crisis may indicate that a hospital cannot provide optimal patient care at all, or at least cannot provide safe patient care—the sole reason for its existence. The leadership's vision and actions to help navigate the time of uncertainty are critical and determine the outcome of the crisis and its long-term impact.

11.1.3 Causes of Crises

There are many causes of crises that cover a wide range of possibilities and that vary in nature. These causes can be categorized as follows:

1. Environmental disasters: For example, fire, which may inflict harm on patients and staff in addition to destroying the physical structure of the facilities. As an example, a recent fire at Jazan hospital in Saudi Arabia claimed the lives of 24 people and injured 123 (Arab News 2015).
2. Natural disasters: An earthquake, flooding, or a hurricane leading to facility damage and sometimes total shutdown. After Memorial Hospital in New Orleans was hit by Hurricane Katrina, at least 45 bodies were found days after the hasty evacuation of the staff and patients (Washington Post 2005).
3. Biological causes, including outbreaks of infections such as Ebola and MERS–CoV: For example, Ebola has closed hospitals in Nigeria and Liberia (NPR 2014; ABC News 2014), and MERS–CoV outbreaks have led to the closure of hospitals in the United Kingdom, Korea, and Saudi Arabia, including our own center as described in this case study (Crofs Blogs 2015; Mail Online 2015; The Korea Herald 2015).
4. Financial and economic reasons might lead to hospitals shutting down, restructuring, or being taken over by another healthcare organization (Sussman et al. 2010).
5. Major sentinel event: Serious events that create a major public outcry and media frenzy can force a system to change. For example, the Betsy Lehman incident at the Dana-Faber Institute in the United States shocked the healthcare system. Betsy, a 39-year-old award-winning health columnist at the *Boston Globe* newspaper, died from a chemotherapy overdose (Patient Safety Network 2005). In another example, the course of history for Virginia Mason Hospital, Seattle, was forever changed on November 23, 2004, when Mrs. Mary L. McClinton died from a preventable medical error. Mrs. McClinton was 69 when she was treated for a brain aneurysm at Virginia Mason, yet was mistakenly injected with chlorhexidine, an antiseptic, which resulted in her death (Virginia Mason Institute 2014). Finally, the U.S. government shut down Johns Hopkins research activities in 2001, including 2400 experiments and over $300 million in grant funding, after the death of a healthy volunteer in an asthma study (SF Gate 2001).

6. Man-made disasters such as civil war, chemical or nuclear disasters, terrorism, and bioterrorism will disturb normal hospital functions (Harvard College Global Health Review 2013).
7. Functional crises: For example, staff shortages and employee strikes. Management challenges may lead to service shutdown (The Telegraph News 2016, Independent).

11.1.4 Types of Crisis

Each crisis presents different and unique challenges, patterns, and magnitudes. Crises can be of any of the following types:

- Expected versus unexpected: An expected crisis has early warning signs that should alert leadership to start thinking of contingency plans and to be prepared to take remedial action. For example, in response to earlier outbreaks of MERS–CoV, we have an emergency preparedness plan that has three levels of escalation based on the number of diagnosed cases.
- Short-term versus long-term: A short-term example is a sentinel event. A long-term example is a financial or economic crisis, or permanent damage to the facility by a natural disaster.
- One-time isolated event versus a recurring incident: An isolated incident that is less likely to recur, such as a fire, or likely to recur, such as an infection outbreak or medical error.

11.2 Managing Crisis

Crisis management is a combination of art and science that is impacted by many factors. The leadership role is essential in the successful management of crisis to minimize the negative impact on the outcome.

11.2.1 Types of Organizational Responses to Crises

A crisis may have a long-term negative impact on the organization's image, function, staff, and public perception of the organization. Leadership has a major role to play, not just in the immediate recovery of function, but also in restoring or improving the image and performance of the organization.

Organizations can respond to crises in different ways, and the type of response may determine the fate of the organization as shown in Figure 11.1.

The initial response of all organizations is to slow down and decrease the performance from baseline to absorb the shock of the crisis. This period can be short and transient or prolonged, and it can be a partial slow down or complete shutdown. Based on the how the crisis is handled, organizational performance can go in different directions. The organization may collapse completely if the crisis is more than the organization can handle or if the crisis is not handled properly. Other organizations may recover from the crisis but will not return to baseline and will continue to underperform in the aftermath of the crisis. On the other hand, many organizations recover from the crisis and return to their default baseline functions as if nothing has happened. Finally, the best response is when the organization's leaders use the critical event as a fulcrum to excel and transform the organization. Therefore, appropriate and timely action by the organization's leaders is a major determinant of the outcome of the crisis and the long-term impact on the organization.

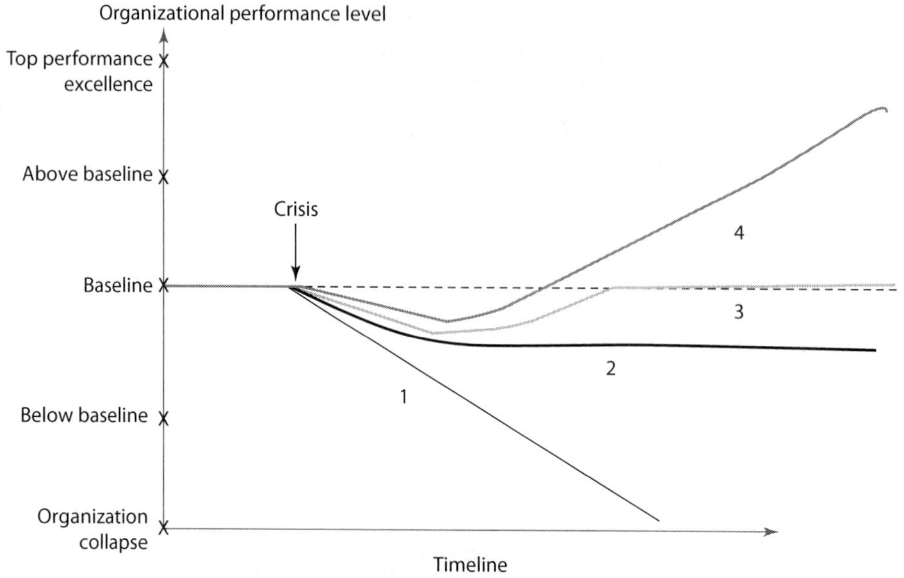

Figure 11.1 Organizational performance after crisis. (1) Organization collapses, (2) organization performs worse than baseline after crisis, (3) organization returns to baseline performance, (4) excelling organization.

11.2.2 Stages of Crisis

Crisis trajectory or course can be divided into multiple stages or phases (Table 11.1). The *pre-crisis stage* precedes the occurrence of the crisis. Usually, there will be warning signs of an impending crisis if the crisis relates to organizational functions, or sometimes the crisis can be unpredictable such as in the case of natural disasters. In our example, the increase in MERS–CoV infection cases was a warning sign that was recognized by the organization and prompted response planning.

The next stage is the actual *crisis stage*, when the events peak, drastic events take place, and everyone realizes the threats faced by the organization. *Post crisis* has stages that reflect the response to the crisis and the outcome. The *emergency response stage* aims to absorb the shock of the crisis and minimize its impact on the organization and, most importantly, the patients. The *building resilience stage* is an early recovery phase that puts the organization back on track. The *excellence stage* is for healthy recovery, as the organization leaders will not accept a return to the old comfort zone but rather push the organization to a new level of excellent performance and achievement.

These represent the stages for healthy recovery of the organization. Organizations that do not do well after crises have different stages that result in a precipitous decline in performance at a varied pace and total organizational collapse.

11.3 Roles of Leaders in Managing Crisis

The leader of the organization during a crisis is like the captain of a ship in a stormy sea. Leaders must be able to rally staff toward the shared vision and common goal of overcoming the immediate challenges posed by the crisis and to take the organization forward to the desired outcome. To

Table 11.1 Leaders Roles in Managing Crisis Successfully

Stage	Pre-Crisis	CRISIS	Emergency Response	Building Resilience	Excellence
Primary goal	Prevention		Containment and damage control	Early recovery with strategic vision	Growth and transformation
Leaders' roles	1. Institutional disaster preparedness 2. Recognition of early signs		1. Early identification 2. Vision 3. Setting priorities 4. Eliminating patients' harm 5. Team approach 6. Command center 7. Transparency 8. Communication (internal and external)	1. Having a clear plan 2. Redesigning the process 3. Implementing QI projects 4. Competence	1. Monitoring 2. Sustainability 3. Vigilance 4. Growth 5. Public trust

achieve this task effectively, leaders need to have a vision, adopt a team approach, and be flexible in playing evolving roles based on the situation.

a. *Vision*: Leadership vision is of the utmost importance, as it provides a clear direction and destination for the team in a time of uncertainty. It is very important that this vision is clear and it must be communicated well to all staff.
b. *Team approach*: Although the role of leadership is front and center in the process, it is obvious that managing crisis is not a one-man show. Creation of a leadership team is critical to tap into the power and collective wisdom of the senior and middle managers and frontline staff.
c. *Evolving leadership roles*: Leadership roles are dynamic and change based on the stage and the magnitude of the crisis. Leaders have to be able to respond to new data and feedback from frontline staff and adapt their responsibilities accordingly (Table 11.1).
d. *Think creatively and clearly when faced with details:* In a crisis, it is easy to become mired in details and layers of complexity when discussing various solutions, but it is more important to help the team to see the wider perspective. During a crisis, leaders are bombarded with a lot of information and data, and it is therefore critical to prioritize this information and the sequence of decision-making. One should aim to combat the disruptive nature of a crisis with creative—and simple—thinking.
e. *Ensure clear and visible senior leadership*: It is essential that all senior staff are visible. Although the Chief Executive Officer and the executive board are ultimately responsible for communication, they must ensure that senior and middle managers also play their part in displaying leadership, conveying confidence, and demonstrating that the situation is under control. Recognizing the need for our immediate reports to lead, the role of the executive team during the MERS–CoV infection crisis was to provide support, resolve differences, ensure focus, and make timely decisions.
f. *Communicate actions internally and externally*: Clear communication to staff and customers should be the normal way of doing business for any organization, but in the event of a crisis it becomes paramount. The CEO, supported by the organization's board of directors, should immediately communicate the crisis situation *within the organization* along with clear protocols for action. Visible and tangible changes are necessary. In our scenario, we regularly e-mailed bulletins to all staff with updates and guidance (e.g., the need to undergo infection control training and an update on the crisis situation), displayed posters in all buildings, and established an online portal providing staff with the ability to ask questions. In addition, senior managers undertook site visits and updated frontline staff.

   Communication *outside the organization* should be transparent and should aim to minimize the impact of the crisis on the wider community. In our case, we ensured that all the relevant public healthcare authorities were kept appraised of the situation as it developed, and we convened ministerial-level meetings to keep discussions open. This meant that the experts in the field felt involved and in a position to comment and also ensured confidence that our organization was responsive and transparent.

   Clear and prompt communication showed the public and the media that the crisis was being addressed. We explained what actions were being taken and the results achieved. This should be an ongoing task, even after the crisis has ended, as reputation and trust take time to rebuild. Our media plan included press releases, regular updates through the national health authorities, scheduling media visits, and updating social media.

To communicate with our patients, we established a call center to inform them of the current situation, rebook outpatient appointments, and reschedule surgeries, imaging, and other procedures. In addition, the call center facilitated the triaging of patients to nearby hospitals and clinics.

g. *Gain support and acknowledge staff*: Staff members are the most important asset of any organization. In a crisis, their support is critical to the successful resolution of the crisis. It is not enough simply to keep staff informed; leaders must also express an understanding of the difficult situation in which the members of staff find themselves, acknowledge the disruption the situation has caused, and, above all, show gratitude for their continued support.

A leader should thank staff members, teams, and team leaders for their cooperation and achievements. Staff should feel valued and protected by their leader and feel that their safety is of paramount importance to the organization. It is important to anticipate that morale might be low and to act swiftly to ensure that the visibility and gratitude of the leader has a calming effect. One needs to take the time to show staff that they are appreciated, and letting them know that someone is there for them is a simple way of improving morale.

I, and the executive team, made a point of thanking all members of staff personally rather than having this gratitude and reassurance cascaded down as just another message "from on high." This approach proved successful, as we received many messages of support—often as simple as an e-mail reassuring us that we were not alone—from all levels of staff. These messages revealed a strong desire to be part of the movement to resolve the crisis, something that any leader should seize as a golden opportunity.

This overwhelming support buoyed morale and ensured that we were all working together as one team toward a common goal. Indeed, in many ways, the crisis had the effect of strengthening relationships within the organization.

Table 11.1 depicts the stages of crisis when managed successfully and the roles of the leaders at each stage.

11.3.1 Leaders' Roles in Pre-Crisis Stages

The primary aim at this stage is prevention and preparedness. Like other healthcare concepts, prevention is much better than management. Leaders should have the organization ready and prepared to avoid crisis but, if it occurred, they should be ready to handle it well. It is critical for leaders to perform the following tasks:

- Disaster-containing plan and drills. It is very important to make sure that an organization is always "crisis ready" by performing disaster drills and staff training.
- Recognition of early signs. It is also very important to recognize the early warning signs of impending crisis, such as weather warnings, to take the appropriate action to prevent or minimize the impact of the crisis.

11.3.2 Leaders' Roles in the Emergency Response Stage

The primary aim of this stage is crisis containment and minimizing damage to the organization. Leaders and hospital staff should be able to identify the crisis at an early stage if it is not expected. Early characterization of the crisis in term of the causes, nature, magnitude, and potential impact on the organization is critical. Performing a thorough root cause analysis is an important step in understanding the crisis and will help to clearly list the efforts required to address this crisis. The following are some of the leaders' roles and expectations at this stage:

1. *Vision:* It is paramount for leaders to have a well-defined and clear vision to guide staff on what is expected from them to get the organization out of the crisis and to reach safe ground.
2. *Setting priorities:* The leadership, in consultation with senior leaders and frontline managers, should set priorities on how to approach the crisis and in what order. For example, in our case, we decided to stop the spread of the infection first to minimize harm to patients and staff and to provide help to patients who needed care in a prioritized fashion. Other causes were then addressed as a lower priority.
3. *Eliminating patient harm:* As mentioned above, the top priority of any organization should be to limit harm to patients that exist in the system and those who will be using the health-care system. Harm can arise from the reason for the crisis (i.e., infection) or from patients' lack of access to care for their disease.
4. *Leadership team:* It is crucial that the approach to the crisis is team based. The team should include clinical and nonclinical staff, senior leaders, and frontline staff.
5. *Involve all stakeholders:* All stakeholders including staff, patients, the public, and others should be involved in addressing the crisis.
6. *Transparency:* The leaders should be transparent in all communications to earn the trust of all stakeholders in order to align efforts toward achieving true success in countering the crisis and controlling it.
7. *Communication:* Communication is an essential tool in containing any crisis, and it should improve in all directions during crises. Communication should be very clear between the leadership teams and staff, between staff and their patients, and between the institution and the community and authorities. The communication should be factual, accurate, and transparent.

11.3.3 Leaders' Roles in Building Resilience

The primary goal of leaders at this stage is to initiate the early recovery of the organization after absorbing the shock of the crisis and to set the organization on the path to recovery with a strategic vision.

1. *Developing a clear plan:* After the emergency response and control of the crisis, the leadership should focus on making sure that there are long-term plans to lead the organization toward better outcomes and safer care. The plan should have very clear short- and long-term objectives and outline the responsibilities and accountability of those who are assigned to the projects.
2. *Redesign process:* Leaders should review the patient care process and work flow and modify or redesign it based on root cause analysis and understanding of the situation.
3. *Implement improvement projects:* Based on the process redesign, building structures can be changed or specific projects implemented to enhance organizational resilience.

11.3.4 Leaders' Roles in the Excellence Stage

The leaders' goal at this stage is to maintain momentum in a long-term fashion to transform the organization and assure its growth.

1. *Continuous monitoring:* It is very important to have measures and indicators that are monitored, reported, and shared with all the stakeholders to make sure that the organization is on target.
2. *Sustainability:* Maintaining the improvement gained by the momentum generated after the crisis is critical; therefore, sustaining improvements and continuing to provide the best and safest care to patients are critical. This was achieved in our hospital by changing the culture of the organization, making it a learning organization and incorporating the positive changes into the healthcare delivery system. Culture changes are essential in sustaining any improvement that is achieved after crisis. Figure 11.2 illustrates various factors that may contribute to the successful transformation of organizations into a permanent state of excellence in performance.
3. *Maintaining vigilance:* It is very important to recognize any early signs of recurrence of the crisis or deterioration in the situation and to implement early interventions to prevent it from recurring.

11.4 Crisis Management Plan

To achieve a vision, one must have an implementation plan. The plan will translate vision into actionable items. The plan should contain:

1. Clear and achievable objectives: short-, intermediate-, and long-term objectives
2. Detailed processes with accountability to achieve the set objectives
3. Monitoring and corrective measures to assess how close the organization is to the desired target

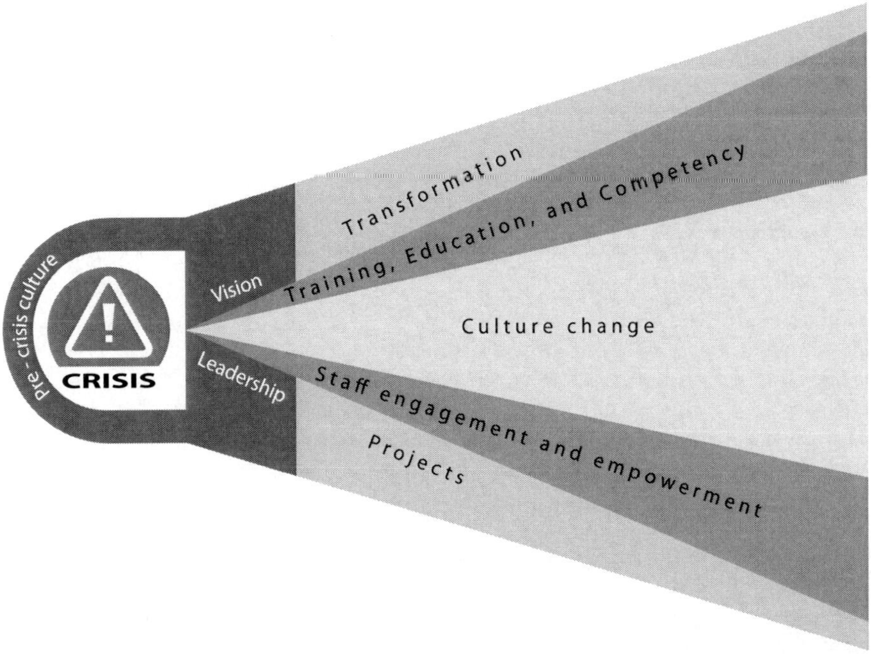

Figure 11.2 Components of successful organizational transformation to excellence following a crisis.

11.4.1 Stakeholder Involvement

Identifying and involving stakeholders is essential to the success of crisis management. Stakeholders may include

1. *Staff*: Involving staff is critical for the success of any plan, and this should be through clear communication, empowering, training, and development.
2. *Patients and families*: Being transparent with patients and their families is important to obtain their input and feedback to help the organization stay on the right track. This should be coupled with actions to assure the safety and well-being of patients and their families.
3. *Public and community*: The public outcry inflamed by media coverage including social media is a strong force that shapes the crisis and frames it within a larger scheme.
4. *Authorities*: Whether national (Ministry of Health) or international (World Health Organization [WHO]), it is critical to have open and direct channels of communications, which was the case in our event. We kept both organizations abreast of developments of the outbreak and the measures we were taking to contain it. This action is important for many reasons including the sharing of experiences and resources and the dissemination of important knowledge on a large scale to prevent extension of the crisis to other areas and to help develop future policies and procedures for wider use.

In summary, the role of leaders in managing crisis is critical, not just to contain the crisis but also to reshape the future of the organization. Although each crisis is different in its nature and impact, the principles discussed in this chapter apply to most scenarios and provide insights for leaders on how to manage a crisis.

References

ABC News. 2014. Ebola outbreak: Hospital where Nigerian victim Patrick Sawyer died shut down and quarantined as virus spreads. http://www.abc.net.au/news/2014-07-29/ebola-hospital-in-nigeria-shut-down-and-quarantined/5631028.

Arab News. 2015. Deadly fire strikes Jazan hospital in southern Saudi Arabia. http://www.arabnews.com/featured/news/855066.

Crofs Blogs. 2015. Saudi Arabia: KAMC emergency department closed over MERS. http://crofsblogs.typepad.com/h5n1/2015/08/saudi-arabia-kamc-emergency-department-closed-over-mers.html.

Harvard College Global Health Review. 2013. Securing health care in war zones. https://www.hcs.harvard.edu/hghr/online/securing-health-care-in-war-zones/.

Independent. 2016. Surprised an A&E is closing because of doctor shortages? We warned you we would leave – now it's happening. http://www.independent.co.uk/voices/nhs-hospital-closing-accident-emergency-department-junior-doctors-contract-jeremy-hunt-theresa-may-a7185041.html.

Mail Online. 2015. Manchester Royal Infirmary closed after an outbreak of deadly breathing illness MERS. http://www.dailymail.co.uk/news/article-3176276/Manchester-Royal-Infirmary-closed-outbreak-deadly-breathing-illness-MERS.html.

NPR. 2014. Ebola shuts down the olders hospital in Liberia. http://www.npr.org/sections/goatsandsoda/2014/08/12/339863749/ebola-shuts-down-the-oldest-hospital-in-liberia.

Patient Safety Network. 2005. Organizational change in the face of highly public errors—I. The Dana-Farber cancer institute experience. https://psnet.ahrq.gov/perspectives/perspective/3/organizational-change-in-the-face-of-highly-public-errorsi-the-dana-farber-cancer-institute-experience.

SF Gate. 2001. Shutdown puts spotlight on human research/Experts say Johns Hopkins case reflects problems across U.S. http://www.sfgate.com/health/article/Shutdown-puts-spotlight-on-human-research-2898348.php.

Sussman, J. B., L. K. Halasyamani, and M. M. Davis. 2010. Hospitals during recession and recovery: vulnerable institutions and quality at risk. *Journal of Hospital Medicine* 5 (5): 302–305.

The Korea Herald. 2015. Korea names MERS-affected hospital, tracks all visitors. http://www.koreaherald.com/view.php?ud=20150605001037.

The Telegraph News. 2016. NHS hospital becomes the first to shut down specialist maternity services because of junior doctors shortage. http://www.telegraph.co.uk/news/2016/09/01/nhs-hospital-becomes-the-first-to-shut-down-specialist-maternity/.

Virginia Mason Institute. 2014. Terrible Tragedy—and Powerful Legacy—of Preventable Death. https://www.virginiamasoninstitute.org/2014/03/terrible-tragedy-and-powerful-legacy-of-preventable-death/.

Washington Post. 2005. 45 bodies found in La. hospital. http://www.washingtonpost.com/wp-dyn/content/article/2005/09/12/AR2005091202035.html.

Chapter 12

Health System Innovation and Reform

Tara Donnelly

Contents

12.1 A Reputation for Discovery and Innovation 218
12.2 Innovation and Improvement in the NHS 218
12.2.1 Defining Innovation 218
12.2.2 History 218
12.2.3 About Academic Health Science Networks (AHSNs) 221
12.2.4 Combinatorial Innovation 223
12.3 Great Global Examples of Innovation 223
12.3.1 India 223
12.3.2 Europe 224
12.3.3 The United States of America 224
12.4 Digital Health 224
12.5 Starting to Scale 224
12.5.1 Successful Scale Case Study: The NHS Innovation Accelerator 226
12.5.2 A Checklist for Scale 226
12.5.3 Scaling Up 226
12.6 What Next? 227
12.6.1 Investment in Scale and Complex Systems Change 227
12.6.2 Creating the Right Environment 228
12.6.3 Opportunities through Precision Medicine 228
12.6.4 Playing the Long Game 228
12.6.5 Make the NHS the Go-To Place on the Planet for Medical Innovation 228
Acknowledgments 229
References 229

12.1 A Reputation for Discovery and Innovation

Britain has a great tradition in healthcare invention and discovery: William Harvey describing blood circulation in 1628, the discovery of antibiotics, development of the smallpox vaccine, DNA and sequencing, inventing computed tomography (CT) and magnetic resonance imaging (MRI) scanners, conducting the first blood transfusion, and having more Nobel laureates in medicine and physiology than any country other than the United States. British clinicians and scientists have innovated since long before the inception of the National Health Service (commonly referred to as the NHS) in postwar Britain in 1948.

The NHS—itself an innovation—was forged by a passionate Welshman called Aneurin Bevan, who sought to create universal health coverage regardless of an individual's ability to pay. Originally established by the Labour Party (the principal center-left political party in the United Kingdom), the NHS is iconic of Britain and has cross-political party support. In polls, the NHS consistently scores as one of the top three issues for British citizens (YouGov 2016).

The NHS is unique in several ways including being the world's largest publicly funded health service. No other country has a health system that provides universal free coverage, is semi-integrated, and achieves prompt care for citizens both in emergencies and on a planned basis. As Simon Stevens, chief executive of NHS England, said:

> The fact is that we hold ourselves to a very high standard, rightly so. [...] there is no other major industrialised country in the world that over the course of the last year can claim to have treated nine out of ten of its patients within four hours in an A&E (Accident and Emergency; Emergency Room) department, or provided 9 out of 10 of its citizens with access to needed planned surgery within 18 weeks.
>
> **Stevens 2016**

However, a number of themes emerge from a study of healthcare innovation in the United Kingdom, as shown in Figure 12.1.

This chapter considers the strengths of the innovation and improvement work in England; describes the quality journey the NHS has undertaken; reflects on some of the themes described in Figure 12.1, particularly that we have been better at discovery than spread and adoption; what has taken place to address these themes, and what next steps are required in this work.

12.2 Innovation and Improvement in the NHS

12.2.1 Defining Innovation

When we talk about "innovation" in the NHS, what do we mean? In the author's opinion, the most useful is "an idea, service or product, new to the NHS or applied in a way that is new to the NHS, which significantly improves the quality of health and care wherever it is applied" (Department of Health 2011).

12.2.2 History

For the first 40 years of the NHS, services were run in a similar manner to when the service was first established, with major population healthcare improvements linked to medical discoveries, vaccination programs, and new medicines.

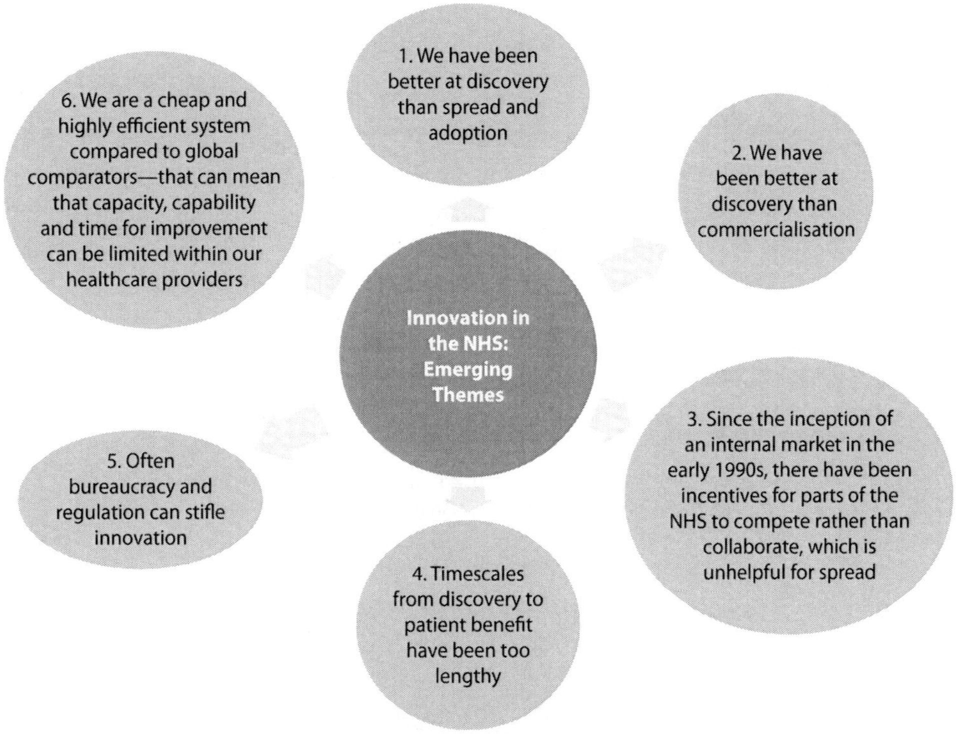

Figure 12.1 Innovation in the NHS: emerging themes.

In 1992, "The Patient's Charter" was published by the government, which set a number of rights and responsibilities for the NHS and patients and included, for the first time, a maximum treatment time of two years for planned surgery. This standard was universal across the service and required all hospitals to review waiting lists and undertake additional surgery to reduce waits to within the new level. This waiting list reform was important, as until this time "routine" cases deemed not to have clinical urgency could (and did) wait for many years. Waiting list management was not seen as a distinct skill and was frequently undertaken by the operating surgeon.

This was the first of a number of standards that established a clear direction for the NHS to better meet expectations and build public confidence and trust. Others that followed were a maximum four-hour wait in A&E (see also Chapter 9) and the system that remains in place today that states that total waiting time from general practitioner (GP, the family physician) referral to treatment completion must be less than 18 weeks. These standards have been significant in shaping the focus for improvement work and also in preserving the supply of NHS care to the vast majority of British people. Other countries experiencing increases in waiting times have seen similar increases in the proportion of people selecting private healthcare, but the United Kingdom has not experienced this increase.

At the same time, the NHS introduced an "internal market" so that the healthcare-providing parts of the NHS would trade with those that commission it. Designed to bring business principles and discipline into healthcare administration, hospitals were required to establish themselves as separate "Trusts," part of the wider NHS but run as distinct, independent entities with a chair and nonexecutive board members, the ideology being that this could lead to the recruitment of people with business skills into local health systems.

While advantages of the internal market exist, it has a number of disadvantages from an improvement and spreading perspective. The requirement for institutions to compete is not highly compatible with encouraging universal spreading of innovation through collaboration, the transaction costs and necessary bureaucracy of the market consuming bandwidth that could otherwise support improvement activities. Furthermore, the payment of providers for activity rather than outcomes encourages them to perform more chargeable treatments and disincentivizes radical change that may well involve investment in keeping people healthy.

The NHS Plan was published in 2000 as a 10-year plan for the NHS. It combined a commitment to substantial investment over the period with some quite radical changes including strengthening the internal market and introducing greater private sector capacity as a means to reduce waiting times.

Professor Sir Bruce Keogh, medical director of NHS England, reflected on the approach to innovation over the past 20 years: If you go back to the early 2000s, we had a focus on innovation for very specific conditions. We introduced the national service frameworks, for example, which, using best practice, outlined how specific clinical services should be shaped.

The areas where there's been the most innovation improvement have been very specific, and I would highlight:

- Focused psychological therapies for very specific conditions
- Primary angioplasty for heart attack—we now achieve among the best outcomes in the world
- The way we organise and deliver trauma services, which has resulted in a substantial increase in survival
- The change in the way we deliver stroke services, particularly in London
- The way we treat old people with fractured hips

These achievements have been based largely on a combination of evidence and consensus among the people that run the health service and were associated with strong clinical support" (Keogh 2016).

In 2001, a central improvement support function was created for the NHS, originally the Modernisation Agency (MA), then the National Institute for Innovation and Improvement (NII; 2005–2013), NHS Improving Quality, and subsequently the Sustainable Improvement Team (SIT). The aims of these agencies were very similar: to provide capacity-building support to the NHS and a range of tools. However, ambition, scale, and budget varied markedly. For example, the MA and NII were large organizations capable of directly supporting clinical teams through improvement programs such as the Productive Ward series—the NHS's most significant export of an improvement product to other countries—and were run as independent improvement organizations. SIT and its predecessor are markedly smaller, with four program areas, and are part of NHS England.

In 2007, the colorectal surgeon Professor Sir Ara Darzi was asked to undertake a review that became "High Quality Health for All—NHS Next Stage Review." This review "set out how the NHS should move away from centrally driven, target-based management to [...] empowered local services focusing on quality as well as activity" (Broad 2009) and introduced requirements for hospitals to publish "Quality Accounts" in addition to annual financial accounts.

There was a sense that while targets could be useful they were a blunt instrument and perhaps contributed to a culture where leaders were rewarded for hitting the target but missing the point. The scandal that emerged at Mid Staffordshire Hospital proved the case in point, where a focus on achieving coveted "Foundation Trust" status in 2008 and hitting highly visible targets including financial balance were at the cost of care quality. The investigation into the Trust by Sir Robert Francis found distressing evidence of very poor care when it began reporting in 2010.

Sir Bruce Keogh notes that "High Quality Care for All" trigged the inception of Academic Health Science Networks (AHSNs): "Ara's review considered 'how do you implement innovation even more rapidly in the NHS?' The drivers for this were that we weren't doing so well in treatment in certain areas as other countries, but also the fact that there was a recognition that the 'N' in the NHS gives a subliminal perception that we should be able to marshal the whole country for research and innovation, but that the structures—as they were then—don't necessarily allow that."

"The concept of Academic Health Science Networks (AHSNs) emerged from this, having all the right people, in the room, talking about all the right stuff, with the right size of population. The idea was that you could have a relatively constrained geographic area with contained patient populations, and populations of around 3–5 million were selected, so similar to a small European country, such as Norway or Ireland, based around 15 natural patient flow groupings in England. The opportunity to bring together the innovators and the system: med-tech industry, academia, different parts of the NHS, the pharmaceutical leads, voluntary sector, and social care locally. Each had decent universities in their region, a number had an Academic Health Science Centre, and they all had different strengths or areas of distinct contribution, like the aerospace industry in the west and the academics in the east."

He continues, "So we sought to start moving from national service frameworks and very specific areas of innovation improvement to a strategy of larger scale collaboration. One of the drivers at the time was the political sense that not only does innovation drive improvement, but that if we got it right, we could turn the UK into the 'go to' place for the pharma/med-tech industries, for entrepreneurs and for ideas—it would be the testing ground. I would like to see that someone sitting in a board room in Boston would think 'where could we test this out?' and the NHS would be right at the top of the list" (Keogh 2016).

AHSNs were formally created following the publication of Innovation, Health and Wealth in 2011, a review undertaken by Sir Ian Carruthers, then chief executive of NHS South of England. AHSNs were seen as a crucial vehicle to help the NHS cross the identified "barriers to innovation" (Figure 12.2), and were established the following year in 2012/2013 (DoH 2011).

In 2014, the "Five Year Forward View" was published, a strategy for the NHS endorsed by its regulators and which included testing new models of care across England. The current and immediate future challenge for all developed healthcare systems is the management of chronic diseases, with many of the new care models—50 currently being tested across the country—focusing on new ways of integrating healthcare for populations (NHS England 2016).

12.2.3 About Academic Health Science Networks (AHSNs)

AHSNs were conceived as neither providers nor commissioners of healthcare, the idea being that they would act as honest brokers within their region and mobilize expertise and knowledge across the NHS, academia, and industry to help improve lives, save money, and drive economic growth through innovation. In this way, they would deliver the Five Year Forward View locally. England's connected network of 15 AHSNs is now working in new ways across health and care, helping partners to deliver change in pace and scale.

AHSNs work across their diverse regions to fulfill four goals: improving population health, supporting collaboration, speeding up the adoption of innovation, and improvement and wealth creation

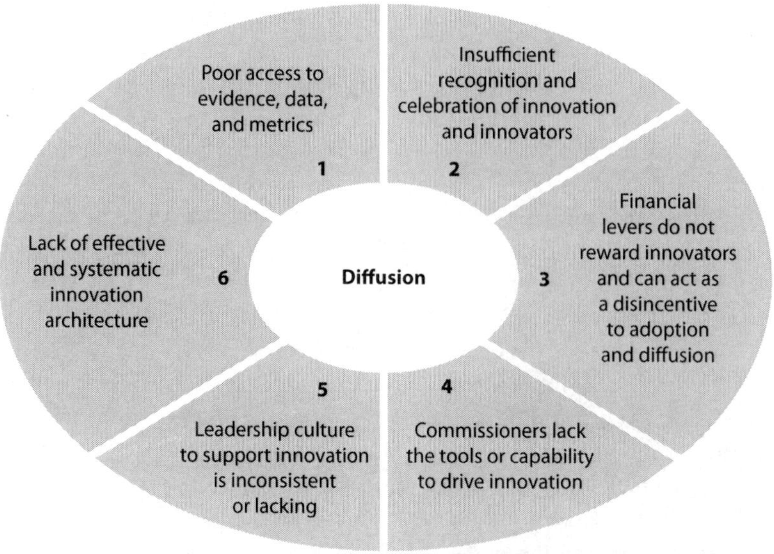

Figure 12.2 Barriers to innovation. (Source: DoH, NHS Improvement and Innovation and Service Improvement, 2011. Innovation Health and Wealth, Accelerating Adoption and Diffusion in the NHS, page 10, http://webarchive.nationalarchives.gov.uk/20130107070708/http://www.dh.gov.uk/prod_consum_dh/groups/dh_digitalassets/documents/digitalasset/dh_134597.pdf.)

for UK innovators. They develop work plans that focus on areas of highest priority to their members; for example, in our case in South London, these are diabetes, digital health, dementia, stroke prevention, alcohol, exercise for joint pain, and patient safety. They also run a number of national programs.

As mentioned in the themes shown in Figure 12.1, finding the headroom to think carefully about improvement in a busy clinical career can be taxing, and as Ian Dodge, Lead Director for AHSNs at NHS England and National Director for Strategy and Innovation says: "The lack of capacity and capability in the service to actually do some of this is one of our biggest constraints. People are busy with their day jobs. There isn't the infrastructure and support—so people trying to innovate have to do so on a shoe string" (Dodge 2016).

Suzie Bailey, Director of Leadership and Quality Improvement at NHS Improvement, agrees: "I think there's a huge amount to do around building capability and capacity for improvement. We've got staff across the NHS who are incredibly value-based, with strong intrinsic motivation to do the right thing—but we're bringing them into busy day jobs and are not giving them the headspace or skillset necessary to understand when or how to undertake improvement" (Bailey 2016). AHSN improvement programs provide help in practical terms through, for example, collaboratives, and also help build capacity through quality improvement skills development.

Professor Tony Young, a consultant urologist and the National Clinical Lead for Innovation, is struck by the "policy to practice" gap and the role AHSNs play in helping to close this. He reflects that "The system's full of really good, nice people, who are really well intentioned and want to make a difference and do it—but just because it's simple policy, doesn't mean it's going to have the impact on the frontline that the people who ideated that policy meant it was going to have. That is one of the things I love about Academic Health Science Networks—because it connects you to the frontline. If we give them enough of a chance, and if we give them the opportunity to grow, and support them to evolve and change like every organisation does, they can start to show real value to the local clinicians that they can practically help you" (Young 2016).

12.2.4 Combinatorial Innovation

Sir Bruce Keogh adds: "The Five Year Forward View takes us a step further than where we got to with establishing the AHSNs in two senses: it tries to create a permissive environment for innovation and it talks about combining innovations—and this is a really important step forward" (Keogh 2016).

The Forward View includes a term new in healthcare—"combinatorial innovation"—which are those innovations that integrate new technologies and other novel approaches that offer the prospect of better care, and better patient experience of care, at the same or lower overall cost. Or, as musician Brian Eno puts it, "You should stay alert for the moment when a number of things are just ready to collide with one another" (Eno 2015). The Forward View states "The NHS will become one of the best places in the world to test innovations that require staff, technology and funding all to align in a health system, with universal coverage serving a large and diverse population. [Over the next five years we will] develop a small number of "test bed" sites alongside our Academic Health Science Networks and Centres. They would serve as real world sites for 'combinatorial' innovations that integrate new technologies, bioinformatics, new staffing models and payment-for-outcomes" (NHS England 2017).

One of the best examples of a combinatorial innovation, in Sir Bruce Keogh's view, is that "in the early sixties something called a mouse was invented. Then, 25 years later, Tim Berners-Lee invents hypertext markup language and launches something that's now called the World Wide Web. But essentially, in the in-between time, someone needed to invent the uniform resource locator or URL, which would enable you to identify where documents are—and it's the bringing together of those three of those things that creates what we think is the normal interface with the Internet as we know it. And that's combinatorial innovation. There are multiple opportunities to use combinatorial innovation to good purpose in healthcare—an example could be, how do you bring together things that measure your physiology/fitness [and] mobile platforms and link that to your own goals as well as general healthcare data to help you better manage your own long-term condition. These are the sorts of experiments we want our Test Bed programme to explore" (Keogh 2016).

12.3 Great Global Examples of Innovation

Although the focus of this chapter is how the UK NHS undertakes innovation, impressive work is, of course, being undertaken in every healthcare system across the world. Interviewees highlighted the following examples of global innovation.

12.3.1 India

Ian Dodge highlights India and notes its ability to leapfrog: "If you talk to Apollo [an Indian hospital chain], when they were rolling out expansion of health coverage, they'll say that in these Himalayan villages they used two bits of technology: they made a deal with the Indian air force about flying people in and out with their helicopters, and mobile phones. That was it. There is something about—particularly in primary care services—how we have our legacy systems set up and it can be hard to migrate onto the mobile models" (Dodge 2016).

In his book *In Search of the Perfect Health System*, Mark Britnell describes that in designing his perfect health system he would take elements from the best of the world's healthcare systems and for "innovation, flair and speed" he would choose India (Britnell 2015). The chapter on India, however, is titled "One country, two worlds" because of the striking disparity between the "islands of excellence"—examples of industrially scaled frugal healthcare excellence at Narayana Health, Apollo, and Aravind Eye Care—and how the one billion people in the rest of the country fare (Britnell 2015).

12.3.2 Europe

Suzie Bailey finds it valuable to look to Europe: "We need to deeply understand what it takes to help innovations to be developed, nurtured, scaled, shared—the NHS needs to do more of looking across the country and to other settings. We tend to look to the U.S.—but there is a lot to learn from Europe, which is why we are getting involved in a group of European organisations committed to working collaboratively to sharing learning on quality improvement" (Bailey 2016).

The Buurtzorg system in the Netherlands is a terrific example of innovation in a service model, where independent, self-managed teams of nurses, using good tablet-based technology, provide high-quality home care, which was very well evaluated by patients and was delivered at relatively low cost (Royal College of Nursing Policy and International Department 2016).

12.3.3 The United States of America

Sir Bruce Keogh notes that: "Improvement science is a big issue—and this was learned from abroad—mainly the impressive Institute for Healthcare Improvement in Boston" (Keogh 2016). Dr Helen Bevan, OBE, Chief Transformation Officer, NHS Horizon Team, highlights that systemic work across the Kaiser Permanente health system in the United States and its rigorous approach to spread is what the NHS can learn most from: "As a system, Kaiser are doing the stuff we need to do, and doing it well" (Bevan 2016).

12.4 Digital Health

The advent of smartphones, mobility, and machine learning is bringing enormous change to healthcare systems. The sci-fi writer William Gibson coined a great expression: "The future's already here, it's just not very evenly distributed" (Gibson 1999). Sir Bruce Keogh echoes this, and when meeting with health tech thinkers involved in machine learning and artificial intelligence to support clinicians making quicker diagnoses noted: "The thing about those guys, was our future was their present. They were just in a different time zone" (Keogh 2016).

12.5 Starting to Scale

The key stages of invention, adoption, and diffusion as described in Innovation, Health and Wealth are shown in Figure 12.3.

Ian Dodge reflects that while we are strong at the top, we get weaker as we descend the diagram: "The NHS is quite good at individual clinical innovations in terms of initial invention, less good about rapid systematic spread of clinical innovations, and much, much poorer about diffusion of innovation in terms of reaching across management and delivery systems" (Dodge 2016).

Helen Bevan diagnoses the issue as follows: "What I think is one of the biggest problems that I see now, is the issue between start-up and scale-up. We have, in my mind, a system that is primarily designed for start-up—and what we keep doing is to put in charge the kind of people that love doing early-stage invention and early innovation. They're your pioneers, your early adopters. What we keep doing is going over and over the cycle, of start-up again to attempt to spread and scale. But we've only got so far. We need a lot a lot of additional thinking … and need to find the

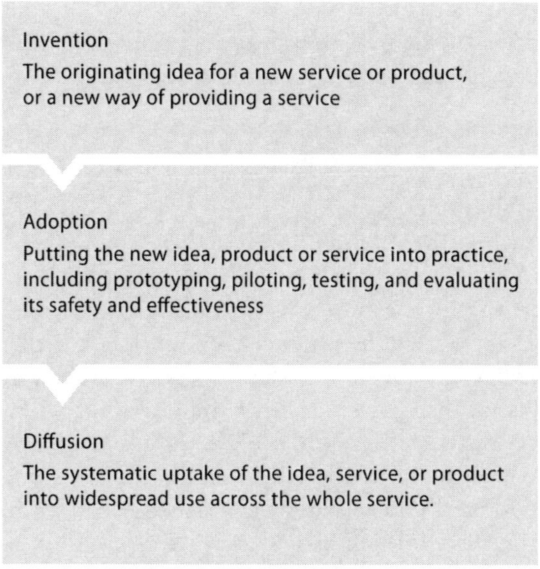

Figure 12.3 Key stages of innovation. (Source: DoH, NHS Improvement and Innovation and Service Improvement, 2011. Innovation Health and Wealth, Accelerating Adoption and Diffusion in the NHS, page 11, http://webarchive.nationalarchives.gov.uk/20130107070708/http://www.dh.gov.uk/prod_consum_dh/groups/dh_digitalassets/documents/digitalasset/dh_134597.pdf.)

people who are good at scale-up, and put them in charge of this activity, not the people who are good at start-up" (Bevan 2016).

Ian thinks that this has been the case for many years, and why "Academic Health Science Networks are potentially such interesting innovations in themselves, around how actually do we drive the spread piece" (Dodge 2016).

In an article published in the *Health Service Journal*, I highlighted the role AHSNs were starting to play in spread: "Spread is not simple and indeed it can be tough. The results from an innovation need the application of local intelligence to work elsewhere. The science of spread tells us that to emulate the success of others' changes is likely to require time, energy, and resources. Networks need to be effectively activated. Leadership judiciously selected. Hearts as well as minds persuaded. Data is often essential. Implementation engineering skills are needed to support staff make changes that are sustainable" (Donnelly 2016).

Ian agrees about the data: "We're also systemically atrocious at using data systematically. For instance, looking at population outcomes of what's happening at the end of a service line change, getting rapid feedback, iterating. Some of the initial bit of improvement science is so vital to getting stuff off the ground, but then typically we see really poor engineering discipline, factory style, around how do you actually convert this at scale" (Dodge 2016).

Sir Bruce Keogh observes that sometimes the spread can be more important than the innovation in terms of making a difference to peoples' lives. He offers that perhaps the most important single technical innovation to impact the health service is the microscope, invented by the Dutchman Antonie van Leeuwenhoek ("the father of microbiology") in 1683. But what made a huge difference to adoption was that the president of the Royal Society, Robert Hook, wrote a beautifully illustrated book in English about it called *Micrographia*, understanding the significance this breakthrough could have in understanding disease. His book became "the first scientific best-seller" and "captured the public's imagination in a radically new way; Samuel Pepys called it 'the most ingenious book that I ever read in my life'" (Wikipedia 2016).

12.5.1 Successful Scale Case Study: The NHS Innovation Accelerator

In 2015, the NHS launched the NHS Innovation Accelerator (NIA) to take a number of proven innovations and work with the NHS to scale them. The program was designed to provide bespoke support to the innovators and help build evidence so that it was more attractive to those in the NHS to access the products and services. Sir Bruce Keogh recalls: "The thought was conceived by one of the junior doctors, Ben Maruthappu, who worked as a clinical fellow in NHS England, then driven largely through Sir David Fish [Managing Director at UCL Partners AHSN] initially" (Keogh 2016). The NIA went on to accept 17 fellows into its first cohort and has been supported by all 15 AHSNs. A year on, the program has been a notable success; the products and services had reached over 345 organizations within the NHS, impacting roughly three million people, and improving health and driving economic growth.

Sir Bruce Keogh adds: "The bit we mustn't forget is that unless [the NIA] leads to a place where we understand the barriers and are in a place where we are willing to take those barriers down, then it won't have succeeded. It is an attempt by our system to work out where the barriers are, break them down, and make the spread of innovation much easier" (Keogh 2016).

12.5.2 A Checklist for Scale

In *The Checklist Manifesto*, Atul Gawande witnesses the immense power of checklists in aviation and surgery (Gawande 2011). Helen Bevan (2016) wrote about a checklist that was developed for successful scale based on work being done by David Albury from the Innovation Unit. Helen found it so useful she adapted it for local use, with the "what this means for us" column in her version, as illustrated in Table 12.1.

12.5.3 Scaling Up

The Health Foundation, which supports innovative healthcare, has over recent years established a specific fund to support the scale-up of ideas. One of the major changes Suzie Bailey identifies over the past 20 years is the trajectory of how patients are being more actively involved in their care, "recognising that patients are their own main carers, have far more hours 'with themselves' than with health professionals. So I am most impressed by innovations that have truly 'flipped' the way healthcare is delivered" (Bailey 2016).

Bailey cites as an example a scheme that Scaling Up Finds from the Health Foundation supported, involving the scaling of work and hemodialysis—how to get patients more involved in their own dialysis care, including some performing their own dialysis care at home, a concept that originated in Sweden. Seven teams are now scaling this model up to around 40 organizations in England and Scotland (Bailey 2016).

Table 12.1 Successful Scale and What It Means for Us

Successful Scale Happened Where:	*What This Means for Us…*
• There was either a critical problem that the innovation was addressing or a major opportunity that it was realizing	• Is the problem/opportunity big enough and well recognized? Does it support the needs of enough of our members to garner support?
• There was wide engagement in the design and development of the innovation (of patients and potential adopters)	• Do we think that the innovation has been developed with adopters and patients so that our members and patients will want it?
• There was strong evidence of desirability (relative advantage), feasibility (ease of integration into current working practices and systems, and/or adaptability to local context), and viability (compelling business case)	• What evidence is there that the innovation is better than the status quo? • How feasible is it that it will be able to be adopted? • Is there a compelling business case?
• It was prioritized above other innovations, either by having an influential champion(s) or being 'top down' (commissioner-led)	• Does it have a strong enough champion?
• It harnessed professional and/or user-patient networks	• Have we the support of the clinical or patient network?

12.6 What Next?

Considering "what next in innovation within the NHS" seems to be a mix of making the most of both local opportunities and the advantages we hold as a national system. The following themes emerge:

- Investing in scale and complex systems change
- Creating the right environment
- Opportunities through precision medicine
- Playing the long game
- Making the NHS the go-to place on the planet for medical innovation

12.6.1 Investment in Scale and Complex Systems Change

There is resounding agreement that getting scale right requires immediate focus, as well as supporting systems: "We've come such a long way—and what we ought to be doing now in an era of STPs*—is putting, in terms of the massive investment that we've made in technological innovation, we should be making the same investment in innovation with complex systems change. We won't be able to implement what we need to implement otherwise" (Bevan 2016).

* Sustainability and Transformation Partnerships, the name for place-based plans that cover a geography rather than focus on single institutions.

12.6.2 Creating the Right Environment

This is a leadership and skills challenge. In "Leading High Performing Health Systems," Professor Becky Malby writes: "In a review of the literature on leadership of high-performing health systems and systemic improvement and innovation networks, Mervyn and Amoo (2014) found the that leadership of the collaborative was the most important variable in operating and sustaining the collaborative venture, and that key issues for systems leadership were: the time needed for the participating organisations to learn and adapt to one another; the requirement for managers to relinquish aspects of their territory in service to a greater common purpose; the focus at an early stage in the collaboration on the plan for sustaining the capacities the collaboration creates; and enabling a professional culture of teamwork and working with the public as partners. These are the 'conditions' that foster successful systemic change" (Malby 2016).

Suzie Bailey frames it in terms of ensuring a supportive culture grows within the NHS such that senior teams make the most of the talent and ideas that exist at every level within their organizations and "would like to help boards to have a deeper understanding of the role that they have in creating those right environments. If they can let go a bit, and create the right environments, then the talent within the organisations can do fantastic things" (Bailey 2016).

12.6.3 Opportunities through Precision Medicine

Professor Richard Barker writes in his book, *Bioscience: Lost in Translation?*, that "if we are bold enough to take [the] seven steps to sustainability and shape more positively the environment in which life sciences R&D takes place, then we can unleash forces that will lead us to a much more productive innovation ecosystem. At its heart will be precision medicine, broadly defined—using the new tools of biology, engineering, and informatics to match patients with therapies more accurately, and to track their outcomes more consistently" (Barker 2016).

12.6.4 Playing the Long Game

Continuity of vision is incredibly important: "The big opportunity that we have is how do we make sure there is a longer term attention span in the different NHS bodies. Where there will be results for patients but also continuity of service. Some of this will take three to five years, and we need to keep doing the same things and see them through. My biggest historic frustration is the extent that people get attracted to things and run out of time and patience and then move on to something else. You can't possibly deliver deep systematic change in a very short space of time. You have to start an inch wide and go a mile deep. The forward view can help with this—but there is still a risk, considering the context we're in financially. There will be impatience for results. The question is how do we combine this impatience for change with a willingness to see it through and do the learning and be systematic about how we do this" (Dodge 2016).

12.6.5 Make the NHS the Go-To Place on the Planet for Medical Innovation

In addition to this being one of Sir Bruce Keogh's goals (see Section 12.2.2), Professor Tony Young adds: "The NHS is the single largest unified healthcare system in the history of the human race. This gives us some opportunities that no one else has had the chance to do—and one of them is to innovate at scale. It's complex and divided—but that's what gives us the opportunity to say well let's have a go at it. If you really want to do this at scale, then we can do this in the NHS. Recently 103 of the brightest clinicians you could ever want to meet were selected to be a part of the Clinical Entrepreneur programme and came together for their first weekend recently. Never before has there been a cohort at such a scale of clinical entrepreneurs who've worked together on the planet, ever" (Young 2016).

While there is plenty to do, it feels as though there is reason for optimism that the entrepreneurial zeal at the heart of our health system will continue to burn brightly and that more recent learning and focus on collaboration and scale will help us to ensure that the best ideas in health and care are disseminated more widely across the NHS.

Acknowledgments

I am very grateful to Suzie Bailey, Dr Helen Bevan OBE, Ian Dodge, Professor Sir Bruce Keogh OBE, Professor Becky Malby, and Professor Tony Young for the generous support they have lent to this chapter and to Stephanie Kovala for all her assistance in compiling it.

References

Bailey, S. 2016 Development Director at NHS Improvement. Personal interview, conducted 19 October 2016.

Barker, R. 2016. *Bioscience—Lost in Translation?: How Precision Medicine Closes the Innovation Gap*. Oxford: Oxford University Press.

Bevan, H. 2016. Chief Transformation Officer, Horizons Group, NHS Improving Quality. Telephone Interview, conducted 6 September 2016.

Bevan, H. 2016. From Spread to Scale Up. Unpublished Research.

Britnell, M. 2015. *In Search of the Perfect Health System*. London: Macmillan Education.

Broad, M. 2009. Darzi Review and NHS Modernisation—At-A-Glance Guide. NHS England. http://www.hospitaldr.co.uk/blogs/guidance/darzi-review-an-at-a-glance-guide

Department of Health, NHS Improvement & Efficiency Directorate, Innovation and Service Improvement. 2011. Innovation, Health and Wealth, Accelerating Adoption and Diffusion in the NHS. http://webarchive.nationalarchives.gov.uk/20130107105354/http:/www.dh.gov.uk/prod_consum_dh/groups/dh_digitalassets/documents/digitalasset/dh_134597.pdf

Department of Health and Social Security. 1992. The Patient's Charter. http://webarchive.nationalarchives.gov.uk/20090811143745/http://www.bristol-inquiry.org.uk/final_report/annex_a/footnotes/HOME/0001/0001-0013.pdf

Dodge, I. 2016. National Director for Commissioning Strategy, NHS England. Personal interview, conducted 16 August 2016.

Donnelly, T. 2016. We're serious about innovation—now let's get serious about spread. *Health Serv J*. https://www.hsj.co.uk/topics/technology-and-innovation/were-serious-about-innovation-now-lets-get-serious-about-spread/7010344.article

Gawande, A. 2011. *The Checklist Manifesto: How to Get Things Right*. New York: Henry Holt and Company.

Keogh, B. 2016. National Medical Director, NHS England. Personal interview, conducted 5 October 2016.

Malby, B. 2016. Systems Innovation—Disruption or Adaptation. Learning Journals Blog. https://beckymalby.wordpress.com/2016/08/04/systems-innovation-disruption-or-adaptation/

Mervyn, K., and N. Amoo. 2014. *Brief Literature Review on Improvement at Systems Level*. Leeds Institute for Quality Healthcare. http://www.leedsqualityhealthcare.org.uk/wp-content/uploads/2014/04/LIQH-Literature-Scoping-Review-Sept-2014.pdf

NHS England. 2015. Real World Testing of Combinatorial Innovation a Global Invitation to Innovators. https://www.england.nhs.uk/wp-content/uploads/2015/03/test-bed-prospectus.pdf

NHS England. 2016. New Models of Care—Vanguard Sites. https://www.england.nhs.uk/ourwork/futurenhs/new-care-models/

NHS England. 2017. Next Steps on the NHS Five Year Forward View. https://www.england.nhs.uk/wp-content/uploads/2017/03/NEXT-STEPS-ON-THE-NHS-FIVE-YEAR-FORWARD-VIEW.pdf

Royal College of Nursing Policy and International Department. 2016. The Buurtzorg Nederland (home care provider) Model. Observations for the United Kingdom. https://www.rcn.org.uk/-/media/royal-college-of-nursing/documents/policies-and-briefings/uk-wide/policies/2015/br-0215.pdf

Stevens, S. 2016. Simon Stevens's Speech to NHS Confederation Conference 2016. https://www.england.nhs.uk/2016/06/simon-stevens-confed-speech/

Wikipedia. 2016. Micrographia. https://en.wikipedia.org/wiki/Micrographia

Young, T. 2016. National Clinical Lead for Innovation, NHS England. Personal Interview, conducted 26 September 2016.

YouGov. 2016. Issues 2 (Most important now + Most important your family). www.yougov.co.uk

Eno, B. 2015. Tweet by @dark_shark on 17/10/15. https://twitter.com/dark_shark

Gibson, W. 1999. The Science in Science Fiction. Talk of the Nation.

Chapter 13

The Financial Aspects of Leading a Reliable Healthcare System

Chris Hurst

Contents

13.1 Why Is Money Important? 231
13.2 Funding Health and Healthcare.... 232
13.3 Allocation of Healthcare Funding 233
13.4 Understanding Business Activities, Income, and Cost....235
13.5 Understanding the Dynamics of Cost 236
13.6 Understanding Income.... 237
13.7 Continuous Improvement, Value, and the Efficiency Contribution.... 237
13.8 Financial Planning.... 238
13.9 Budgeting and Financial Management.... 239
13.10 Concluding Points.... 239
References 240

13.1 Why Is Money Important?

Money is the blood that flows through the "arteries and veins" of an organization and, of course, through any health system. There are very few parts of an organization that money does not pass through or touch in some way. As with the human body, when the flow (of financial resources) is constrained for a sustained period or becomes "arrhythmic," problems start to arise. The pressure or distress that follows results in organizational "trauma" that, in turn, can be expected to impact on the efficient functioning of other parts of the organization or system. In the course of responding to this trauma, valuable management time and focus are diverted. Importantly, for a healthcare organization this response is also likely to consume and divert significant clinical time away from patient care.

A leadership culture which accommodates the myth that costs and income are something for only finance staff to worry about is unlikely to be successful over the longer term. This chapter describes why a health system's ambition to achieve and sustain *reliable healthcare* must be built on a culture that promotes good financial understanding and strong financial management as integrated components of service and clinical management. In summary, it is important that cost and reliable healthcare are recognized as being *two sides of a single coin*.

The use of terms *organization*, *health body*, and *health system* in this chapter are to be regarded as synonymous.

13.2 Funding Health and Healthcare

A nation's healthcare costs are typically funded from one, or a combination of, the following three sources:

- *Private sector resources*: Principally reimbursed by health insurers which are in turn funded by member and employer premiums
- *State revenues*: That is, publicly funded health services
- *The individual*: Including insurance policy deductibles, exclusions, and excesses and co-payments for services (e.g., for an appointment with a primary care doctor)

There is no single model for the funding of healthcare and citizens' access to healthcare services vary considerably around the globe. Access to healthcare services and the range of the services available to the citizen are influenced by factors such as government spending priorities, health and social care policy, and a country's ability to attract experienced and qualified clinical staff.

Global healthcare costs have increased significantly in recent decades. Between 1995 and 2014, world per capita health expenditure more than doubled from US$462 to US$1,061 (World Health Organization 2017). The principal drivers of healthcare costs are well understood but, unfortunately, there is no "silver bullet" that can fully mitigate the financial challenges most governments now face as they respond to the pressures that their healthcare budgets are under due to

- Changing demography (an aging population)
- The costs of technological advancement and the ever-increasing scope of treatable conditions
- Rising patient expectations
- Increases in populations (in some countries)
- The growing impact of the largely lifestyle-related chronic health challenges of the developed world

Changing demography represents the most significant long-term economic pressure on government spending and brings with it the potential for declining tax revenues as a larger proportion of a country's population move into retirement.

In 1965, the over-65 cohort accounted for circa 5.1% of the world's total population. Over the past five decades, this figure has increased to 8.3%, an increase of nearly 63% (United Nations 2015). This trend is forecast to continue and it is expected to create further pressures on healthcare capacity and costs. However, this factor can be expected to have a differential impact around the globe as the growth rate of the over-65 population is projected to vary significantly across countries. To illustrate the extent of this variation, Table 13.1 summarizes the changes in the percentage of the over-65 population over the past five decades for a few countries.*

* These countries have been selected to illustrate the range of variation and do not have any statistical significance as a group.

Table 13.1 Changes in over 65 Population, 1965–2015.

Country/ area	%age of total population over 65 in 1965	%age of total population over 65 in 2015	Increase over 50 years
Japan	6.3	26.3	x 4.2
Greece	8.3	21.4	x 2.6
Sweden	12.7	19.9	x 1.6
Netherlands	9.5	18.2	x 1.9
United Kingdom	12.2	17.8	x 1.5
Poland	6.8	15.5	x 2.3
Australia	8.6	15.0	x 1.7
New Zealand	8.1	14.9	x 1.8
United States	9.5	14.8	x 1.6
Singapore	2.6	11.7	x 4.5
China	3.4	9.6	x 2.8
India	3.2	5.6	x 1.8
South Africa	3.9	5.0	x 1.3
Saudi Arabia	3.6	2.9	x 0.8
World (average)	*5.1*	*8.3*	*x 1.6*
OECD members (average)	*8.9*	*16.2*	*x 1.8*
European Union (average)	*10.6*	*19.2*	*x 1.8*

Source: World Bank—staff estimates, based on age distributions of United Nations Population Division's World Population Prospects. (From United Nations, 2015). www.dataworldbank.org | Health Indicators | Population ages 65 and above (%age of total.)

In 2014, total health expenditure—expressed as a percentage of a country's gross domestic product—ranged from as little as 1.5% (Timor-Leste) to as high as 17.1% (United States). The proportion of total health expenditure defined as public health expenditure ranged between 17% (Sierra Leone) and 99.2% (Tuvalu) (World Health Organization 2017). Table 13.2 provides these statistics for the countries listed in Table 13.1.

13.3 Allocation of Healthcare Funding

It is usual for national governments to retain certain health-related responsibilities and, therefore, to set aside part of their total health budget to cover the costs of these functions and for other purposes (e.g., for policy initiatives and contingencies). Nationally retained responsibilities typically include health policy, health information/informatics, public health, performance monitoring and management, and government administration (e.g., finance, human resources, etc.). However, some of these functions may be organized and operated at a regional or state level (such as in the United States and Australia).

A government's arrangements for distributing the balance of its total health budget to service providers and other organizations (after budgeting for the above costs) are influenced by the configuration of its healthcare infrastructure. For example, responsibility for commissioning healthcare services for a local population may be vested in an organizational tier which is independent of the organizations that provide healthcare. Under this configuration, money is allocated to the commissioning bodies, which then commission and pay for services for their population

Table 13.2 Total and Public Health Expenditure 2014.

Country/area	Total health expenditure as age of total GDP	Public health expenditure as %age ot total health expenditure	Life expectancy at birth (years)	
				Variation from highest
Netherlands	10.9	87.0	81.3	-2.3
Sweden	11.9	84.0	82.0	-1.6
Japan	10.2	83.6	83.6	
United Kingdom	9.1	83.1	81.1	-2.5
New Zealand	11.0	82.3	81.4	-2.2
Saudi Arabia	4.7	74.5	74.3	-9.3
Poland	6.4	71.0	77.3	-6.3
Australia	9.4	67.0	82.3	-1.3
Greece	8.1	61.7	81.3	-2.3
China	5.5	55.8	75.8	-7.8
United States	17.1	48.3	78.9	-4.7
South Africa	8.8	48.2	57.2	-26.4
Singapore	4.9	41.7	62.3	-21.3
India	4.7	30.0	68.0	-15.6
World	*9.9*	*60.1*	*71.5*	*-12.1*
OECD	*12.4*	*62.2*	*80.1*	*-3.5*
European Union	*10.0*	*77.8*	*80.7*	*-2.9*

Source: World Bank [www.dataworldbank.org | Health Indicators: | Health expenditure, total (%age of GDP) and | Life expectancy at birth (total years)].

from (both state and private sector) service providers using a payment tariff (e.g., as in England). However, in some countries, health funding is allocated directly to healthcare systems which have comprehensive service responsibilities* (e.g., in Wales), or may be allocated to a number of separate, specialist service organizations.

The basis for distributing funding to healthcare organizations (be they commissioners or providers of healthcare) is normally carried out in one or a combination of the following three ways

- By politicians, to reflect political and government policy priorities
- Using a formula(e), typically using population size as its starting point with some adjustments for local health need†
- Based on historical allocations of funding, adjusted incrementally each year (e.g., to allow for inflation)

In addition to these funding distributions, it is common for part of the overall health budget to be set aside and separately distributed for the education and training of health professionals, for research and development, for ministerial policy priorities and for other time limited initiatives. Resources may also be held back centrally as a financial contingency (e.g., for the cost of responding to a pandemic).

Whatever funding arrangements are in place, for a health system to be able to provide reliable healthcare it is important that these arrangements operate in a reasonably predictable and transparent way and can be understood by the organizations in receipt of the funding. It is also essential

* For example, for secondary, tertiary, community, mental health, and learning disability services.

† Statistics for the past utilization of services are typically used as proxy indicators of health need.

that health systems have competence in strategic and financial planning and can make realistic estimates of their future operating costs and funding (see also Section 13.8).

13.4 Understanding Business Activities, Income, and Cost

In business, an increase in activity will normally generate an increase in income, however an increase in income will not always result in an increase in profit. Profitability is a function of both income *and* expenditure. To have a reasonable prospect of running a successful business, it is essential that those leading and managing the business have a good understanding of

- The *level of income* generated by each department from its principal services and product lines
- The *cost* of the resources being used to provide services and/or products
- The *contribution* that each area of the business must make from its income toward the organization's overheads and fixed costs (e.g., for corporate support services and to cover building running costs)

This intelligence requires a business to have reliable systems for capturing and counting business activity *and* arrangements in place for monitoring product/service quality and customer satisfaction.

In the global healthcare sector, the resources and processes that health bodies have in place to capture and count service activity (and to gauge patient satisfaction) vary considerably in their comprehensiveness, timeliness, and reliability. For some services—for example, community-based care and mental health services—it can be more difficult for managers and professionals to identify meaningful measures of activity. Quality metrics and patient feedback can also be difficult to obtain in these areas. In the secondary and tertiary hospital sector, these arrangements tend to be more mature and better resourced, although the resources devoted to understanding quality and patient satisfaction are not always proportionate to the challenge.

A private sector organization uses its understanding of profit (at a product and service level) to inform important business decisions, for example

- The most effective way to allocate finite business resources and assets (such as space, equipment, and staff) across its different business activities
- The most beneficial* areas for investment
- The areas it may be appropriate for it to disinvest in

Monitoring service and product profitability can also help to alert management to problems within the business (and/or in its market) and prompt it to take timely action.

Although the concept of profit is unlikely to be viewed as directly relevant for a publicly funded health system (or for a not-for-profit provider), it is just as important for every publicly funded system to understand its costs and income if it is to provide reliable healthcare over the medium to longer term.

* Including considerations like short-term profitability, shareholder return, and strategic positioning; for example, extending the existing range of products or entering a new market.

13.5 Understanding the Dynamics of Cost

It is important for senior health staff to be aware of the principal factors that influence local operating costs and the relative impact of these factors. For example, the growth in the number of ward admissions, an increase in average length of stay, or an increase in qualified nursing staff vacancies. *At what point does each of these factors impact adversely on the efficient running of our service, and what would be the impact on our running costs?*

Without a broad understanding of these dynamics, there is the potential for the delivery of reliable healthcare to be put at risk, as unforeseen (but predictable) financial pressures arise and consume staff time to resolve them. A good understanding of cost behaviour also strengthens service and corporate planning capability.

Cost behavior* needs to be understood at a level which is practically useful for each local service and departmental team. The greatest benefit comes from understanding costs at a service line† level. An understanding of how service costs are influenced by changes in the number and mix of patients seen and treated is the foundation of good service planning and financial modeling. This, in turn, helps to support effective budget setting.

For example, a significant or sustained change in the volume of service activity can be expected to result in physical resources being put under increasing pressure on a day-to-day basis; including bed capacity, staff workload, waiting times for diagnostic imaging or laboratory tests. These pressures quickly increase quality and patient safety risks and rapidly drive financial pressures and budgetary overspending. As a consequence, local management and clinical time is quickly diverted away from care activities to crisis management and recovery planning.

Understanding the relationship between service activity and operating costs can offer significant benefits for operational managers. An examination of the relationship between activity, capacity, and cost is likely to reveal a number of operational trigger points or thresholds that, when breached, become very challenging and costly for a service to manage. By identifying these trigger points in advance, it is possible to adapt operational policies to use these thresholds—for example, to trigger the flexible deployment of staff or bed capacity across service departments to help maintain patient flow and to sustain quality and safety until equilibrium has been restored.

As in a private sector environment, this understanding also helps to inform and strengthen the quality of business cases for investment and, when necessary, can be used to help assess the impact of proposals for service disinvestment.

This understanding is the foundation of *service line management (SLM)*, an approach that was originally developed in healthcare management in the United States, drawing on examples of good private sector practice. SLM provides for the greater devolution of decision-making powers to local teams in exchange for their acceptance of greater direct accountability and for greater responsibility for resource management, quality, and ensuring service sustainability. While SLM falls outside the scope of this book, a useful summary of the United Kingdom's early experience of its introduction in the 2012 publication *Service-line management: Can it improve quality and efficiency?* (www.kingsfund.org.uk/publications/service-line-management). This report summarizes the English NHS's initial experience and the comments of a small number of healthcare leaders in provider trusts. The principal aim of the study was to examine the potential for SLM to improve service quality and efficiency.

---

* How costs change in response to a change in service activity; for example, costs may be fixed, semi-fixed, or variable with changes in activity (similarly, income).

† Services managed as distinct operational units, typically by clinicians.

13.6 Understanding Income

Public funding for healthcare tends to be relatively fixed over the short to medium term as it must managed alongside other national priorities for spending, such as education and defence. That is, heathcare funding is unlikely to automatically increase in direct response to any growth in the level of service activity or to changes in the overall complexity of clinical workload. While many countries operate a payment tariff system to reimburse their healthcare providers, tariffs tend to be crude in both their calibration and operation.* Tariffs also tend to be "unaffordable" to governments unless financial caps, discounts, and penalties are used to dampen down the reimbursements sought by providers.' These adjustments tend to create perverse incentives and generate management activity which works against "whole system" working.

It is important for managers and clinicians to understand how their services are funded and to have an understanding of the relative security and stability of that funding. They should also be aware of any factors that may put their funding at risk, for example, breach of quality or minimum waiting times standards.

At a macro level, the relative inelasticity of public funding for health and the upward pressure on healthcare costs are creating a significant financial challenge for many governments around the globe. This is beginning to result in an increased pressure on healthcare providers to deliver greater cost efficiencies.

For example, after many years of real terms funding growth, the National Health Service (NHS) in England has been set very challenging levels of cash-releasing efficiency improvements over the past five or so years, which are not being fully delivered (Gainsbury 2016). The UK government and the NHS are not alone in this growing challenge.

13.7 Continuous Improvement, Value, and the Efficiency Contribution

Publicly funded healthcare organizations are likely to come under increasing pressure to deliver efficiency improvements that generate real financial savings. While improvements in service productivity and quality are important, realizable financial savings are required to help fund the escalating costs of meeting the more complex health needs of an aging population in the developed world.

A culture of *continuous improvement* requires managers and clinicians to have a joint appetite to learn from within and outside their organizations *and* to learn from past experience and mistakes. The benefits of delivering improvements typically flow in a number of different "currencies," including

- *Quality gains/risk reduction*: For example, improved patient satisfaction or a reduction in clinical risk
- *Cost avoidance*: For example, a change in working practice that avoids the need for additional staff to be recruited following an increase in team workload
- *Capacity-releasing benefits*: For example, a reduction in average length of stay on a ward, which frees up bed capacity for additional patients to be admitted

* Partly because of the underlying complexity of healthcare activities and treatments and because the individual needs of patients with the same condition can also vary, requiring different levels of clinical "resourcing."

- *Cash-releasing efficiencies*: For example, a change in staff rotas that reduces the use of locum doctors or agency nurses, or a change in the local prescribing formulary that results in substitutions with lower cost drugs

Cash-releasing improvements are also important because they can be used to create a financial contingency within an organization to manage future pressures, to invest in services, and/or to fund further improvement initiatives.

13.8 Financial Planning

The challenge for an organization to make sustained improvements increasing by efficiency—for example, by using value management* and using process improvement tools—cannot be satisfied by imposing savings targets on departmental service budgets. The organization's strategy, its medium-term plans, and its operating and management cultures must also embrace the leadership's ambition for ongoing improvement. Improvement programmes must be integrated into the organization's strategy and operational plans, thereby signposting for staff where these improvements are to be delivered.

To have the greatest chance of success, local teams must be meaningfully involved in the identification of these opportunities and in shaping the changes required to secure improvements. Leadership's responsibility is to help provide the organizational capacity, capability, and support required by local teams to deliver the changes and benefits.

An organization that sustains such success will have developed a competence in medium-term planning, which requires both corporate and local management teams to

- Have a good understanding of the business it is in
- Have a good understanding of how the business is performing
- Make realistic assumptions about its future levels of activity, income, and costs

This is not a science and requires judgments to be made at a senior level. When dealing with uncertainty, it is important that a number of feasible scenarios/futures are examined, as time will reveal that a number of the final planning assumptions used are inaccurate to some degree. A good planning process deals with this risk by using high-level modeling to assess the broad impact of changes in key planning assumptions. A good process draws on the input and views of senior managerial and clinical staff.

An effective annual planning process can be expected to significantly enhance the leadership's understanding of the *financial dynamics* of the business, which will provide a strong platform for reliable healthcare.

---

* "The concept of Value is based on the relationship between satisfying needs and expectations and the resources required to achieve them ...." "Value Management is concerned with improving and sustaining a desirable balance between the wants and needs of stakeholders and the resources needed to satisfy them" (The Institute of Value Management).

13.9 Budgeting and Financial Management

Budgeting flows from planning but, when implemented unintelligently, is viewed as a mechanical and technical process which is inflicted on service managers and clinicians by the organization's finance team, with little or no recognition of the local operational pressures. This *does not* describe an effective budget-setting process.

There are many definitions of "a budget," but, at its simplest, a budget is a sum of money allocated for a particular purpose. The purposes or objectives of a budget are typically described as

- A mechanism for controlling the use of resources
- A mechanism for communicating a plan to those responsible for its delivery
- A tool to motivate managers to achieve the budget goals set for them
- A basis for evaluating management performance
- A basis for understanding an organization's performance
- A tool of accountability

To satisfy any or all of these objectives, a budget must have certain basic qualities. First, the basis for setting the budget must be understood by those accountable for its management, including any assumptions about cash-releasing efficiency savings. Second, it should be set using realistic assumptions and parameters that demonstrate a reasonable link with other deliverables (e.g., workload and quality targets and any assumed productivity improvements). Third, there should be explicit agreement about the degree of autonomy the budget manager has to work within his/her overall budget (as opposed being required to contain spending within each budget line). Finally, the budget should be set after there has been a dialogue about the principal risks that could impact on costs and income over the budget period. This dialogue should result in broad agreement about where and how these risks will be managed if they crystallize. These considerations do not preclude an organization from setting a challenging or "stretch" budget, but it is essential that there is a reasonable degree of confidence that the budget is capable of being delivered at the time it is set.

There are times when significant external factors or other uncertainties make it challenging to satisfy these budget-setting criteria. In such circumstances, it is important that the uncertainty and risks are acknowledged in the dialogue with budget holders and senior clinicians. It may be necessary to give the budget holder additional flexibilities within their budget to secure the overall commitment from staff that they will work together (across departmental boundaries) to manage resources and pressures within the organization's overall budget.

13.10 Concluding Points

Cost and reliable healthcare are two sides of a single coin, and financial resources must be managed well in partnership with clinicians for a health system to be able to deliver reliable healthcare on a sustained basis.

There is a growing requirement for healthcare organizations to deliver year-on-year improvements in the way they use resources to deliver patient care. Some of these improvements will enable financial savings to be made and these savings will be essential to maintaining financial stability. Translational research and the enthusiastic adoption of proven innovation is also becoming an increasingly important characteristic of successful health systems.

It is important that the annual business processes used within a health system are consistent with and reinforce its internal leadership culture, because in the final analysis *the difference between a plan and what actually happens is people*.

References

Foot, Catherine, Lara Sonola, Jo Maybin, and Chris Naylor. 2012. Service-line management: Can it improve quality and efficiency? *The King's Fund* [ISBN 978 1 85717 631 5].

Gainsbury, Sally. 2016. *Feeling the Crunch: NHS Finances to 2020*. London: The Nuffield Trust.

United Nations. 2015. World population prospects, the 2015 revision. https://esa.un.org/unpd/wpp/.

World Health Organization. 2017. Global health expenditure database. http://apps.who.int/nha/database.

Index

Abnormal uterine bleeding (AUB), 144
Academic health centers, 125–127
Academic Health Science Networks (AHSNs), 221–222
Academic primary care, 149
Acute illness care
- cardiovascular disease (CVD) prevention, 139–141
- and child health, 148
- chronic disease prevention and management, 138–139
- overview, 137–138
- stroke prevention in atrial fibrillation, 141–142

Adult HCAHPS. *see* Adult Hospital Consumer Assessment of Health Care Providers and Systems (Adult HCAHPS)
Adult Hospital Consumer Assessment of Health Care Providers and Systems (Adult HCAHPS), 66
AHSNs. *see* Academic Health Science Networks (AHSNs)
AI. *see* Artificial intelligence (AI)
Albury, David, 226
API. *see* Application program interface (API)
Application program interface (API), 117
Artificial intelligence (AI), 113
Atrial fibrillation stroke, 141–142
AUB. *see* Abnormal uterine bleeding (AUB)
Automation, and operational excellence, 34–36

Barcode technology, 120–121
Benchmarking
- patient outcomes, 75–77
- and performance management, 183–185

Best Value Contract Review approach, 169–171
- application of, 172–173

Bevan, Helen, 224, 226
BI. *see* Business intelligence (BI)
BMI. *see* Body mass index (BMI)
Body mass index (BMI), 43
Boelen, Charles, 124
Boston Globe newspaper, 206
Budgeting, and healthcare, 239
Business activities, and healthcare, 235
Business intelligence (BI), 174–177

Cardiovascular disease (CVD), 139–141
Centre of Excellence for Pediatric Quality Measurement (CEPQM), 67
CEPQM. *see* Centre of Excellence for Pediatric Quality Measurement (CEPQM)
The Checklist Manifesto (Gawande), 226
Child health, and primary care
- child protection, 147
- chronic diseases, 148
- mental health, 148–149
- routine surveillance and vaccinations, 147
- serious illness, 148

Child protection, 147
Chronic diseases
- and child health, 148
- prevention and management, 138–139

Cleaning and disinfection, 73
Clinical outcome trending, 74–75
ClinicalTrialsMatch, 119
CLMA. *see* Closed-loop medication administration (CLMA)
Closed-loop medication administration (CLMA), 120
Cloud computing, 113
Combinatorial innovation, 223
Competence-based medical education, 130–131
Computed tomography (CT), 56
Computerized physician order entry (CPOE), 120
Continuous improvement, 237–238
Contraception, 144
Cost, and healthcare, 235
- and decision-making, 198–199
- improvement circle
  - cash, 201
  - footprint, 200–201
  - outcome, 200
  - productivity, 201–202
- overview, 189–190
- success strategies
  - clinical teams to treat high volumes of patients, 192–193
  - and minimally invasive techniques, 193–195
  - overview, 190–191
  - patients in self-managing their health, 195–196

scale in clinical and administrative support systems, 191–192
and target interventions, 197
value-based healthcare, 50–55
Cost dynamics, 235
CPOE. *see* Computerized physician order entry (CPOE)
Crisis/crises
causes of, 206–207
description, 206
overview, 205–206
types of, 207
Crisis management
leaders' roles
in building resilience, 212
in emergency response stage, 211–212
in excellence stage, 212–213
overview, 208–211
in pre-crisis stages, 211
planning
overview, 213
stakeholder involvement, 214
stages of, 208
types of organizational responses, 207–208
CT. *see* Computed tomography (CT)
CVD. *see* Cardiovascular disease (CVD)

Decision-making, in healthcare, 198–199
Departmental performance management program, 31–34
Department of Plastic and Oral Surgery (DPOS), 52
Digital health, and health system innovation, 224
Disinfection and cleaning, 73
Distal radius fractures (DRFs), 61
Dodge, Ian, 224
DPOS. *see* Department of Plastic and Oral Surgery (DPOS)
DRFs. *see* Distal radius fractures (DRFs)

ECMO. *see* Extracorporeal membrane oxygenation (ECMO)
Efficient clinical practice
overview, 46–47
and value-based healthcare
cost, 50–55
employee engagement, 64–66
evidence-based guidelines (EBGs), 55–58
and outcome measurements, 48–50
overview, 47–48
pediatric patients and their families, 66–68
process mapping/timing, 51
quality improvement (QI), 63–64
Standardized Clinical Assessment and Management Plans (SCAMPs), 58–62
time-driven activity-based costing (TDABC), 51–55
unit costs, 52
EHRs. *see* Electronic health records (EHRs)
Electronic health records (EHRs), 113–116
Electronic medical record (EMR), 114
Electronic medication administration record (eMAR), 120
EMAR. *see* Electronic medication administration record (eMAR)
Emergency response stage, leaders' roles in, 211–212
Employee engagement, 64–66
EMR. *see* Electronic medical record (EMR)
Enhanced recovery after surgery (ERAS), 77–79
ERAS. *see* Enhanced recovery after surgery (ERAS)
Europe, health system innovation in, 224
Evidence-based guidelines (EBGs), 55–58
Excellence stage, leaders' roles in, 212–213
External environmental factors, in HROs, 89
Extracorporeal membrane oxygenation (ECMO), 62

Fast Healthcare Interoperability Resources (FHIR), 117
FIHR. *see* Fast Healthcare Interoperability Resources (FHIR)
Financial aspects
budgeting and financial management, 239
business activities, income, and cost, 235
and continuous improvement, 237–238
cost dynamics, 235
and financial planning, 238
funding health and healthcare, 232–233
allocation of, 233–235
and income, 237
overview, 231–232
Financial management, and healthcare, 239
Financial planning, and healthcare, 238
Fish, David, 226
Foundational interoperability, 116

Gawande, Atul, 226
GDP. *see* Gross domestic product (GDP)
GPOs. *see* Group purchasing organizations (GPOs)
Gross domestic product (GDP), 189
Group purchasing organizations (GPOs), 28
Gynecological cancers, 145–146

Hale Family Center, 68
Hand hygiene, 72–73
Healthcare-associated infections (HAIs)
cleaning and disinfection, 73
hand hygiene, 72–73
needlestick and sharps injuries, 73
personal protective equipment (PPE), 73
respiratory hygiene, 74
waste disposal, 74
Healthcare education and training
and competence-based medical education, 130–131
interprofessional healthcare delivery, 127–129
leadership, management, and governance, 130
overview, 123–124
professional learning and development, 131–132
regionalization and academic health centers, 125–127

research, clinical investigation, and data in, 129–130
and skills-upgrading, 131–132
social accountability, 124–125
talent acquisition and management, 131–132
and technology-enabled learning, 130–131
Health Information Technology for Economic and Clinical Health (HITECH) Act, 114
Health information technology (HIT)
and barcode technology, 120–121
and electronic health records (EHRs), 113–116
evolution of, 112–113
and interoperability, 116–120
overview, 111
patient engagement and experiences, 122–123
and radio-frequency identification (RFID), 120–121
Health Service Journal, 225
Health system innovation
Academic Health Science Networks (AHSNs), 221–222
checklist for scale, 226
combinatorial innovation, 223
continuity of vision, 228
creating right environment, 228
defining, 218
and digital health, 224
in Europe, 224
history, 218–221
in India, 223
investment in scale and complex systems change, 227
and National Innovation Accelerator (NIA), 226
opportunities through precision medicine, 228
overview, 218
scaling up, 226–227
stages of, 224–226
in United States of America, 224
Heck, Jeffery, 124
High reliability organizations (HROs)
components of, 85
implementation, 87
leadership commitment
challenges, 94–95
external environmental factors, 89
improvement spread and scale-up, 93–94
improving and redesign, 92–93
internal environmental factors, 88–89
measurement, 91–92
role of middle managers, 89–90
situational awareness, 87–88
standardization and simplification, 90–91
strategies toward, 96–97
overview, 84
principles of
commitment to resilience, 86
deference to expertise, 87
preoccupation with failure, 85–86
reluctance to oversimplify, 86
sensitivity to operations, 86
HIT. *see* Health information technology (HIT)
HITECH. *see* Health Information Technology for Economic and Clinical Health (HITECH) Act
HL7 International, 117
Hook, Robert, 225
HROs. *see* High reliability organizations (HROs)

ICHOM. *see* International Consortium for Health Outcomes Metrics (ICHOM)
ICU. *see* Intensive care unit (ICU)
IMGs. *see* International medical graduates (IMGs)
Improvement circle, for cost and quality
cash, 201
footprint, 200–201
outcome, 200
productivity, 201–202
Income, and healthcare, 235, 237
India, health system innovation in, 223
Infertility, and women's health, 144–145
Intensive care unit (ICU), 60
Internal environmental factors, in HROs, 88–89
International Consortium for Health Outcomes Metrics (ICHOM), 49
International medical graduates (IMGs), 125
Interoperability, 116–120
Interprofessional healthcare delivery, 127–129

KAMC-R. *see* King Abdulaziz Medical City in Riyadh, Saudi Arabia (KAMC-R)
Keogh, Bruce, 225–226
Key performance indicators (KPIs), 164–167
King Abdulaziz Medical City in Riyadh, Saudi Arabia (KAMC-R), 205
KPIs. *see* Key performance indicators (KPIs)

Layers of culture model, 5–6
Leadership, and organizational safety culture, 10–11
Leadership commitment, in HROs
challenges, 94–95
external environmental factors, 89
improvement spread and scale-up, 93–94
improving and redesign, 92–93
internal environmental factors, 88–89
measurement, 91–92
role of middle managers, 89–90
situational awareness, 87–88
standardization and simplification, 90–91
strategies toward, 96–97
Leaders' roles, in crisis management
in building resilience, 212
in emergency response stage, 211–212
in excellence stage, 212–213
overview, 208–211
in pre-crisis stages, 211
Lean management/Six Sigma, 39–40
Leeuwenhoek, Antonie van, 225

Length of stay (LOS), 60
LOS. *see* Length of stay (LOS)

Management accounting system for hospitals (MASH), 52
Maruthappu, Ben, 226
MASH. *see* Management accounting system for hospitals (MASH)
Menopause, 145
Mental health, of children, 148–149
MERS-CoV. *see* Middle East Respiratory Syndrome Corona Virus (MERS–CoV)
Micrographia (Hook), 225
Middle East Respiratory Syndrome Corona Virus (MERS–CoV), 205
Mobile health (mHealth), 113
Multilevel model of safety climate, 6–8
Multimorbidity, and primary care, 142–143

National Guard Health Affairs (NGHA), 16–17
National Innovation Accelerator (NIA), 226
Needlestick injuries, 73
Never Events, 161–163
NIA. *see* National Innovation Accelerator (NIA)

Obstetric care, 145
Operational excellence
- and automation, 34–36
- departmental performance management program, 31–34
- and Lean management/Six Sigma, 39–40
- overview, 25–26
- and patient satisfaction, 36–39
- policies and procedures, 26–28
- and staff engagement/empowerment, 40–44
- and staff recruitment/retention, 40–44
- supply chain management, 28–31

Organizational safety culture
- barriers to developing and sustaining, 16
- description, 3–5
- interventions and strategies, 14–16
- layers of culture model, 5–6
- leadership and, 10–11
- multilevel model of safety climate, 6–8
- National Guard Health Affairs (NGHA) case study, 16–17
- overview, 2–3
- patient safety culture
  - and outcomes, 10
  - tools for measuring, 11–14
- 3 Es model, 8–10

Outcome indicators, 162–163
Outcome measurements, 48–50

Patient care committee, 72
Patient engagement, and HIT, 122–123
Patient outcomes
- benchmarking, 75–77
- clinical outcome trending, 74–75
- enhanced recovery after surgery (ERAS), 77–79
- healthcare-associated infections (HAIs)
  - cleaning and disinfection, 73
  - hand hygiene, 72–73
  - needlestick and sharps injuries, 73
  - personal protective equipment (PPE), 73
  - respiratory hygiene, 74
  - waste disposal, 74
- measurement, 160–163
- overview, 71–72
- patient care committee, 72
- quality improvement (QI) program, 75
- and safety culture, 79–80

Patient safety culture
- and outcomes, 10
- tools for measuring, 11–14

Patient satisfaction, and operational excellence, 36–39
PECARN. *see* Pediatric Emergency Care Applied Research Network (PECARN)
Pediatric Emergency Care Applied Research Network (PECARN), 56
Pediatric patients and families, 66–68
Performance management
- and benchmarking, 183–185
- and Best Value Contract Review approach, 169–171
  - application of, 172–173
- and business intelligence (BI), 174–177
- clinical quality
  - defining, 158–160
  - key performance indicators (KPIs), 164–167
  - Never Events, 161–163
  - outcome indicators, 162–163
  - patient outcomes measurement, 160–163
  - process indicators, 162
  - qualitative and quantitative approaches, 163–164
  - structure indicators, 162
- measurement of value, 169–171
- overview, 156–157
- and performance metrics, 177–183
- and return on investment (ROI), 171–172
- reward, 173–174
- and robust service management, 176
- staff, 167–169
- three M's, 157, 185–186

Personal health record (PHR), 114
Personal protective equipment (PPE), 73
Pharmacy information system (PhIS), 120
PhIS. *see* Pharmacy information system (PhIS)
PHR. *see* Personal health record (PHR)
POCRnet Patient-Powered Research Networks (PPRNs), 119
Positive patient identification (PPID), 120
PPE. *see* Personal protective equipment (PPE)
PPID. *see* Positive patient identification (PPID)

PPRNs. *see* POCRnet Patient-Powered Research Networks (PPRNs)
Precision medicine, and health system innovation, 228
Pre-crisis stages, leaders' roles in, 211
Primary care
  academic primary care, 149
  acute illness care
    cardiovascular disease (CVD) prevention, 139–141
    chronic disease prevention and management, 138–139
    overview, 137–138
    stroke prevention in atrial fibrillation, 141–142
  and child health
    child protection, 147
    chronic diseases, 148
    mental health, 148–149
    routine surveillance and vaccinations, 147
    serious illness, 148
  description, 136–137
  and multimorbidity, 142–143
  and women's health, 143–146
    abnormal uterine bleeding (AUB), 144
    contraception, 144
    gynecological cancers, 145–146
    infertility, 144–145
    menopause, 145
    obstetric care, 145
Process indicators, 162
Process mapping/timing, 51
Professional learning and development, 131–132

QI. *see* Quality improvement (QI)
Qualitative and quantitative approaches, 163–164
Quality, in healthcare
  and decision-making, 198–199
  improvement circle
    cash, 201
    footprint, 200–201
    outcome, 200
    productivity, 201–202
  overview, 189–190
  and performance management
    defining, 158–160
    key performance indicators (KPIs), 164–167
    Never Events, 161–163
    outcome indicators, 162–163
    patient outcomes measurement, 160–163
  success strategies
    clinical teams to treat high volumes of patients, 192–193
    and minimally invasive techniques, 193–195
    overview, 190–191
    patients in self-managing their health, 195–196
    scale in clinical and administrative support systems, 191–192
    and target interventions, 197
Quality improvement (QI), 75
  and value-based healthcare, 63–64

Radio-frequency identification (RFID), 120–121
Randomized controlled trials (RCTs), 61
RCTs. *see* Randomized controlled trials (RCTs)
Real-time location systems (RTLS), 121
"Referral to Treatment Time" (RTT) KPI, 166
Regionalization, and academic health centers, 125–127
Reiman, T., 5–6
Relative value unit (RVU), 51
Resilience building, leaders' roles in, 212
Respiratory hygiene, 74
RFID. *see* Radio-frequency identification (RFID)
RTLS. *see* Real-time location systems (RTLS)
RTT KPI. *see* "Referral to Treatment Time" (RTT) KPI
RVU. *see* Relative value unit (RVU)

Safety culture, and patient outcomes, 79–80
SDO. *see* Standards development organization (SDO)
Semantic interoperability, 116
Sharps injuries, 73
Simplification, 90–91
Situational awareness, 87–88
Skills-upgrading, and healthcare education, 131–132
Social accountability, 124–125
Social networking/social media, 113
Staff engagement/empowerment, 40–44
Staff performance management, 167–169
Staff recruitment/retention, 40–44
Standardization, 90–91
Standardized Clinical Assessment and Management Plans (SCAMPs), 58–62
Standards development organization (SDO), 117
Structural interoperability, 116
Structure indicators, 162
Supply chain management, 28–31

Talent acquisition and management, 131–132
TBI. *see* Traumatic Brain Injury (TBI)
TDABC. *see* Time-driven activity-based costing (TDABC)
Technology-enabled learning, 130–131
3 Es model, 8–10
Time-driven activity-based costing (TDABC), 51–55
Traumatic Brain Injury (TBI), 56

Unit costs, 52
United States of America, health system innovation in, 224

Value-based healthcare
  cost, 50–55
  employee engagement, 64–66
  evidence-based guidelines (EBGs), 55–58
  and outcome measurements, 48–50
  overview, 47–48
  pediatric patients and their families, 66–68
  process mapping/timing, 51

quality improvement (QI), 63–64
Standardized Clinical Assessment and Management Plans (SCAMPs), 58–62
time-driven activity-based costing (TDABC), 51–55
unit costs, 52
Vanderbilt-Ingram Cancer Center, 119
Virtual Advisors Program, 67

Waste disposal, 74
Women's health, 143–146
abnormal uterine bleeding (AUB), 144
contraception, 144
gynecological cancers, 145–146
infertility, 144–145
menopause, 145
obstetric care, 145

Young, Tony, 228

Zohar, Dov, 6–8